HISTORY OF MODERN MORALS

BY

MAX HODANN

A Central Participant in the European
Weimar-Era Sexual Reform Movement

TRANSLATED BY

STELLA BROWNE

*" Error of opinion may be tolerated
when reason is left free to combat it."*

With a new Introduction by
James DeMeo, PhD

Historical Reprint Series

Natural Energy Works
Ashland, Oregon, USA

ISBN: 978-0-9891390-2-1

Other works by Max Hodann: (most are in the German language)
* *Boy and girl. Conversations Among Friends About the Issue of Gender*, 1924
* *Where Children Come From*, 1926
* *Sex and Love in Biological and Social Relationship*, 1927
* *Fornication! Fornication! Mr Prosecutor!* 1928
* *Adult Sexual Misery*, 1928
* *Sexual Misery and Sexual Advice. Letters From a Clinical Practice,* 1928
* *The Art of Making Love*, 1928
* *Sex and Love. With Diagrams and Sixteen Drawings,* 1932
* *Sex Life in Europe: A Biological and Sociological Survey,* 1932

About Max Hodann:
* *Max Hodann (1894-1946): Sozialist und Sexualreformer,* by Wilfried Wolff, Von Bokel Verlag, Germany 1993.

Introduction to the 2013 Republication

Short Biography of Max Hodann

Max Julius Carl Alexander Hodann (1894-1946) was born in Neisse, Germany. He began a study of medicine in 1913, and soon became an active and leading member of various socialist youth and sexual reform organizations. His medical specialty was sex-education, birth control, and the prevention of sexually transmitted diseases. From 1922 to 1933, Dr. Hodann held the post of Head City Physician for Berlin-Reinickendorf, where he worked as an independent scholar and with various European sex-reform organizations. He wrote books on sexual education aimed at working-class people, and for adolescents.

As is reflected within *History of Modern Morals*, Hodann's books, articles and lectures of the period advocated for a reform of sexual, family and marriage laws towards greater freedom and equality for women, and stood as a counterpoint to Church propaganda of that day which promoted sexual superstitions, guilt and fear, as well as compulsive lifelong and frequently arranged, loveless marriages. As an educator and practicing physician, Hodann worked for legalization of contraception and abortion, and in affirmation of premarital sexual love as natural and healthy. He worked with Magnus Hirschfeld at the Institute for Sexual Science in 1926, and with Wilhelm Reich in the broader Sexual Politics (SexPol) reform movement.

Like many social reformers of the pre-Nazi Weimar period, Hodann joined ranks with various Marxist and socialist organizations in efforts to spread sexual knowledge, particularly in the face of opposing and growing Nazi power. He wrote

and spoke against old Kaiser laws which frequently carried over into the Weimar Republic, and later against new Nazi laws limiting everyone's general freedoms, including basic sexual and marriage freedoms. In 1933, shortly after Hitler became Chancellor of Germany and the Reichstag was burned, Hodann was arrested in a massive roundup of intellectuals and anti-Nazi political activists, and held in a concentration camp for six months. Upon release he fled to Switzerland and later to Norway, working for a time as a physician in the International Brigade during the Spanish Civil War, and with short periods of residence in London and Palestine.

Hodann continued writing and speaking out for sexual freedom, legalization of contraception and abortion, women's rights, secular marriages, freedom to divorce, and other sexual and family reform measures. In 1940, he fled to Sweden where he remained over the course of World War 2. He died in 1946.

Reasons for this Republication

The decision to reprint this book was not difficult. To clearly see the way forward, one must know from where one came. Hodann's *History* covers early scientific investigations into human sexuality and the mysteries of procreation, and development of the sexual reform and women's rights movements in Weimar Germany and Europe generally, in the early decades of the 1900s. However, unlike many contemporary works on this subject, *History of Modern Morals* is authored by a man who lived the struggle, was a leader in it, got arrested by the Nazis for it, was betrayed by the Communists for it, and intimately worked with other professionals who also had personally suffered for their work in the same social-sexual reform movement. His writings are therefore filled with a strong passion and vitality, and with many personal observations, anecdotes, and clarifying information not found elsewhere.

Hodann's *History* is also unique in that he openly and frequently discusses the work of his contemporary and associate, Dr. Wilhelm Reich. While maintaining his independence, Hodann assimilated Reich's important and controversial clinical sexual research findings, and helped to promulgate them as unofficial participant and supporter of the *SexPol movement*, which Reich created and led starting in 1928. Of the many scholarly texts addressing this interesting subject and period, most mention Hodann, but few mention Reich. Or if they do, Reich is diminished or misrepresented, even slandered. By contrast, Hodann's *History* is generous in its discussion of Reich, which is especially important given Reich's life-positive emphasis upon love and emotion in sexuality, and his distinction between natural-healthy *heterosexual genitality* versus neurotic or pathological sexual expressions. In this modern era of anti-scientific "political correctness", this essential distinction has been either diminished or erased from public discussion – which is another good reason for this republication.

History of Modern Morals gives us a glimpse into an important period of Weimar sexual reform history, and the ideas and aspirations of some of its most central luminaries. Also in the clear hindsight of history, it exposes the weaknesses and errors in some of their naive positions regarding Marxist political agendas, as discussed below.

Max Hodann, Wilhelm Reich and SexPol

Hodann mentions Reich with praise in many parts of his book, and certainly was moving along similar directions. Both men were psychoanalytically-oriented medical doctors, and both advocated for greater sexual freedom and responsibility, as well as for political freedoms and democracy, during the 1920s and 1930s. In spite of the dethroning of the German Kaiser and Austrian Emperor after WW-1, both Austria and Germany still retained many of the same over-arching moral verbots and sexually-repressive, anti-child and anti-woman attitudes and legal codes. Those reforms in sexual and family law as were made during that time, were due to the hard work of numerous social reformers and organizations, including Reich and Hodann, and SexPol. Unique to SexPol, however, was a clear line of clinically-developed understandings on exactly how reforms in family and sexual law could influence behavior and character structure, and thereby end much of the mental health crisis and social violence associated with ungratified sexual needs and miserable marriages. SexPol also directly addressed the role of poverty and laws against contraception, which exacerbated such problems as multiple unplanned pregnancies, alcoholism, spouse abuse, and abandoned mothers with children.

Hodann and Reich placed a primary emphasis upon heterosexual genitality, wherein sexual discharge and gratification had their own importance to biology and health, separate from mere procreation. Reich's clinical work clarified how the chronic absence of complete sexual discharge in uninhibited *full-body genital orgasm* would lead to chronic tensions, neuroses, and even violent or sadistic/masochistic behaviors. Sexual gratification thereby became an indicator and regulator of mental and emotional health. These and other aspects of Reich's sex-economic theory clashed with the ideology and goals of the Church moralists, as well as with other political factions (ie, the Nazis) opposing contraception or women's liberation, or motivated by desires for more children as future workers or cannon-fodder for wars. SexPol also constituted a first attempt to merge the ideas of Freud with Marx, though most Freudians and Marxists barely tolerated the merger, or actively opposed it.

Both Hodann and Reich joined ranks with the socialists and communists in efforts to counter these trends, during the same approximate period as when the Nazis rose to power. The same was true of other European intellectuals and artists of the time, most of whom rather blindly joined various Marxist or socialist parties. Marxist communism was popularly, though ignorantly viewed as a transformative doctrine towards a better and freer society. Therefore it is not surprising how most of the family and sexual-law reformers looked to the organized socialist or Marxist parties for help in promoting their reform legislation, and in the struggle against Hitlerism.[1] I will return to this point momentarily.

On the one side, SexPol reformers like Hodann and Reich worked towards the prevention of neuroses through a healthy love-based and non-compulsive sexual life, where couples would marry only for love. They aimed to uplift the status of women by improving their economic situation, and also by greater sexual freedom for youth and elimination of arranged loveless marriages. This would, by observable examples, dry up the demands for prostitution, and the economic plight which drives women into it. A man or woman is not likely to seek out different sexual partners if their present relationship is loving and gratifying. And a women is not likely to offer herself for money if she already has decent work and pay, and is not struggling to feed her children under conditions of abandonment.

Through legalization of contraceptives, or abortion if it became necessary, families could have only as many children as they wanted and could care for. Children would then be given a non-authoritarian upbringing and education, which included sexual information, and the rights of adolescents and young unmarried people to their own privacy. Secularized marriage and divorce laws, providing help to impoverished or homeless mothers with children, and protecting children and adolescents from adult seducers, rapists, and the prostitution trade, were also key elements in the reforms championed by Hodann and Reich, through SexPol and otherwise.

Another goal was the ending of Church-borne distinctions between "legitimate" and "illegitimate" children, created by the crushing dictates of the Baptismal Certificate. That reform alone would open up new opportunities to the under-classes of formerly denounced "bastard" people. The unwed mother was then shunned as "immoral", and in some regions her children were forbidden access to legal marriage, education, the professions, government jobs, officer status in the military, and other upwardly-mobile pathways.

Such was the social stranglehold of the politically-powerful Church moralists at the time, as a carry-over from older periods of feudalism and Tsars, Emperors and Kaisers, whose laws on family and sexual life were formulated by prior warlords or theocrats. SexPol therefore worked for expanded rights to secular civil marriages, outside the controls of the Church, which historically had forbidden marriage across class, religious or racial lines, and supported compulsive arranged marriages, with a forbiddance of divorce. SexPol worked in opposition to all such laws which stood in the path of human happiness and freedom in sexual and family matters, and also fought for the rights of women towards a full economic and social equality.

Hodann and Reich also considered childhood masturbation as natural and healthy, and it was accepted that, quite on their own, adolescents would gradually move towards full sexual intercourse within their peer groups as teenagers, typified by the young lovers in Shakespeare's *Romeo and Juliet*. Contraceptives and hygiene would insure against unplanned pregnancies or venereal diseases. This would result in vibrant, happy and non-authoritarian character structures in the subsequent adult personality. In this regard, SexPol took much from Freud and psychoanalysis, though Reich's emphasis upon sexual freedom for adolescent couples was something which alarmed both his Marxist and psychoanalytic associates.

Hodann and Reich also stood against pornography, and against the persecution of homosexuals, even while viewing homosexuality as primarily the product of neurotic compulsions and anxiety or rage towards the opposite sex, due to ferocious child caretakers, or from child rape or seduction. Protection of children from adult seduction and pedophilia was also a central part of SexPol, frequently discussed in the opposition to widespread traffic in women and children for prostitution. This was viewed as a by-product of the larger sex-repressive patriarchal authoritarian social order. As children grew up in households with abusive fathers and cold affectless mothers, they tended to both tolerate and crave a similar situation within adulthood, as seen in their selection of marriage partners and political leaders. State structure mirrored family structure, Reich argued. Hodann's views basically agreed with those of Reich on all these aspects, though he was slow to accept Reich's views on homosexuality as having a cultural-social causation.

On the other side, the SexPol movement adopted socialist and Marxist rhetoric, which at that time of post-WW-1 chaos, economic depression and turbulence, was promising quite a lot to people hungry for social improvements and an end to old repressive laws. The "Great War" (WW-1) brought an end to the various authoritarian Empires that had dominated the political and social landscape of large parts of the Old World for centuries.

The German Kaiser, the Austro-Hungarian Emperors, the Tsar of Russia, and the Ottoman Caliph were all swept away. In the European parts of these former Empires, new democratic institutions were soon declared into place, without much awareness for how the authority-craving character structure of the average citizen, who had no experience in democratic voting or representative government, would react to it. This led to the appearance of some political parties clinging to the status quo – notably those who had benefited from the system of Empire, and who also looked to the Church for inspirational authority on how society and families ought to be governed. Others demanded quick and certain reforms in economy, working conditions, and an immediate end to Church autocracy and the lingering class system. This latter group was mostly, though not entirely, attracted to the socialist parties.

The original Russian Revolution of February 1917, with its democratic *Duma* and Russian Provisional Government, lasted only 8 months until the Bolshevik communists shot their way into power, in October of the same year. Thereafter, they dominated and controlled, either openly or covertly, the other Communist Parties (CP) of the European nations, all of whom promised a "worker's paradise", and great revolutionary changes beyond what was already in development without Marxism. At the time and for many people impatient for change, after centuries of oppressive, class-structured and restrictive Empire, these promises fell on fertile ground. The CP betrayals became apparent only later on, around the same time as the Nazi rise to power in c.1933, as discussed below.

Before the Nazi ascent, however, the Weimar years allowed for open development of multiple sexual-social reform groups, putting the new democratic governments under pressure for legal changes. A plethora of organizations openly fought for women's rights, birth control, sex-education, child welfare and marriage reforms, with conferences, public meetings, and political actions, and with books and pamphlets spreading their messages. SexPol was one of the most comprehensive of these organizational efforts, seeking to better people's lives through a merger of two of the most socially radical doctrines of the period,

Freudian psychoanalysis and Marxist socialism. The Marxists capitalized upon these social movements in the formation of a specific "Unity" umbrella organization, which for a time served as a vehicle for reforms as Reich, Hodann and others were already promulgating. Any uplifting of a suffering humanity required sexual liberation, changes in family law, and Marxist socialism, they argued. However, other social and sexual reformers, notably from Britain and the USA, rejected the necessity for Marxist ideology to advance their goals.

In the end, both the *National* Socialists (Nazis) and the *International* Socialists of Marxist Communism made open war against all the social and sexual reformers, just as they did, on and off, against each other. SexPol and the larger sexual reform movement enjoyed its largest following for only the few years of Weimar, notably from c.1925-1932. By 1933, they were all under open public assault from both the Nazis and Communists. Both Hodann and Reich wrongly believed they would obtain shelter and support from the communists. However, their ideas on the central importance of sexual health, freedom and happiness went against Marxist doctrines on class warfare, or the superiority of the "proletariat" over the "bourgeoisie". Reich told them, bluntly, both were equally neurotic and sexually impotent. For such commentary, he was thrown out of the German CP.

Hodann was arrested and spent 6 months in a Nazi concentration camp. Upon release, he was sent into exile, his German citizenship and medical degree revoked. Reich fled Germany just days before the Nazi roundup of their opposition, and he was also expelled from both the German CP and the International Psychoanalytic Association (IPA). His writings were denounced, banned and/or burned by all of them.[2] The IPA was then trying, unsuccessfully as history shows, to accommodate itself to the new Nazi rulers.[3] When Hodann and Reich later fled separately to Scandinavia, they were further assaulted in the Nazi press as "sex-Marxists" or "foreign Jews", even while being rejected and attacked by the Communists as provocateurs.

The Nazis finally crushed out the social-sexual reformers across Europe, and the Stalinists did likewise across Russia and in other areas under their controls, as they reversed most of the original sexual and family reforms passed before their respective seizures of power. All the reformers were driven into submission, into exile, or sometimes caught into the respective Nazi or Stalinist prisons and death-camps. WW-2 and the Cold War ensued thereafter, during which time new generations dedicated themselves towards social, economic, and sexual reforms that spread globally. These new efforts in fact proceeded faster and farther within the capitalist liberal democracies than in the hard socialist or Marxist-Communist dictatorships, a point I will return to momentarily.

Old Sexual Revolution Versus Modern Sexual Chaos

Today, looking back, one might ask if the older goals of SexPol were ever achieved within the Western democracies. The answer is a qualified "yes", but with complications. The basics of legalized contraception, abortion, secular marriage, divorce, women's rights and a greater sexual freedom overall, have been realized across much of the world (lagging decidedly in Muslim, Hindu and Buddhist regions, however). These changes were generally pushed along by sex-reform organizations which had no direct connections or historical roots in SexPol, or which predated it. However, some of the more critical aspects of SexPol led to Reich's later scientific discovery of the bioelectric/ bioenergetic nature of sexual tension and discharge, while working at the University of Oslo in 1934-1936, just before the outbreak of WW-2 and summarized in his 1942 work *Function of the Orgasm*. Reich's experimental findings were never significantly adopted into the sexual science of the late 20th Century, however, and this had very clear consequences in how sexual research and social reform efforts would develop. This is especially so where "politically correct" New Left social activism in large measure has supplanted the older Church moralism with a normalization of sex-pathology. Natural science and medicine have thereby been corrupted, with severe consequences in public policy-making and social development.

For example, modern "sexology" is today most clearly characterized by the problematic work of Alfred Kinsey, whose basically unscientific ideas became the vogue. Unlike Hodann and Reich, who emphasized sexual health and gratification over neurotic un-health and un-gratification, and how people were frequently trapped in unhappy compulsive marriages and neurotic sexual activity in efforts to compensate, Kinsey advocated for an equality of all sexual varieties and experiences, including the compensatory ones, without clear distinctions between healthy versus neurotic expressions. He promoted a vague and crude "discharge theory" of human sexuality, where no distinctions were made between the lesser sexual "climax" as one might get from exclusively non-genital or pre-genital excitation, and the more specific *full genital orgasm*.. Erection and ejaculation in the male, from Reich's clinical findings, were merely prerequisites for a full orgasm. By contrast, Kinsey defined "orgasm" by the mere presence of ejaculatory reaction. Masturbation, homosexuality, sodomy and genital heterosexual intercourse were all placed on the same level of emotional, biological and bioenergetic importance by Kinsey, without attention to their obvious differences – especially as regarding the passive-receptive partner in oral or anal copulations. Kinsey's conclusions and theories were also reliant upon raw data over-representing sexually neurotic and criminal populations, whose behavior was then unscientifically generalized to the larger population as "normalcy".[2,4]

Worse, Kinsey also secretly consulted with pedophiles to obtain "time to orgasm" computations for the youngest age groups, and argued for decriminalization of pedophilia as "normal" conduct. It was as far removed from the earlier determinations of Hodann, Reich and SexPol as one could possibly go. As history shows, Kinsey's unscientific and even criminal calculus, promoted under a cloak of "scientific study of human sexuality", received large public attention and approvals, especially from the pornographic industry, mainstream media and Hollywood.[2,4] By contrast, Hodann died a forgotten man, while Reich was publicly slandered by CP operatives in America, dying alone in a prison cell, his books burned by the US government. Continuing slanders are heaped on his grave every year, by the same pedo-porno journalists who celebrate Kinsey.[2]

Reich's clinical findings of the 1930s, which Hodann endorsed but in later years Kinsey opposed, thereby reflect an older line of scientific investigation, of sexual and emotional health versus unhealth, which was rooted in the early concepts of Freudian libido theory (but not Freud's later ideas on sublimation, latency and the death-instinct). Reich's clinical sex-economic findings, and his laboratory experiments on the bioelectric and bioenergetic nature of emotion and sexual excitation, marked the logical and more scientifically developed extension of the larger sexual reform movement in which even the young Freud had at one time been a participant. It is a badly-neglected line of research and empirically-founded theory, stretching back to early biology, through Darwin and other natural scientists on the physiology of reproduction, and hence through Freud and Reich, who clarified the emotional-social dynamics and eros of sexuality. This is well articulated in Hodann's *History*.

The consequences of this repression and neglect of the earlier research findings from SexPol are profound. One can go on to internet today and find all sorts of extreme pornography, including child-porn and other shocking materials of a clearly psychopathological nature. Progressive-leftists following the Kinsey model have largely supported this, even gone to the courts demanding that highly deviant extreme pornography be accessible in public libraries. Public homoerotic "love" parades and street festivals with open sodomy thereafter appeared. By the Kinsey model, "all sexual contacts and discharges are equal", including sadomasochism and the disease-prone homosexual bathhouse subculture. These have been elevated in public and legal standing, frequently over the strong objections of physicians specializing in sexually-transmitted diseases. And from this, it is not surprising to see pedophilia/child-rape and bestiality en-route to legalized status as "alternative sexualities", normalized in the universities. This is the new anti-love "sexual freedom", resultant from the Nazi-Communist obliteration of SexPol, and the subsequent poorly-considered adoption of the Kinsey model.

Aside from Kinsey, we also see today many parallel anti-sexual, anti-child, and profoundly *anti-scientific* trends in modern medicine and education. These are not only the antithesis of what the early SexPol reformers were advocating, but indicate a loss of emotional and intellectual clarity on the part of the professionals, who themselves are frequently highly neurotic or pathological in personal conduct and ideology.

Expressions of widespread sexual fears and hatreds persist within the general populations of the Western liberal democracies. This includes sexual sadism within the professions, albeit glossed over with academic language and scientism. For example, genital mutilations (circumcision) for baby boys persists in North America as a purely cultural or religious fetish, with no defendable scientific justifications. Attitudes towards female reproduction are still stuck in Medieval premises, where pregnancy is treated as if it were a disease requiring medical intervention in our modern hospital sick-houses. Midwives helping with natural and gentle home births, robbing ob-gyns of their high fees, are still put into prison in many states, reminiscent of the Medieval burning of such women. Risky surgical obstetrics, meanwhile, commands that ~33% of all American births be undertaken by scientifically unjustifiable C-sections, with a related epidemic of unnecessary hysterectomies. Unethical and anti-scientific surgeons also do horrific "preventative" mastectomies – full breast amputations – on perfectly healthy women based upon a deeply-flawed and Medieval "genetic" calculus, no better than if they used astrology or the I-Ching to make their cancer predictions. Women are thereby being surgically "cured" of their "evil" and "sinful" sexual organs, via "modern medicine". A similar scientism spreads into male sexual health, as with unreliable "marker tests" being abused to justify ever-more prostate surgeries, after which erectile disorders and incontinence are a common result.

New Medieval "hiding virus" theories also predominate, in a wholesale discarding of basic principles of scientific causality and proofs. A health problem today can be blamed on a nearly undemonstrable or hypothetical "supervirus" to which you were allegedly exposed some 20 years earlier – as with the unproven "infectious HIV" theory of AIDS[5] and its decidedly anti-sexual social messages and impacts. Sex is no longer a mere "sin" as preached by black-robed priests; now "sex can kill". So say the new priests in white-coats, and their small army of fingerwaggers in Big Education and Big Media. "Hiding invisible viruses" now replace "The Devil" or "invisible demons".

These new taboos about genital sexuality are taught to schoolchildren, in a schizophrenic manner along with encouragements towards non-genital homosexuality, and are spread socially by massive media propaganda in Orwellian "anti-sex" style. Claimed HIV infections are now also thrown up as an excuse for doing even more male genital mutilations than already occur, and for denying children breast milk (again, the "evil" sexual organs). People who are declared as "infected" then receive the new Scarlet Letter "A", even as promiscuous sex-clubs for both heteros and homos are given full legal approvals under "civil liberties" rhetoric. Even worse, but perhaps more revealing, the white-coats today also perform *full genital amputations* on confused teens and slightly older youth, the so-called "sex-change surgery". In this, they emulating the worst of the old Saharasian slave-traders, where kidnapped boys destined for the harems of pedophile rapist warlords had their external genitalia completely cut away, while girls' genitalia were sewn shut.[6] Today, young boys and girls, confused by years of heterosexual repression and porno-homoerotic propaganda, can be roped into believing they are "gay" through aggressive marketing by pedophile-oriented homosexual activist groups, who are also allowed into the public schools to spread their poison. Parents and professionals who have spoken out against these destructive trends typically find themselves accused of "hate speech" and become targets for personal attacks – not too different from what happened in the Middle Ages when priestly authority was challenged. Big Medicine, Big Government, Big Media and Big Science have all thereby been recruited to support and encourage the trends *against heterosexual genitality*, which also gets funding from public sources, making the situation all the more intractable, and likely to persist and grow.

Related social customs of an alarmingly repressive nature are also being directly imported from the Islamic world, such as female genital mutilations, polygamy, arranged child marriages and the veil. Strange "feminists" have even praised Islamic female sexual slavery, proclaiming forced polygamy and the veil as "liberating". "Civil libertarians" also form political alliances with Islamic groups, to promote the totalitarian desert warrior's creed of Sharia Law and male supremacy, as merely "religious practices" or as some new kind of bizarre "spirituality", as in the "religion of peace" nonsense.[6] They don't use the same clear and stark terms as I do, but once their fuzzy wording and smiley-faced facade of smoke and mirrors is peeled away, what I give here is a very clear description of the real situation.

There is likewise no real end to authoritarianism in the schools, where old practices of spanking disobedient children are today replaced by putting them into Ritalin-drug straightjackets, based upon psychiatric genetic hocus-pocus about "attention disorders" in frequently boring windowless and microwave/EMF contaminated and agitated classrooms, to keep them sitting still in their school chairs, or docile at home. Other teens get antidepressants, to put a smiley-face on their misery, just as their parents have learned to do. It is hard to say which is worse, the spankings or the psycho-drugs. Teachers who dare to speak out risk being fired, and get no support from the civil libertarians or teacher's unions either, who make open war against the parents who try to home-school their kids, to spare them such madness, including the increasingly leftist Big Government brainwash. Not surprisingly, teenage sexual misery, revealed in widespread drug-abuse, binge-drinking, seeking of empty sexual activity, with murderous bullying, school violence and suicides, have persisted. Children frequently run away from such abusive or dysfunctional homes and schools, making for permanent populations of runaway teens in the major cities of the world, who in turn are exploited for prostitution.

And yet, in spite of all this sexual chaos and insanity, *it is the rarely-implemented proposals from Reich, Hodann and SexPol which are attacked as unrealistic or morally objectionable!*

Adults in Western society, having suffered through such things, not surprisingly exhibit high levels of sexual impotence and ungratification. To compensate, and add to the profits of the pharmaceutical houses, popular media celebrates the "remedy" of Viagra pills, as if the issue of male sexual impotence and premature ejaculation was something other than a tragedy.

Inorgasmic and depressed women are, in turn, put on Prozac or Luvox in high numbers, a chemical smiley-face painted over their sexual misery. Prostitution meanwhile flourishes, stimulating the same problem of traffic in women and children for sexual purposes as described by Hodann and Reich back in the Weimar days. The roots of these problems in sexual repression and associated sexual license and misery are no longer addressed in any serious manner, the professional classes being hardly better today than they were in the 1930s. American and European movies further exacerbate the problem by misrepresenting porn, pedophilia, homoeroticism and prostitution as something "cool" or "hip", giving them social legitimacy.

The original SexPol efforts towards a *real sexual revolution distinguishing sexual health from unhealth*, was therefore never fully realized. The old compulsive Church moralism preaching sexual sin diminished in influence, for certain, but has frequently been replaced with a new brand of *compulsive sexual promiscuity and violence*. Love and emotional considerations are diminished, as empty pre-genital eroticism with sadistic elements is elevated.

The 1960s youth culture of my own generation, now grown to adulthood, bears much of the responsibility for this situation. Hodann, Reich and SexPol never had the goal of filling human societies with pornographic "swingers", wife-swappers, bisexuals, polygamists, prostitution, S&M whippers, bathhouse promiscuity, child-porn and pedophiles. But that is what one finds frequently openly endorsed, or claimed to be "harmless activity" by professionals who often come from those same pathological social networks. At foundation they merely seek to normalize their sickness. With justification from the unscientific Kinsey theories, they grabbed the public microphone and got praise and support from Hollywood, Big Media and Big Government, wreaking a havoc within society that has not yet reached its pinnacle, but which most assuredly has nothing to do with authentic sexual freedom, love or health. The political consequences of this unsettling trend have yet to be fully appreciated, as the cross-cultural evidence suggests such societies collapse into authoritarianism and rationalized wars of aggression, eventually self-destructing.[6]

By contrast to Hodann, Reich, and other physicians following the precepts of SexPol, or to the clear-minded anthropologists such as Bronislaw Malinowski and Verrier Elwin, and educators such as A.S. Neill, these expressions of loveless sexual hyperactivity and Medieval anti-sex medicine as given above are psychopathological, derived from sexual repression and sex-frustration which, in turn, generates sadistic and masochistic behavior. They are not something one finds in authentic sexually free societies where genital sexual gratification is predominant.[6]

Marxist-Communist Betrayal of the Weimar Sex-Reformers, and Everybody Else

While the seizure of Nazi power in Germany led to an expected destruction of the Weimar-era sex-reform movements, the various European Communist Parties (CP) which took their orders from Moscow, turned out to be just as hostile, but not immediately so. The various freedom movements which appeared across Europe after the destruction of the German and Austro-Hungarian Empires, were at first supported by European socialist organizations. With the clear hindsight of history, however, today we know how the Marxist-communists acquired organizational controls over critical social reform movements, using freedom-slogans and deceit to gain influence. Only a facade of interest in human welfare or the advancement of liberty existed, and freedom-oriented social reforms of all kinds were thereby undone. All the decent social reformers who had formed the backbone of the original reform movements, like Hodann and Reich, were pushed out and frequently attacked by the same CP organizations which once hosted their lectures and sold their books.

Shortly after the 1933 Nazi takeover in Germany, most of the sexual reformers of Weimar were in prison, in exile, on the run, or dead. The Soviet Union followed suit shortly thereafter, banning abortion and shutting down or taking over remnant independent sex-counselling clinics, schools and organizations for psychoanalysis and sexology, replacing their leaders with political functionaries. Stalin, like Hitler, wanted more babies for cannon-fodder and planned wars of conquest – eventually they both passed out medals to mothers with the most children. We also know today how *the Soviets under Lenin and Stalin were secretly working and cooperating with the German High Command and later Nazis towards larger totalitarian agendas*, in which independent sexual reform organizations had no place. The Bolshevik-CP betrayal of the original Russian Revolution and independent Soviets after October 1917 was initiated by the Russian traitor Lenin, whose power-grab was facilitated and financed by the Kaiser and the German High Command, and for which he rewarded the Kaiser with vast stretches of Russian territory. Deadly betrayals and massacres of freedom-seeking working-class people in the Soviet Union followed quickly thereafter, carried out by Lenin's executioner Trotsky and others. Starting around 1921, the Soviets began secret negotiations with the German military, towards mutual rearmament, in violation of the Versailles agreements. Top Secret factories were built with German technology deep in Soviet territory, which later provided Hitler's Wehrmacht with massive numbers of tanks and artillery, and his Luftwaffe with squadrons of the latest fighter aircraft and bombers.[7] The world awoke in the mid-1930s to a fully re-armed German totalitarianism, against which Stalin pretended to be a threatened victim, rather than the collaborator he was.

The Soviet-CP also betrayed the Spanish Revolution, selling defective weapons (for hard gold) to the Republicans, attacking allied but non-Soviet-controlled Republican divisions, and delivering Spain into the hands of Franco, whose military was well-supported by the Nazis. The Stalinist-CP organized the gulag labor-death camps, the starvation-genocide of millions of Ukrainians, and numerous other atrocities. All of this was covered up by the Comintern and their Western left-progressive allies, who dutifully parroted Soviet propaganda (ie, the *New York Times* willful cover-up of the Ukrainian genocide). Later came the Hitler-Stalin Pact for the division of the world in bloody conquest, starting with Poland and the Baltic States, and the ugly spectacle of various European-CP cadres welcoming the invading Nazis as "fellow socialists", even as they goose-stepped and shot their way across Europe. The Soviets continued supplying the Nazis with grain and raw materials, even after the invasions of Poland, France, and the mass-bombings of British and other European cities. Large numbers of social reformers and freedom fighters in every case were sent to a slow death in Soviet gulags, or simply head-shot into open pits.

By 1939, the Marxist-CP betrayals were fully obvious to everyone with open eyes. But this was not so obvious during the Weimar years of the 1920s and early 1930s, when the hideous lie was being successfully propagated among left-progressives, that the Soviet Union slave-state was some kind of utopia.

And truth be told, today we also know how neither Marx nor Engels had authentic sympathy for the working-class peoples whom their totalitarian ideology and CP organizations would later conquer and dominate. Only in the private letters and more obscure writings of Marx and Engels did they expose their hatred, contempt, and bloody plans for a ruthless totalitarianism and liquidation of all who opposed them.[8] Neither Hodann nor Reich, nor any of the early sex-reformers knew about those materials, nor about the crimes of Lenin and Trotsky, nor of Stalin's long cooperation with Hitler, which were all hidden and concealed from the outside world. These only got a wider public attention after WW-2, with the lion's share of documentation coming available only after the opening of Soviet and East German archives, following the 1991 collapse of the Soviet Union. The German-speaking world during Weimar remained blissfully ignorant of these facts, and for awhile, Marxism could still be paraded around as fashionable, reasonable, and untarnished.

Irrespective of the widespread appeal of Marxism, every social reformer of the Weimar period opposed class divisions and exploitation of workers, Marxist or not. The British, American and French systems of liberal democracy for example had a long history of self-reform, including the anti-slavery movements, the women's rights and sexual reform movements, and the older trade guilds and unions. They owed nothing to Marx. But in Germany, where the warmongering autocratic Empire of the Kaiser had only recently ended, there was an impatience with chaotic Weimar democracy and a hunger for quick social change. Marxist rhetoric slandered the Western democracies and preached violent revolution, at the same time the Nazis spoke with similar socialist zeal, in what surely was an irredeemable situation. Both promised the Moon, inflamed people's hatreds, and society fractured. The Nazis won, temporarily.

The sex-reformers thereby suffered critically from their ignorance or miscalculations about the benefits or necessity of joining their reform efforts to the Marxist parties. Reich, for example, was by 1936 placed on an NKVD death-list[2,9] for daring to suggest such things as how the "new man" of Soviet communism was just as sexually disturbed and neurotic as the "old man" of capitalism. He unforgivably emphasized freedoms in sexual and family life over Marxist class-warfare rhetoric. By 1939, Reich held decidedly anti-communist views and fled to America, revising his old papers and books so as to reduce or eliminate prior Marxist language. He also began calling the Communist Party *Red Fascists*, emphasizing their similarities to the *Black Fascists* of Nazi psychopathology. He continued to be publicly slandered by old European Marxists and cloaked CP agents in his new homeland. A scandal was fabricated in American left-wing magazines and the yellow press, leading to a phony "investigation" of his pioneering biophysical research by the socialist-oriented and Roosevelt-empowered US Food and Drug Administration (FDA). The FDA lied to the US Courts, got Reich's scientific books and research journals burned, and threw him into prison on a technicality, where he died in 1957.[9]

Hodann, as mentioned, was slow to realize the Marxist betrayals. When he was finally released from incarceration by the Nazis in late 1933, he traveled and for a time acted as physician for the International Brigade during the Spanish Civil War, witnessing the Soviet-CP betrayals first-hand. He later wound up isolated and trapped in "neutral" Nazified Sweden where he was called the "sex-Jew from Weimar". He bravely dared to continue with his speaking and writing, and giving help to war refugees and German military deserters. *"The old slogans have lost their meanings"* he declared with depression, knowing how so many of his old comrades in the sexual reform movement had been destroyed or killed by the Communists, who disowned him as well. Impoverished and in poor health, he died in 1946, possibly by suicide.

For those readers who know the authentic ugly and very bloody history of the Communist movement and Soviet Union, and the calculated concealment of their many crimes, it is fairly clear that Hodann, Reich, and so many others in the Weimar sexual/social freedom and reform movements had a terribly naive and superficial understanding of Marxist concepts and agendas. For those who don't know that history, and who might believe Marxism still has rational merit, it is well past time for them to confront the ugly facts about how the Marxist-CP factions the world over killed many times what the Nazis did, but somehow have got away with it, avoiding the public stigma of genocidal butchery, or taking of responsibility. However, this awful history of 20th Century fascism, Red and Black, is no rational cause for rejecting the scientific works on human sexuality, family and society as developed by workers such as Hodann or Reich, who for a time were peripherally attracted to the collectivist illusion. In any case, Hodann's European work, like that of Reich, was predominantly aimed at sexual reform issues, and not overtly or purely political agendas. Economic stability retains a central importance for family happiness and social harmony, but is proven more readily achievable without Marxist thuggery – as seen in Western democratic societies with trade unions. We can look back on the turbulent Weimar period and gain important lessons, as we head into new periods of social turbulence.

There are a few errors of fact in the Hodann text, such as the derogatory reference to the "monkeyville" trial (p.viii of Hodann's Preface). This trial in fact was carefully planned in advance by both prosecution and defendant, aimed at bringing a legal challenge before the American courts against certain laws opposing the teaching of Darwin; it was no expression of spontaneous religious fanaticism as popular newspaper accounts and Hollywood films have misrepresented. Darwin and evolution were being taught in most American school biology classes, even in the states having such archaic laws, but without enforcement. Also, there is discussion by Hodann about eugenics that, for him, carried the emphasis of ending the transmission of scientifically proven hereditary disorders. Only after the Nazi takeover of German medicine did the stain of genocidal race-theory appear. That brand of murderous eugenics was never advocated by Hodann, Reich, nor by others working within the larger Weimar sex-reform movement. Hodann also cites some statistics from the Soviet Union which should be viewed with caution as to their accuracy. Again, Hodann remained a dedicated socialist until quite late, changing views only after his bad experiences with the Communist factions during the Spanish Civil War, and later after the 1939 Hitler-Stalin Pact and onset of WW-2. That, along with learning of the arrests or assassinations of so many of his former socialist associates by the Soviet NKVD. His *History* was written in 1936, before Hodann came to such critical realizations, and so contains the occasional declaration in favor of short-lived conditions or reforms within the early Soviet Union which did not last for long, except as illusions maintained by Politburo propaganda.

And finally, Hodann makes an amazing statement about Ernst Roehm, leader of the Nazi SA Brownshirts, suggesting that maybe if he had won the battle with Hitler, things might have turned out differently.(p.313) Roehm was in fact a violent pedophile homosexual, as were most within his SA units, and that is the only reason why he occasionally made statements opposing "moral cranks" critical of his behavior. The SA were Hitler's henchmen, street thugs and killers who after Roehm's death were absorbed into the equally ruthless SS.

These errors are left standing in the translation without comment, other than here, and will find corrections in historical texts which have not succumbed to modern revisionist deceit.

The manuscript for *History of Modern Morals* was completed in c.1936, apparently without any published German edition, which was impossible during the Nazi period. The English translation was published in 1937, by William Heinemann Medical Books in London, which at the time carried several titles on the sexual reform movement.

James DeMeo, PhD
Ashland, Oregon, USA
June 2013

Introduction References

1. The alternative social-reform pathway, of a liberal capitalist democratic republic – following the ideas of the American example, as from the inspirational writings of Jefferson, Franklin and Adams, or even the French model – never "caught on" within German speaking nations, due to language barriers, cultural biases and Marxist utopian propaganda.

2. For more details, see: James DeMeo: *In Defense of Wilhelm Reich*, Natural Energy Works, Ashland, Oregon 2013. Myron Sharaf: *Fury on Earth: A Biography of Wilhelm Reich*, St.Martin's/Marek, NY, 1986.

3. Bernd Nitzschke: "Psychoanalysis and National Socialism, Banned or Brought into Conformity? Break or Continuity?" *International Forum of Psychoanalysis* 12, 2003, p. 98-108.

4. Judith Reisman, et al.: *Kinsey Sex and Fraud*, Lochinvar-Huntington House Publications 1990; Judith Reisman, et al., *Kinsey - Crimes and Consequences*, Inst. for Media Education, 1998.

5. See: Peter Duesberg: *Inventing the AIDS Virus*, Regenery, NY 1996. Also consult www.duesberg.com and www.virusmyth.com

6. See my extensive cross-cultural and geographic review of over 1100 different societies from around the world, confirming Reich's findings. James DeMeo: *Saharasia: The 4000 BCE Origins of Child-Abuse, Sex-Repression, Social Violence and War, In the Deserts of the Old World*, Natural Energy Works, 2nd Revised Edition, 2006. Social variables indicating high levels of violence and warfare correlate strongly positive with infant neglect, childhood trauma, adolescent and adult sexual repression, strict marriage rules, low women's status, and high levels of political and religious hierarchy.

7. See: Ulrich Albrecht: *The Soviet Armaments Industry*, Harwood Academic Pub., 1993, p.13-17, 57, 62-67. Viktor Suvorov: *The Chief Culprit: Stalin's Grand Design to Start World War II,* Naval Institute Press, Annapolis, 2008, p.17-18. Edward E. Ericson: *Feeding the German Eagle: Soviet Economic Aid to Nazi Germany*, Praeger, 1999. Gerald Freund: *Unholy Alliance: Russian German Relations from the Treaty of Brest-Litovsk to the Treaty of Berlin*, Harcourt Brace & Co., 1957. Hans W. Gatzk: *Stresemann and the Rearmament of Germany*, Johns Hopkins Press, 1954.

8. James DeMeo: *"The Hidden History of Marx and Engels: Genocide Quotations"*, www.orgonelab.org/MarxEngelsQuotes.htm

9. James DeMeo: *"New Information on the Persecution and Death of Wilhelm Reich"*, www.orgonelab.org/ReichPersecution.htm

Notes on unusual terms in this translation:

"Dread" – a meaning of anxiety, sexual avoidance or fear.

"Sexual Oekonomie" – the Sex-Economic theory of W. Reich

HISTORY OF
MODERN MORALS

BY
MAX HODANN

TRANSLATED BY
STELLA BROWNE

*" Error of opinion may be tolerated
when reason is left free to combat it."*

To
LISE LINDBAEK,
MY FRIEND AND FELLOW-WORKER,
IN GRATITUDE AND REGARD

PREFACE

IN all civilized countries people are aware that there is a growing contrast between tradition and law regarding morals and sex life on the one hand, and the real behaviour of men and women on the other. Our modern age has changed the social fabric, especially since the Great War, in fundamental and far-reaching ways. Changes of the social and economic structures imply changes in the ethical structure as well ; and this inherited structure of ethical codes is now so undermined that the defenders of its " objectivity " and intrinsic validity have been driven to the defensive. The world has grown more worldly, more exclusively preoccupied with its own conditions, organisms and institutions, and therefore less apt to listen to and obey the Churches. From Copernicus to Darwin, and from Darwin to Freud, the results of scientific discovery and deduction have shown a cumulative contradiction to the traditions of the Middle Ages, though certain survivals of these traditions are still deeply entrenched and vigorous among us to-day. And it is due to these mediæval traditions that the investigation of human instincts and emotions is still impeded by the deepest inhibitions in the individual, as well as by social customs and prejudices. The individual repressions and inhibitions are manufactured by education ; and this education is in harmony with the class-division and the class spirit of the Community ; at least in so far as education is noticed or assisted or directed by the State. Certainly the " bourgeois " Community of the mid-twentieth century is no longer Victorian ; but it still possesses the most sensitive antennæ for all things that might endanger its prosperity or permanence.

The institutions of this Community are subject to the dogma of " the impartiality of science " ; or feel themselves bound to respect this legacy of the French Revolution, an epoch in which the " Third Estate," now the nominal ruler in democratic states, had to fight for its very existence. Individual liberty and scientific impartiality were by no means accepted truisms in high places in 1789.

But in the early nineteenth century, when the Third Estate began to hold the casting vote in the destinies of European peoples, it made its peace and drove its bargain with the inheritors and survivals of feudalism ; and more especially with the Church. So it was no chance surrender, but a sociological necessity, when Rudolf Virchow, the world-famous pathologist, demanded fetters and gags for science (for natural science and for his special branch of knowledge in the interest of the State) in his celebrated lecture on " The Freedom of Science in the Modern State." The theory of evolution and human descent was an unscientific and speculative hypothesis, and might not be taught in schools. It was dangerous to constituted authority.

In 1877 the fight against the Darwinian theory of Evolution was in full swing, for Darwinism proclaimed and proved Man's animal descent and inheritance, and dethroned Man " made in God's image " from a unique position of privilege. And Darwinism has conquered ; the civilization of to-day accepts his conclusions, tacitly if not explicitly ; and the famous " Monkeyville " case in the most backward regions of the United States of America is merely an instance of provincial ignorance in so-called " educated " people.

The focus of conflict and emotional tension for the nine-teenth century was the Darwinian theory. In the twentieth, the stress has shifted to the scientific investigation and discussion of sexual matters. Thus, even to-day, the definite statement of sexual facts seems to many (otherwise intelligent) people in bad taste and unnecessary. Even so distinguished a representative of the intellect and spirit of England as Havelock Ellis had to suffer the stigma of treat-ment as an " obscene writer " at the hands of the official authorities of his country. And on March 10th, 1932, the leading progressive daily of France, L'Œuvre, noted that the science " sexology " was a " new branch of know-ledge," in recording the foundation of the Société de

Sexologie in Paris. Indeed, this new science bears an uninviting name : " Sexology," is a hybrid, neither good Latin nor good Greek. But the development of the language and the thought of mankind does not follow the rules of the schoolmen, but the needs of life itself ; and so we shall have to accept and occasionally use this term, which is already " current coin."

Sexology is a new science. But its official recognition is delayed and still refused. Why ? Why are Magnus Hirschfeld, Havelock Ellis, Margaret Sanger " outsiders " to the hall-marked university science of to-day ? And Sigmund Freud, who was permitted to occupy a " Chair " at Vienna, had to go through years of mockery and insult as a " charlatan," before Society made terms with him—and before he, to some degree, adapted himself to Society's requirements ? Why these incongruities ?

Because the last remnant of human divinity and transcendentalism threatened to dissolve and vanish, when Science discovered—and began to teach—that the intellectual self, the mind and emotional qualities of each and every one of us, are intimately dependent on the chemistry of his or her body, *i.e.*, on the Endocrine Glands ; and further that the religious fixations of various races and ages are only intelligible as manifestations of collective neuroses. And, from another angle, the belief in the Soul and the Moral Order of the Universe forms the most impregnable bulwark of the bourgeois state.

And in spite of all resistance and attacks, the framework for our new science has been set up, the ground plan drawn. Attacks on the status of sexual knowledge will be swept away as triumphantly as the onslaughts led by Virchow against Darwin.

There is a further significant parallelism between to-day and 1877 ; in that year the Evolutionary Theory of Human Origins was already basically established and of gigantic scope and suggestion ; but detailed confirmation and application were to take place in the ensuing decades. This process of working out general principles involved many revisions ; and the same is true already, and doubtless will be true in future, in the sexological domain. Perhaps the most significant and suggestive development is already visible to-day : the linking-up, the demonstrable interaction, between sexology in general, sexual-psychology in particular, and sociology. In other words, the expansion and evolution of Psychoanalysis into " Sexual-Oekonomie " (Reich) and " Clinical Sociology " (Schmalhausen). And so we have perhaps arrived at the right moment for a survey and a synthesis of our available knowledge regarding the bases of present-day morality. The history of sexology is simply the history of the changes in the customs and codes of the Occident, under the stress of social and economic forces and scientific discoveries. This history of sexology is by no means exclusively a record of research. It is concurrently a record of suspicions, accusations, prosecutions, persecutions, legal and illegal, and savage penalties. Hunger strikes and attempts at murder lend their peculiar savour to its pages. It is, in fine, the record of the resistance of the champions of obsolete ideas and customs, threatened in their security and supremacy by the pioneers of constructive progress. It is the record of the expansion of library and laboratory to fill the stage whereon moves the drama of our modern world.

TABLE OF CONTENTS

xi

HISTORY OF MODERN MORALS

CHAPTER I

THE SECRET OF GENERATION

I

DARKNESS reigns in the great Hall of Assembly in the Masonic Building at Oxford. But there is a reflection from the cone of light thrown by the softly crackling film camera on the screen at one end of the hall; and this dim gleam serves to show that the available space is packed with people. Their tense silence is only broken by the occasional comments and explanations of the demonstrator.

The film unfolds its marvels; for the first time the audience sees the process of cell-division, and the emergence of a new cell, the beginning of what is to grow to a living creature. The date is August 15th, 1935, and the occasion the session of the Department for Visual Education of the Synchronized International Educational Conferences. The film is of German origin. It was composed with infinite thought and effort. It was the triumph of technique crowning a century of active biological research into the process of reproduction in dimorphic or bisexual species. The previous stages of this long search for truth were not less dramatic than the significant and memorable demonstration of the fertilization of the rabbit egg before the representatives of fifty-two nations, assembled in Conference on education, in that illustrious and ancient University town.

As the film displayed its marvels, I remembered a late afternoon on a summer's day in the Berlin University Institute for Microscopic Anatomy. The year was 1913. We had just had the advantage of a lecture in a series or

Embryology, delivered by Professor Oscar Hertwig. We students listened to him and revered him ; we realized his greatness. The little fellow with the white torpedo beard had asked three of us, of whom I was one, to stay behind after the lecture and speak to him. We sat on one of the long tables, still strewn with microscopes and materials, and we were highly excited. What could " Henny " want to see us about ? His nickname was the result of his intense preference and frequent use of the chicken-embryo as laboratory material for study and illustration. Hertwig appeared and we sprang to our feet. He seemed in the best of spirits, and so talkative and genial that we hardly recognized the concise, formal, matter-of-fact style of his lectures and discussions in his unofficial affability.

" Will you be good enough to come to my workroom, gentlemen ? That's right ! Now, I want to talk over a suggestion with you. You have all shown more skill and interest in our joint work than the rest of your class mates. Would you care to work as assistants at my Institute ? We shall hardly be able to afford any remuneration, but you will have the chance of a much more thorough grounding than from the lecture series alone. What term are you in ? "

One of us three was in his third, another in his fourth. " And you ? " I was nonplussed, but blurted out : " My first, sir ! " The course of lectures in question was generally attended by members of more advanced classes, and I had really been " gatecrashing " Embryology, before the officially appointed hour. Hertwig stared in surprise. " Your first ! Where did you learn the technique ? " So I had to explain that I had done a good deal of microscopic work as a school-boy, following the mental stimulus of a visit which I had managed to pay to the great arch-zoölogist Haeckel himself, at an absurdly early age. Hertwig showed lively interest at the mention of that great name. He was associated with Haeckel's work at Jena University, not only by years of mental interchange and correspondence, but, above all, through the greatest discovery of his life.

" Tell me how you got into touch with Haeckel ? "

I was just ten years of age when I had the opportunity

of spending a few months in Jena. From my early childhood I had taken a lively interest in both animals and plants, and had listened to, and wondered at, the mention of Professor Haeckel's name : the " Ape-investigator." What a wonderful man he must be ! And so, one day, it befell that I stood full of longing and curiosity just outside the gate of his garden ; and an elderly gentleman broke into my daydreams with the brisk but kindly question : " Well, my boy, what are you here for ? " The gentleman wore a big black slouched hat and looked as though he might be an artist.

My audacity almost failed me, but finally I got out a statement that " I really wanted to see the man who knows all about animals." The gentleman shouted with laughter, and said : " Well, well ! perhaps that can be arranged. Come along." And forthwith led me through the garden and into the house, and into a room crammed from floor to ceiling with books, skeletons and skulls, human and simian. And then, turning to me, he introduced himself : " I happen to be Ernst Haeckel, by the way ! " He told me about the different kinds of apes and monkeys, and showed me his water colour sketches of Indonesian scenes and people. For he was an artist of individuality and graphic power, and my first impression was therefore correct, though not complete ! Hertwig was delighted to hear of this incident and became more conversational than ever before or since— in my experience of his ways.

" Ah, yes, Haeckel ! Yes, yes ! how well I remember the results of his public acceptance of the new discoveries and doctrines that came to us, from England, in the 'sixties, and roused such a storm for and against ! "

2

And indeed the distress and confusion among the tradition-ally minded representatives of science was indescribable, for Haeckel drew conclusions, with unswerving logic, from the premises of Darwin's discoveries as to the Origin of Species. He left us an account of their reception. In his *Kampf um den Entwicklungsgedanken*, Haeckel said : " In

1863, I attended the Naturalists' Congress at Stettin, and gave the first public exposition of the Darwinian theory of Evolution in Germany. I was almost alone in my acceptance ; the overwhelming majority of those present regarded me with regret and pity, as the victim of a misapprehension and delusion. What a fantastic theory, how could it be taken so seriously ! ' A dream in an after-dinner nap ' was the comment of Keferstein, the well-known zoölogist of Göttingen University ! "

In 1874 Haeckel published a comprehensive statement of the theory of evolution, applied to all living species, under the title *Anthropogonia*. The Roman Catholic Bishop of Bonn, Michelis, promptly stigmatized the book as " a murderous assault on the Truth of Revelation and the essential Conditions of Morality ; a disgrace and a blot on our German name ; and a symptom of scientific hallucination and senile dementia."

But we need not go back half a century in order to realize the severe conflicts and the tremendous results implied by the biological discoveries of the Origin of Mankind and the secret mechanisms of generation. On January 26th, in the year 1935, the Protestant cleric Pastor T. S. Valen, writes as follows in *Aftenposten*, the leading Conservative paper of Norway, concerning the Darwinian theory : " Such a doctrine can lead to the overthrow of moral principles, and teach men contempt for the God given laws of Right and Wrong ; that is for His Ten Commandments."

In the 1870's the Conservative Press of Germany rejoiced greatly at the attack launched by Rudolf Virchow, the famous anatomist, in his lecture on " The Freedom of Science in the Modern State " (Munich, 1877). The lecture suggested the need to limit the aforesaid freedom, and stigmatized the Darwinian theory as an " unscientific hypothesis, unsuited to educational purposes and dangerous to the constituted authority." " We must not and ought not to teach that Man is derived or descended from the Ape or from any other animal species." In the revolutionary year 1849, young Virchow emphatically proclaimed a monistic philosophy, and his conviction that " he would never find himself compelled to deny the unity of human personality and all its implications." But twenty-eight years after, the adroit politician and man of the world rejected Evolution with equal emphasis, and proclaimed : " Soul, not cells." And as Haeckel pointed out in 1905 : " The crown of this reactionary recantation was his accommodation with those churches which he had so resolutely attacked twenty years before. With the coolest suavity, he finds ' the only safe basis for education are the doctrines of established religion '."

When this speech became known in England, Darwin declared Virchow's conduct disgraceful, and expressed the hope that he might have occasion to be ashamed of it.

No, there was no exaggeration in Hertwig's account of the emotions and reactions provoked by the new theory that Darwin and Wallace had given to the world. The problem of human origins was vital and topical to the highest degree ; and it is as fundamental now as on that summer evening in 1913.

3

Hertwig had preferred to specialize in the ontogenetic aspects of biology. These were less associated with public and philosophic conflict than their obverse (phylogenetic). He said : " I began by trying to clarify what the microscope could reveal of the structure of gametes (reproductive cells) in order to trace the process of fertilization. You can hardly imagine how much more difficult microscopic work was in those days, with the comparatively primitive instruments and lack of micrographic control."

Then the great biologist told us of his sudden idea, of exposing the eggs of the sea-urchin to the action of sperms of the same species, in a liquid medium. His frail, small figure trembled as he recalled the intellectual tension and the joy of creative research.

" I was on an expedition to Corsica, you know, with Haeckel and my brother Richard, the zoölogist. At Ajaccio I began to examine the ova of the sea-urchin, you know they are in profusion in those waters: *Toxopneustes lividus*, gentlemen. When Haeckel returned to Germany, Richard

and I stayed on, throughout April and May, 1875, and
continued our research work. I sat at the microscope,
while the light lasted, from dawn till nightfall.

" At that date we were still in the dark about the minute
and delicate details in the process of fertilization. I was
able to ascertain, for the first time, that the two merging
and conjoining cells were the gametes of the two parent
beings of different sexes ; namely, ova and spermatozoa.
Both were genuine structural cells, both consisted of protoplasm and nuclear substance. And as both these gametes
united to form a new cellular entity, we concluded that the
process of fertilization and reproduction might be summarized
not only as ' omnis cellula e cellula ' (every cell comes from
another cell), but also ' omnis nucleus e nucleo ' (every
nucleus from another nucleus).

" This superseded the view hitherto enunciated by Haeckel,
that in the process of fertilization a fresh cellular nucleus is
developed out of a hitherto undifferentiated homogeneous
globe of protoplasma. Haeckel's Monads don't exist,
gentlemen ! My observations in Corsica and Villafranca
were incorporated in my thesis ' Fertilization consists in
the conjunction and merging of sexually differentiated
nuclei '."

His enthusiasm was infectious. One of us asked : " So
you were the first human being to behold the actual invasion
of an ovum by a spermatozoön ? " " Well no, not exactly.
That precise process escaped me, but was observed and
recorded by my colleague Hermann Fol, a Swiss."

Hertwig went to a bookshelf and drew out an old volume
of the proceedings of the Genevan " Société de physique
et d'histoire naturelle."

The date was 1879, and the volume contained Fol's
" Recherches sur la fécondation chez les divers animaux."

" Look here ; you have the first drawings illustrating the
invasion of the ovule and the formation of the receptive
cone. Fol used a new stain which clearly revealed the
identity of the invading spermatozoön in structure and
nature with the other spermatozoa surrounding the ovule.
In his own words : ' The comparison of this male cell with

those which abounded in the liquid medium, swarming around the ova, left no possible doubt as to its nature; the aspect of all sperms was identical.'

" After these confirmations of my Corsican research there could be no doubt that we had made the first steps towards elucidating and understanding the secret of generation."

4

The *savant* was silent for a while and lost in memory. Then he continued :

" Yes, it was forty-six years after Karl Ernst von Baer had discovered the first human ovule. Research means time, gentlemen, and much, very much, patience; you'll have to get used to that ! And he who discovers anything new is generally considered a mental case by his contemporaries. You'll get accustomed to *that*, too ! "

" Were your conclusions attacked too ? "

" Of course, of course ! Though not so offensively as Haeckel's, for he was called ' Antichrist ' and ' the Plague of Jena ' and—a forger. And even honoured with stone-throwing, by devout hands, in March of the Year of Grace 1908. No, it wasn't so bad as that for me. But there was considerable discussion, in scientific books and periodicals, about Fol's work and mine. Meanwhile research went on steadily, while reaction raged ! We were able to obtain definite facts about the central core of the gametes, the nucleus and its substance. Fleming found a new method of staining, and in 1879 he saw that the nuclear substance, so stained, formed threads during the process of fertilization, and then fell into portions which split longitudinally—as is now well known. These he christened chromosomes—in 1888. The basis for our knowledge of the maturation and development of gametes was furnished by Eduard van Beneden, who worked in Brussels, on the parasitic form, *Ascaris megalo-cephala*, and confirmed the specific differences in the chromosomes of various living beings. In 1884, Naegeli pointed out the difference between ' Idioplasm ' and ' Protoplasm ' and Strasburger reached the same conclusions in his research on plants ; so we know that chromatin must be the permanent essential substance of heredity. Waldeyer had described the morphological process of cellular division as karyokinesis. But the actual genetic mechanism was still a riddle.

"We knew by human experience, throughout centuries, that hereditary influences operate fairly equally as between the two parents of any child. But we were confronted by the strange disproportion of the two mating cells ; the ovule was so much larger that we were forced to the conclusion that the genetic factors were a function of the nuclear chromatin : *i.e.*, Naegeli's idioplasm.

"And then there was the numerical constancy of the chromosomes ; we asked ourselves why the chromosomes did not double themselves at every merging of the gametes, and then quadruple in the next generation, *ad infinitum ?*

"Well, now we know : we have just considered this subject in the lecture room. But we split our heads over it in the 1880's, I can tell you ! In 1888 I made the first observation of the reduction of chromatin during the maturation of the gametes of *Ascaris*—incidentally the best available material in matters of cell-division ; these observations were exact and repeated, thus enabling us to confirm Beneden's conjecture—or prophecy ?—that ' fecundation consists in the transformation of the female gamete into a complete cell ; and in the replacement of the eliminated elements by fresh elements furnished by the spermatozoön '."

So we know that there is no cellular disintegration in fertilization, but cellular motions and readjustments, karyokinesis, and the distribution of the essential chromatin by means of raylike structures. We know that there is no non-nuclear stage in this chain of evolution, but rather a permanent and typical number of chromosomes for each living species. We know that fertilization implies the merging of one ovule and one spermatozoön and that the multiplication of chromatin is prevented by the ensuing divisions and subdivisions of the developing chromosomes.

5

The discovery of the reproductive mechanisms by means

of the microscope was a scientific milestone, but for the practical life of every day it meant comparatively little. For instance, stock breeders, both of animals and plants, have always had a positive interest in the knowledge of how to " cross " in order to be able to rely on the reasonable probability of perpetuating certain characteristics. They want to know when they may expect improved results— or on the other hand inferior offspring.

Medical men, politicians dealing with the quantity and quality of populations, and students of human psychology all alike wish to know which special combinations of individuality in parenthood are dangerous in perpetuating and accentuating frequent and therefore probably hereditable defects ; and which human " blends " are advantageous. The general tendency of heredity was known, in its broad outlines, since 1871, when Quêtelet applied mathematics to biology and discovered that in any population or group of living creatures the range of variation of special characteristics tends towards a mean average. Let us take as an example bodily stature in a group of persons delimited socially or ethnically. We shall find, as a rule, relatively few " very tall " or " very short " people, but many " average people " of " medium height." As Quêtelet puts it, in his *Anthropométrie* : extreme departures from the " mean average," both in excess and defect, are rare. Approximations to the average, if not the exact average itself, are in the majority.

The creator of British Eugenics was Francis Galton. He thought Quêtelet's law of averages afforded a foundation for a so-called " Regressive Law." If the parents both show a divergence from the average in a certain characteristic, this quality is also displayed by their offspring, but as a rule to a lesser degree, *i.e.*, with a tendency to revert to the group average (1889). Biologists felt that the tendencies they had observed were in correspondence with the facts ; there was a trail to follow. But the riddle of heredity was by no means solved.

Then, in 1900, the Dutch investigator, Hugo de Vries, published an essay entitled " Sur la loi de disjonction des hybrides " in the *Proceedings of the French Académie de Science* (March, 1900) which appeared simultaneously as a note in the third number of the periodical of the German Botanical Society for 1900. De Vries pointed out that an Augustine Father in the monastery at Brno (Brünn) had made extensive observations and annotations on the crossing of sweet-peas (*Pisum sativum*) and even formulated a set of rules for this genus, which deserved the closest attention from investigators. This had happened as early as 1865, and the cloistered botanist had remained totally unknown to the world of science till 1900. When Gregor Mendel, who lived from 1822 to 1884, passed away, his friends mourned a most kindly and helpful character, but no one dreamed that a classic authority on natural science had died with him. By a curious chance the German botanist Focke had read—somewhere—where he could not remember—in the seventies of last century, Mendel's great work *Versuche über Pflanzenhybriden* (*Experiments in Hybridization of Plants*) and had mentioned it in his book on *Plant Hybrids* (Berlin, 1881) : " Mendel believes he has found constant numerical ratios between the different types of hybrids."

Keen botanists, experimenting continuously with crossbreeding, could not miss so suggestive a comment ; and in the issue of the German Botanic periodical following that containing De Vries' contribution there appeared a communication by Carl Correns, who was at that time at Tübingen University : " *Gregor Mendel's Law on the Results of Hybridization.*" In June, 1900, this was further elucidated by documents and reports from Erik Tschermak, the Viennese savant, also dealing with sweet peas ; Tschermak's experiments confirmed the discoveries of Mendel in his monastery garden a whole life's span before ; discoveries on which Mendel's Laws are based. They are as follows :

In the first hybrid generation all the individuals exhibit a uniform appearance (law of uniformity) ; in the second hybrid generation the characters split up in accordance with the proportion of $1 : 2 : 1$ (law of segregation) ; in all subsequent hybrid generations the characters are inherited independently of one another and combine in hybridization in all possible ways (law of independence).

The simultaneous rediscovery and resurrection of Mendel's work of the year 1865 by three entirely independent investigators, De Vries, Correns, and Tschermak, was a real scientific " sensation." Mendelism was born ; and the bridge was formed between the fundamental processes of cellular subdivision and conjugation and the empiric observations of hereditary characteristics in successive generations. Now, at last, we began to understand how it was possible for parents to bequeath to their offspring characteristics which were not apparent in themselves ; their phenotype—their special individual aspect and constitution—could not give free play to all the qualities of their inheritance, i.e., their genotype.

Shortly before the war of 1914–1918, Eugen Fischer put on record the first anthropological evidence—collected on an adequate numerical material—that Mendel's laws are valid for human populations. Fischer had made a careful study of the half-Boer, half-Hottentot cross-breeds of Rehoboth, in what is now the South-West African mandated territory of the South African Union. These people are known as the Rehoboth Bastards, and this was the title of his book published in 1913. At the same time, Professor Iltis, the careful and devoted executor of Mendel's scientific material, found the original manuscript of the work on hybridization, stuffed away in a chest full of other papers destined for the flames as " rubbish " !

I have never had a more pathetic realization of misunderstood and unrecognized greatness than on the occasion of my visit to the Mendel Museum at Brno in the company of Professor Iltis, to whose labour the foundation of this Museum is due. There I beheld the documents relative to Mendel's unsuccessful examination for the University of Vienna ! The investigator of nature's secrets whose name has become identified with modern biological knowledge was not considered worthy in his lifetime, and by constituted authority, to adorn an academic " Chair " !

6

The discovery of the laws of inheritance in hybrid forms made it possible to " link-up with " Darwinism. Even in pre-war years, the leadership in this branch of research had passed to the United States of America, where Th. H. Morgan had concentrated on the *Drosophila* or fruit fly. As material for experimental research, *Drosophila* soon beat the Ascaris hollow ! In 1928 Morgan thus summarized the results of fifteen years' research on successive *Drosophila* generations :

" If, as Darwin supposed, and if, as is generally accepted to-day, the process of evolution has taken place by the slow process of accumulation of small variations, it follows that it must be the genetic variations that are utilized, since these, and not those due to environmental effects, are inherited " (*Theory of the Gene*, p. 315). And again : " The evidence from the Drosophila-work, which is in accord with that from all other forms that have been critically studied, shows that even in those cases where one part is especially modified, other effects are commonly present in several or in all parts of the body. The subsidiary effects not only involve structural modifications, but physiological effects also, if one may judge by the activity, the fertility, and the length of life of the mutants." . . . " Each gene may have an effect on a particular organ, but this gene is by no means the sole representative of that organ, and, in extreme cases, perhaps on all the organs or characters of the body."

Thus Morgan was led to enquire " are genes of the order of organic molecules ? " In spite of the initial difficulties of accepting so bold an hypothesis : " it nevertheless is difficult to resist the fascinating assumption that the gene is constant because it represents an organic chemical entity. This is the simplest assumption that one can make at present and since this view is consistent with all that is known about the stability of the gene, it seems, at least, a good working hypothesis " (*l.c.* p. 321).

At this point we reach the borderline of exact knowledge to-day ; beyond is doubt, conjecture, hypothesis. But practical eugenists are quite aware of the significance of research into cells and chromosomes, as was shown by their invitation to Professor C. F. McClung of Pennsylvania, an expert on Cytology, to address the Second International Congress of Eugenics in New York (1921). McClung spoke on " The Evolution of the Chromosome Complex " and stressed the share of Cytology in making possible " a real recognition of the relation existing between the material substratum of hereditary processes and their visible somatic manifestations " (Report, p. 65). He ventured to claim that the theory of chromosomes had the same basic importance for biology as the atomic theory for chemistry and physics. And indeed, the proof of the specific and constant number of chromosomes, in different animal forms, cleared the trail for the discovery of sex determination. *For genetically, sex is an inherited quality, descending from father to son, from mother to daughter.* But its mechanism remained obscure for a long time ; and was finally detected through observations on the fruit fly, *Drosophila* : one chromosome appeared to be an exception to the rule of subdivision, to which all the others conformed, and subsequent tests have confirmed this exception and demonstrated that this particular X chromosome is indeed the determinant of sex in the embryo. Thus we know that " sex " is not " a physiological phenomenon, independent of the genetic situation " (Morgan, 1934, p. 208).

Of the essential factors in sex determination for the genesis of sex we are no longer in doubt, especially since the basic observations of Correns—one of the joint re-discoverers of Mendel's law. There appear to be no grounds for revision of the results summarized by Goldschmidt in his work on *Sexual Intermediacy (Sexuelle Zwischenstufen,* 1931). The clearest account of the function of the X chromosome is that of the Spanish sexologist, Gregor Marañón, who has devoted years to this branch of research :

" The nucleus of the male gamete or spermatozoön, as well as that of the female gamete or ovum, is composed of a certain number of chromosomes or chromatic filaments, which, when the two gametes unite to form the zygote or egg, merge and give birth to the nucleus of this zygote. Study of these chromosomes shows that they are of two kinds : some of great number and similar size, which we call ordinary chromosomes, and another single one of large size, which we call chromosome X. Upon the combination of the chromosomes depends the sex of the new being, in accordance with the following schema :

" The ova all have a given number, n, of ordinary chromosomes plus one chromosome x $(n + x)$. The spermatozoa, on the other hand, belong to two types : in some there exist, as in the ova, a number, n, of ordinary chromosomes, plus one chromosome x $(n + x)$. In others this chromosome x is lacking and there are only the ordinary chromosomes (n). According to whether one or the other of these two types of spermatozoön unites with the ovum, the chromosome composition of the egg which results will be different, in the manner indicated by the following formula :

Ova	Spermatozoa	Egg	Sex
$(n + x)$	(n)	$(2n + 1x)$	male
$(n + x)$	$(n + x)$	$(2n + 2x)$	female

"According to this theory, the sex of the individual is decided by this chromosomal mechanism at the moment of fecundation " (pp. 248f).

To follow the terminology of Haecker, the German geneticist, the mechanism described by Marañón means the " syngamic determination of sex." But we are extending our knowledge of sexual intergrades, thanks mainly to the work of Goldschmidt, and are beginning to ask how far this syngamic determination is capable of " epigamic " modification. For in the higher forms of organic life, this " epigamic determination or modification of sex " is clearly discernible.

" The sexual alternatives for individual cell clusters . . . depend directly on the XX or XY composition of the cell. But in higher forms this function passes—at least partially— from the individual cell to a special centre, which stimulates one or the other essential substance (i.e., hormone), and thus decides to which sex the individual organism shall belong.

When and to what extent this centre can function, and to what extent primary XX or XY process takes place simultaneously in the individual cell are special questions" (*l.c.*, p. 11).

These special questions are the gateways to a fresh field of knowledge : that of the influence exerted on the sexual characteristics of living species by the chemical processes of their bodies.

7

In the year 1910 E. Steinach of Vienna published three contributions to the *Zentralblatt für Physiologie* (No. 24) on " The sexual impulse and genuine secondary Sex Characteristics, as products of the internal Secretions of the Gonads." Ten years later the great biologist could thus summarize the results of his experimental work :

" If female gonads are implanted in castrated males, they develop the typical characteristics of the female ; if male gonads are implanted in spayed females, the typical characteristics of the male appear." . . . " The psyche of a feminized male animal is eroticized on female lines ; behaviour and reactions are those of the normal female " and *vice versa* (*Rejuvenation*, Berlin, 1920, p. 20).

The first experimentalist on gonadic transplantation was Berthold, who made successful experiments with domestic fowls, at Göttingen, in 1849 ; but Steinach definitely proved the relativity of sexual characteristics and their dependence on the chemistry of the internal secretions. Steinach has shown us that " neither the psychic nor somatic sex characters of adult mammals can be regarded as fixed and irreversible. He proved that some of these characters are reversible and that the gonads are intimately connected with such transformations. This early attained result has been of much value in the chief task of studies on the biology of sex during the past fifteen years, namely, to supply full proof that sex itself, the primary and secondary character alike, is plastic and reversible " (Riddle, Ingese Congress, 1926. Report I, p. 223).

The first working hypothesis to which investigators

inclined was that of an organic substratum, which must be either virilizing or feminizing and from which arose the development of the respective secondary characters. And the general sense of this view has been verified, although many more complex factors are involved than was at first believed. As early as 1775 Borden wrote, " Every organ serves as a workshop for the preparation of a specific substance which enters into the blood ; such substances are useful to the body and are needed in order to maintain its integrity." Here, indeed, was the germ of the idea of internal secretion, which was, however, to lie dormant for more than a century. For although Claude Bernard is generally regarded as the originator in 1855 of the idea of internal secretion, his concept was limited to the maintenance of a constant composition of the blood by this means. Brown-Séquard started the modern interest in the subject, though his data were both inadequate and inaccurate.

Brown-Séquard was half American, half French. On May 15th, 1889, at the age of seventy-two, he performed a remarkable exploratory experiment on himself. He gave himself several injections of the filtration from the amputated testicle of a dog, over a period of weeks, finally supplemented with the testicular secretion of guinea-pigs, in a state of vigorous health. In June of the same year he recorded the results before the Biological Society of Paris. He reported an amazing improvement in his general health, and mitigation of the typical symptoms of senescence ; and the progress of this recovery was unmistakably associated with the regular and frequent injections. Brown-Séquard's contribution had the most sensational " press " ; particularly in the United States. The professor's exalted rank in the world of science, his American father, his birth on the Island of Mauritius (a British Colony) were all proclaimed as proof that he must have found the long-sought and much desired Elixir Vitæ, the draught that bestowed immortal youth ! The Western world " lost its head " over Brown-Séquard, just as it did after the war of 1914–18, when the experimental results of Steinach and Voronoff were made into a " publicity stunt." The professor was forced to protest in the interests of science and his personal honour. He spoke of "espérances absurdes" and declared "j'ai seulement dit et je crois encore qu'il est parfaitement possible de réparer des ans les outrages réparables."

But there was this basis of fact : there were evidently substances in the injected preparation which activated both the general and the sexual capacities of the organism.

When in 1905 Starling introduced the word "hormone" at Hardy's suggestion for the chemical messengers produced in ductless glands, the name gained immediate and general acceptance. "Schaefer pointed out that, by derivation, this term should be restricted to stimulating substances, and tried to introduce the name 'chalones' for secretions having an inhibitory effect ; but all in vain—the first-comer was already an established favourite" (*British Medical Journal*, 1935, p. 667).

At the Centenary of University College, London, on February 28th, 1927, Ernest Starling spoke as follows on the memorable subject and name of hormones : "It was not till the discovery of secretin by Bayliss and myself in 1902 that we recognized that these so-called internal secretions were merely isolated examples of a great system of correlation of the activities, chemical and otherwise, of different organs, not by the central nervous system, but by the intermediation of the blood, by the discharge into the bloodstream of drug-like substances in minute proportions which cooked an appropriate reaction in distant parts of the body." . . . "These hormones, as we called them, we concluded must be of a fairly simple chemical nature, more or less diffusible and easily eliminated or destroyed in the body" (*A Century of Physiology*, pp. 25–26).

8

The study of the hormonic substances started with investigations into "Secretin"—the product of the duodenum discovered by Bayliss and Starling. Then, under the influence of Steinach, inquiry was concentrated on the interactions between the general economy of the organism, the circulation of the blood, and the specific gonadic secretions.

The problem of chemical "erotization" arose, and a somewhat misleading clarification set in with the working hypothesis advanced by Steinach of the localized significance of the interstitial gonadic tissues, which he considered carried the endocrine or hormone substances, which were distinct from the "generative," *i.e.*, gametic products of ovary and testis respectively. Steinach termed this interstitial portion of gonad "the puberal gland"; but even in 1926 this cytological view of the hormonic secretions regulating sex was not completely confirmed, as was shown at the first Ingese Congress. The Russian reflexologist, Vladimir Mikhailovitch Bechterev, for instance, was sceptical of Steinach's theory of cellular specificity, till his death in 1927. But the main work of Steinach is accepted as valid; and may be summarized in the words of his promising pupil, Peter Schmidt, who died quite young as the result of acute melancholia :

"(1) The action of the sexual glands is specifically sexual ;

"(2) Hormopoiesis in the sexual glands is independent of the formation and excretion of procreation cells ;

"(3) The hormone of the sexual glands is of the greatest importance for the formation and the maintenance of the physical and mental sexual characters ;

"(4) Interference with the sexual cells (transplantation, ligation, Roentgen rays) causes an increase or a restoration of hormonic processes ;

"(5) Increase of hormonic processes in individuals with signs of old age, premature or not, partial or total, causes a regeneration which may be termed rejuvenation " (*Theory and Practice of the Steinach Operation*, 1924, p. 36).

Once more, as after Brown-Séquard's autoinjections in the late nineteenth century, the longing of humanity for length of days and immortal youth was brought into contact with the intensification of sexual power. We will consider some of the preliminary studies and observations which have established the main thesis of Steinach. These preliminary investigations were made by veterinary surgeons, and were read only in a close circle of their colleagues.

Tandler and Keller contributed an article to the German professional organ of veterinary surgeons in the year 1911. They described a peculiar form of genital abnormality, known to cattle-breeders as the " twixter " (German : " Zwicke "). Lillie, the American biologist, then made a full study of these creatures, especially in a contribution to *American Science* (No. 45, 1916), and they were termed " free-martins." The name and fame of the free-martin have spread beyond the confines of science, into the more untrammelled fields of fiction. In Aldous Huxley's *Brave New World*, a wide and precise knowledge of cytology, endocrinology and the results of experimental surgery has been woven into a fascinating pattern, with streaks of rich comedy against a sinister background ; for Huxley " gives damnably to think " of what may be the results of our biological indiscretions and reckless experimentations, but his novel has presented facts and ideas to circles unwilling to receive the minute statistics and cautious records of the typical scientific monograph. We are dealing with the subject on the basis of science, so though the free-martin has been introduced into the world of *belles-lettres*, we will quote Lillie's matter-of-fact account of its genetic peculiarities :

" When twin calves are born, one of which is a normal male and the other a female, the latter is generally sterile. It is called a free-martin. The external genitalia of the free-martin are female—or at least more female-like than male-like, but the reproductive organs resemble testes. It has been shown that each of these twins comes from a single egg, and that later the blood systems of the two embryos are in communication through connections established between the embryonic envelopes. The evidence shows convincingly that the free-martin started as a genetic female, and that the connection with the male through the circulation has suppressed the development of the ovary, under which circumstances the testicular structures develop " (Morgan, 1934, p. 220).

The free-martin is " freak " or anomaly in which an alien (male) hormone has begun to operate at a certain stage of pre-natal development, producing an "intersex," in the term coined by Richard Goldschmidt in 1915. He described an "intersexual" form as follows : "an individual who or which ought to be a definite male or female (XX or XY) according to genetic components, but has only developed on the lines peculiar to this sex up to a certain point. At this point, which is crucial, evolution proceeds and is completed on the lines of the other sex " (1931, p. 12).

Goldschmidt attempted a classification of "intersexes," although he readily admitted that it was not as yet possible to construct a complete scheme embracing all possible modifications. He established the dependence of the actual degree of anomaly on the period of time in fœtal development at which the " turning-point " occurs. If the turning-point comes early in fœtal existence, the abnormality is pronounced ; if late, the abnormality is slight.

Goldschmidt's five grades of intersexuality are as follows :

1. Female intersexuality. Turning-point occurs after the individual has reached maturity. The external organs of the woman are unchanged, but the inner genitalia atrophy. No male hormones are active in these cases ; they present an appearance suggesting a female eunuch.

2. Weak or slight intersexuality. Turning-point occurs before puberty, or sometimes at the end of the pre-natal stage. The internal genitalia are infantile ; there are tissues secreting testicular hormones. The general appearance shows a masculine trend, and there is sometimes considerable enlargement of the clitoris, like a miniature penis.

3. Medium intersexuality. Turning-point occurs before the Wolffian ducts degenerate. There are more or less complete Mullerian ducts and vasa deferentia. The gonads are ovotestes or testicles which do not secrete sperms.

4. Pronounced intersexuality. The turning-point here occurs before the differentiation of the organs derived from the Mullerian ducts. Vestiges of the vagina, and uterus masculinus. The female gonads have completely changed into testicles, sometimes functionally active. Sometimes the testicles begin to descend.

5. Sexual transmutation. Internal organs wholly male, but externally sometimes very slight virility. Morphologically very difficult to diagnose (1931, p. 410).

All these intergrades develop more or less far, but in a definite direction ; from an original female form to a more or less pronounced maleness. Male intersexuality, changing from the original male to a more or less complete female, has not yet been recorded among either avian or mammalian species. And the evidence so far available is enough to establish the *rôle* of the organic chemistry in moulding and modifying the sexual characteristics. Sex is not absolute, it is relative and plastic. But what are these potent hormones, these ingredients of our veins and tissues that can initiate changes comparable to the magic brews of the sorceresses of ancient myth ?

9

It was soon realized that the sexual endocrines are not a simple antithetic pair, and with every year of research fresh complexities seem to arise. We may summarize the present state of knowledge thus : Male individuals appear to owe their organic determinism to one specific substance and so far there is neither evidence of a vital endocrine cycle in the male, nor of male intersexuality, although we must keep an open mind here, and remember the comment of Moore : " It is interesting to speculate upon the possibility of a hormonal cycle in the male, which has not yet indicated itself. It is entirely possible that with more exact methods, such a hormonal cycle may be demonstrated " (Paper on *Sex Hormone Antagonism*, II Ingese Congress, London, Report, p. 293). On the other hand, the vital cycle in females is evidently due to the interaction of various hormones.

Moreover, these hormones are opposite in their action ; they function alternately and balance one another. In the first cyclic phase, there is a flow of ovarian or œstrous hormone ; in the second phase, of corpus luteum (follicular or luteal) hormone. And Fraenkel has proved that the latter substance is necessary for the reception and nidation of the ovule in the uterine wall. G. W. Corner and William

M. Allen were the discoverers of the luteal hormone, in 1929. They called it " Progestin," it is the same substance as that termed " Luteohormon " by Carl Clausberg (*American Journal of Physiology*, No. 92, 1930).

Progestin is balanced in the female organism by the original sex hormone œstrin, which is found in the ovaries, placenta, blood, urine and gall bladder (Frank, 1929). When ovulation has taken place, the secretion of Progestin sets in and replaces or supplements the original flow of œstrin. Should no pregnancy occur, the supply of Progestin automatically diminishes. The hormonic cycle affects the whole genital tract ; there is a regularly recurrent follicular atresia, caused by the action of the corpus luteum. Frank claims that only one human ovum in 300 becomes functionally mature, the rest are resorbed (Frank, 1929, p. 290). His chemical analyses convinced him that :

" We may accept the presence of two sex hormones, the one mainly fat soluble, the female sex hormone produced by the ovary, corpus luteum and the placenta ; the other mainly water soluble, elaborated by the corpus luteum alone " (Frank, 1929, p. 293). The exact operation of this recurrent hormonic alternation is still obscure, both in the pregnant state and otherwise ; indeed there is much that is not yet elucidated in the whole field of endocrinology.

We already know that there are potent " extragonadal sexual factors " (Marañón, 1930, *Revue française de l'Endocrinologie*). Thus the products of the thymus are antagonistic to genital functions ; they retard or even inhibit puberty. The cortex of the renal capsules exudes a hormone which increases virility in males, and accentuates masculine characteristics (*e.g.*, hair distribution) in females. But so far as we know, the real mainspring in this complicated mechanism is the anterior pituitary hormone, which " touches off " the endocrine secretions in the gonads in both sexes. Moreover, we know that there must be reciprocal action, for castration leads to cellular changes (degeneration ?) in the anterior lobe of the pituitary gland (Dohrn-Hohlweg, II Ingese Congress Report, p. 436) ; but the exact mechanism here is as yet unknown.

Thus endocrines are the elements in an intricate pattern ; even the exact source of the pregnancy hormones (which saturate the organism at an early stage in gestation, as discovered and utilized by Aschheim and Zondek) is still unknown. There appears to be sound evidence for their placental origin. According to Aschheim neither the œstrus hormone which is responsible for the phenomena of " heat " and therefore the basic hormone of desire and sexual congress, nor the corpus luteum product " progestin " which causes follicular and luteal growth are active during gravidity. But endocrine substances which form and determine the growth of the fœtus are produced during pregnancy.

Butenandt of Göttingen has isolated and described the distinctive hormone of the male (*Nature*, 1932, No. 130, p. 238). According to a personal communication from Professor F. A. E. Crew, " The most recent suggestion for the formula is $C_{19}H_{30}O_2$; and this appears to be identical with the crystalline hormone extracted from human urine." So far, there have been no appreciable clinical applications of this important biochemical discovery. But the observation of the corpus luteum and its rhythmic appearance and degeneration have become the basis of suggestions and controversies of keen human interest.

10

In October, 1924, Dr. H. Knaus, at present Professor in Prague, began some research work in London on the physiology and pharmacology of the uterine muscle, and continued it at Cambridge in April, 1925. These studies led him to make a closer investigation of the corpus luteum as a gland of internal secretion, and in 1927 he discovered a reaction of the uterine musculature determined by the hormone of that body. This reaction takes place in the rabbit twenty-four hours after ovulation, being stimulated by the secretion of the newly formed corpus luteum. In the early part of 1928, therefore, he attempted to fix the time limit of ovulation in healthy women with regular menstrual periods by noting the onset of this change in the function of the uterine musculature. Certain other investigations into the problem of fertility, undertaken to clear up various minor questions which had arisen during the course of the work, ended by revealing a periodic fluctuation between fertility and sterility.

In crucial scientific research it has often happened that two or more separate investigators have been engaged on the same line of research and have made corroborative discoveries, independently and unknown to one another. This was the case with Knaus on the one hand and the Japanese biologist, Professor Ogino, of the Takeyama Hospital at Niigata, on the other. Following Ogino's independent investigations, he came to these conclusions :

" 1. The period of probable conception is generally the eight days between the twelfth and nineteenth day before the next menstrual period : the eight days include the five days after the maturation of the ovule and three before.

" 2. During the period between the twenty-ninth and twenty-fourth days before the probable date of the next menstruation, conception is rarely possible.

" 3. During the period between the eleventh and first days before the next menstruation, conception cannot take place " (*Zentralblatt für Gynäkologie*, 1930, p. 478).

Ogino's statements are almost identical in substance with the formulation of the results obtained by Knaus, as printed in the documents of the Austrian Public Health Bureau (Vienna, 1931, No. 10) : " The woman who menstruates regularly at intervals of between twenty-eight and thirty days, has been experimentally proved to ovulate between the fourteenth and sixteenth day of her cycle. This means, according to the biological processes which we have described, that conception can only occur with her between the eleventh and seventeenth days of her cycle. For such spermatozoa as may enter the female tract before the eleventh day will have lost their functional potency by the time the woman's ovule is liberated, and the ovule which may be extruded on the sixteenth day of the cycle can no longer be fertilized on the seventeenth. This means that such women (with regular cycles of twenty-eight to thirty days)

are physiologically infertile in the first ten days of their
cycle and after the seventeenth, as well."

There are two factors to be reckoned with in effective
fertilization. Apart from the date of ovulation, we have
also to consider the functional activity of the sperms. The
most detailed and so far still authoritative work on this
subject is that of Hoehne and Behne, as long ago as 1914
(*Zentralblatt für Gynäkologie*, 1914, I., pp. 5*ff*).

"We conclude that there is no sure ground for the
assumption that functional spermatozoa survive and remain
fertile for several weeks or even days in the normal oviducts
of living and sexually mature women. On the contrary, it
is most probable that spermatozoa remain functional within
the oviduct for a short time only ; probably for not more
than three days" (*l.c.*, p. 15).

The exact degree of temperature is decisive here. We
know that the male scrotum acts as a protective and regu-
lative encasement, and that human spermatozoa can only
mature in a temperature lower than that of the abdominal
cavity. In agreement with Moore, the American investigator,
and Fukui, the Japanese, F. A. E. Crew made this dependence on temperature clear at the Congress of 1926 in Berlin
(Report I., p. 72). The fact that relatively low temperatures
are necessary for the efficient elaboration of functional
spermatozoa does not only account for the sterility of
Cryptorchids—in whom the descent of the testicles is
incomplete—but also offers an additional reason for believing
that the spermatozoa only survive for a brief while after
emission into the female receptaculum.

According to Knaus, the following factors are requisite
in calculation of the alternate periods of feminine fertility
or sterility :

1. Accurate knowledge of the individual characteristics
of the woman's menstrual cycle, from which the dates of
ovulation and conception are calculated.

2. There must be no kind of sexual congress whatever
during the time of possible conception.

3. Temporary abstinence loses its contraceptive value if
a change takes place in the character of the menstrual cycle,

the most important factor in its safe use. Deviation from the normal rhythm may take place under the following conditions :

(a) After confinement or miscarriage.

(b) After febrile and debilitating diseases.

(c) After any drastic alteration in the ordinary routine of life such as prolonged travel in a strange climate, mountaineering or other strenuous sports (*Periodic Fertility*, 1934, p. 109).

In subsequent chapters we shall have occasion to refer to the most socially significant of all possible causes of deviation from the normal rhythm : a cause which Knaus himself has ignored ; namely, the *repression and denial of regular sexual activity in a very large number of adult women.*

Knaus's theory has found enthusiastic and unqualified support in the Roman Catholic church, for the social and political reasons indicated in our fifth chapter : " Birth Control." Gynæcological and sexological experts, on the other hand, have published detailed reports furnishing serious ground for doubt of any complete periodic sterility in genus homo. Felix Thieme has taken the trouble of collating these significant objections (*Marriage Hygiene*, Vol. II, Bombay, 1936, pp. 320 *ff*).

In his study of "The Prevention of Conception" (*Empfängnisverhütung*, Stuttgart, 1932) Ludwig Fraenkel sums up as follows : " The period immediately before menstruation is not very fit for conception for physiological reasons as shown by the opinions of experts, printed in the medical literature. A safe period, however, *i.e.*, a period within the menstrual cycle, the careful restriction to which, as regards sexual congress is a real contraceptive, does not exist. Thus there might exist periods in a woman's life very favourable for fertilization, mayhap also periods extremely unfavourable for the same purpose, but no periods totally free from the possibility of fertilization " (p. 22).

Similar considerations have been put forward by Professor M. Bolaffio (*Zentralblatt für Gynäkologie*, 1932, p. 1510) and Emil Novak (*Journal of the American Medical Association*, 1934, Vol. 102, p. 452). Perhaps the most exhaustive criticism was that by F. Weinstock, the pupil of Fraenkel (in the *Zentralblatt* of 1934, p. 2947). Weinstock has examined 416 cases where pregnancy had occurred after a single intercourse, the date of which was exactly known. A comprehensive table shows that not one single day within the menstrual cycle was free from fertility.

The " safe period " lies at present in that borderland where speculation and laboratory experiment have not yet been fully clarified by actual practice in the circumstances of everyday life, and where the clash of opinions is coloured by emotion. Unfortunately, Knaus was not always able to be objective and open-minded in his treatment of criticism, although intellectual detachment is the first requisite of scientific research. There was a regrettable instance of his vehemence, at Frankfurt-am-Main, during the Gynæcological Congress of 1931, in reply to remarks by Stoeckel. Knaus permitted himself the retort that the methods recommended by him were possibly not generally accepted, for the simple reason that birth control by means of contraceptives " was praised and supported by medical men of mediocre gynæcological knowledge and proficiency, as an easy source of considerable gain! " (*Z. für G.*, 1931, p. 2856).

II

We shall have to make many excursions into this debatable land between what is actually known and what is willingly believed. But let us return for the moment to the relatively serene atmosphere of therapeutics. Any outline of what is known about the hormones of sex should include mention of the use of these hormones as healing substances.

There are three groups of " indications " for the pharmaceutical use of these hormones :

1. Disturbances of the monthly cycle in women.
2. Disturbances of potency in men.
3. Symptoms of age in both sexes.

The best " taking off ground " for tests of the female cycle was obviously the normal phase of disturbances and irregularities preceding the menopause ; for the climacteric, with all its individual variations, is a biological event, whereas the bewildering diversity of symptoms in the reproductive life of individual women may be caused by a variety of reasons. L. Fraenkel used tablets of lutein from the corpora of cows in the treatment of climacteric disorders, with good results. But in cases of genital hypoplasia (infantilism, arrested development) and acute amenorrhœa this preparation had no effect. Mainzer, Landau, Chrobak and Mond have administered ovarian preparations by the mouth and with varying success. Then Hermann and Fellner had relative successes with ovarian, luteal and placental extracts, used on virginal rabbits ; and Schroeder, Gerbig and Zondek were able to prove that such results were far from being due to the specific extracts, but were also produced by extracts from the liver.

There followed a pause in this sequence of investigation, and then the American biochemists began to use test material for the effect of endocrine preparations. Stockard-Papanicolaou ; Long-Evans; Allen-Doisy, obtained helpful results in the histological alterations of the tissues and smears from the vaginæ of spayed white mice. At about the same time Butenandt succeeded in crystallizing the male hormone, simultaneously with Doisy in the U.S.A.

There followed the elaborate research on the hypophysis (pituitary gland), which revealed at least four distinct functions of its secretion, or four distinct endocrines produced by the pituitary :

1. Hormones of general growth (Evans).

2. Substances stimulating the follicles to mature. These have been termed " Prolan A " by Zondek, " Rho 1 " by Wiesner of Edinburgh.

3. Substances causing luteinization : (" Prolan B " or " Rho 2 ").

4. A hormone influencing metabolism by the increase and reactivation of the specific function of the albumens, when this function diminishes.

Further interesting results have been obtained by Shapiro (1930) in cases of arrested development of the male genitalia by the administration of anterior pituitary hormone. There was later confirmation of this energizing property in the frontal lobe of the pituitary, in stimulation of the testicles to full function, after a surgical operation for the cure of Cryptorchism (Shapiro, 1935).

Harry Benjamin of New York contributed a report to the Ingese Congress of 1930 (p. 462), on his hormonic treatment of genital impotence. He injected the male hormone, as derived from the urine of young men. But impotence, whether complete, partial or occasional, is a complex symptom, neurotic as well as gonadic, and we have treated its main causes in dealing with the work of the Sex Consultation Centre (Chapter IV).

There remains the therapy of senescence by means of hormonic preparations. In 1924, Norman Haire summarized what was known about the clinical surgery of this subject in a concise monograph. He came to the conclusion that in many cases vasoligature or vasectomy (sometimes even only on one duct) had appreciably good effects. Even in cases of organic disease or advanced senility the operation often ameliorates the condition to some extent. Haire also tested transplantations of living tissue. On July 20th, 1920, Serge Voronoff transplanted and grafted the testicle from a chimpanzee into the groin of a man of seventy-four with amazing short-time results. After three months, the patient was reported to look like a normal man of forty-five. Voronoff performed about a thousand similar operations between 1920 and 1927. They did not wholly fulfil the hopes raised by the first striking hit ; but in theory the method is apparently quite sound. Both Haire and Peter Schmidt are of opinion that the transplantation of a testicle has no ill-effects, and the same is true of the transplantation of ovaries. Sometimes grafts succeed where ligature and vasectomy fail. According to Haire, transplantation should always be carried out as a prophylactic measure where a woman's own ovaries have to be removed owing to some disease.

Steinach and Peter Schmidt have also obtained similar results by the application of radiant heat to the whole body, and especially to the gonads (diathermy), although the influence of increased blood supply on endocrine secretion is not yet fully understood. Finally, there have been pharmacal experiments by Doppler, who smeared the gonadal artery with phenol, thus obliterating the nervus sympathicus. In this manner the spasm was prevented and the consequent congestion led to the same results as Steinach's heat treatment.

What is the mechanism producing the incontestable " rejuvenations " which have been observed and recorded ? Vladislav Ružička, Chief of the Institute of Biology at the University of Prague, contributed observations to the Archiv for Cytology as early as 1908. He pointed out that the cells of juvenile or adolescent organisms differed from those of organisms in middle life or advanced age by (1) their amount of chromatin, and (2) by the greater solubility of their components. The cells of mature or senescent bodies were richer in plastin or protoplasm, so that the process of age may be described in organisms as the increasing density and concentration of the bio-colloids, and death itself as the coagulation of bio-colloids. Ružička's term for this fundamental organic process is " protoplasmic-hysteresis." Metabolic activation interrupts this process for the time being, and such metabolic activation is without doubt the direct result of the endocrine superflux caused by hormonic injection (Ružička, Ingese Congress 1/2, 1928, pp. 162 ff). We may therefore doubt whether endocrine increase means further length of life. But there is no sound reason to suppose that more intense vitality need imply a shorter lease of life ; that a " merrier " life is necessarily " shorter."

12

We may claim that the main mechanisms and functions of sex are understood to-day, though there are many points still to be elucidated. The chief revelatory agents here have worked in quiet laboratories ; with microscopes, scalpels and chemicals. Public attention has only been aroused —as was the case in the days of Darwin and Haeckel— when religion, one of the " pillars of the social fabric," was menaced by unwelcome truth, or when the secret longing of mankind for eternal life and eternal youth received sensational or tantilizing stimulus in early exaggerated accounts of the work of Brown-Séquard, Steinach and Voronoff.

But one conclusion cannot be avoided here, and mental and social honesty alike require its formulation. The sexual activation or re-animation of an organism or an individual means their all-round activation, bodily and mental. The curve of genital efficiency in individuals and their curve of social and professional efficiency are almost congruent. They rise and fall together. The tragic conflicts and consequences that often arise from this interaction have been poignantly expressed in imaginative literature, whereas sociologists, though equally aware of them, have generally kept silence, oppressed by mountains of statistics and the pressure of " that public ignorance, mis-called public opinion."

In the years 1921–22, the poet and dramatist Ernest Toller wrote his excruciatingly painful play " *Hinkemann*," as a prisoner in Niederschönenfeld fortress. The play depicted the fate of a man whom " war casualty " deprived of his virility, and whom conditions arising from the war proceeded to deprive of his human status and his right to work and citizenship because of his emasculation. Therefore, the ideal of asexuality is no ideal ; there are no better proofs of its inadequacy and inhumanity than the results of scientific research.

In the following chapters we must pursue and dissect the contradictions and cruelties which have grown out of the sexphobia of the nineteenth century, in spite of the simultaneous growth of scientific research and method. Sexual knowledge has still to wage constant battle with the vestiges of Victorianism ; and these are often the more powerful for being implicit and subconscious. We must overcome this peculiar legacy of the nineteenth century, to which even the most enlightened amongst us are co-heirs. To do so thoroughly and consistently will be a task worthy of the best brains and most undaunted courage ; and it can hardly be achieved by the methods of logical demonstration and persuasion alone, without recourse to something more drastic and more definitely constructive.

BIBLIOGRAPHY

ALLEN, E. a. o., *Sex and Internal Secretion*, London, 1932.
ALLEN and DOISY, " Ovarian Hormone," *J. Am. M. Ass.*, 81, 1923.
ASCHHEIM, *Hypophysen Vorderlappen Hormon*, 2, Ingese Congress, London, 1931.
ASCHHEIM and ZONDEK, cf. *Klinische Wochenschrift*, 1927, 6, 248 ff.
BAER, C. E. v., *Ueber die Zielstrebigkeit in den organischen Körpern*, St. Petersburg, 1876.
BECHTEREV, W. M., *Die Geschlechtstätigkeit vom Standpunkt der Reflexologie*, 1, Ingese Congress, II., Cologne, 1928.
BENJAMIN, H., *Standardized Male Hormone*, 2, Ingese Congress, London, 1931.
BERNER, " Hermaphroditismus und Geschlechtsumwandlung," *Handb. Inn. Secr.*, Vol. II., 1930.
BIEDL, *Lehrbuch der inneren Sekretion*, Berlin, ab 1913.
BOUIN and ANCEL, *Quels sont les éléments testiculaires qui élaborent l'hormone sexuelle ?* 1, Ingese Congress, I., Bonn, 1917.
BUTENANDT, " Ueber die chemische Untersuchung der Sexual. hormone," *Ztsch. f. angew. Chemie*, 1931, 44, 905. *Cf. Nature*, 130/1932, and *Wien. Klin. Wschr.*, 47, 1934.
CHAMPY, C., *Sexualité et hormones*, Paris, 1924.
CONCLIN, E. G., " Karyokinesis and Cytokinesis in the maturation of Crepidula and other Gastropoda," *Ac. Nat. Science*, Philadelphia, 1902.
CREW, A. E., *The Scrotum*, Ingese Congress, I., Cologne, 1927.
DICKINSON, R. L., *Human Sex Anatomy*, New York, 1933.
FISCHER, E., *Die Rehobother Bastards*, Jena, 1913.
FLEMING, " Beiträge zur Kenntnis der Zelle," *Arch. mikr. Anat.*, 16, 1879 ; 18, 1880 ; 20, 1882.
FRANK, R. T., *The Female Sex Hormone*, London, 1929.
GALTON, A., *Natural Inheritance*, London, 1889.
GLEY, *Les grands problèmes de l'Endocrinologie*, Paris, 1926.
GOLDSCHMIDT, R., *Die sexuellen Zwischenstufen*, Berlin, 1931.
HAECKEL, *Kampf um den Entwicklungsgedanken*, Jena, 1905.
HAIRE, N., *Rejuvenation*, London, 1924.
HERTWIG, O., *Präformation oder Epigenese*, Jena, 1894.
HERTWIG, O., *Mechanik und Biologie*, Jena, 1897.
HERTWIG, O., *Kampf um Kernfragen der Entwicklungslehre*, Jena, 1909.
HERTWIG, O., *Dokumente zur Geschichte der Zeugungslehre*, Bonn, 1918.
ISCOVESCO, H., " Les Lipoides," *Presse méd.*, 30, 1922.
KNAUS, H., *Periodic Fertility and Sterility in Woman*, Vienna, 1934.

LILLIE, " The Free-martin," *Journ. exp. Zool.*, 23, 1917.
LILLIE, *cf.*, *Biol. Bull.*, 44, 1923.
MARAÑÓN, G., *Problemas actuales de la doctrina de las secreciones internas*, Madrid, 1922.
McCLUNG, G. E., *Evolution of the Chromosome Complex*, II. Congress of Eugen., New York, 1921.
MEISENHEIMER, J., *Geschlecht und Geschlechter im Tierreich*, Jena, 1921 and 1930.
MORGAN, TH. H., *Theory of the Gene*, Yale University, 1928.
MORGAN, TH. H., *The Scientific Basis of Evolution*, New York, 1932.
MORGAN, TH. H., *Embryology and Genetics*, New York, 1934.
RUŽIČKA, V., *Ueber Altern und Lebensdauer*, 1, Ingese Congress, II., Cologne, 1928.
RUŽIČKA, V., *cf. Helv. Chim. Acta*, 17, 1934.
SHAPIRO, *Wirkung d. Hypophysen - Vorderlappenhormons*, W.L.S.R. Congress, Vienna, 1931.
SHAPIRO, " Chirurg. od. hormonale Therapie d. Kryptorchismus," *Schweiz. med. Wschr.*, 65, 1935.
SCHMIDT, H., *Haeckel, E., Denkmal eines Lebens*, Jena, 1934.
SCHMIDT, P., *The Theory and Practice of the Steinach Operation*, London, 1924.
SCHMIDT, P., *The Conquest of Old Age*, London, 1929.
SCHRADER, F., *Die Geschlechtschromosomen*, Berlin, 1928.
STARLING, E. H., *A Century of Physiology*, London, 1927.
STEINACH, E., " Geschlechtstrieb als Folge der innersekretorischen Funktion der Keimdrüsen," *Ztsch. Physiol.*, 24, 1910.
STEINACH, E., Willkürliche Umwandlung von Säugetiermännchen in Tiere mit weibl. Geschlechtscharakteren," *Arch. Physiol.*, 144, 1912.
STEINACH, E., *Verjüngung durch experimentelle Neubelebung d. alternden Pubertätsdrüse*, Berlin, 1920.
TOLLER, E., *Brokenbrow*, London, 1926.
VORONOFF, S., *Transplantation der Geschlechtsdrüsen von Affen auf den Menschen*, Berlin, 1926.
WALDEYER, W., " Ueber Karyokinese," *Arch. mikr. Anat.*, 32, 1888.
ZAVADOVSKI, M. M., " Aequipotentialität der Gewebe des Männchens und Weibchens bei Vögeln und Säugetieren," *Endocrinologie*, V, 1929.
ZONDEK, B., *Diseases of the Endocrine Glands*, London, 1935.

TABLE OF EVENTS

1828 C. E. V. BAER discovers the Human Ovule.
1849 BERTHOLD performs the first transplantations, at Göttingen.

1859 DARWIN's *Origin of Species.*
1863 HAECKEL champions Darwinism in Germany.
1865 MENDEL discovers the mechanism of Genetics.
1871 QUÊTELET's *Anthropométrie.*
1874 HAECKEL's *Anthropogonie.*
1875 O. HERTWIG observes the fertilization of the Sea-Urchin.
1877 VIRCHOW opposes the theory of Natural Selection.
1879 FOL observes the conjunction of Sperm and Ovum.
FLEMING discovers the Chromosomes.
1884 NAEGELI formulates the theory of Idioplasm.
1889 F. GALTON formulates the law of Recessives.
BROWN-SÉQUARD's Hormonic Injections.
1900 Rediscovery of Mendelian Laws.
1905 STARLING coins the term " Hormones."
1908 RUŽIČKA's theory of Protoplasmic-Hysteresis.
1910 STEINACH's first account of the Internal Secretions.
1911 TANDLER's account of the Gonads (Free-martin).
1913 E. FISCHER's work on the Rehoboth Bastards.
MORGAN discovers the X Chromosomes.
First Congress of Eugenics in London.
1914 HOEHNE and BEHNE's publication on the Vitality of Sperms.
1915 GOLDSCHMIDT's theory of Intersexuality.
1916 LILLIE's investigations on the Free-martin.
1920 VORONOFF grafts Ape's Glands into Human Subjects.
1921 Second Congress of Eugenics in New York.
1927 BUTENANDT and DOISY crystallize the Male Hormone.
KNAUS discovers the reaction of the Uterine Muscles to the Corpus Luteum.
1928 KNAUS and OGINO formulate the theory of the " Safe Period."
1929 CORNER and ALLEN demonstrate the substance Progestin.
FRANK's monograph on the Female Hormones.
1931 GOLDSCHMIDT's classification of Intersexuality, in a sequence.
1932 ALLEN's monograph on Sex and Internal Secretions.
1935 The process of fertilization in the Rabbit Ovum, depicted at Oxford.

CHAPTER II

PEOPLE WHO ARE—DIFFERENT

I

IN the year 1895 a strange suicide occurred in the German provincial town of Magdeburg. A young officer shot himself on the evening before the date fixed for his wedding day. On the morrow of this tragedy, a general practitioner, recently settled in Magdeburg, whom the dead man had consulted professionally, received a mass of documents, bequeathed by his patient. A letter accompanied the manuscript material expressing the wish that the doctor should keep and use it in the interests of science, and for the benefit of the writer's companions in misfortune.

The documents left no doubt as to the inherent tendencies and most intimate feelings of the writer. He was emotionally stirred by, and attracted to, his own sex, he was homoerotic or inverted. The pressure of his family and conventional considerations had led to an engagement to a normal girl, but on the eve of his wedding day conscience overcame convention. He chose to die rather than face the inevitable conflict between his inherent nature and the innocent and legitimate expectations and rights of his betrothed bride.

The young medical man who received this tragic legacy had been quite unaware of his patient's idiosyncrasy. He was overcome with horror and grief as he took up the revolver which lay besides the pile of manuscript. Just at that very time the Oscar Wilde case was rousing London ; and the petted poet was receiving a sentence of two years' penal servitude for actions which were only made penal offences in the eleventh section of the Criminal Law Amendment Act of 1885, ten years before the date of his trial and sentence. This Act had been passed as a result of the revelations of

Mr. W. T. Stead in the *Pall Mall Gazette*, under the title
" Modern Babylon." His exposure of the traffic in quite
young children as well as boys and girls in their teens, for
purpose of sexual exploitation, had roused public opinion,
which is apt to concentrate on symptoms and ignore causes.
A similar storm broke loose against the successful playwright
and " society " favourite. We must, in fairness, admit that
Wilde was warned of his impending arrest and given forty-
eight hours to leave the country. The authorities were
anxious to avoid the scandalous publicity of really sordid
details. But Wilde had persuaded himself that no one would
dare to arrest and charge him. He let the forty-eight hours
pass, the law took its course.

Frank Harris who was at that time editor of the *Saturday
Review* tried to put in a word for Wilde as an artist ; but
both printers and owners of the paper refused to accept this
tribute to facts and fair play : " It would be better not even
to mention this name." In the face of this public attitude
it is comprehensible that Harris should remark in his book
published in 1930 :

" The right of free speech which Englishmen pride themselves on had utterly disappeared, as it always does disappear
in England when there is most need of it. It was impossible
to say one word in Wilde's defence or even in extenuation of
his sin in any London print."

2

In the same year, a broad-minded and warm-hearted
social reformer, Edward Carpenter, published a brief essay
with the Labour Press in Manchester. It was dated 1894,
and entitled : *Homogenic Love*. He stressed the fact that
this pamphlet " was among the first attempts in this country
to deal at all publicly with the problems of the ' Intermediate
sex ' "—for so he termed the homosexuals. He had made
an agreement with the well-known publishers, Fisher Unwin,
to produce a further and fuller work : *Love's Coming of Age*.
Let us quote from Carpenter's own account, written twenty
years later, in his autobiography *My Days and Dreams*, of
what followed Wilde's arrest in April, 1895.

" From that moment, a sheer panic prevailed over *all* questions of sex, and especially of course, questions of the Intermediate Sex. I did not include Homogenic Love in my proposed new book ; but when the mere existence of the thing came to the knowledge of Fisher Unwin, he was so perturbed that he actually cancelled his agreement with me, with regard to the book *Love's Coming of Age*, and broke loose from it. All publishers shook their heads. The Wilde trial had done its work and silence must henceforth reign on sex subjects."

No London publishing house would touch the small book and Carpenter had to return to the little Labour Press in Manchester.

The panic that had seized the British public opinion did not extend to the Continent, although exact scientific knowledge of the nature and symptoms of homosexuality was still very meagre. In 1876 Westphal had published a detailed description of a case, which was followed, in 1882, by the studies of Charcot and Magnan, and in 1886 by a small manual in which the Austrian psychiatrist, R. von Krafft-Ebing, treated the subject from the standpoint of forensic medicine, and for professional readers, under the discreet title *Psychopathia Sexualis*. At a later date, this little book was enlarged by several hundred pages. But already in the first edition some lines had been dedicated to " Reversed Sexual Emotion " (*Conträre Sexualempfindung*).

But the first modern monograph on homosexuality was composed by Albert Moll, a doctor practising in Berlin. His book appeared in 1891, with an introduction by R. von Krafft-Ebing.

All these essays and studies approached their theme as a medical matter, and with extreme hesitation ; they left its social effects and implications severely alone. But the young general practitioner in Magdeburg was haunted by the responsibility of the Community for tragedies such as those of his patient, self-slain on the eve of marriage, and of Oscar Wilde's trial. He felt that something must be done to enlighten this obstinate refusal to understand, till an entirely false and harmful situation was created, and then met by desperate measures and Draconic penalties. And to this task of enlightenment he devoted his life.

He took up the task swiftly. In 1896 there appeared a slender paper-covered booklet, published under a pseudonym, and entitled *Sappho and Socrates*. Both these intellectual stars of the Ancient World, the Lesbian singer and the Athenian sage, were homosexuals or inverts. Socrates loved honourably and helpfully boys and young men, such as Alcibiades : Sappho loved the maidens whose names are immortal through her genius. The author of the pamphlet demanded the same right of emotional expression for those modern men and women whose instinctive urges were in the same direction, rather than on " normal " lines, towards their opposite sexes. And this author himself was Magnus Hirschfeld.

3

The year 1896 brought forth a new monograph in Germany, translated by the distinguished editor of the *Centralblatt für Nervenheilkunde*, Dr. Hans Kurella. The English original was the work of Havelock Ellis, who was hardly known as yet, even in his own London. On March 15th, 1927, Hirschfeld paid this tribute in a letter to Houston Peterson, the American biographer of Ellis :

" The book *Sexual Inversion* by Ellis and Symonds [1] was very important for the homosexual question in Germany. The spirit of this book was so noble and scientific that we have preferred it to Moll's *Conträre Sexual-Empfindung*. Since this time the name of Havelock Ellis has been very popular in Germany."

In 1897 Magnus Hirschfeld, having moved to Berlin, founded the " Humanitarian Scientific Committee " (*Wissenschaftlich-Humanitäres Komittee* or *W.H.K.*), which aimed at " the scientific study of homosexuality and associated manifestations, and further of the whole range of human emotions, and the utilization of the results of such study for the progress and welfare of humanity."

For Magnus Hirschfeld definitely intended to use the

---

[1] In later editions Symonds' contributions were omitted.

knowledge gleaned in his consulting room in order to arouse the conscience of the public. He coined the term " Sexual Intergrades " as a comprehensive title for all the shades and phases of aberrant instinct that he encountered in the course of his work of research, classification and defence. Accordingly, the first action taken by the new Committee was to arrange a petition against Paragraph 175 of the Penal Code of the German Empire : this paragraph corresponded to the British Law of 1885. The petition was intended to bring enlightenment as to the facts to wider circles than those immediately interested, and to start discussion. And it had definite success in both respects. Among its signatories were August Bebel, the leader of the German Social-democratic Party ; the poets, Richard Dehmel, Gerhart Hauptmann and Ernst von Wildenbruch, and the eminent jurist Franz von Liszt, but only one doctor of special celebrity, namely, Krafft-Ebing. The general public maintained an attitude best shown in the reply of H. von Kupffer, the personally courageous editor in chief of the *Berliner Lokalanzeiger*, a paper in close touch with Court Circles ; Herr Kupffer's letter to the W.H.K. was dated August 30th, 1889.

" I have no objection to the inclusion of my name among the signatories to the Petition concerning homosexuality, addressed to the Reichstag. But I see no opportunity of raising this highly important subject in my paper, without causing great offence, owing to the prevalent misconceptions."

4

In spite of these prejudices, the petition rallied experts and sympathizers enough to enable Hirschfeld to found a special periodical, the *Annual for Sexual Intergrades* (*Jahrbuch für Sexuelle Zwischen-Stufen*). This first appeared in 1900, and over twenty volumes were published. In the third of these, Krafft-Ebing tackled a question of profound significance, but as yet unsolved. He asked whether homosexuality or " inversion " was congenital or acquired. In 1886 he had drawn a sharp distinction between these two groups, when first treating the subject. But the study and sifting of case material which had taken place in the subsequent seventeen years seemed to indicate that homosexuality was a constitutional, inborn aberration from the normal impulse of sex. The term itself was first employed in an anonymous memorandum to the Prussian Ministry of Justice ; the author of this document—as is now known—was a Hungarian medical man, Karl M. Benkert. Carpenter had used the term "intermediate sex" in his work on *Homogenic Love* and Carpenter's friendship and cooperation with Hirschfeld brought much mutual inspiration and information. On the Continent the homosexuals themselves generally preferred to be called "the third sex"—without attempting any scientific elucidation of the riddle their emotional life presented. But the collection and collation of first-hand material (both contemporary and historical) continued, and the results published in the *Intergrade's Annual* enabled the following conclusions to be drawn :

The numerous types of personality which show pronounced "feminine" characteristics in persons anatomically or genitally male, or pronounced "masculine" traits in persons anatomically and genitally female, are admittedly liable to neuroses, and to a greater psychic and mental instability than the average : but they are in no sense necessarily criminal. On the contrary, this instability often implies extreme sensibility to impressions and inspirations, which may be gloriously active and creative in music and art. Some examples of artistic genius or taste above the average among homosexual or bisexual persons are Byron, Walter Pater, Tchaykovsky, Hermann Bang, Winkelmann, Count von Platen-Hallermund, Hans Christian Andersen, Frederick the Great of Prussia, Michelangelo and Leonardo Da Vinci—who was proceeded against and punished for homosexual relations four hundred years before Wilde. Even to-day, many normal persons have food for thought in these words of Carpenter's—himself so highly cultured and widely read, and emotionally so expert, with first-hand knowledge of this subject : "I have said that the Urning men in their own lives, put love before money-making, business-success, fame and other motives which rule the normal man. I am sure that it is also true of them as a whole, that they put love before lust. I do not feel *sure* that this can be said of the normal man, at any rate in the present stage of evolution."

5

Hirschfeld had the opportunity of putting the knowledge he had gained and the case for tolerance before the forum of the world in the years 1907–9. At that date a remarkable series of judicial proceedings took place in Germany, centring round Prince Philip von Eulenburg, a courtier and aristocrat known as " Philli " among his intimates. " Philli " was a personal friend of the Emperor William II, a man of sensitive sympathies, an advocate of moderation in home and foreign policy, and indeed of Peace ; and therefore, a thorn in the flesh of the sabre-rattling junkers who were to dominate events.

His silent but persistent foe was " the old Privy Councillor " Holstein, the mainspring of the German Empire's Foreign Office, who aimed at continuing and expanding Bismarck's " Blood and Iron " policy, and therefore detested the " Round Table at Liebenberg," where pacific and artistic influences gathered round the Kaiser, when he was guest in Eulenburg's home.

Holstein himself was an adapt at political intrigue ; he kept in the background and let others do his work.

On November 17th, 1906, the storm broke. A highly offensive article appeared in a political magazine *Die Zukunft* (*The Future*)—ably edited by Maximilian Harden, a well-known publicist who upheld the Bismarckian traditions. This article attacked the " Camarilla " or clique which surrounded, and to some degree influenced, the sovereign, and whose abnormal personal tastes and habits were notorious : for the influence of these persons had been so unfortunate and against their country's interests that public opinion must take cognizance of their activities. There followed a second and a third article, with quite unequivocal attacks on the intimate life of Prince Eulenburg and on that of the Military Governor of Berlin, Count Cuno von Moltke. The name of Hirschfeld was mentioned, as an expert authority in a position to confirm these statements.

Eulenburg left Prussia for the shores of Lake Geneva, hoping against hope that the scandal would die down. The Court ignored the articles, and unfortunately for himself Eulenburg ventured to return within a few weeks, at the beginning of 1907. On the second of February, Harden returned to the charge in more extreme and definite terms.

The anti-Eulenburg faction persuaded the heir-apparent to inform the Emperor of the attacks on his friend and the details of the charges. William II was a man of pathological impulsiveness and irritability ; and all his decisions on matters of moment were the result of personal hyper-sensitiveness and personal predilections. On May 23rd he gave Moltke his *congé* and a week later he " dropped " his former friend and host Eulenburg, in the brusquest manner possible. In later days, after the war and all it brought, he sincerely regretted this unfair and precipitate action.

Moltke brought a lawsuit against Harden for defamation of character ; and the defendant cited Hirschfeld as an expert witness to corroborate the charges. The Court was to decide whether the plaintiffs had been defamed and aggrieved through the accusation of criminal homosexual conduct. And the Court—an insignificant lower tribunal—decided in Harden's favour, for he had not, so they decided, accused Eulenburg and Moltke of specific acts, but of an erotically tinged or tainted friendship, which had not been without effects on political decisions and events in the Prussian State. *Zukunft* became a document of international importance ; the vanity of Harden, a man of brilliant intelligence but of an egotism and conceit rivalling his Emperor's, was gratified.

The first trial was followed by a second. In the interval between the two events, the Chancellor of the Empire, von Bülow, brought an action against a homosexual author, Adolf Brand, an extremely effeminate and pronounced type of " æsthete " ; and Brand was condemned to a term in prison for defamation of character, although Hirschfeld had vouched for his *bona fides* in the remarks for which he was put on trial. Then there came suddenly a stream of public references to the indiscretions of Eulenburg's youth ; to obscure and intimate relationships with persons of humble station, men of the people : affairs which had been experienced, finished and up till then, forgotten, decades ago. From the analytic and forensic standpoints, these documents were far from inspiring confidence in their author's good faith ; but they served the purpose of drawing attention to the sexual " past " of a prominent public man.

Harden's paper emphasized the first of these documents published in Munich. He admitted that in late middle age Eulenburg might pass for a man, but in his youth he had been " a girl in a Cuirassier's uniform " (" *une fille déguisée en cuirassier* "). That sufficed ; a charge of perjury was made and the prince was arrested. His health had broken down, and he was carried on a stretcher into the Law Court, and kept under police supervision for months in a hospital ward. Sensational rumours, strongly flavoured with sex and crime, were in every newspaper and on every tongue ; and the jealousy and self-esteem of the middle class philistines gloried in the consciousness of their own normality, in the reprobation of " evil in high places." The purpose of Eulenburg's enemies was achieved. A public man who stood in the way of a certain political group was " removed " by lashing moral indignation into action.

Looking back at the Eulenburg case, it is all too clear that Harden's vigorous personal vanity and self-esteem were utilized by the extreme militarists in order to rivet their hold on the Emperor. Harden had a wide and detailed knowledge both of the diplomacy and the military establishments of Europe, having been the legatee of Bismarck's papers ; and he made constant use of these unrivalled sources of information. Another factor also influenced Harden's conduct. He was of Hebrew origin and had had to contend with anti-Semitism, both avowed and concealed, throughout his career. After the war there were even attempts on his life. His reaction to constant hostility took the form of " over-compensation," he longed for power, and rejoiced in its exercise ; he considered himself the heir and successor to Bismarck, destined to implement Bismarck's policy in Kaiser Wilhelm's despite.

In his attack on Eulenburg, Holstein even went so far as to put the former Countess Moltke (who had obtained a divorce from Count Cuno) into communication with Harden. Many years ago, in the course of a personal interview, in the charming setting of Harden's study at Grunewald, on the outskirts of Berlin, he assured me that he had kept the material placed in his hands by the Countess (and including certain correspondence between Eulenburg and Count Cuno) —" strictly private and confidential " for years. Stroking his yellow kid gloves with meditative fingers, he declared that he wished to avoid even the appearance of making political capital out of sensational manifestations of sex. But he had done just that and nothing else against Eulenburg, and his method of attack gives the unhappy affair its very grave significance, both as regards history and psychology.

6

On June 30th, 1934, a catastrophe incomparably more violent and tragic again drew the world's attention to the rulers of Germany. The mass-murders within the Nazi Party were a continuation and intensification of the former methods of perjury and slander and judicial condemnation. The slaughter organized by Goering and Hitler on genuine St. Bartholomew's Eve lines, was made acceptable to the people by sensational reports and lurid details. Meanwhile, it is common knowledge that Hitler's best friend Streicher, editor of the notorious and scurrilous anti-Semitic publication *Der Stürmer*, suffers from pornographic mania ; a pathological obsession with ideas of crime and dirt. From a strictly impartial point of view, therefore, the Führer would seem to have no tenable cause for moral indignation at sexual aberrations in the service of political aims. But . . .

Yes,—*but*. In a social order, such as that now prevalent, the emotions and even needs of sex are subjected to repressions, associations and traditional customs, which influence not only conduct, but consciousness as well. In the dim labyrinth of secret curiosities and desires, of which the daylight mind is unaware, there is always the risk of stimulating the unconscious urge by hints and suggestions which release a torrent of emotional energy, at the disposal of the clever tacticians who pull the strings. Holstein and Hitler both speculated in moral indignation—moral indignation of which the origin is a mystery veiled from the comprehension of its devotees. And of course this psychic camouflage can and does take a variety of forms. Thus, as in the case of Hirschfeld, opponents of sexual enlightenment consider it almost criminal for a doctor to deliver public lectures on sexual subjects ; it is assumed to be a form of advertisement for his own professional competence. Those who argue thus always profess much sympathy with sex in itself : " a natural and necessary part of life as every reasonable person must agree, etc., etc. : but such methods of exploiting sex ignorance are unfair and unworthy." I fear that in the case of medical men who charge extortionate fees in other branches of the profession, no protests are raised. And why not ? Obviously, because they avoid the tabooed subject of sex. Or, if they deal with it, they do so in exclusively professional circles, and with the double safeguards of Greek and Latin terms. But to speak of sex so as to be understood by the general public is still regarded as offensive. Hence the many attacks on Hirschfeld by the leaders of official medicine in Germany. And I have had cause to know the regret and vexation of my opponents at their inability to raise the cry of " fee-snatching " against me ; for thanks to earlier circumstances, I was in the happy position of being able to give advice and information on sex matters *gratis* to those who sought such help.

7

As the opposition to Hirschfeld's activities grew more vocal, so also grew the amount of material relevant to the actual facts and needs of the situation. There appeared a range and diversity of sexual manifestations, such as may perhaps have been partly known before, but had certainly never yet been systematically studied or classified. Hirschfeld felt obliged to extend the field of his research to the whole subject of sex, and no longer to confine himself to the intermediate types. In 1908 he founded a second scientific periodical, under the title *Sexus*. His collaborators in this work were Rohleder of Leipzig and the anthropologist F. S. Kraus of Vienna : the latter was known as expert in Slavonic folk-lore. In 1913 an International Medical Congress was held in London, at which Hirschfeld exhibited scientific material illustrative of homosexuality, for the first time, at the Imperial Institute. In the same year he founded the Berlin Society for Sexual Science (" Gesellschaft für Sexual Wissenschaft ") in collaboration with Iwan Bloch— (whose early death was a great loss to science and humanity) —and with H. Koerber, the psychoanalyst, and Albert Eulenburg. Bloch had already written a monograph of extreme significance, the first scientific study of the inter-actions between sex and the sense of smell—*Osphresio-logie ;* the book appeared under the pseudonym " Hagen " in 1906. In 1912 there appeared Bloch's *magnum opus, The Sexual Life of our Time*, followed by comprehensive studies on the origin and development of Prostitution. After the war, G. Loewenstein continued this particular research. Koerber was a disciple of Freud, at a time when psychoanalysis was regarded with profound suspicion. A. Eulenburg was co-editor of the *Deutsche Medizinische Wochenschrift* and a prominent figure in his profession.

It was at a session of the Berlin Society of Sexual Science that I first met Hirschfeld in 1915. We arranged a meeting and talked over the subject thoroughly, and as a result I became his collaborator. I learned the immense range and the shades of difference in sexual constitutions and proc-livities, among human beings ; I learned also that ignorance and fear may prevent many who most need medical diag-nosis and help, from venturing to claim them.

At that time I was serving in the German army and my regiment was stationed at a small country town, an hour and a half's journey by rail from Berlin. Suddenly there was a scandal that rocked the whole place. Two young fellows, privates in my own company, had been arrested in the town for "having been guilty of espionage, disguised as women." I succeeded in getting permission to visit them while they were under arrest ; and my suspicions proved correct. Both these youths were members of that large group of " variant " individuals, who can only feel happy and at ease, wearing the habitual dress of the sex to which, anatomically, they do *not* belong, and assuming the habits customary to that " opposite " sex. They were " Transvestites " or " Eonists." There was not a shadow of justification for treating them as spies. Both were in despair at their misfortune and disgrace ; but when I put the matter before the " experienced " army doctors, the response was : " Incredible rubbish—keep your hands out of this, young man."

Now Hirschfeld had published the first special monograph on this form of aberration as early as 1910 ; the work was entitled *Die Transvestiten*. I recollected our discussions as to whether such variant types could be considered " disguised " in any costume in which they felt " at home " and really themselves. But alas, when I referred my Olympian chiefs to Hirschfeld's monograph—already five years in circulation—their provincial self-satisfaction and self-righteousness remained unmoved. So I wired to Hirschfeld, and he came at once. A committee of all the resident medical men, and all the military officers of the little garrison, was called, and Hirschfeld displayed appropriate photographic material and gave a convincing statement of what was already known about transvestitism. The two suspects were summoned and questioned. And the result brought light and help—they were released and their military service was remitted. One of them became a " female impersonator " in the cabarets and variety theatres of Berlin, and was a grateful friend to us and our work.

8

To dress or " disguise " oneself " as man " or " as woman " respectively, is only the most evident symptom of the attempt to become man or woman, as the case may be. Therefore " transvestitism " is an inadequate descriptive term, and it is advisable to use the name coined by Havelock Ellis in 1920 for these types, *i.e.*, "eonism."[1] This term is derived from the personal name of a characteristic individual, just as "sadism" derives from the Marquis de Sade (1740–1814) and "masochism" from Leopold von Sacher-Masoch (1836–1895). The Chevalier D'Éon de Beaumont (1728–1810) was a French aristocrat and diplomat in the reign of Louis XV. He passed for a woman until his death, which took place in London; the post-mortem proved that his external bodily structure was entirely male.

Eonism is not a mere "freak" as some, otherwise intelligent, medical men are still apt to believe. It is one among the many divers manifestations of the sexual constitution of humanity. It forces those persons who thus "deviate" from the average, into combat with the traditional customs and conduct of "men" or "women" respectively. This aberration is instructive as regards one of the unsolved problems of modern knowledge. For, by our laws, a "male" eonist may only appear in public dressed as a man, and a "female" eonist in woman's attire. Recently, in London, a man was arrested in a cinema, betrayed by his masculine voice; he was in woman's clothing and the arrest was justified by the police on the plea of public safety and order. It is feared, by those who do not understand the distinctive psychology of the eonists, that a man in woman's clothing might begin a conversation or acquaintance with a normal woman, and then proceed to some sexual aggression or attack. I have had the opportunity of observing an extremely large number of cases of this deviation (as of others also), and have been convinced that their sexual urge is far from predominant, in fact they appear to be "under-sexed" as compared with the majority of normal persons; and they are apt to be very shy and diffident in their general and social attitude, quite apart from sexual matters. Another complexity in their natures is this: they are by no means always homosexuals. But even when their sex and love life are normally directed,

---

[1] Conspicuous recent cases in England were the boy Augustine Hull (sentenced 1931) and the woman known as "Colonel Barker" (1927–28). Both were extreme examples of their respective tendencies.

they are ultra-modest and shame-faced, and unwilling to reveal or display their physical sex attributes.

In his one-volume *Psychology of Sex*, published in London, 1934, Havelock Ellis analyses the eonist deviation in these terms : " It is normal for a man to identify himself with the woman he loves. The eonist carries that identification too far, stimulated by a sensitive and feminine element in himself which is associated with a rather defective virile sexuality on what may be a neurotic basis." The same is true, *mutatis mutandis*, for eonist women, who wish to pass for men. Some sound knowledge of the result of modern research on this subject would save patients much persecution and the police much bewilderment—were such knowledge mastered in official and authoritative circles.

9

At the beginning of Hirschfeld's investigations he had to rely on material collected by others. But after twenty indefatigable years he issued a three-volume study *Sexual-pathologie*, which appeared in 1917, and was calculated to bring the first principles of the new science of sex to the knowledge of students of law and medicine in graphic and practical form. The book was published by a firm of high repute, specializing in medical works ; Marcus and Weber of Bonn, who afterwards moved to Berlin and Cologne. This firm had published the periodical *Zeitschrift für Sexualwissenschaft* since 1913, and in 1926 Max Marcuse's *Dictionary of Sex Terms* (*Handwörterbuch der Sexualwissenschaft*). In spite of these unimpeachable auspices I have never heard any reference to Hirschfeld's book from any Professor of Medicine. The academic gates were closed to Hirschfeld, and even after the fall of the Hohenzollern Empire in 1918 the Weimar Republic had no chair anywhere for the tireless investigator.

Hirschfeld's work was more unwelcome to the political reaction in Central Europe than even Sigmund Freud's. He was simply labelled as a " propagandist for homosexuality," and the anti-Semitism so strongly developed in Germany, even before Hitler's advent, was also an element

in consolidating opposition to his work. Moreover, Hirschfeld's political sympathies were always definitely " Left,"
i.e., liberal and progressive, although he took no active part
in politics, and he never denied his firm belief that the medical
man's duty is to enlighten and protect, not only in his
consulting room, but in public as well. He was a great
popularizer of knowledge, and differed in this respect from
Albert Moll, whose studies covered much the same field, but
whose attitude and method of treatment remained strictly
academic and, sò to speak, " orthodox." Moll constantly
stressed the seriousness of his scientific status although (!)
he specialized in sex questions. Indeed, there is often an
almost apologetic and deprecatory note in his works when
dealing with these " regrettable subjects."

Hirschfeld was quite independent of the judgment of
Scribes and Pharisees ; he never hesitated to call things by
their names, and was always ready to explain the results of
his investigations to the mass of the people, and to appeal
to their interest and answer their enquiries. The contrast
in methods and approach was very evident on the occasion
of International Congresses, organized independently by
both savants : Moll's organization was the International
Society for Sexual Research (*INternationale GEsellschaft
für SExualforschung, or* " INGESE ") and Hirschfeld's, The
World League for Sex Reform on a Scientific Basis, or
" W.L.S.R.," of which Hirschfeld, August Forel and
Havelock Ellis were the first Presidents. A brief glance
through the respective Reports and Proceedings will leave
no doubt that Moll registered the exact results of investigation, while Hirschfeld rallied the world to fight for fundamental reforms.

10

The great reformer had hoped for a more civilized and
favourable climate of thought after the change of government in Germany, in 1918. But the opposition grew, and
took a malignantly aggressive form. In 1919 he was knocked
down and injured by a gang of Nationalist roughs in Munich ;
fortunately his injuries were not fatal, and he replied to the

brutal mediævalism of his aggressors by opening the Institute of Sexual Science to the public, and by presenting his matchless collection of material to the Prussian State. In the section specially dedicated to homosexuality was preserved the revolver of the young Magdeburg suicide, whose personal tragedy had drawn Hirschfeld's attention to the problem of the Intergrade and thus sown the seed of enlightenment.

The Institute, once established, enabled us to review the whole position and progress of this work, and the theoretical basis of the Science of Sexology. Steinach had contributed to the forty-sixth volume of the *Archiv für Entwicklungsmechanik* (periodical dealing with evolutionary biology), in 1920, an essay on the "Histology of the Gonads in Male Homosexuals." He stated and proved his contention that :

"If in the course of fundamental differentiation puberal glands are developed whose elements are predominantly male or female, the resultant individual is definitely man or woman, as the case may be. But if the genetic differentiation is imperfect, and the puberal glands of intermediate type, then intermediate individuals result. And there may even be physical hermaphrodites due to the activity of the bisexual puberal glands, in any of the numerous phases of this anomaly."

The practical application of Steinach's discoveries is restricted, as we are at present unable to detect cellular hermaphrodism, except by means of a post-mortem. Long before Steinach proved him right, Hirschfeld had put forward the working hypothesis that the specific tension between the sexes is the result of chemical substances in their bodies. He termed these (at that time conjectural) substances "Andrin" and "Gynækin" respectively. It was an obvious corollary to make chemical tests in cases of intermediate structure and temperament, in order to ascertain whether the theory was biologically sound.

And now the laboratory work of Professor Abderhalden, of Halle, has substantiated the theory in several cases of "perversion." One instance was that of a young woman interested in art and by profession a painter. From the time

E 3

of her birth she was deemed to be a boy and educated accordingly. Then marked tendency to eonism revealed itself and she took to women's clothes and habits, but remained somewhat of a recluse and almost " sexless " in her instincts and emotions. Both for practical purposes, as a citizen, and as a matter of principle, she wished to adopt a woman's name, and accordingly I had several blood tests made in Abderhalden's laboratory clearly showing the presence of ovarian elements. In spite of this proof of her femininity, or, at least, of her intermediate constitution, the Prussian Ministry of Justice refused to permit the change of name, as the person in question had the external physique of a man. The change of name was permitted, however, in certain rare cases of patent physical anomaly or deformity, such as clitoridal enlargement resembling the male organ in women, or hypospadias and infantile penis in men. Such extreme physical evidence was irresistible, even by the logic and intelligence of the Prussian Ministry of Justice. But characteristically the patients were not allowed to choose their new names ! The Ministry had gradually collected a list of " suitable " names, which might be used indiscriminately for either boys or girls (such as, for instance, Tony, which might be either Antony or Antoinette)—and required the patients to select from a very restricted field.

A recent case of psychic hermaphrodism has become known throughout Europe ; here sex, was voluntarily changed by the use of modern surgical technique. For four decades the Danish artist, Einar Wegener, had passed as a man, but had always longed to be a woman, and had shown very typical feminine tendencies and tastes. The Dresden surgeon, Professor Warnecross, performed a complicated operation, with complete success ; including castration, transplantation of ovaries, and plastic remodelling of the external genitalia. Four separate operations were performed, and after the first the patient took the name of Lili Elbe : a thoroughly " feminine " woman, a new-born personality with ardent hopes for this new life. Most unfortunately an old kidney trouble led to her demise within a year. But the case demonstrated that Steinach's tests were perfectly valid for our species as well.

II

In 1920 Hirschfeld issued the second edition of his monograph on homosexuality in both men and women: an encyclopædia of knowledge, which will long remain the basis for our work in this field. Hirschfeld also tried to use the cinema as a means of instructing public opinion and arousing public sympathy. The firm Oswald produced a film entitled "Different from the others" ("Anders als die Andern") under Hirschfeld's direction, and Conrad Veidt took the part of the hopeless invert, whom blackmailers hounded to his death. Hirschfeld remained firmly of opinion that sexual aberrations or anomalies arise on a somatic or constitutional basis in the individual, *i.e.*, that they are organic, not acquired, and therefore not strictly speaking "curable." Therefore, in his view, only a compromise with the uncongenial and hostile environment is feasible, and such a procedure should be attempted by the physicians in charge of these cases.

A strong argument for this view of sexual anomalies was presented by the comparative measurements made and recorded by Arthur Weil. These tests were incorporated in Weil's paper, entitled *Bodily Proportion and Intersexuality as results of Endocrine Secretion*, at the First International Congress for Sexual Reform (Berlin, 1921). Weil found two groups of measurements to be directly dependent on endocrine constitution, namely, (*a*) the ratio of the upper part of the body (trunk) to the limbs, that is, the distances from the crown of the head to the base of the spine (the os coccygeum) and from the coccyx to the ground respectively ; and (*b*) the ratio of shoulders to hips. The mean averages of these measurements were as follows :

	Trunk to Limbs.		Shoulders to Hips.	
	in.	in.	in.	in.
Men ..	100	95	100	81
Women ..	100	90	100	97

Among Weil's cases were 200 male homosexuals. In

these there was a distinctly more feminine type of hip measurement than in the " normal " men. Moreover, their ratio of trunk to limbs was on the average 100 : 108.

Weil was able to confirm that in cases of trunk to limbs ratio of over 100 to 103, there was no active attraction towards women ; and that measurements beyond this boundary line denoted the constitutional intergrade.

Since Steinach's work in sexual metamorphoses, we know that " sex " is not a fixed and unalterable state of being, but a function of the whole endocrine apparatus and its hormones (activating electric forces) [1] on the basis of the sex chromosomes. Thus, Weil's results are only what we might expect, they afford useful evidence in the great question as to whether homosexuality be constitutional (inborn) or acquired. For this question is of crucial significance in the medical estimate not only of active inversion, but of all other forms of intersexuality as well.

12

The general result of our investigations to date appears to be that the sex chromosomes supply the tendency according to which the embryo in its early stages evolves as a male or a female. But that this basic tendency is more or less susceptible to endocrine modification, and in human beings to strong psychic and cerebral influences, in the post-natal and juvenile stages of growth. Thus sexual intergrades may be both constitutional or endocrine and psychically determined. The most comprehensive summary of what we know at present on this matter is that of F. A. E. Crew (1931) :

" It would seem that the ovary does not exert any appreciable influence upon the soma before the individual has attained a certain age, and that the sex-equipment of the female becomes developed because the impulse to this differentiation is innate in the soma of the embryo. In other words, the female type of sex-differentiation owes nothing to the female sex-hormone. This is not to say that when once that sex-equipment has been developed, it does

<hr>

[1] W. Reich, 1936.

not depend upon the female sex-hormones for its maintenance. In contrast with this, the male type of differentiation demands the presence of the male sex-hormone elaborated by the testis. . . . From the experiments which permit these conclusions to be drawn, the fact emerges that the differentiation into a female is a function which every embryo can perform, so long as no male sex-hormone is present to impose upon the body a male type of differentiation. The female sex represents, in the early stage of its development, the neutral form—that is, the form which the soma assumes in the absence of the male sex-hormone. On the other hand, every embryo would become a male, if it were exposed during its early development to the action of the male sex-hormone.

" If this be so, it follows that in cases in which the male sex-hormone appeared in the body at a later stage of development than was usual, a form of intersexuality would result, and that the degree of this intersexuality, as measured by the amount of femaleness in characterization, would be an indication of the extent of the delay—the later the effective production of male sex-hormone, the more femaleness."

So we may accept the distinction drawn by Albert Moll and accepted by Havelock Ellis, as between (1) psychosexual hermaphrodism, a form of more or less patent bisexuality and (2) complete inversion, *i.e.*, a biological variation or anomaly.

In about a third of the cases of complete inversion, there is evidence of heredity.

Many psycho-analysts are of opinion that " there is no such thing as ' inborn inversion '," in spite of the facts already cited. In the course of the first Ingese Congress (Berlin, 1926) the Viennese psycho-analyst, K. G. Heimsoth, declared that : " In the light of contemporary research,—homosexuality is impossible and an untenable hypothesis. But there is only and always bisexuality, according to Freud, Stekel and all practising psycho-analysts."

Although Stekel's authority is thus appealed to, he himself is much more cautious than Heimsoth. In his study, *The Homosexual Neurosis*, on p. 314, he says :

" My personal experience has convinced me that here
and there psycho-analysis is successful in effecting a cure.
But only under certain conditions. The homosexual must
be genuinely willing to be cured. He must actively desire
a change in his leaning. . . . The will to health is found
only in the lighter forms of homosexuality."

A third pronouncement is of interest. The New York
specialist, Harry Benjamin, spoke as follows at the second
Ingese Congress which took place in 1930 in London (*Report
of Congress*, p. 463) :

" In one case, a physician of thirty-one, homosexual
inclinations gradually disappeared and definite heterosexual tendencies developed during nine months' treatment
(with male sex-hormone), consisting of about fifty injections.
This was the case after prolonged psycho-analytic treatment
had failed."

13

These different views indicate the possibility of effective
treatment in the medical sense of the word. Many homosexuals feel perfectly healthy and desire no " cure " nor
change of their condition ; this is certainly adequate ground
for leaving them in peace, and refraining from unwelcome
advice or, of course, compulsion. But their subjective
condition gives little indication of the exact nature and origin
of their anomaly. Where the anomaly is not solely of endocrine origin, but due to psychic influences, there is the possibility of treatment, and possibly also the need of treatment.
Perhaps in the future, physicians will advise a combination
of analysis and endocrine injections. But also in these cases
of " pseudo-homosexuality " we should remember the warning Ellis uttered in 1934 : " We have to recognize that the
homosexuality rests on a natural germinal basis, and cannot
therefore be regarded as completely acquired, but as the
development of a latent aptitude."

And while giving full weight to the significance of hormones, we must not underrate the psychological and associative factors which may determine the direction of emotion.
All cases with strong psychological elements should be

regarded as potentially alterable or curable : if for no other reason than for that clearly and bravely stated by Wilhelm Reich (1932), that " As a rule, sexual satisfaction in healthy heterosexual persons is much more acute than in homosexuals, even if healthy." Reich, who has had much experience in psycho-analysis, thinks he is justified in concluding that most " homosexuals " owe their peculiarity to deficient development in childhood, and that the fixation is generally acquired round about four years of age ; therefore its origin remains below the level of consciousness in those so affected. Reich was able to achieve a cure in twelve cases, so that men previously homosexual experienced spontaneous sexual desire for women. In a personal communication of the present year, he stated that the opposite process could not be carried out (*i.e.*, heterosexuals could not be made homosexual through psycho-analysis). The last word has not been spoken on this problem, nor have we as yet any " acid test " as to which cases are " neurotic invalids " and which biological variants, on an obvious endocrine basis ; and, therefore, respectively " curable " or the reverse.

14

One form of " treatment " should only be suggested after the most careful and thorough diagnosis and preliminary psycho-therapy—if at all : for there are already numerous examples on record of most tragic results to both parties. That " cure " is—marriage with a " normal " woman or man. Unfortunately, even to-day some doctors recommend this step, in total disregard of the profound organic differences in these deviations, and without any previous instructions or suggestions to either partner. As an example of the grave consequences, let me quote verbatim from a letter written by the " normal " wife of a man who was certainly not " normal " :

" Honoured Sir,

" It isn't easy for me to say what I have to say, briefly and clearly, and especially because I have never mentioned it to anyone, before to-day. My husband is the director of a travelling theatrical company, and we have been married nearly five years, with not the slightest prospect of offspring. I looked forward so keenly to my married life, I prepared myself, in mind and body, to be fit for motherhood. Shortly before our wedding day, my husband seemed very depressed about something, and I asked the reason. He explained that he felt very anxious about the difficult times ahead and our financial position, and was afraid we could not rightly afford a child. I laughed his doubts aside and said lightly : ' Oh, well, then, don't let us have one for a while, anyway ! ' We spoke of other things and I must confess I thought no more of the matter, though I suffered from the cool reticence and self-restraint of my fiancé during our engagement. But I told myself that marriage would bring a change, and was glad to believe it, for I am a much more impulsive and intense person emotionally than he is, and react more quickly to things and people. Oh, doctor, how can I describe the first few days of my married life ! I was in such a state of tense expectancy that I shook like a leaf. And a week went by, and my husband's manner and conduct remained as before ; I was still a maiden and not his true wife ; and then —very strange questionings began in my mind.

" I am not accusing him of anything and I am not just ' letting myself go ' to you. But—still nothing happened and then I remembered our talk during our engagement, about a child and financial difficulties, so I felt relieved— surely that was the explanation.

" However—our position improved from the money point of view. Even my husband admitted things were looking rosier. So I began to hope for the child, and—I admit it frankly—for the experience I had missed.

"But nothing happened. My husband is very taciturn and reserved. He has many staunch friends, and is very much respected and liked, but he has no intimates. We ' got on ' very well together, and our minds and spirits grew ever closer and dearer to one another, and I appreciate this, but our bodies did not meet. Night and morning he kissed me gently and I felt deeply happy when he stroked my hair.

" But—I wondered and thought and puzzled my brain.

And nevertheless I was able to keep up appearances ; to seem happy and at peace. Until the strain proved too much ; the recurrent tension every evening and then—the disappointment. My pride and will broke, and I asked him, straight out : ' Berthold, why don't you come to me and stay with me ? ' I could see that he was not at ease—but struggling in his mind. Once he spoke of a ' temporary trouble ' which prevented him—without being any more explicit : and I was ' tactful '—or cowardly ? I didn't ask further questions. Oh, you cannot know what it cost me, even to ask the question I did ! Then there came a time when he said ' Be patient, bear with me, dear ! ' and I reproached myself for not having kept silence. It was a terrible time of pain and perplexity : my vanity and my pride were so deeply wounded. I got quite morbid and used to stare at myself in the looking glass, with bitter despair. I felt he did not love me, and knew not where to go or what to do. But I managed to hide my desperate hurt from my husband.

" Then came an experience which roused me from this Slough of Despond. A young man of our acquaintance began to seek my company and desired to possess my body. And my self-esteem returned, the primitive Eve in me rejoiced in being wanted and I had a very narrow escape from catastrophe, for my physical passion was for a while almost stronger than my love for my husband. Almost, but not quite, for at the crucial moment, when he tried to approach me, I grew so cold and remote that he did not dare to take me. But after that episode I felt wiser and happier, more mistress of my own fate and tenderer and more understanding to my husband. You see, he was thirty-five when we married, and had never been with a woman in that way : his parents and people were all severe upright folk, and he had all kinds of repressions and inhibitions as a child. He met his own troubles without anyone's help or advice. And he is not impulsive or a creature of moods. Surely you see that such a temperament cannot approach and possess a woman at once—without being a weakling or incapable ? And I vowed to myself that if he was not himself drawn to

my body, I would never beg or try to force his approach.
You know, while he is on tour, he often thinks of me, he
writes to me every day and often contrives to see me. He
is really a very fine and genuine person, and I know how
much he means to me, and I cannot leave him——.

" Well, one night two years ago, came the happiest moment
of my life, for he said : ' I want to have a child by you,
more than anything.' I forgot all that had gone before,
and was ashamed of my doubts and happier than words can
say. But, doctor, you can hardly believe it, can you ?
everything went on as before, and to-day, five years a wife
in name, I am still physically untouched. It is very hard
for both of us. My husband's work on tour tires him out, he
comes back in great need of rest. I consider him, tend him,
arrange for him to have long hours of sleep. Then, as soon
as he feels better and fitter—my desire for him wells up in
me. I force it down, I won't thrust myself on him—then
he has to go off again, and I feel such depression, such despair.
Do you know, I offered to cease any bodily proximity ; to
sleep in separate rooms. And he wouldn't agree. I have
entreated him to seek medical advice, but there again his
inhibitions make it so difficult. He says he has never met
a doctor in whom he could feel the necessary confidence.
Oh, what shall we do ? We both want a child so terribly.
And another strange thing : there is no fire, no primitive
ardour in my husband, either for hate or love. He is so
equable and so independent : won't let me mother him, but
does everything for himself. I mustn't be a mother or a wife
either ! And both would be such blessings—I hoped for them
so.

" There is a marriage rather like mine among our circle
of acquaintance. My husband knows the man well ; he is
quite an invert and only married in order to have an housekeeper. He just neglects his wife and is always surrounded
by a crowd of youths. And of course she too is still *virgo
intacta*. I am so sorry for her, and wonder that she fails
to see what causes all this. Berthold disapproves thoroughly
of this man's conduct in marrying for a housekeeper. The
woman is not quite free from blame, for she weeps and shows

how unhappy she is. Oh, I would never let myself do that.
"Now, doctor, you may perhaps think me an evil-minded
person, but this marriage of our acquaintance has got on my
nerves, and I am wondering whether my husband may not
possibly have some similar tendency. He likes the company
of boys and there are two who are special pals of his. As
yet, I have not mustered up courage to ask him or broach
the subject, but I notice things. For instance, being in these
boys' company and talking to them, stimulates him and
makes him quite lively and vigorous : he puts everything
else aside when they come along. When we are by.the sea,
no ' bathing belle ' ever gets a glance from him, but he often
watches the naked boys and young men on the beach.
He just isn't interested in women, either in others or in me.
But there was a torchlight procession one night, hundreds
of lads together, and I felt him trembling as I stood beside
him, though it wasn't a bit cold—I know that all this is
surmise—nothing tangible ! And what about this—it may
be quite all right, perhaps I ought to be ashamed of my suspicions. But my husband told me one day he had a business
appointment with a young fellow, in whom he showed
evident interest. They were to go to the theatre together—
so he told me—and when I asked him where they had spent
the night, he said at a friend's house. Some days later, I
met the youth, by chance, and forthwith he gave a most
comical and humorous account of the four flights of stairs
at the hotel where he and Berthold had spent the night.
I tackled my husband and he had to admit that they went
there together. The petty falsehood made me so sad ! I
don't ask questions any more, now. Why couldn't he have
told the truth ? He seemed so uncertain and contradicted
himself more than once. And my suspicions grew—perhaps
it is quite all right and then again—perhaps my husband is
in love with the young fellow and so he felt guilty and unsafe
when I asked about it.

"There is lots I haven't told you about, and I don't know
whether this is clear enough. But if I don't post it I shall
burn it—Doctor, please, please help us ! Tell me what I
ought to do."

15

The husband of this poor bewildered woman refused all medical inspection or consultation, so I could only advise her to apply for a dissolution of her marriage. We shall never know whether psycho-therapy could have helped them both. But the pathetic letter is a veritable contemporary human document, showing the intricate inhibitions and the lamentable ignorance which still surround the essential facts of sex. And the frequent uncertainty as to the advisability of treatment arises simply because we cannot distinguish between innate and acquired. Of course cases which are not biological " sports " are much easier to diagnose. Manifestations which are abnormal in degree, but essentially only extreme developments of sexual trends which are found in most people, are much more easy to study and " place " than the more divergent forms of sexual inversion.

All rigid classification must be inadequate, but the following synopsis, drawn up by L. Klages in 1924, may be of use, as applying to and defining the average in man and woman respectively. The synopsis shows definite tendencies, and may be serviceable in judging the presence or degree of " psycho-sexual hermaphrodism."

MASCULINE TRAITS OF CHARACTER

Masculine Trait	Corresponding
Differentiation . . .	Dualism.
Enthusiasm, power of objective feeling . .	Liability to Illusion and Delusion.
Imagination . . .	Neglect of actual Facts.
Energy	Insensibility or Cruelty.
Activity and versatility .	Restlessness.
Power of Conviction . . Abstract thought . .	Fanaticism and Pedantry.
Impartiality . . .	Lack of Individual Consideration.
Dignity	Arrogance and Mental Vanity.

FEMININE TRAITS OF CHARACTER

Unity and Harmony . .	Instinct dominating Reason.
Personal devotion : Love of Individuals . . .	Partiality and personal prejudice.
Equable nature . .	Limited range of feeling.
Sympathy and Compassion	Lack of Initiative.
Persistence and Tenacity .	Pettiness.
Acute intuitive Perception	Indifference to logic.
Emotional spontaneity and honesty . . .	Blindness to Values of a general nature : " Subjectivism."

I must again stress the provisional and imperfect nature of these suggestions ; but they do indicate what we may reasonably expect in men and women in our present stage of social evolution. For certain psychological differences depend on the differing chemistry of the metabolic and endocrine functions. In cases of aberration and variation, we must ask what degrees are " still normal " and which are " morbid." Havelock Ellis suggests " deviations " as a suitable term for the " morbid " manifestations.

" In order to remain within the normal range, all variations must at some point include the procreative end for which sex exists. To exclude procreation is perfectly legitimate, and under some circumstances morally imperative. But sexual activities entirely and by preference outside the range in which procreation is possible may fairly be considered abnormal ; they are deviations " (*Psychology of Sex*, p. 126).

16

The typical feature of most sexual aberrations or deviations is the appearance of a Symbol or Substitute : an accessory feature of the normal content of the sexual emotion or function becomes the centre of attraction, and finally replaces the natural goal of sex. Binet used the term " erotic fetishism " for certain special deviations, as early as 1888, but as Lombroso pointed out, in 1897, this term is inadequate.

Most forms of fetish-symbols are to be found, latent but recognizable, in the complex emotions of normal sex attraction. " Fetishisms are, in a slight degree, entirely normal. Every lover becomes specially attracted by some individual feature of the beloved or to some of the various articles that come in contact with her. But this tendency becomes abnormal when it is exclusive or generalized, and it becomes a definite deviation when the fetish itself, even in the absence of the person, becomes completely adequate not only to arouse tumescence, but to evoke detumescence, so that there is no desire at all for sexual intercourse " (Ellis, *l.c.*, p. 144, 1934).

But all the sexual ardour of the pronounced case of deviation is focused on possessing the object which has become his or her sexual symbol. The results may be such social injuries as theft, burglary, assault and battery or even arson. There are shoe-, foot-, stocking-, clothes-, hair-fetishists. Krafft-Ebing interpreted shoe- and foot-fetishisms as rudimentary Masochism, but this is by no means invariably the case.

Animals may become objects of sexual attraction to human beings, as well as inaminate objects or substances (such as textile fabrics). The emotional interest in animals may be a highly wrought sympathy and understanding or may take the grossly primitive and direct form of attempted intercourse ; zöerasty or " bestiality." The term " sodomy " is sometimes used in this sense, but it is ambiguous and should be avoided in a scientific discussion. Scientists and criminologists all agree that crude zöerasty manifests in actions only perpetrated by mental defectives or by extremely primitive persons, and may be therefore considered rather as a " substitute " gratification—a human partner being inaccesible—than as a genuine deviation of impulse.

Two groups of deviation, in particular, have excited the public imagination and played a *rôle* in literature : these are the association of sexual excitement with theft ; and its association with pain, whether suffered or inflicted.

As early as 1825 Gall made and recorded the discovery

that thefts may be committed in order to provoke an erotic sensation, and this form of symbolism was almost exclusively found in women. This deviation was known as kleptomania and was studied by Stekel in 1908 by psycho-analytic procedure. In 1917 the American psychiatrist Kiernan used "Kleptolagnia," an analogous term to "Algolagnia," Schrenck-Notzing's designation for pain perversions. Algolagnia includes both the active and the passive types of pain fetishism and is derived from the Greek names for pain = Algos (cf., analgesia) and Lagnos = sexual excitement. The most concise analysis of Kleptolagnia has been made by Havelock Ellis (l.c., p. 486).

"The act, far from being motiveless or in a strict sense irresistible, has a definite and intelligible motive and is carried out with reasonable precaution. The instinctive desire is to secure sexual excitation which cannot be obtained—for whatever reason—in more normal ways, by reinforcing the feeble sexual impulse by the stimulus furnished by the emotions of fear and anxiety, which necessarily accompany the perpetration of a theft. There is no desire to appropriate the stolen object for purpose of gain, and when its sexual effect has been obtained, either in the act of stealing or by subsequent masturbation, it is hidden away or destroyed."

A similar compulsive urge is found in erotic arson or Pyrolagnia; Lacassagne described a case of this fire-mania in Lyons in 1896.

17

Algolagnia has two forms or two facets, active and passive; the former is known as Sadism following the confessions of the Marquis de Sade, the latter as Masochism, so called after the Austrian writer, Sacher Masoch. In their most definite and genuine form they both provoke the acme of sexual sensation and relief, without functional intercourse, and are therefore incontestable deviations or "perversions." There does not seem to be any clear demarcation between activity and passivity here. But Hirschfeld pointed out that male Sadism and female Masochism represent highly exaggerated developments of trends already characteristic

of the respective normal *rôles* of the sexes, whereas female
Sadism and male Masochism were transpositions of these
normal tendencies, and therefore in a class by themselves. He
termed female Sadism and male Masochism, " Metatropism."
But there has been no adequate and satisfactory classification of available case-material to this day.

The source of the pain perversions lies very deep. It has
been found that the actual sex impulse of these deviants is
weaker than the normal average, as is also the case in
Kleptolagniacs. It is a widespread error to assume that
Sadists are impelled to their crimes by a volcanic force of
lust. Pain, suffered or inflicted, serves as a lash to bring
on the detumescence which the normal endocrine or psychic
mechanism cannot achieve. Havelock Ellis, in Volume III
of his great *Studies*, has traced this pathological deviation
to its sources, and stressed the late recognition of Masochism, which was first recognized and recorded by Krafft-
Ebing in a masterly passage of his *Psychopathia sexualis*
(1886).

We may completely endorse Ellis's view that Algolagnia
is " a great subdivision of erotic symbolism " ; " it includes
all the cases in which pleasure is associated actively or
passively, in reality or in simulation or in imagination, with
pain, anger, fear, anxiety, shock, constraint, subjection,
humiliation, and allied psychic states. For all these states
involve recourse to a great reservoir of primitive emotion
which may be utilized to reinforce the sexual impulse."

18

The most widely diffused and therefore most socially
important deviation is—exhibitionism. Lasègue was the
first recorder of this manifestation, in 1877. Those who have
had occasion to give advice and instruction about sex, and
to receive the confidences of many individuals, must all
have marvelled at the number of times they have had to
observe the growth of psychic traumata in girls and women,
based on sudden encounters with male exhibitionists. In
the dark lobby of some apartment house, in narrow alleys,
or secluded glades ; these women—often as quite young

girls—have come suddenly face to face with a man, who exposed his genital organs to their gaze. Every woman with normal sexual responses will instantaneously assume, very naturally so, if she has no special knowledge of psychopathology, that this exposure is only the prelude to an attack on her person, an assault or a rape, and seeking to escape such an outrage she will probably make her complaint to the police.

Of course, the policeman goes on the same very natural assumptions as the terrified woman ; arrests the man and brings him before the court as a dangerous criminal in intention. The defendants behave with remarkable unanimity : they deny all criminal intent with obvious sincerity. They often, and less honestly, deny any sexual or erotic purpose. They declare that they were about to perform another necessary function.

The genesis of exhibitionism derives partly from actual mental deficiency and partly from an infantile fixation, which has focussed in itself the whole sex urge of the individuals in question, and becomes a compulsive reflex. Epilepsy appears to be excluded, though exposure sometimes occurs during epileptic seizures. But the subjective and substitutional factors which make the exhibitionist a " deviant " do not affect the epilept, who exposes himself as he loses consciousness.

In such cases, it is no prelude to, or preparation for, a brutal attack, but the *final and adequate expression* of the exhibitionist's individual sex desires. There is no bodily danger to other persons, but there is the public nuisance and the psychic effects on some girls and women.

Sentences in courts of law are, of course, in no way therapeutic measures, and perfectly ineffectual as a cure for deep-seated emotional fixations and regressions. Exhibitionists need skilled medical treatment and, to say the least, advice. But they receive one sentence of imprisonment after another, and always revert to their " criminal " practice. The sentences are increased. They wander from police-court to prison, although apart from their special

anomaly they may be wholly law abiding persons, and even
affectionate and conscientious marriage partners.

19

My first experience of these people as a consultant left
me at a total loss what to do or advise. My hapless patient
had been sentenced twenty-one times ; then Fate and an
exceptionally intelligent judge sent him to my consulting
room. It appeared to me that a prolonged analytic procedure
might bring relief ; I asked Hirschfeld's view, and he, the
most practical of men, and in his own words the " environmental therapeutist " said to me :

" Yes, of course, my dear colleague, we could send him to
a psycho-analyst. But it will take a very long time ! We
can't expect a profound mental disturbance to vanish sooner
than T.B. ! and doctors always insist on several years'
treatment for T.B. So—psycho-analysis is a preserve for
the wealthy. This poor chap is an unskilled labourer. He
can spare time but certainly not money, for he has very little.
We must try a cruder and more material method ; it is
certainly empiric, but it should work more quickly."

Hirschfeld had the man brought to his study and said :
" Now look here, you know quite well that you can't be
sure of yourself. Don't you just have to expose yourself
willy-nilly, when the fit is on you ? "

" Yes, sir."

" When do you generally feel this fit coming over you ? "

" Oh, in the evening, about dusk."

" Yes, of course." He turned to me : " We don't know
why, but that is generally the hour." Then to the patient :
" So you see, you mustn't wander around alone in the evening,
but your wife will come and fetch you from your work. And
she needn't wait just in front of the factory gates, or your
pals will start making fun of you both. Do you understand ? "

" Yes."

" That is all right, then. And you must ask her to make
you a special kind of pair of trousers, no slit in front, but
closed like bathing drawers, and with bands over your
shoulders under your jacket. No braces—those are too easy

to unfasten. The way this will help you is by preventing you from being able to expose yourself whenever the fit is on you. The sheer material external difficulty will prevent the action until you come to your right mind again. And, what's more, to *know* that there *is* this obstacle will make the fits come much less often. We don't know why it should, but it does! So why not use this knowledge to help our patients? And then: no alcohol at all! Last time it happened you'd had a drop, hadn't you?"

" Yes," was the reply in tones of depression and regret.

" Now you've got to leave that alone, or you'll excite yourself and have more trouble. There's one thing more : we'll give you a paper, a personal certificate, that you are known to us as an habitual exhibitionist and that you are being treated by us for your trouble. So the police will know that, if anything should go wrong, they've got to bring you back to us, and not put you in quod."

The man was sent home, his wife was requested to attend and given instructions, and I am bound to say that however superficial and " external " this method seems—and is— it nevertheless proved effectual in hundreds of cases, and saved hundreds of good and loyal wives from the humiliating shock of a police visit, with the announcement that " your husband's been caught again."

The testimony of all serious students is that the exhibitionist does not aim at sexual injury to the woman's person, nor at shock to her mind. So far as he possesses normal mental faculties, he regrets having shocked and disgusted other people. He is much pleased and elated if girls and women respond to his exposure with amusement, and laugh or smile as they pass by. The act of exposure may be a symbol of sexual initiation or defloration, but for that very reason it is calculated to cause severe psychic shock to girls who have had no instruction nor warning, and thus may lead to serious social repercussions, as this particular form of symbolism is widely diffused and frequent.

20

I would refer readers to the remark of A. L. Wolbarst in

his article in the *Medical Journal and Record* for July, 1931, on " Sexual Perversions, their Medical and Social Implications " : " We may possibly find ourselves on the correct road if we act on the theory that any sexual deviation which has always given satisfaction without injury to a particular individual must be considered normal for that individual."

Of course there must be effective safeguards of the interests and welfare of other persons, especially of young persons and children. On this essential point the laws of various states differ widely. While safeguarding the public, the weak and the young, we must ask for thorough revision of existing laws, on the basis of modern scientific knowledge. Our motto should be the sentence chosen by Hirschfeld for the Haeckel Hall of his Institute : " Our Question is not ' Who is at fault ? ' but ' What is at fault ? ' "

When sex experts judge and estimate the emotional urges of those who have broken traditional and current laws, they tend to very different conclusions to the majority of judges, who are apt to share the ignorance and bias of the general public and not infrequently have profound unconscious repressions of their own.

The mental process in question is one and the same, whether applied to a homosexual person (in countries where homosexuality is a penal offence), to an exhibitionist, or to an impotent elderly, or prematurely senile, man, who attempts sexual practices on children, as a result of the simultaneous *débâcle* of his mental and genital powers.

The frequent incompatibility of the judgment pronounced by psychological experts with the verdict of the law tends to make the honest sexologist far from popular in juridical circles. But in countries with official " expert advisers " these *savants* are apt to consider themselves obliged to echo and confirm the verdicts of tradition.

I have often been in a position to note the sharp contrast between tradition in the seat of judgment and modern science ; when Hirschfeld expressed his deep sense of human solidarity and sympathy with the unpopular minority whose cause he pleaded, and tended to adopt a view altogether favourable to the accused. His evidence was refused, on various occasions, because of " previous bias," for he was wholly convinced that the majority of cases of sexual deviation were as much matters of individual constitution as hair or eye-colour and shape of skull. He persisted in his championship, however, and during his active period he was able to achieve some wholesome results in the operation of the German Criminal Law.

Immediately after the war of 1914–18, Hirschfeld and other experts began to draw up a scheme for the revision and reform of the German Penal Code in sex matters, based on the material they had already been able to collect. Throughout the lifetime of the Weimar Republic there were suggestions and discussions and debates for legal reform, and the same was the case in neighbour states, such as the Republic of Czechoslovakia.

In 1927 Kurt Hiller published a most careful and detailed companion project to the official Penal Reform Bill, containing much important improvement, but since then the political history of Central Europe has made it impossible to carry out any progressive suggestions.

In the same year as Hiller's judicial reform project appeared Magnus Hirschfeld's four-volume work on *Sex Science* or *Geschlechtskunde;* this treated not only the deviations, but the biologically normal manifestations as well. It is curious but characteristic, that the path to scientific investigation and discussion of normal phenomena had to pass by way of the study of abnormality and morbidity. This is the reason for the stupid and reactionary assertion, which has more than once appeared in print, to the effect that Sexual Science was a deliberate " cult of the Perverse." As this term " perverse " is apt to appeal to the prejudices and to titillate the repressed curiosities of philistines, it is totally unsuited for scientific or responsible discussions. And the lack of generally used and yet accurate and adequate terminology serves to increase the psychological confusion and delusions and the ignorance of actual causes in this sphere. Again and ever again we hear that foolish calumny, that responsible scientists are " encouraging homosexuality," " making propaganda for abnormality," and so forth.

Although there can be no doubt of the neurotic and associative factors in certain cases of inversion, we do not need to know very much in order to know that no one becomes homosexual through " encouragement," " incitement," or " propaganda " alone ! But ignorance and repression produce a mass-misunderstanding which secures a hearing and acceptance for the grossest stupidities, provided they are flavoured with the condiment of sexual sensation.

21

In 1928 the second International Congress for Sexual Reform took place in Copenhagen, with Hirschfeld in the chair. (The first Congress took place in Berlin in 1921.) The World League for Sexual Reform was founded on this occasion ; in 1929 the Congress met in London and in 1930 in Vienna, while the Ingese met in London in 1930, dealing mainly with endocrinological problems ; the Viennese meeting of the W.L.S.R. was devoted to the various projected reforms in the Penal Codes of many European states and to the sociological aspects of sex. The last W.L.S.R. Congress took place in 1932, in the Anatomical Institute of the University of Brno (Brünn) in Czechoslovakia.

Hirschfeld had just returned from a trip round the world, where he had been the guest of Universities in Japan, China, India and the U.S.A.

Before he started on this voyage, I had felt impelled to warn him to stay out of Germany until there was a definite improvement in the political situation, for even at the end of 1930 I was extremely sceptical of the prospects of any cultural progress under the prevailing conditions. On his return to Europe, Hirschfeld realized the situation, and went to Vienna and thence to Switzerland. The *débâcle* of Central European science and civic life cut him to the heart, for quite apart from his own admitted speciality, he had always been one of the first to acknowledge and help the forces of progress in every sphere. The tragic farce that is now being played on the stage of public life in Germany is calculated to wipe out the memory of his work. Yet many thousands of blind followers of Hitler and Streicher owe to

Hirschfeld's investigation and agitation their liberty from imprisonment, their recovery from degradation and despair.

On May 11th, 1933, Fascist students of the University of Berlin deliberately and thoroughly destroyed the material collected at the Institute of Sexual Science, the graphic and MSS. *dossiers* and the Library of over 20,000 volumes. The students seized all combustible material in the place, books, photographs, files, MSS., flung it out of the windows into great lorries drawn up in readiness, to the sound of shouts, yells, and anti-Semitic songs, and then burnt the major part of this unique testimony in public : a kind of psychic and mental *auto-da-fé.*

This was done under the auspices of the then Minister for Propaganda and even the bronze portrait bust of Hirschfeld by Isenstein was committed to the flames, as a final "gesture" of hatred and contumely. The building itself was dedicated to the use of the National Socialist Association of German Jurists and Lawyers !

What an irony of fate that Hirschfeld should have suffered so flagrantly insulting a repudiation, for during his voyage round the world, a few years previously, he was received by German diplomatic representatives abroad, with all the honour due to one of the country's most distinguished *savants.* And it is more than irony, it is tragedy of the deepest and most savage kind, that the Nazis should have made him their scapegoat-in-chief, for the Nazi ranks are still—after the murderous *coup* of June 30th, 1934, as before it—thoroughly honeycombed with homosexuality, both in sentiment and active practice ! Hirschfeld is the man *par excellence* to whom the two per cent. of inverted persons in modern communities owe the fact that their right to survive, to exist, to live and love after their natures is a discussible and mentionable problem, and not forever a *chose jugée* as under mediævalism !

Hirschfeld's last refuge was on the soil of France ; his former colleagues were either scattered to the four winds or imprisoned. On his sixty-seventh birthday he died, in Nice. But in Germany, Streicher, the vulgar specialist in hate-mongering and pornography, enjoys the highest favour and friendship of the leader.

22

Let none of my readers suppose that deep-seated opposition to the scientific study of sex is peculiar to the new barbarism enthroned in Central Europe. On May 31st, 1898, one year after Hirschfeld's Humanitarian-Scientific Committee had been founded in Berlin, the London police arrested George Bedborough, and he was charged forthwith at Bow Street, with issuing an " obscene book " entitled *Sexual Inversion*. On reading the notices in the British press, Dr. Hans Kurella, of Breslau, wrote as follows to Havelock Ellis :

" Honoured Colleague, I read a few days ago in the *Daily Chronicle* that a book with the title of yours had given rise to a public prosecution. I wondered at the identity of the title, but could not imagine that a purely scientific work like yours should be subjected to such treatment.

" For us on the Continent, such a proceeding is altogether incomprehensible. What would become of science and of its practical applications if the pathology of the sexual life were put on the index ? It is as if Sir Spencer Wells were to be classed with Jack the Ripper.

" No doubt the judge (unless suffering from senile dementia) will accord you brilliant satisfaction. But in any case the whole of scientific psychology and medicine on the Continent is on your side."

There was no error ! The sedulously respectable police of the Victorian era had procured Havelock Ellis's great book, through the instrumentality of a disguised detective, and the indictment of October 31st, 1898, at the Old Bailey came to the conclusion that " the whole book from the first page to the last, and every line," was charged as " wicked, lewd, impure, scandalous and obscene."

The judge was the Recorder, Sir Charles Hall. He is not known to have been suffering from senile dementia, but he pilloried himself forever by the following pronouncements :

" You might at the outset, perhaps, have been gulled into the belief that somebody might say that this was a scientific book. But it is impossible for anybody with a head on his shoulders to open the book without seeing that it is a pretence and a sham, and that it is merely entered into for the purpose of selling this filthy publication."

It should be borne in mind that the book in question was the first volume of the world-famous *Studies in the Psychology of Sex*, accepted in all enlightened circles to-day as the standard classic on the subject in the English language.

It was an expensive, detailed and wholly scientific publication, the last kind of treatise in the world to " popularize " or " advertize " its theme, although some sound and intelligible instruction on the subject would have been not a moral outrage, but a public asset.

After the trial, the medical press " got busy " and Ellis was actually told that reviews had been refused, because the book appeared through a little-known publisher and not with the hall mark of one of the " accepted " firms. But Havelock Ellis was able to put this hypocrisy to flight by the simple statement of fact which he repeats in the preface to his latest edition (1936).

" I had not yet found an English publisher, though I had approached several London medical publishers; they were all afraid of the subject, though one at least said he would have been glad to accept the book if he had not the privilege of being an English publisher."

Houston Peterson, the biographer of Ellis, informs us that " The wounds Ellis received in that trial have never entirely healed. He could not cease to feel that the work of his life had been smirched by a poisonous monster, and there hung over him the possibility of similar attacks " (*Biography*, p. 263).

The present writer was a guest in England, and he does not feel it becoming to venture any judgment on the present " official " view of sexual science in this country. He will content himself with quoting the judgment passed by the most eminent and informed of living sexologists, namely, of Havelock Ellis himself. After the deplorable *début* in 1898, he took measures to have his further volumes published in the United States of America, where they are issued for the benefit of doctors and other responsible persons, and not in any way accessible to all and sundry ! In 1898 he wrote about the position in England ; doubtless after deliberate reflection and with the characteristic reserve and moderation of his temperament and years :

" In this country it is a sufficiently hard task for any student to deal with the problems of sex, even under the most favourable circumstances. He already, as it were, carries his life in his hands. He has entered a field which is largely given over to faddists and fanatics, to ill-regulated minds of every sort. He must, at the same time, be prepared to find that the would-be sagacity of imbeciles counts him the victim of any perversion he may investigate. Even from well-balanced and rational persons he must at first meet with a certain amount of distrust and opposition. . . . Certainly I regret that my own country should be almost alone in refusing to me conditions of reasonable intellectual freedom. But I must leave to others the task of obtaining the reasonable freedom that I am unable to attain."

BIBLIOGRAPHY

BAUMONT, M., L'Affaire Eulenburg et les Origines de la Guerre Mondiale, Paris, 1933.
CARPENTER, E., Homogenic Love, Manchester, 1894.
CARPENTER, E., Love's Coming-of-Age, Manchester, 1895.
CARPENTER, E., Intermediate Sex, London and Manchester, 1908.
CARPENTER, E., My Days and Dreams, London, 1916.
CREW, F. A. E., Sex, in Outlines of Modern Knowledge, London, 1931.
ELLIS, H. H., A Note on the Bedborough Trial, London, 1898.
ELLIS, H. H., Psychology of Sex, London, 1934.
ELLIS, H. H., Studies in the Psychology of Sex, II, III, VII.
ELLIS, H. H., Preface to the Studies, Ed. 1936.
HARDEN, MAXIM., Die Zukunft, 1906, 1907, 1908, 1909.
HIRSCHFELD, M., Die Transvestiten, Berlin, 1910.
HIRSCHFELD, M., Sexualpathologie, Cologne, 1917.
HIRSCHFELD, M., Homosexualität des Mannes und des Weibes, Berlin, 1920.
HIRSCHFELD, M., Geschlechtskunde, Stuttgart, 1927.
HOYER, N., Man into Woman, London, 1933 (Lili Elbe).
INGESE, First Congress, ed. MARCUSE, I–V, Cologne, 1927–28.
INGESE, Second Congress, ed. CREW, London, 1931.

KLAGES, L., *Psychologie der Handschrift*, Stuttgart, 1924.
KRAFFT-EBING, V., *Psychopathia sexualis*, Stuttgart, ab 1886.
KRAFFT-EBING, V., in *Jahrb. f. sex. Zwischenstufen,* III, Berlin.
MARAÑÓN, GR., *Estudios de fisiopatología sexual*, Barcelona, 1931.
MOLL, A., *Die conträre Sexual Empfindung*, Berlin, 1891.
PETERSON, H., *Havelock Ellis*, New York, 1928.
REICH, W., *Der sexuelle Kampf der Jugend*, Berlin, 1932.
SCHRENCK-NOTZING, *Zeitsch. f. Hypnotismus*, XI, 1899.
STEKEL, W., " Ueber die sexuelle Wurzel der Kleptomanie,"
    Ztsch. f. Sexualwiss, 1908.
STEKEL, W., *Der Fetischismus*, Berlin, 1923.
STEKEL, W., *The Homosexual Neurosis*, Boston, 1922.
STEINACH, E., *Arch. f. Entwicklungsmechanik*, 46, 1920.
W.L.S.R., First Congress, ed. WEIL, Stuttgart, 1922.
W.L.S.R., Second Congress, ed. LEUNBACH, Copenhagen, 1929.
W.L.S.R., Third Congress, ed. HAIRE, London, 1930.
W.L.S.R., Fourth Congress, ed. HERBERT STEINER, Vienna, 1931.
WOLBARST, *Med. Journ. and Record*, July, 1931.

TABLE OF EVENTS

1869 BENKERT first uses the term " Homosexual."
1870 WESTPHAL publishes particulars of a Homosexual case.
1877 LASÈGUE'S monograph on Exhibitionism.
1885 Criminal Law Amendment Act in Great Britain.
1886 KRAFFT-EBING publishes *Psychopathia sexualis*.
1888 BINET coins the term " Erotic Fetishism."
1891 MOLL'S monograph, *Die conträre Sexualempfindung*.
1895 Wilde case in London.
    CARPENTER'S *Homogenic Love*.
1896 First (German) edition of Havelock Ellis' work.
1897 Scientific Humanitarian Committee founded in Berlin.
1898 Bedborough case in London.
1900 *Annual for Intermediate Types* founded.
1907–09 Eulenburg case in Germany.
1910 HIRSCHFELD'S monograph on Transvestitism.
1913 *Zeitschrift für Sexualwissenschaft* founded in Berlin.
1917 HIRSCHFELD'S *Sexualpathologie*.
1919 Institute of Sexual Science founded.
1920 H. ELLIS introduces the term " Eonism."
1921 First Congress for Sexual Reform on a Scientific Basis,
    in Berlin.
1926 First Congress of the International Society for Sexual
    Research (" Ingese "), Berlin.
1927 HIRSCHFELD publishes *Geschlechtskunde*.

1928 W.L.S.R. founded at Copenhagen during Second Congress
for Sexual Reform.
1929 Third W.L.S.R. Congress in London.
1930 Second Ingese Congress in London.
Fourth W.L.S.R. Congress in Vienna.
1932 Fifth W.L.S.R. Congress at Brno.
1933 Nazis destroy the Institute of Sexual Science, in Berlin.
1934 Massacre of Homosexuals in Germany.
1935 Death of Hirschfeld. Dissolution of W.L.S.R.

CHAPTER III

THE FIGHT AGAINST VENEREAL DISEASE

I

In his book *Sexual Truth versus Sexual Lies, Misconceptions and Exaggerations* (New Jersey, U.S.A., 1932) Dr. William J. Robinson publishes a letter which he received from one of his patients. I quote the letter here, for many readers of the summary of events and research in the previous chapter will no doubt feel just as Dr. Robinson's correspondent :

" I am much more interested in the fearful heartaches, in the unquenchable longings of normal men and women of all ages than I am in the sufferings of perverts and degenerates. Not that I pity the latter less, but I pity the former more. For we must bear in mind that taken all in all, the perverts, including in this term the homosexuals, sadists, masochists, nymphomaniacs, etc., do not constitute more than five per cent. of the population."

This is not only an intelligible reaction, it is even justifiable. Sexual science is a much greater thing than the systematic description of constitutional or neurotic aberrations. But even when following up our knowledge of normal development we find that the first impetus to genuine investigation was given by morbid phenomena ; by the venereal diseases contracted through sexual intercourse.

In the words of Ernst and Seagle (p. 163, 1929) : " If the Age of Faith adopted the Index of Heresy, the Age of Divine Right the Index of Treason, it was inevitable for the Age of Democracy to adopt the Index of Sex."

And this imperative taboo was not infringed until modern medicine began the campaign against venereal diseases. It was realized that the discovery of the infective organisms and the perfection of methods of treatment were inadequate to deal with syphilis and gonorrhœa ; that it was necessary to explain the nature of such diseases to the general public, their symptoms and sequelæ and the possibility of preventing them. And if the public is to be told—then it must be told not only by private consultation but by public instruction.

Of course, this medical and social campaign against the strongest taboo of western civilization had to meet bitter oppositions and profound inhibitions. In Great Britain the best known aspect of this struggle for knowledge is associated with that fearless pioneer, Josephine Butler (1828–1906), and her fight against one-sided discrimination against woman. Let us remember, as an example of one point of view, the words of Mr. Solly, a member of the College of Surgeons, who " far from considering syphilis an evil, regarded it, on the contrary, as a blessing. Could the disease be exterminated, which he hoped it could not, fornication would ride rampant through the land " (Irene Clephane, *Towards Sexual Freedom*, 1935, p. 135).

It is not easy to realize that Mr. Solly's view has advocates in the twentieth century. But let us quote one instance from the history of 1914–18. During the German occupation of Belgium, in 1917, the textile industry collapsed, and thousands of women were thrown out of work. There followed an immense increase of promiscuous intercourse between these workless women and the womanless conquerors in occupation of Belgium. General von Bissing, in command at Brussels, had some forethought and sense of realities. He established a Consultation Centre for Venereal Diseases, and he ordered wholesale supplies of condoms (sheaths or " French letters ") from Germany for free distribution to the troops. For he understood that men who habitually faced death in horrible forms, and who had been for years removed from the influences of all civic order and all domestic affection, were not likely to forego sexual gratification as a result of moral sermons, but that preventive hygiene might save their health, if suitably applied.

But Bissing failed. Once more Imperial influence turned the scale against knowledge and humanity. Her Majesty the former German Empress, Augusta Victoria, learnt through some secret court or church channel that a German General " was inciting our soldier heroes to immorality by distributing indecent appliances." The ethical views of the Empress-Consort were ultra-Victorian, although she had nothing like the personality or authority of the British Queen who impressed so much of her character on the age. In military circles the lady was given other, less respectful titles, but—the prophylactic condoms were not sent to Belgium and the venereal disease statistics leaped to incredible devastation and destruction—to the glory of Piety and Virtue !

Another example ; an eminent British authority, Dr. Robert A. Lyster, Chairman at the Annual Meeting of the British Society for the Prevention of Venereal Diseases, has declared, in 1929, that " it is true that we have to contend with ignorance in connection with preventing venereal diseases, but our chief obstacle is a bitter organized hostility founded entirely on misrepresentation and fanatical prejudice. We meet malice and slander and lies, and the misconstruction of evidence to an enormous extent, directly we approach this subject, owing to its associations with various strongly felt social and religious views."

In 1932 this Society protested in a letter to the Press, as follows :

" In spite of the fact that the Committee appointed by the Government, presided over by Lord Trevethin, reported ten years ago in favour of chemists being authorized to sell approved preventives, no Government has yet implemented the findings of this Committee. . . . For too long now, officialdom, urged by fanaticism and prudery, has withheld this vital knowledge from the people."

No one can deny that these comments are objectively correct and ethically justified. Years ago, in 1868, Sir William Jenner blocked out our programme, as follows : " I think that syphilis is a disease entirely preventible. I think that children and other persons suffer largely from it without any sin of their own and therefore I think it ought to be prevented."

M.M.   G

2

In 1879, when bacteriology was in its infancy, the Breslau medical man Albert Neisser (1855–1916) detected the pathogenic organism which causes gonorrhœa. He termed this the " Gonococcus." Six years later, Bumm succeeded in isolating this organism and Neisser proved its susceptibility to the action of silver salts, thus laying the foundation of effective treatment for " clap " or " gleet " as the populace calls this complaint.

For gonorrhœa is a much commoner complaint than syphilis, although the latter can cause graver individual symptoms. A minute analysis and " follow up " of available statistical material after the war of 1914–18 convinced Blaschko, of Berlin, that the average ratio of syphilis cases to gonorrhœal cases was as 2 to 7. But this frequency is aggravated by the ignorance and indifference still prevalent, and the social significance of gonorrhœa is very grave, quite apart from the superficial nonsense still talked by the man in the street, and by certain cliques of irresponsible youths. Even after fifty years' research, medical men must agree with a leading specialist, when he states that : " The vast majority of cases of gonorrhœa in the male are treated by practitioners who have not the slightest interest in venereal disease, and who make no pretence at being qualified in this branch of medicine. Worse still, there are those chemists who hand treatment across the counter . . ."

The crucial point here is—the date at which a cure can take place. We know that in the course of this disease a relative auto-immunization of the infected person takes place ; an immunization, that is, against his own gonococci. It follows that these micro-organisms are, as it were, encapsulated, or hidden away in some portion of the genital apparatus, and do not cause the typical discharge any longer. The ignorance of many doctors, the recklessness or stupidity of many patients, and the totally inadequate provision for public treatment in most countries (for only Great Britain, Scandinavia and the Soviet Union are sufficiently enlightened to provide any free treatment !) lead to the most deplorable lapses in the final tests before a " clean bill " can be given. A few smears are taken often with simple methyl blue staining, and not even subjected to the (sometimes fallible) Gram technique. And all is said to be well, once more. At the first occasion of sexual intercourse following this happy verdict, the local congestion leads to the break up of the old encapsulations ; the gonococci flood through the natural secretions, and the sensitive mucous membrane of the—generally unsuspecting —partner is attacked by a freshly acquired " clap."

It may therefore be of help to summarize the considered opinion, formed after drastic criticism of available material, as to the absolute minimum necessary tests for the cure of gonorrhœa, at least in the male.[1]

1. Dilatation of the urethra and inspection by means of the urethroscope.

2. Microscopic examination of the prostatic fluid before and after provocation.

3. Serological examination by the so-called complement fixation reaction. The negative result here does not necessarily mean freedom from infection ! During the first fortnight after initial infection with gonorrhœa the reaction is always negative.

4. Cultural examination of the prostatic fluid, before and after provocation.

These complex clinical procedures require an armamentarium of technical appliances in the public health dispensaries, such as few states outside England at present even contemplate. In spite of the earlier triumph of bacteriology in detecting the active organism of gonorrhœa, the practical success of social therapy is not in any way comparable to what we are able to record about syphilis ; and this in spite of the difficulties and delays in ascertaining the actual cause and epidemiology of syphilis.

3

In the lower left-hand corner of Mathias Grünewald's

---

[1] Both actual diagnosis and actual cure are much more difficult in women, owing to their special structure.—Translator's Note.

famous altarpiece, portraying the Temptation of St. Antony, we behold a ghastly form, a livid greenish-blue in colour, the face covered with festering ulcers : a portrait from life of the malignant syphilis of the sixteenth century. Few living authorities can have encountered anything like this, for in the four centuries since Grünewald's observations the symptoms of syphilis have changed incalculably. Syphilis is known to be the very Proteus of Pathology.

As long ago as 1868 Sir William Jenner distinguished between three characteristic stages, and Neisser elaborated the diagnosis of " primary," " secondary " and " tertiary " symptoms. These views held the field till 1917, when doubts as to the rigidity of this classification began to be expressed. And the actual cause of this appalling disease, the theme of so much study and controversy, remained a riddle throughout the nineteenth century.

Animal experimentation with guinea-pigs, mice and rabbits revealed nothing. Suddenly it occurred to the Russian biologist, Elia Metchnikoff, in the course of his studies in Paris, that anthropoid apes would give better clues. He consulted Pasteur, who agreed with him, but Pasteur's Institute was not in a position to supply the necessary funds. Let us quote Olga Metchnikoff (1921, p. 190) : At this time Metchnikoff gained a prize of 50,000 francs on the occasion of the Congress in Madrid, and " utilized this money in the acquisition of two anthropoid apes. The same year M. Roux won the Osiris prize of 100,000 francs, which he devoted to the same object, and it was decided that the two together would undertake researches on syphilis. Other donations, 30,000 francs from Morosoff, of Moscow, and 250 roubles from the Society of Dermatology and Syphilography of the same city, completed the capital required to execute the projected plan.

" The inoculation of anthropoid apes with syphilis was successful. The chimpanzee was found to be most sensitive to the disease ; it manifests primary and secondary symptoms identical with those of man. . . . Owing to the ability of apes to contract syphilis, experimental vaccination and serotherapy could be attempted on them ; but, though these experiments were sometimes encouraging, the results obtained were not constant enough to justify their application to man."

But the actual causative agent had not been detected. Then the Hamburg specialist on protozoal forms of life, F. Schaudinn, was persuaded by Edward Hoffmann, the syphilologist, to take up the search. In a few days, or rather hours, Schaudinn succeeded, where a whole generation of medical men and bacteriologists had laboured in vain. "Prepared by extraordinary eyesight, extraordinary skill with the microscope, unlimited energy and enthusiasm of genius" (Stokes) he identified the spirilliform protozoön to which he gave the name spirochæta pallida. This organism is 7/1000 of a millimetre long and 0·25/1000 "thick." (Red blood corpuscles are 7/1000 millimetre in diameter.) The tiny spirochæte was the pathogenic organism of syphilis.

When the spirochæte had been perceived and its dimensions recorded, Metchnikoff discovered that the French observers Bordet and Gengou had been the first to see the micro-organism (in 1903) but had failed to realize its significance.

Schaudinn's method was used and revealed the same microbe in apes, inoculated with human virus, which confirmed the specific character of the "treponema"—an alternative name used by some savants, instead of spirochæta pallida, to this day.

To quote Olga Metchnikoff (*l.c.*) : "An observation was then made which was of great importance on account of its consequences : it was ascertained that the syphilis microbe was absorbed by the less mobile mononuclear phagocytes, and remained localized near the entrance point long enough to allow of a local treatment which might succeed in being curative, as it had time to act before the microbes had passed into the general circulation of the organism. This supposition was proved to be correct by a series of experiments on monkeys ; and, in 1906, a young doctor, M. Maisonneuve, inoculated himself with syphilis and applied the treatment with a perfectly satisfactory result."

Obviously it was necessary to give the earliest possible

treatment to every case of syphilitic infection. Hence the importance of reliable tests to be applied in the necessary prompt diagnosis. A remarkable advantage was gained as soon as the serologists were in a position to make use of the specific changes caused in the blood by the influence of syphilitic toxins.

Bordet, in 1898, was the first to clearly demonstrate serum hæmolysis in the test tube. Kolmer describes Bordet's first application of complement fixation in his work with Gengou, carried out with *Bacillum pestis:* " to settle an argument with Ehrlich and Morgenroth as to unity of complement " as Stokes remarks (1934, p. 108). " In the race for the development of the possibilities of this new type of diagnostic procedure, it is once more interesting that Bordet and Gengou . . . again lost the pre-eminence that would have come from the initial application of complement fixation procedure to the diagnosis of syphilis. Instead, the distinction, so far as our field is concerned, fell to Wassermann, Neisser and Bruck."

August von Wassermann (1866–1925) completed the technique known by his name henceforward in 1906. Rigid tests proved that the reaction is by no means only applicable to syphilis, but remains a valuable diagnostic procedure, especially after certain improvements have been affected. Moreover it became possible to test and control the reliability of individual " Wassermann's " by means of the " flocculation test " ; and the most dependable of the methods here proved to be Kahn's. The lead went to the U.S.A., both in the investigation of sera and of chromosomes, though both lines of research were of mixed Franco-German origin. The proceedings at the Second Serological Conference organized by the League of Nations in Copenhagen (1928) indicated that Kahn's test was positive in 61 per cent. of all tested and positively syphilitic cases, and remained negative in all (100 per cent.) the tested negative cases. The Conference held at Montevideo three years later (1931) confirmed these results.

Therapy went hand in hand with diagnosis. Since the turn of the century, Paul Ehrlich had worked at his Institute of Experimental Therapy at Frankfurt am Main to solve the problem of effective treatment. He was an ardent believer in Paracelsus' doctrine of the specific affinities and antidotes. He combined one blend of substances after another to find something that would attack the spirochæta pallida without injuring the normal cells of the human tissues.

He based his triumphant series on arsenic, and composed a substance which has become world famous under the name of its experimental number : " Ehrlich-Hata 606." His colleague in these experiments was the Japanese Hata, and the date was 1910. " Ehrlich-Hata 606 " is better known, perhaps, as Salvarsan. It too has been altered and improved, and similar chemical combinations have been patented outside Germany. Arsenic is the basis of them all, and has won an equal *rôle* in the campaign against syphilis with the traditional mercury, bismuth and iodides.

4

But since 1917 we have learnt more of the actual process of infection. What we now know is summed up by Stokes in these terms (1934) : " The limitation of the syphilitic process to a local inoculative phase is so extremely short as to be practically non-existent for therapeutic purposes. The chancre, accepted by traditional syphilology as the first manifestation of syphilis, is in reality a rather late affair " (p. 44).

The increased clinical material available and adequately recorded has shown us that we can no longer keep to the rigid chronological classification of " primary," " secondary " and " tertiary " symptoms. There are cases in which typically " tertiary " symptoms appear a few weeks after the initial infection ; without any intervening " secondary " phenomena.

This new knowledge has deep practical value. Formerly we were entitled to believe that " primary cases " could be regarded as cured after one " abortive test " ; to-day we know that the only safeguard against recrudescence is to be found in prolonged observation in every case. There is a

complete *volte-face* in professional opinion, above all in
Central Europe. Neisser's successor at Breslau, Jadassohn,
warned his colleagues over the wireless not to trust the
" abortive test." Before 1933, the German medical profession accepted this warning from a Jew. Since then,
Jadassohn has left Breslau for Zürich ; and Neisser, Ehrlich
and Wassermann are all dead. They were fortunate enough
to complete their life work before German laws and German
medicine became sacred preserves of " Aryans " only.

5

The general embarrassment of self-consciousness artificially
induced by the educational system still prevalent in Europe
and America handicaps the fight against venereal diseases
in ways of which the public is not aware. The clinical and
technical requisites in this fight are known and accepted in
their main portion ; but all workers for actual instruction
and enlightenment of the general public on these subjects
will be able to recall experiences exactly parallel to that
recounted by Mr. Wansey Bayly at the W.L.S.R. Congress
in London (1929), as follows :

" On one occasion in the discussion that followed a lecture
that I gave, a clergyman said, ' Venereal disease is God's
punishment for sin,' but was rendered speechless and foolish
by a private soldier at the back of the hall who rose and said :
' Am I to conclude from the reverend gentleman's remark
that irregular sexual relations with a virgin or a respectable
married woman is not contrary to God's laws, seeing that
such are never visited by His punishment of venereal disease ?
When I was young I was taught that while irregular sexual
relation with a loose woman was wrong, that with a virgin
or a decent married woman was infinitely more wrong.'
The reverend gentleman collapsed like a pricked bubble as
every chatterer must when up against stern facts " (Congress
Report, p. 248).

In my personal experience a scene took place which also
illustrated the gulf between the verdicts of science and the
prejudices founded on traditional theology. Some years ago
I addressed a public meeting on Sex Education at Aix-la-

Chapelle ; it was an occasion specially arranged for working-class people. But evidently the preliminary notices had reached other hands, for some of the teachers and students at the Technical College of Aix, most of whom were of course Catholics, turned up among the audience. So I had to deal with sex questions before a group of theologically prejudiced and sensationally excited opponents, instead of an audience with comparatively ready susceptibility to reason and facts, as is the case with working-class assemblies.

I used my unsought opportunity by starting from the doubtless welcome fact that venereal diseases had considerably decreased in most countries to-day. Why was this ? Well, first of all, through the improved knowledge of medicine and the better public recognition of the possibility of treatment ; a knowledge and recognition which we owe first and foremost to Neisser, Schaudinn, Ehrlich and Wassermann. And in the second place, to a change in the sexual habits of the peoples of Northern, Western and Central Europe. For hitherto, the sex needs of the majority of young unmarried men had been met by fairly frequent and active intercourse with professional prostitutes, of lower social status. This still takes place, but there is a steady increase of another type of relationship, namely, between unmarried men and girls of their own social class ; and this avoids the mechanical frequency and promiscuity of the sheer physical act which spreads both direct and " mediate " contagion far and wide among professional prostitutes and their clients. I stated my view that these developments were highly desirable in the interests of health, and suggested that those who deplored them were faced with the dilemma of either advocating the decrease of these diseases and the increase of so-called " immorality," or the decrease of " immorality " and the further diffusion of disease ; and I awaited with eager attention, the verdict of the Catholics among my audience.

They advocated nothing ! Neither *pro* nor *con.* They just went home " deep in thought." Perhaps one or two may even have begun to doubt the divine and infallible origin of their " moral standards."

6

The prejudices against the clear analysis and control of contemporary conditions, are not only theological. The class divisions of the present social order provide further restrictions to thought and action. The chief official of the German Society for Combating Venereal Disease (Gesellschaft zur Bekämpfung der Geschlechtskrankheiten) in Czechoslovakia, Dr. Leo Dub, made the following significant comment (in a medical publication, *Beiträge z. ärtzl. Fortbild. Praha*, No. 22, 2.11.32, p. 368) : " The abolition of the licensed brothels in our country has accelerated the almost unrestricted promiscuity in which modern youth has its being. The former customers of the licensed houses were mostly young men of the middle classes, whose sexual aggressiveness has now turned towards the formerly safeguarded women of their own social stratum."

The safeguarding and protection of these middle-class girls and women in the past meant a deep psychological cleavage and contradiction. It meant that love and physical sex experience were divorced, and that the latter was obtained under humiliating circumstances with " inferiors." For the antithesis between sex and love is the stronger and cruder, the more highly the pre-nuptial virginity of girls is prized and the more stringently it is exacted. And another factor is important here, the relatively late age at which legal marriage is contracted in our civilization of the West. One has only to study the customs of Roman Catholic countries, to verify this attitude of young men towards the special class of venal women who supply their demands.

But even in non-Catholic countries, the repression due to traditional religion makes the fight against venereal disease much harder than would be the case were the problem purely medical, as, for instance, in the case of typhus. Even in England the work has been made more difficult and less effective by such opinions as that " advocating self-disinfection encourages vice by making it safe." But every sociologist must agree with the late Lord Chief Justice Trevethin when he said : " It is urged by some that any system of disinfection would tend to increase the number of exposures and to raise the disease rate. We have received no evidence of facts in support of this view and we are inclined to think that those who hold it attach too much weight to the deterrent effect of the fear of disease."

These wise words were spoken in 1923. Two years later, in the course of the International Social Hygiene Congress, the representatives of the British Admiralty and the British War Office both agreed that the ultimate elimination of venereal disease depended not on treatment after infection but on prophylaxis after risk. Nevertheless the Ministry of Health did nothing on the lines indicated, even after a deputation of experts had been received by Mr. Neville Chamberlain, then in charge of the Department, in May, 1925. The deputation tried to obtain official sanctions for prophylactic measures, but in vain. After some correspondence, the Minister dropped the matter. And at the London Congress for Sexual Reform, four years later, it was regretfully recorded that " the undemocratic, unscientific and anti-social attitude of previous Ministries of Health in this country, due almost certainly to the narrow, pathetically narrow, religious views of certain prominent permanent officials in the Ministries, cannot fail to be looked upon by future generations as a blot upon our times and as a clear indication of the need of sexual reform."

7

Similar pronouncements from what ought to be responsible quarters might be collected from most other countries ; and this in spite of the obvious fact that effective prophylaxis against venereal disease can be made available with perfect decency and discretion. For years, in Germany, a group of medical men who realized facts, and among whom I had the honour to be numbered, tried in vain to have automatic machines containing condoms and chemical disinfectants set up in the men's lavatories of the principal pleasure resorts of pre-Hitler Berlin. Our efforts were wrecked on the protesting barrier of the " Public Morality Societies "— those lairs of stupidity, repression and hypocrisy ! In one quarter of the city, mainly inhabited by industrial workers, the local Borough authorities were enlightened enough to give instructions that the automatic machines should be set up, but the Central Office cancelled this order.

And all this folly and misery prevailed in spite of the completely sound and clear scientific basis for prophylactic hygiene ! The relevant measures are most succinctly put in the twopenny pamphlet issued by the British Society for the Prevention of Venereal Diseases :

" 1. Pass water as soon as possible after sexual intercourse.

" 2. Then wash thoroughly the sexual organs with soap and water if possible.

" 3. Then bathe thoroughly with solution of potassium permanganate (easily prepared either from crystals or tablets by adding sufficient to colour the water a deep pink, or easily carried about ready for use in a bottle) all parts exposed to infection. In case of females a syringe should be used. This is the most important of all measures, and even when used alone has proved to be effective. The other measures are additional precautions.

" 4. Then apply thoroughly to all parts exposed to infection an ointment or cream containing 33 per cent. calomel. This ointment or cream, as well as the above tablets, can be obtained from chemists.

" 5. It is an excellent additional safeguard to apply the above ointment or cream before sexual intercourse. Any chemist will supply at small cost the materials in this prescription."

Please supply—

A half-ounce tube of ointment :

Calomel	3 parts
Hydrous Lanolin	4 ,,
White Vaseline	2 ,,
25 Tablets Potassium Permanganate	5 grains

Similar instructions have been issued by Health and Welfare Societies in other countries as well. It is, of course, difficult to follow up their exact operation. The health of the individual or group must be supervized and tested continuously, in order to get reliable results. But the armies and navies of the great powers have been given systematic instruction of this kind, and have shown an appreciable improvement, decreased disease, and better general health, thus proving that the propaganda of enlightenment and the practical measures have been well worth while. " It pays to advertise," said Colonel L. Harrison at the Social Hygiene Congress of 1933, and he was right.

Of course, objections may be raised as to the manner of presentation in the instructions given, for some governments now in existence become morally perturbed at any mention of anything to do with sex. The wisest way out of this difficulty was found and followed by the founder of the great Berlin rubber-factory " Fromms Act." Mr. Fromm has certainly done more to prevent venereal disease than many learned societies rolled into one. He sells all his firm's specialities under the same patented title, " Fromms Act " : from sponges and babies' teats and hot water bottles to condoms, and is able simply, directly and decently to advertise his wares, for even the most fervent moralist would make himself too ridiculous by agitating against the advertisement and sale of bath-sponges made of that equivocal substance, rubber !

Yes, the venereal diseases are on the decrease ; in Europe, in America, in the Soviet Union. Not, of course, solely through preventive prophylaxis, but certainly in part because of this. The other decisive factor here has been the great change in sexual habits, to which reference has already been made.

8

The traditional form of prostitution implies comparatively indiscriminate sexual supply—on the woman's side—for payment. This ancient institution is diminishing in all countries of contemporary civilization, always excepting those under the complete sway of the Roman Catholic Church. This statement may appear too sweeping, but at the London Congress in 1929, R. G. Randall made an acute psychological diagnosis. He said : " Thus, wherever teaching of sex is in the hands of the Roman Catholic

Church there seems also to be a big demand for prostitutes. Prostitution does not, however, at any point help to clear up the muddle of sensibilities created by religious teaching and by chivalrous and mediæval superstitions about sex. It seems merely to vitiate it. The practice of confession in the Roman Catholic Church seems also to provide an avenue by which the process of vitiation is facilitated by permitting compromise and by refusing to face psychological facts" (p. 256 of *Congress Report*).

In other words, the modern revolt against the so-called " double standard " has left Catholic communities practically untouched, in spite of certain theoretical subtleties. The revolt against the double standard of sexual morality is the central ethical current of our times ; it links together all the modern tendencies which favour the fight against venereal diseases. It implies the repeal of all special police control of prostitution, in favour of the hygienic treatment of the whole community, on the basis of scientific knowledge and sexual equality. It fulfils the programme of the Abolitionists and is largely their achievement.

The beginning of this movement was in the year 1869, when Mrs. Josephine Butler began her struggle against the British Contagious Diseases Acts. The essential nature of her struggle is best stated by Irene Clephane, in her vital and illuminating historical survey *Towards Sexual Freedom* (p. 135) : " That which had been taken for granted—the chastity demanded for women, the unchastity palliated in men—began to be questioned, and the questioning thus initiated has not yet been silenced or satisfied."

In 1864 the periodic inspection of women of the prostitute class was introduced into England ; but although the C.D. enactments were made in the interests of the soldiers who were the prostitute's clients, there was no corresponding measure for inspecting and supervizing them, although in their case it would have been perfectly feasible. The reason for the C.D. Acts was known and recognized by all, and the prostitutes called themselves " Queen's Women " because they said " they were kept clean by the Government, for the benefit of the Queen's soldiers." A committee set up in

1868 " to enquire into the working of the C.D. Acts " certainly did recommend similar sanitary control for the soldiers, but nothing was done to enforce this advice, for the medical examination of the men in the services " so far as the army was concerned, had been abrogated in 1859 on the recommendation of a committee presided over by Lord Herbert because it was said to offend the modesty of the men, and so far as the navy was concerned, had never existed " (Clephane, p. 113).

9

I am quoting the first important public document of the Abolitionists in full, for it throws a flood of light on the conditions and tendencies of the time. It is the Manifesto published in the *Daily News* for New Year's Day, 1870, on behalf of the Ladies' National Association for the Repeal of the Contagious Diseases Acts. It calls things by their true names, although it takes the moral or ethical view much more definitely than the hygienic. This Manifesto, drafted by Harriet Martineau, stirred up enthusiasm beyond as well as within her native country. Yves Guyot, Mazzini and Victor Hugo all expressed their sympathy and agreement :

" We, the undersigned, enter our solemn protest against these Acts.

" 1. Because, involving as they do such a momentous change in the legal safeguards hitherto enjoyed by women in common with men, they have been passed not only without the knowledge of the country, but unknown in a great measure to Parliament itself ; and we hold that neither the Representatives of the People nor the Press fulfil the duties which are expected of them when they allow such legislation to take place without the fullest discussion.

" 2. Because, so far as women are concerned, they remove every guarantee of personal security which the law has established and held sacred, and put their reputation, their freedom, and their persons absolutely in the power of the police.

" 3. Because the law is bound, in any country professing to give civil liberty to its subjects, to define clearly an offence which it punishes.

" 4. Because it is unjust to punish the sex who are the victims of a vice, and leave unpunished the sex who are the main cause both of the vice and its dreaded consequences ; and we consider that liability to arrest, forced medical treatment, and (where this is resisted) imprisonment with hard labour, to which these Acts subject women, are punishments of the most degrading kind.

" 5. Because by such a system the path of evils is made more easy to our sons, and to the whole of the youth of England, inasmuch as a moral restraint is withdrawn the moment the State recognizes and provides convenience for, the practice of a vice which it thereby declares to be necessary and venial.

" 6. Because the measures are cruel to the women who come under their action—violating the feelings of those whose sense of shame is not wholly lost, and further brutalizing even the most abandoned.

" 7. Because the disease which these Acts seek to remove has never been removed by any such legislation. The advocates of the system have utterly failed to show, by statistics or otherwise, that these regulations have in any case, after several years' trial and when applied to one sex only, diminished disease, reclaimed the fallen, or improved the general morality of the country. We have on the contrary the strongest evidence to show that in Paris and other continental cities, where women have long been outraged by this system, the public health and morals are worse than at home.

" 8. Because the conditions of this disease in the first instance are moral, not physical. The moral evil, through which the disease makes its way, separates the case entirely from that of the plague, or other scourges, which have been placed under police control or sanitary care. We hold that we are bound, before rushing into experiments of legalizing a revolting vice, to try to deal with the causes of the evil, and we dare to believe that with wiser teaching and more capable legislation those causes would not be beyond control."

Over 120 names were attached to the Protest, but the number very soon reached two thousand, including those of Josephine Butler, Harriet Martineau, Florence Nightingale, Mary Carpenter, Mary Priestman, Ursula Bright, Margaret Lucas, all the most prominent women in the Society of Friends and many others well known in the literary and philanthropic world.

10

We can only outline the main events of Josephine Butler's pioneer work. She began by founding a " refuge " in the Liverpool slums ; and it was considered unspeakably impious, dangerous and disgusting that a lady of her birth and associations should show friendship and concern for women whose profession and whose very existence were supposed to remain as unholy and forbidden mysteries, unknown to the Victorian wife and daughter. But Josephine Butler must have considered and reckoned with this opposition, before she took up her historic work in a time of deep loneliness and depression following a bereavement. Unfortunately she had to meet hostility in some quarters where it might well be deprecated. In Crewe, she spoke for the rights of these pariah women to an assembly of railway workers ; she said that, as the women thus outlawed were the daughters of the working people, she was appealing on their behalf to working men. When she left Crewe, protest meetings were arranged by the leaders of those working men. The infant labour movement of the 1870's had no perception of the political importance of this attack on the *privileged classes* on the moral front ! [1]

But the *Daily News* Manifesto proved the interest aroused and the significance of her attack. In the House of Commons bewildered uncertainty prevailed : " We know how to

---

[1] The same blindness to justice in sexual matters was shown in 1924, at the Annual Conference of the Labour Party in London, when the Chairman made a flippant joke about birth control and was called to order by the delegate from Chelsea, Miss Stella Browne, from the floor of the hall. —Translator's Note.

manage any other opposition in the House and in the country, but this is very awkward for us—this revolt of the women. It is quite a new thing ; what are we to do with such an opposition as this ? "

The Colchester by-election was made use of to support an Abolitionist candidate against Sir Henry Storcks, the official in charge of the administration of the Acts. Storcks was beaten at the polls, receiving 853 votes to his opponent's 1,363. But " that rabid woman " Josephine Butler had to leave Colchester at night, for she was refused admission to houses and hotels, alike.

In 1871 this pioneer woman, whose early environment had been deeply religious, and whose husband was himself an Anglican divine, and a most generous helper of her work, had already passed through many storms, heard many expressions of hate, fear and stupidity. She attended a Church Congress and found her experiences surpassed : in her own words " never so deep and angry a howl as now arose from the throats of a portion of the clergy of the National Church."

In 1875 there came to life in Liverpool the " British Continental and General Federation for the Abolition of Government Regulation of Prostitution " ; now the International Abolitionist Federation. An international Congress was arranged, and the argument that regulation " notoriously promotes national and even international traffic and commerce in prostitutes " struck home. In 1882 it was officially admitted that British girls were lured to foreign countries, often under completely false pretences, and for purposes of prostitution. In 1883 the Acts were suspended. In 1885, after the *Pall Mall Gazette's* revelations, the Criminal Law Amendment Act formally penalized the traffic in women to the Continent of Europe. And in 1886 the Contagious Diseases Acts were finally repealed. A great victory, but a milestone, not a final goal ; and the fight went on against the " White Slave Traffic " (" *Traite des blanches* ").

II

At a private conference held in 1899, the French Government was induced to take a significant step, by calling an official conference, to meet in Paris during 1902. In 1904, thirteen states signed an international agreement for mutual support in measures directed against the traffic in women. These states were Belgium, Denmark, France, Germany, Great Britain, Italy, the Netherlands, Norway, Sweden, Portugal, Russia, Spain and Switzerland. In the U.S.A. an Immigration Commission was at work from 1905 to 1909, enquiring into the Importation and Harbouring of Women for Immoral Purposes. The facts they unearthed led to the White Slave Traffic Act, passed by Congress in 1910.

In the same year a new International Convention was signed in Paris; Austria, Hungary and Brazil joined the signatories of 1904 in penalizing all traffic in women, between citizens of these countries.

The private assembly held in London had several notable results; it gave rise to local and national Committees, independent of their respective governments. These devoted organizations did the spadework which led to the inclusion of the fight against the " Traffic in Women and Children " —a more sober but not less resolute version of the " White Slave Trade "—among the objects of the League of Nations. This recognition is embodied in Article 23 of the Covenant. In June, 1921, a Conference of thirty-four Nations was called at Geneva. In September, thirty-three of them signed an agreement to found a Standing Advisory Committee for the International Prevention of the Traffic. A further step was taken in setting up a body of experts, with powers commensurate to their task, to study and report on the subject. The experts were able to start their work at once, owing to the financial contributions of the American Bureau of Social Hygiene in December 1923.

While this body investigated the sociological aspect of the trade in women and girls, the Red Cross organizations of different countries took up the war on venereal disease. On January 27th, 1923, the *Union internationale contre le péril vénérien* was founded in Paris. This is now the great Central Station for venereological hygiene and prophylaxis. And this Union took the Abolitionist view. The Congress held in Paris, 1926, accepted a resolution in these terms : " Considering that the therapeutic treatment of patients suffering from venereal disease is one of the principal means of arriving at the suppression of syphilis and the decrease of other venereal diseases, considering that regulation of prostitution has never, at any time or in any country, rendered it possible to limit the ravages caused by venereal diseases and that, on the other hand, it is against all justice and all idea of social morality, the Advisory Council recommends, first, the suppression of the regulation of prostitution, and, secondly, the application of measures having in view the whole of the population, men, women and children, and being inspired in so far as possible by the principle, of individual liberty."

The final and unanimous adhesion to these principles and this programme took place in Cairo, during the Congress of 1933.

12

The League of Nations Experts' Commission investigated conditions in twenty-six separate states in Europe, Africa and America. They made their report in 1927. The contents and conclusions of this Report certainly influenced the League against regulation and in favour of Abolitionism. " The existence of licensed houses is undoubtedly an incentive to traffic, both national and international. The fact has been established by previous enquiries, and is admitted to be true by many governments as a result of their experience. The enquiries made by us not only confirm this fact, but show, as other observers have remarked, that the licensed house becomes, in some countries, the centre of all forms of depravity."

In the following year these investigations were applied to Asia, and gave similar results. The new report appeared in December, 1932. It stated that " The principal factor in the promotion of international traffic of women in the East is the brothel. . . . The most effective remedy against the evil, therefore, is, in the Commission's opinion, the abolition of licensed or recognized brothels in the countries concerned."

The League Secretariat then held a further enquiry, issued individually, on the dates fixed for closing down the licensed houses in various states and " the laws and regulations then in force for the protection of public morals and the results of this application " as well as of " measures applied to combat venereal diseases." " The Consultative League of Nations Commission for the Protection and Welfare of Children and Young People " studied the material supplied, and during its session from April 4th to 11th, 1934, came to these conclusions, which the League Assembly accepted in the following September :

" I. The Traffic in Women and Children Committee . . .

" Having carefully studied the report prepared by the Secretariat on the abolition of licensed or tolerated houses, observes with great satisfaction that since the beginning of the Committee's activity considerable progress has been made by many countries throughout the world in abandoning in certain towns or in the whole of their territory the licensed, or tolerated, house system, which, according to the information obtained by the Committee, is one of the main incentives to the traffic in women, and that where this procedure has been adopted, there is no evidence that any increase in the incidence of venereal disease has resulted from the closing of licensed or tolerated houses, or that public order and decency have suffered because of their abolition.

" The Committee wishes to draw the attention of governments to the fact that those authorities which have . . . abolished the system of regulation are unanimous in declaring that the problem of prostitution can be more effectively dealt with when licensed or tolerated houses are abolished, and that there is no desire in such countries to return to the old system.

" II. The Traffic in Women and Children Committee . . .

" Asks the Council to invite Governments to maintain the abolition of the system of licensed or tolerated houses wherever this has been realized, and to consider the desirability of abandoning this system where licensed or tolerated houses still exist.

" III. The Traffic in Women and Children Committee . . .

" Observes that certain countries and certain towns that have abandoned the licensed house system have retained the system of compulsory registration and medical examination of professional prostitutes.

" As the number of the latter forms everywhere but a small part of the total number of prostitutes, the retention of the system of registration would appear to be unnecessary from the point of view of public hygiene so long as adequate provision is made for the general treatment of venereal disease.

" In view of the grave objections to the system of regulation on moral and other grounds, the Committee sincerely hopes that those authorities that still maintain a system of compulsory registration and regular medical examination of prostitutes will abandon this practice in view of recent medical experience" (*League of Nations*, C. 149, M. 62, 1934, IV).

13

The seal was set on the propaganda against the Traffic in Women by the Convention submitted by the League of Nations to the representatives of twenty-seven states, during the Session of 1933, and accepted. In 1921 reformers had limited themselves to seeking protection for girls under twenty-one years of age. In 1933 they aimed at making the commercialized sexual exploitation of adult and mature women, equally impossible :

" Whoever, in order to gratify the passion of another person, has procured, enticed, or led away, even with her own consent, a woman or girl of full age for immoral purposes, to be carried out in another country, shall be punished, notwithstanding that the various acts constituting the offence may have been committed in different countries" (adopted on Oct. 11th, 1933 ; signatories : Albania, Australia, Austria, Belgium, Bulgaria, United Kingdom, Chile, China, Czechoslovakia, Danzig Free State, France, Germany,

Greece, Hungary, Latvia, Lithuania, Monaco, Netherlands, Norway, Panama, Poland, Portugal, Spain, Soudan, Sweden, Switzerland, Union of South Africa, Yugoslavia).

Even so, only a portion of the work to be done has been achieved, and from the medical and sociological standpoint a relatively inconsiderable portion. There are still great discrepancies in the attitudes towards prostitution, and its administrative treatment, from one country to another. And the status and treatment of prostitution necessarily influence the treatment of venereal disease. Fortunately, complete unanimity exists as to the necessary conditions for effective treatment. The *Union internationale* settled the tasks of the medical campaign, in 1930, at the Copenhagen Congress, as follows :

Resolution 10 :

" 1. First and above all else, in the case of the sufferer being infective, aim at reducing as much as possible his infectivity by an immediate course of intensive treatment.

" 2. Strive to prevent the reappearance of contagious symptoms by a further course of active treatment.

" 3. Strive to prevent any possibility of the transmission of congenital syphilis to offspring. In this connection the Union would insist on the fact that the campaign against congenital syphilis should proceed by means of :

(*a*) A systematic search for contact through enquiries within the family circle as well as by clinical and serological tests.

(*b*) Treatment not only of children recognized to be syphilitic, but also of parents before conception and of the mother during pregnancy, these treatments requiring usually to be both regular and prolonged.

" 4. As far as possible, protect the patient himself from the onset of the tertiary stages of syphilis by aiming at the complete elimination of the germ in the infected tissues."

The realization of this clinical programme requires many and varied measures, both sanitary and administrative. The increasing demand and concurrent need for public health and welfare work after the war of 1914–18 have led to a continuous expansion of the mechanism of public health, and to a collection of data, previously beyond our ken. The well-known public health expert, Schwéers, sketched out a plan of campaign for the treatment of venereal diseases, based on the experience of Central Europe and the preliminary work of the German Health Insurance department. He allotted the *rôle* of centre and focus to the Public Welfare Centres (*Dispensaire*, or Health Centre).

He demanded as indispensable conditions :

1. General accessibility of the Consultation Centre for all persons, without preliminary overhauling or interrogatories of any kind. Stringent avoidance of any " Charity " or " Inferiority " atmosphere.

2. The combination of advice with treatment. Genuine individual attention. Any personal humiliations such as were inseparable from the *régime* of the *police des mœurs* to be absolutely barred.

3. Care for externals, in the structure and decorations of the buildings ; cabins where patients can wait their turn in privacy ; good sanitary provision, so that patients may be reassured and soothed and receive an education in bodily care at the same time. Finally,

4. The medical attendance must cost the patients nothing.

The first condition is the result of experience that every intermediary authority, whether a private doctor or an official, increases the hesitations and inhibitions of the patient, and leads away from the welfare centre where help should be sought.

The second condition here laid down as essential may seem strange ; it should be a matter of course, that where treatment is found necessary, such treatment should immediately—nay automatically—follow the recognition of venereal disease. But unfortunately there appears to be a definite conflict of interests here, between the public weal and the livelihood and prosperity of the medical profession. This incompatibility of interests has been perceived in many countries under diverse conditions. The doctors fear to lose patients through the active competition of the centres and they therefore frequently boycott these centres and especially oppose any official permits for treatments as apart from diagnosis. In Berlin the centres had to wage the hardest struggles with the official professional representatives of medicine ; finally the " profession " boycotted such medical men and women as had put themselves at the disposal of the Urban Consultation Centres for the treatment of patients. Their point of view was set forth with startling clarity and shall we say *naïveté* by Professor F. Lenz of the University of Munich. Professor Lenz is a specialist in racial theories, as understood by the National Socialists. He says :

" There cannot be any doubt that the venereal diseases could be completely extirpated. But we must recognize that here, too, weighty economic considerations oppose the achievement of public health. We must clearly understand that a serious and effective campaign against venereal disease would not only reduce hundreds of specialists to penury, but would also make heavy inroads on the precarious incomes of tens of thousands of general practitioners. It would be unjust to demand what amounts to the sacrifice of their livelihood, from medical men, in the interests of our nation's health."

Thus Professsor Lenz. That was before the dawn of the Hitler dispensation. I do not know whether such disarming candour is permitted now in public utterances on this subject, but the " incompatibility " remains ! And is not confined to Germany. In the United States of America John Stokes, in his encyclopædic work *Modern Clinical Syphilodology* (1934, p. 1313), has pointed out that : " The duty of the physician to the state must begin with what is now too often lacking—a co-operative attitude of mind. Figures published in 1930 by the Massachusetts Department of Public Health revealed startlingly this indifference or non-co-operation on the part of the medical profession, as expressed in the single item of reporting or notification of venereal disease. The physician too easily regards the state as his rival in the venereal disease field. While the establishment of free clinics is unquestionably an important function of the state in the control of syphilis, the establishment of such clinics will become less of a necessity in proportion as the practitioner is able by the organization within his own ranks, to raise his standards and lower his costs.   If he fails to do this he has only himself to blame if he finds the state his rival."

The final solution of this real conflict of interests can only come with the Socialization of the Practice of Medicine and from the knowledge that adequate therapeutic treatment is one of the basic good things of life to which all citizens have a claim, irrespective of their private financial position. Austria, Denmark, Italy and Sweden have all accepted this in practice, and the Soviet Union proclaims the principle of Socialized Medicine.   In Great Britain, of recent years, there has been a great extension of practical facilities for antivenereal prophylaxis and treatment.   In 1916 the representatives of the medical profession themselves endorsed the action of the Royal Commission on Venereal Diseases, recommending this programme of socialization.

Comment on Schwéers third " essential condition " is hardly needed.

But we may add one footnote to the fourth, namely, that in many communities and institutions there are enquiries into the financial position of the patient ; and that is, of course, in actual fact the financial status and personal relationships of his family, for treatment is only given *gratis* to the poor or the absolutely destitute.   This limitation is an encouragement to breach of professional secrecy and confidence ; and leads to the greatest difficulty in bringing the urgency of his case home to the patient who has to submit to such inquisitions, and to further danger to third parties, in consequence.

14

There is no branch of medicine in which the preservation of privacy and secrecy is more crucial for successful treatment, than in venereology.   Immediately after the war of 1914–18 there was much discussion about this, for all previous experience of such epidemics as smallpox, typhus and cholera had proved public notification to be essential to effective treatment. But in the case of venereal diseases it becomes extraordinarily hard to demand or enforce notification : a psychological element is involved ; notification implies moral condemnation and something like public exposure. In Norway the treatment of venereally infected persons was made obligatory as early as 1860 ; Denmark followed suit in 1906 ; Sweden in 1918 ; Czechoslovakia in 1922 ; and Germany and Soviet Russia both in 1927. The same is true of the United States of America, Canada and Australia. But up to the most recent date there has been much dispute as to the relative advantages of absolute or conditional notification respectively. As an instance of conditional notification, which has proved strikingly effective, we may quote the rules in force in the State of Massachusetts, as recorded by Cavaillon :

" The doctor who has seen a syphilitic person in his professional capacity makes a statement to the sanitary authorities, but this statement refers to the case by a number only, and does not mention the name. Thus the Commissioner of Health files a document without name or address and strictly an item of statistics if the patient attends for treatment. But if while still requiring treatment and himself in a contagious state, the patient ceases to visit his doctor, and discontinues treatment, either by the first physician or another (for the system applies equally to the medical man in private practice and to the medical man at a public clinic or dispensary)—then and then alone, the doctor in charge informs the Commissioner of Health that the patient number so-and-so has such-and-such a name, and lives at such-and-such an address. Then the Commissioner does intervene—but without having recourse to the police. He verifies the address, he looks up the patient and informs him that unless treatment is resumed, definite coercive and precautionary measures can be taken against him " (Cavaillon, p. 31).

The system achieves the exclusion of police interference in this matter of public health. The general public is afraid of police action as a rule, and fear is not a helpful inducement in the propaganda for health of mind and body. Therefore the police force is not a suitable instrument in the attack on venereal disease, although still so considered and employed in some states to the present day.

The most consistent recognition of the inadequacy and undesirability of police interference here may be found in the Netherlands and Great Britain. Both have abolished the regulation of prostitution and rely solely on an entirely non-coercive system for combating venereal diseases. Both countries have abolished the licensed brothel and the licensed prostitute. They do not register prostitutes nor do they attempt in any way to keep them under special medical control. They have no system of notification of venereal diseases, nor is compulsory detention applied to any class or section of infected persons. In a paper read to the Abolitionist Congress held at Graz in Austria (September, 1924) the Chief Medical Officer for the City of Amsterdam made the following statement :

" At Amsterdam, thanks to the devotion of doctors, nurses and the social workers attached to the polyclinic, we have obtained this remarkable result, that 95 per cent. of the syphilitic men and 85 per cent. of the women have remained continuously under treatment at the clinic and polyclinic during the two years that this system of collaboration, *i.e.*, the non-compulsory system, has been established. These figures are certainly not surpassed by those obtained in countries where compulsory treatment is in force."

In England, the system in force is based on the Venereal Diseases Act of 1917, " To prevent unqualified treatment and quack remedies." This law forbids :

1. Treatment of venereal diseases except by duly qualified doctors.

2. Advertisement in any shape or form, offering treatment or remedies for venereal diseases,

and imposes

3. The maximum penalty of up to two years hard labour and £100 fine.

During the special conditions of war time, " Emergency

Measures " were found necessary, and in 1916 " Public health regulations " instituted :

1. Free diagnostic facilities for venereal diseases.
2. Venereal disease Clinics and free Salvarsan.
3. That all venereal disease treatment records must be confidential.
4. Public instruction and education on the subject.
5. Repayment by the Ministry of Health of 75 per cent. of the expenditure incurred.

These refunds have been altered under the Local Government Act of 1929 : otherwise the provisions are unchanged. In England and Wales there are now 188 Treatment Centres, and in connection therewith thirteen hostels for notorious prostitute girls, one institution for the care of children with vulvovaginitis, and nine homes for venereally infected pregnant women (cf. Empire Social Hygiene Yearbook, p. 440, 1934).

15

Wherever there are available statistics of the sanitary success achieved by Abolitionism and Regulation respectively in the same districts and localities, the result is a striking testimony in favour of Abolitionism. Let us quote the figures for Berlin, for the autumn of 1927 and the ensuing period. Berlin had at that time a population of over 4,000,000.

In 1926 the police had arrested and detained 2,028 women in the Berlin area. Among those 2,028 women, 641 were found to be recent cases of venereal infection. Within the period of time covered by these arrests, at least 60,000 fresh cases of infection occurred in Berlin. The current system of police " control " accounted for 3,337 persons, on October 1st, 1927, the date on which the Health Section of the Municipality of Berlin took over the fight against venereal diseases from the police. These 3,337 women could be identified ; they were the actual survivors after sifting a police dossier for 7,111 persons ; more than half of these had died, changed their address, or in some other manner, dropped out.

From 1st October, 1927, to 30th September, 1930, the largest of the Consultation Centres in Berlin had on its books 4,387 persons, *i.e.*, more than fell to the efforts of the police throughout Berlin in 1926. In all, nineteen Consultation Centres were in existence and they treated 8,823 gonorrhœa cases, 2,096 of syphilis and 623 of chancroid ; *i.e.*, 11,542 definitely proved cases of-fresh infection, compared to the 641 arrested by the police in 1926 (just over 8 to 1).

Since then the progress of humane and scientific methods in Germany has been rudely interrupted. Concurrently with the return to Conscription, Hitler's Government re-introduced the brothel. Unfortunately, in spite of repeated enquiries from scientific societies, those in authority have furnished no definite statistics. But Hamburg, for instance, once more contains four " Prostitutes' Alleys." These are shut off from the neighbouring streets by double gateways ; but the children at play in the streets are quite able to observe the numbers of persons who pass through these gates. The women within the Quarter sit in long rows at their windows ; they are of all ages, from seventeen to fifty ; a Norwegian sailor has given an impressive description of this Quarter (as it appeared in 1935) published in the Oslo periodical *Lördagskvelden*, November 25th, 1935 : " Masklike faces, without a glimmer of expression ; bodies shamelessly exposed ; an indescribably venal display ; an abyss of human degradation."

Of course we can consider the status and treatment of prostitutes and the measures against venereal disease from other angles besides the contrast between Regulation and Abolitionism. Thus, as in the U.S.A., there may be a Prohibition of Prostitution itself [1] apart from the transmission of disease ; or the provision of free treatment may be linked up with far-reaching state supervision, as in Germany, from 1927 to 1934, when brothels were re-introduced, and as in the Soviet Union since 1918. One of the foremost authorities on this subject is Dr. Cavaillon, General

---

[1] In practice the American system, at least in large towns, has tended towards a particularly harsh and unjust form of regulation. *Cf.* Seabury Report and documents in *Shield*.—Translator's Note.

Secretary of the *Union internationale contre le péril vénérien.*
He compares the three systems as follows :

" In theory, the American Prohibitionist system is the best, for if it stops prostitution, it stops the diseases disseminated by prostitution. But in practice, does it stop prostitution ? We must recognize that this aim is not attained and that clandestine prostitution is none the less frequent and dangerous.

" Regulation only touches an infinitesimal percentage of prostitutes ; and does so inadequately, at least so far as gonorrhœa is concerned. It presents a whitewashed but often misleading façade.

" Abolitionism on the other hand is powerless before those prostitutes who are able to exercise their profession with skill and tact. In short, the secret prostitute defies prohibitionists, abolitionists, regulationists, and it is the secret prostitute whom we must tackle. We incline to believe that a State Health Service will obtain better results. Not, of course, perfect success ; we cannot imagine any perfect success or perfect system, but perhaps a State Health Service is the least faulty and inadequate " (*l.c.*, p. 55).

16

In fairness to the complexity of elements in the problem of prostitution, we should mention that certain arguments in favour of regulation have been put forward in France —(the cradle of this system)—which merit some serious attention. The modern advocates of regulation claim that the Anglo-American attitude is merely hypocrisy and also a resignation of effective control over facts. Moreover, that powerful pressure from the unconscious makes this " moral " attitude the mouthpiece of inhibitions and aberrations, treating the prostitute as a creature unworthy of any consideration. Marcel Rogeat criticizes the Anglo-American attitude thus : " Very many Englishmen are, above all, anxious to be ' gentlemen ' in the opinion of others ; to observe certain external forms and rules. They do this with ease, but at the slightest provocation or opportunity, this artificial being ' strips to the buff ' and shows a primitive brutality that disregards all refinement and tenderness. This crude egotism treats what should be the mutual and complex sexual act as on a par with the relief of the bladder and is only too often still the rule in Anglo-Saxon and Puritan marital relations. Their wives, as respectable Puritan women, must on no account look, or touch or try to understand, or take any active interest " (*l.c.*, p. 224).

He is equally sharp in reproof of American ways. " Apart from a few genuine Puritans, the Yankees, both men and women, have such easily stimulated sexual instincts that the motor car must be called in to provide a suitable outlet " (p. 220). He claims that in Latin lands " as may be observed in France, unlegalized sexual relationships are practised with a sort of mutual frankness and fair play on the same level of honesty as prevails in other business transactions " (p. 22). So he proposes to abolish the harsh and derogatory name of prostitution in favour of a more just and charitable term for the " canalization of extra-marital sex relationships " which is unavoidable in our present system. He would speak of the " Service or Supply of Sexual Relief or Solace " ; and of " Ladies of Solace " or " Professional Relievers " (" soulageuses professionelles "). Indeed, Rogeat's arguments and suggestions are such enthusiastic propaganda for the regulation of prostitution, that his book deserves to be subsidized by the business Federation of the French brothelkeepers ! And there is this spark of truth ; the psychological honesty and Latin clarity of Rogeat's analysis are more human and intellectually respectable than the traditional " hush ! hush ! " of the Anglo-Saxons.

Unfortunately facts disprove his case, and throw a very different light on the system idealized in Rogeat's book. In the spring of 1935 the " *Union temporaire* " discovered and exposed a Parisian " *maison publique* " which was a veritable gold mine for its owners. " They employ thirty women, who serve at a charge of six francs per customer, and they levy three francs out of the six on each occasion." " In some of these houses the women come to ' work ' at nine in the morning, returning home by the latest Metro train. The customers wait their turn in a passage known as

' the garage.' Each of these unlucky girls has to receive seven clients before she has earned the money to pay for a lunch, for which the mistress of the house charges twenty-one francs. Girls have been known to receive as many as fifty men each in the course of the working day. And there are always others ready to take the place of those who contract disease."

The Deputy, Vaillant Couturier, vouches for these particulars in *Humanité*. Moral wrath gets us no further here ; practical, radical and carefully considered action is needed to deliver the girls and check the diseases. But official authorities still oppose prophylaxis on " Moral Grounds."

17

On January 25th, 1932, the British National Society for the Prevention of Venereal Disease found it necessary to send the following communication to the press : " For too long now, officialdom, urged on by fanaticism and prudery, has withheld this vital knowledge from the people." Unfortunately, however, this same noxious prudery is upheld and continued by the very usage of such terms as " promote the elimination of commercialized vice "—to quote from the programme of the British Social Hygiene Council. Even the Society for the Prevention of Venereal Disease itself takes a regrettably inconsistent attitude in its Open Letter to Parents and Guardians : " It is precisely the weak-willed who succumb most easily to the temptations which lure them to the vicious courses you condemn."

The hygienic side of the campaign against venereal diseases is in no way promoted by the element of positive sexphobia in much of the current propaganda, and it is strangely inadequate to demand—as does the otherwise valuable and intelligent S.P.V.D.—that instruction for self-disinfection " should only be given to men above the age of eighteen, to adult women on demand, and to younger persons in special cases at the discretion of those responsible for their welfare." Such timid " ifs and buts " can only hamper the giant's task of sexual sanitation. The same malevolent remnants of superstition survive in the rules of some of the

Societies associated with the National Insurance Scheme in Great Britain. To this day, these societies classify and penalize syphilis and gonorrhœa as "misconduct diseases" (*Empire Social Hygiene Handbook*, 1935, p. 78). We must not allow ourselves to ignore the amount that is still to be done in this direction in England. The letter of the Criminal Amendment Act of 1885 still stands, but London is even now one of the chief "key-points" of the Traffic in Women, as the investigations following the murder of Max Kassel, in January, 1936, have clearly shown.

Further valuable and illuminating experiences have been made, in England as to the effect on personal liberty of the "Solicitation Laws" which have been kept in force after other portions of the Act of 1917 fell into desuetude, in order to eliminate erotic aggression and unwelcome intimate advances in the public streets and parks. A case which took place on May 6th, 1930, as recorded in the *Shield* for July, 1930, shows the outrageous results of giving complete power to the police in these matters: "On May 6th, two Liverpool girls obtained £30 damages against four police-officers of that city, and in addition Mr. Justice Mackinnon, after hearing legal argument, awarded the girls costs on the High Court Scale against all the defendants. There seems no reason to suppose the arrest of the girls was made in malice, but we give some details of the case because it offers a striking example of the danger of accepting police evidence that some unknown and absent person was annoyed or molested. The girls, aged nineteen and twenty-one, both in respectable employment, had been to a club dance and were returning home about midnight when they met a young man, a fellow-member of the club, and stopped and chatted with him and then crossed the road to speak to three other young men whom they knew well. Probably all these young people were rather hilarious and chaffing one another. At this point a constable came up to the girls and said he had been watching them, and asked where they lived. They gave the name of a street which, it seems, does contain some undesirable characters. The constable then arrested them, and took them to the Bridewell, followed by the young men, who tried to explain matters, but were not allowed to enter the police station. Meantime, a crowd had collected.

" The girls were charged with annoying men, and, according to their evidence, the police-constable said the annoyed men would not come forward. Eventually the girls reached their homes about 1 a.m., after being told they would probably receive a summons. This never came, but the parents, on behalf of the girls, brought an action in the Civil Court, before a jury, for wrongful arrest and false imprisonment. The ' annoyed ' men gave evidence for the girls, proving that they were all in employment and members of the same club." The pertinent question of Mr. Hemmerde, K.C., who defended the two girls " if people can be arrested in this sort of way, what security has anybody got ? " proves that there are no Abolitionist principles on the pavements, and the same is true of both Holland and Germany. Helen Wilson indicted conditions in English towns, when she spoke at the Abolitionist Conference in Frankfurt am Main in 1926. " Police laws, enacted nearly a century ago, are still in force for all our cities ; they impose a fine of forty shillings or an imprisonment of fourteen days on every common prostitute who in the streets loiters or importunes to the annoyance of the inhabitants or passengers " (Town Police Clauses Act of 1847 ; with special provisions for London under the Metropolitan Police Act). In accordance with these enactments, and in the year 1922 alone, 3,000 women were imprisoned and 3,000 more were fined. Certain cities have by-laws to punish men who annoy women, but these are very seldom applied. These Solicitation laws and their analogues in other countries prove the constant recurrence of attempts at police control instead of hygienic help. Careful collection and comparison of historical data show that, as a rule, police activity and health improvement have varied in inverse ratio to one another. Even in our time very few people can contemplate illicit (i.e., extra-marital) sexual manifestations without strong emotional perturbations, anger or misgivings, and it distressed many serious people when the expert American Sociologist, Dr. William Robinson, of New York, expressed himself in these terms, at the

London Congress of Sexual Reform, in 1929 : " Prostitution is not an immoral, criminal or anti-social occupation. It should therefore be made perfectly legal and should be considered as legitimate an occupation as any other. As the occupation carries with it certain dangers to public health, it should be subject to sanitary control (sanitary, not police), the same as are some other trades endangering public health. The prostitute is just the same sort of human being that her sister is. Morally, mentally and physically, she differs very little from the average of the stratum from which she springs " (*Report*, p. 294).

18

But in spite of Solicitation Acts and other police paraphernalia in various countries, venereal diseases are diminishing almost everywhere. And where social and economic tendencies are re-enforced by really effective sanitary measures, the results are astounding and admirable. Thus, since the new methods have been adopted in Belgium it has been authoritatively stated by the *Ligue contre le péril vénérien*, in its *Appel du Pays :* " In five years, syphilis has decreased by nine-tenths throughout the kingdom, not only among the civilian population, but in the Army as well." From Denmark we have the following illuminating statistics[1] :

Year	Gonorrhœa		Chancroid		Syphilis	
	cases	per 10,000	cases	per 10,000	cases	per 10,000
1923	11,115	33·1	404	1·2	2,496	7·4
1927	11,951	34·4	250	0·7	2,197	6·3
1930	11,658	32·9	230	0·6	1,794	5·1
1932	10,410	29·0	90	0·3	893	2·5

The general trend here is similar to the Belgian : an immense decrease in syphilitic cases, whereas gonorrhœa still remains a grave social peril. The returns for the treat-

[1] As recorded in *Medic. Beretning f. d. danske Stat f. Aaret* 1932, p. 73, Copenhagen, 1934.

ment centres in England and Wales show that the cases dealt with for the first time at these centres, after rising to a maximum of 42,805 in 1920, fell rapidly to 22,010 in 1924 ; from which year the numbers fluctuated till 1932, from 22,019 (in 1929) to 23,395 (in 1927), falling to 21,525 in 1933.

One of the main tasks of contemporary hygiene concerns ports and centres of maritime commerce. The initiative here was taken by the British Government on August 16th, 1920 ; a circular was sent to all ports in the United Kingdom recommending the organization of free treatment for venereal cases in clinics where advisable. This move was extended to the international field through the International Labour Office at Geneva, as well as of the International Seafarer's Federation, the League of Nations and the *Office Internationale d'Hygiène Publique*. On December 1st, 1924, an *International Convention* was signed at Brussels, in the following terms :

" Art. 1 : The high contracting parties undertake to establish and to maintain in each of their principal sea or river ports services for the treatment of venereal diseases open to all merchant seamen or watermen, without distinction of nationality. These services shall have a staff of medical specialists and a technical equipment kept constantly abreast of the progress of science. They shall be so established and worked as to be readily accessible to those desiring to make use of them. Their size shall be proportionate in each port to the volume of traffic, and they shall dispose of a sufficient number of hospital beds.

" Art. 2 : Medical treatment and the supply of medical necessaries shall be free of charge. The same shall apply to hospital treatment when it is considered necessary by the doctor of the service. Patients shall receive likewise free of charge the medical supplies necessary for the treatment to be followed on the voyage till the next port of call.

" Art. 3 : Each patient shall receive a card, which shall be strictly personal to himself, and on which he shall be designated by a number only. On the card the doctors of the different treatment centres visited by him shall enter :—

" (a) The diagnosis, with a summary of the clinical particulars noted at the time of the examination.

" (b) The treatment carried out at the centre.

" (c) The treatment to be followed on the voyage.

" (d) The results of serological examinations undertaken in cases of syphilis (Wassermann).

" Art. 4 : Masters of ships and shipowners shall be required to make known to the crews the existence of the services contemplated in the present agreement. At the time of the vessel's sanitary inspection, or on his first visit on board, the sanitary officer shall furnish the crew with notices showing the time and place for consultations."

Countries which have signed, ratified or adhered to the Agreement : Argentine, Australia, Bahamas, Belgium, Brit. Guiana, Brit. Honduras, Canada, Ceylon, Chili, Cuba, Cyprus, Denmark, Falkland Islands, Fiji, Finland, France, French Cameroons, French Equatorial Africa, French Guiana, French possessions in India, French West Africa, Gambia, Gibraltar, Gilbert and Ellice Islands, Great Britain, Greece, Grenada, Guadeloupe, Holland, Hong Kong, Iceland, Indo-China, Iraq, Irish Free State, Italy, Jamaica, Leeward Islands, Madasgascar, Martinique, Mauritius, Monaco, Morocco, New Zealand, North Borneo, Peru, Poland, Roumania, St. Lucia, St. Vincent, Seychelles, Solomon Islands, Straits Settlements, Sweden, Tahiti, Trinidad, Tunis.

The *Office Internationale d'Hygiène Publique* and the Health Organization of the League have since held three Conferences on the reliability of a number of the methods by which serum is tested for syphilis, and their conclusions are embodied in " Recommendations re Serological Syphilis Tests " in the Quarterly Bulletin of the Health Organization of the League (Vol. 1, No. 4, Dec., 1932). The I.L.O. has been mainly responsible for the further protection of seamen ; in 1931 it issued a Bluebook : *Promotion of Seamen's Welfare in Ports*, with advice on the organization of anti-venereal measures in ports and harbour towns, based on answers to a Questionnaire issued to various Governments

at the Third Maritime Conference in 1929. These recommendations are a successful blend of strictly medical and wider
social demands, for it has been fully understood that the risks
run by seafaring men are mainly due to their own standard
of life and to their exploitation in the " dives " and places
of entertainment open to them. The actual realization of
the I.L.O. programme has, of course, been held up by the
economic crisis. And the urgent request of the *Union
internationale contre le péril vénérien* at the Madrid Congress
in 1934, addressed to such states as had not ratified the Brussels Convention, has also met with most inadequate response.

19

The financial and actuarial aspects of the V.D. problem
prove repeatedly that refusal to provide treatment and social
therapy, on the plea of " initial expense," is indeed " penny
wise and pound foolish." In England syphilis is still
responsible for 11·8 per cent. of all deaths due to " nervous
and vascular diseases," and it is estimated that each year
brings 190,000 fresh infections ! In France, Cavaillon's
evidence is that " syphilis afflicts one-tenth of the population,
3,920,000 French citizens of both sexes. 200,000 babies are
still-born annually, slain by syphilis in their mother's womb.
At least 400,000 miscarriages every year are also due to this
scourge. The French death-rate is at least 80,000 cases a
year. In every hospital 40 per cent. of the chronic cases
under treatment are of syphilitic origin. In Belgium, a
series of hospital entries, taken at random and examined,
showed 22 per cent. of syphilis. Syphilis costs the State
over fifty million francs per annum, not to mention the costs
of hospital treatment, invalidism, and pensions."

These few statistics give some idea of the economic
significance of syphilis. We must remember, however, that
exact statistics have been so far unobtainable, owing to
particular moral and emotional prejudices against infected
persons.

Between November 1st, 1898, and April 30th, 1899, the
questionnaire method was applied to venereal diseases by

Jadassohn in Switzerland, but only one-fifth of the doctors approached sent any replies. On April 30th, 1900, there was a similar effort in Prussia, which brought in replies from 65 per cent. There followed large-scale attempts at some kind of census of venereally diseased persons in several countries ; this took place in Germany in 1919, in Austria in 1920, Czechoslovakia and Switzerland in 1921, but neither these attempts nor the lists of fresh cases at treatment centres were wholly adequate. There was, however, one constant ratio, which has been found in other countries as well : " While in syphilis the ratio of new female cases to new male cases is as 1 to approximately 1·6 (1⅗), in gonorrhœa the similar ratio is as only 1 to 3·9 ; it seems to me that women in general are not awake to its importance " (*Empire Social Hygiene Year Book*, 1935, p. 445).

This means, of course, that the cure of venereal diseases and their prevention are largely dependent to-day on the knowledge and active assistance of women. The realization of these factors has led to two most significant developments, which we shall review briefly, in conclusion. The first is the analysis and comparison of economic motives with other incentives to prostitution. The second is the epoch-making system instituted in Soviet Russia for eliminating prostitution as a social reservoir of disease.

20

At the Ninth International Congress for the suppression of the Traffic in Women and Children, held in Berlin in 1933, Sybil Neville-Rolfe, Secretary of the British Social Hygiene Council, submitted the conclusions reached in a study of " the economic conditions in relation to prostitution." This document was based on the report of the Commission of Enquiry into Traffic in Women and Children in the East (held under the auspices of the League of Nations) and on evidence tendered at the Regional Social Hygiene Conference in New York in January, 1934.

It was expressly stated at the Berlin Congress that :

" in the non-regulationist countries, while there may be no diminution in the volume of promiscuous intercourse, there is undoubtedly a decrease in commercial prostitution." And the deduction is drawn that where women abandon themselves for pecuniary returns, " social rather than economic factors are the preponderating cause."

Mrs. Neville-Rolfe takes her stand here on conditions in India. Certainly India has an almost inexhaustible supply of material for prostitution in its 20,000,000 Hindu widows—often of very tender age—and its many Muslim divorcées. But what juggling with words to attempt any rigid separation between " social " and " economic " factors ! The decisive element is the terrible insecurity of livelihood and the inability to earn enough, whether by so-called skilled or unskilled work, to elude death by starvation. In China it is admitted that " families that do not run into debt do not sell their girls." As regards German conditions, there is the following testimony : " The number of married women among those arrested has increased enormously during the last few years because of the unemployment of the husbands, and in many cases the wife being unable to obtain work herself. It is also noted that the parents being unable to support their younger children," and so on. What are these causes of prostitution, if they are not economic ? Further, it is recorded that the " younger children " " live away from home and partly because of lack of food, partly through lack of supervision, take to a life of prostitution." And this conclusion is drawn : " Here, however, the increase of prostitution is due not only to the economic situation and the lack of employment, but also to bad housing and lack of family life and supervision by the parents."

Surely no serious person will deny that " bad housing " is an economic factor. There remains then the " lack of supervision," the crux of the matter. And Mrs. Rolfe passes judgment thus : " there is no evidence that poverty is in itself the cause of prostitution. There is evidence that an unstable social background, in juxtaposition with a demand supported by wealth, will attract women and girls to

prostitution." In plain words, the " unstable social background " is the economic basis and the wealth of the men
who buy is the economic lure to prostitution. We can only
describe as misleading and superficial such verdicts as those
of F. Sempkins, Secretary of the National Vigilance Association of Great Britain and of the International Bureau for the
Suppression of Traffic in Women, who reported as follows,
on " Unemployment and Prostitution of Young Girls " :
" In general, young girls take to an immoral life to satisfy
their need for money—or perhaps simply because they prefer
free love to marriage."

Such pronouncements arise—perhaps unconsciously—from
the urge to prove that " moral " turpitude or inferiority
rather than economic need or pressure is responsible for
the generally deplorable symptoms of prostitution. This
point of view justifies appeals to sentiment, chivalry, chastity,
religion : but any constructive social approach is treated
as a secondary consideration and hardly put into effect.
And so in actual practice prostitution is accepted, but
prostitutes are despised and persecuted, and moral reprobation frequently becomes physical brutality. We do not
idealize the prostitute, nor dispute that there is a relatively
high percentage of psychopathic individuals in " the oldest
profession in the world." Alienists and psychiatrists agree
on this. But how does it happen that prostitution is so
largely recruited from the ranks of the socially insecure and
undernourished ? Why is it that we so seldom meet professional prostitutes from the middle or upper classes, which
must also contain a certain number of mentally and morally
defective persons ?

21

In Soviet Russia prostitution has been consistently viewed
and treated as of mainly economic origin. In June, 1917, the
Pirogoff Society held a congress of Venereologists at Moscow ;
during this congress Professor Bronner made certain suggestions for the rational treatment of venereal diseases,
but it was not until after the Bolshevik Revolution in

October of 1918 that the Joint Council for the Suppression of Prostitution was founded as part of the Peoples Commissary for Public Health, or " Nar-Kom-Sdrav," and comprising not only the experts of the department, but representatives of both the Trade Unions and the Women. Prostitution was known as the main source of venereal diseases, and therefore the Soviet campaign was directed against Prostitution as a social entity : but it was explicitly stated that the individual prostitute should not suffer any persecution. On the contrary, the first essential measure was to be the establishment of economic equality for women. This aim is worked for through a double method : both sexes are entitled to employment, and paid at the same rate, while concurrently the health of women and their education receive special care. The Venereological Institute in Moscow, established according to plans drawn up by Professor Bronner, became the centre for this work as early as 1921. In 1923 the first All Russian Congress for Combating Venereal Diseases was held, and the constructive measures adopted included not only the Treatment Centres or " Dispensaries," but also the organization of " mobile detachments " or Sanitary Flying Corps, and the " clean-up " of the great plains by means of a network of special " Ven-Points " so-called. These measures were put into operation with the greatest possible amount of publicity. Herewith one example of the methods adopted and the interest aroused.

In the year 1925 a letter was received at the Commissariat of Health by the Department of the Joint Council for the suppression of Prostitution ; this communication bore the signature of " The prostitute, Tania." Tania protested " in the name of many of us " against " the slogan that the campaign against Prostitution must not become an attack on the Prostitute. For as a matter of fact, everything is done to bring down the Prostitute's earnings to a pittance that no longer supports life. Every day our takings grow less, and it becomes more difficult to obtain shelter or houseroom, if we do find any place to live in the rent is so high that all our earnings are swallowed up."

This letter was printed verbatim in one of the chief daily papers of Moscow; and Semashko, Commissar for Health, gave a detailed reply, under his own name, in the *Rabotchay Gazeta.* In this " Reply to the Prostitute, Tania," he said : " You addressed yourself in the name of many other women, to the Central Soviet for Combating Prostitution, and declared that the existence of this Soviet was making the condition of prostitutes worse and worse. You beg the Soviet to leave prostitutes in peace, you stress the fact that prostitutes are not criminals, but you forget that prostitution is a source of venereal diseases, which are among the worst dangers threatening our people. You lament the marked decrease in earnings from prostitution, resulting from the Soviet's activity. This decrease shows that the method adopted is being successful. You implore the Soviet to set free the prostitutes from the ' persecution ' of the special constabulary, and protest that there is no ground for such persecution. But these special officials have the duty of detecting foci of infection and bringing brothel-keepers before the People's Tribunals, and they fulfil these difficult duties with devoted zeal. The constabulary is not entitled to carry out any repressive measures against individual prostitutes ; the Commissary for International Affairs has issued precise instructions about this. We do not deny that it is possible that some constable or other, who is below the standard required, may have exceeded his instructions, but this must not be done with impunity. Any prostitute is entitled to call any worker to account if her rights as a citizen have been infringed ; she can demand to be shown his authority, and then should report him directly to the Soviet for the Suppression of Prostitution.

" Prostitution is a grave sickness of our social organism : a sickness inherited, like other social ills, from the capitalist order, and we shall get rid of prostitution—we hope sooner than of other ills—by improving our economic conditions and habits. We know that no woman is brought to put her most cherished possession up for sale, because she wants to live in luxury, but because she is in direst want. We know, too, that our campaign against prostitution causes the prostitute herself loss, through decreased returns. Nevertheless our campaign will continue ; it is necessary in the interests of the community to which the welfare of individuals and of single groups must give way."

And this campaign has been successful. In the Moscow of 1914, 56·9 per cent. of all fresh venereal infections were communicated by prostitutes. In 1924, 31·7 per cent. and in 1931 only 9·8 per cent. (Semashko, p. 112). The decrease of unemployment in Soviet Russia, and the development and encouragement of women's work in industry, under the first and second Five Year Plans, have had spectacular results. Women supplied a quarter of the total industrial producers in October 1st, 1930, and over a third (33·7 per cent.) on December 31st, 1934. (The exact figures are 3,697,000 and 7,100,000 respectively.) Special institutions were founded, in order to lead and train women to leave the life of prostitution and enter productive service to the community. These were termed Labour Prophylactories (Lyetschebno-trudovye profilaktorii). These homes for diseased prostitutes are equipped with a variety of workshops, dressmaking shops, shops for bookbinding, paper bags, turnery, etc. Whenever a dispensary discovers a diseased prostitute, she is placed in one of these prophylactories. There she works, and with what she earns buys her food and clothing, and she receives medical treatment free of charge. The prophylactories are run by their inmates in a form of self-government. When the diseased woman is cured, she is given a job in a factory, for a while she receives special attention and medical care and then she is regarded as stabilized and restored to citizenship. In the year 1929 there were twenty " Prophylactoria " in the territories of the U.S.S.R. ; in 1931, following the drive to liquidate prostitution, there were thirty-three ; in 1934, at the end of the year, there were twenty-four. The venereal diseases statistics are striking testimony in favour of these methods. Here are some returns, reckoned as per 10,000 of the population :

Year	Tzarist Russia and U.S.S.R.	
	Syphilis	Gonorrhœa
1913	76·8	—
1914	74·7	40
1928	42·8	31
1929	32·2	25·7
1930	29·5	24·3
1931	24·7	20·5

Here are certain figures for Moscow alone, they do not specify but include all three diseases, syphilis, gonorrhœa and chancroid :

Year	Cases per 10,000
1926	168
1928	111·3
1929	107·3
1930	95·3
1931	79·8
1932	63

The Soviet Government gives as much weight to the abolition of all so-called " moral " prejudice against prostitutes—especially " former prostitutes "—in attaining this excellent result, as to the incorporation of these girls into the ranks of industry and the care for their general and technical instruction. This educative policy has enormously quickened the social interests and activities of women. The elections for the Soviets in three sample years show this :

In 1926 only 28 per cent. of women took part.
In 1929   48·5   ,,   ,,   ,,
In 1934   80·3   ,,   ,,   ,,

So much for the progress of women as electors. What about their position as elected persons ?

	In the Town Soviets	In the Village Soviets
In 1926	18·2 per cent.	9·9 per cent.
In 1934	32·1 ,,	26·4 ,,

And in 8·1 per cent. of the Village Soviets women are the Chairmen and leaders. In a later chapter of this book we shall deal with the change in the general position of women and with the special sexual customs and codes of Soviet Russia. But we can definitely summarize their success in tackling prostitution here and now. Economic opportunity for women and the objective and scientific disregard of traditional " moral " prejudices have effectually disposed of prostitution as a large-scale *social* institution, and therefore also as a reservoir of venereal infection. To-day the problem that remains is psychological, and concerns those individual cases who prefer to satisfy their erotic needs or tastes on commercial lines.

BIBLIOGRAPHY

ALMKVIST, J., *Rückgang der Ven. Krankheiten in Schweden und seine Lehren*, Ingese I, Vol. 4, Cologne, 1928.

BATKIS, *Problems of Prostitution in U.S.S.R.*, London, 1929.

Borba c prostitutii w S.S.S.R. (Unpubl. Material of the Embassy of U.S.S.R. in London, 1935).

BRITISH SOCIAL HYGIENE COUNCIL, *Annual Report* (Carteret House, London).

BURCKLAND, *Geschichte der Zoologie*, II. Vol., 1921.

BUSCHKE-JACOBSOHN, *Geschlechtsleben und sexuelle Hygiene*, Berlin, 1921.

BUTLER, Jos., An autobiograph. memoir, ed. by W. George and L. A. Johnson, London, 1928.

CAVAILLON, *Les législations antivénériennes dans le monde*, Paris, 1931.

CLEPHANE, I., *Towards Sexual Freedom*, London, 1935.

DUFOUR, *Geschichte der Prostitution*, Berlin, 1929.

EFRON-FRONSTEIN, *Klinitscheskaya i sozialnaya Venerologiya*, Moskva, 1926.

Empire Social Hygiene Year Book.

ERNST, MORRIS, and SEAGLE, WILLIAM, *To the Pure, A Study of Obscenity and the Censor*, London, 1929.

GARLE, H. E., "Abolition and After," in *Health and Empire*, 1935.

GARLE, H. E., "A Study in Comparative Legislation," *Empire Social Hygiene Year Book*, 1935.

HECHT, H., and HAUSTEIN, H., "Die soziale Bedeutung und Bekämpfung der Geschlechtskrankheiten, *Handbuch d. Haut- und Gesch. Krkh.*, XXII, Berlin, 1927.

METCHNIKOFF, O., *Life of Metchnikoff*, London, 1921.

NEILANS, A., "The International Movement against Regulated Prostitution," *Internat. Rev. of Mission*, 1933.

NEVILLE-ROLFE, *Social Hygiene in the Mercantile Marine*, London, 1934.

NEVILLE-ROLFE and SEMPKINS, *Poverty and Prostitution*, London, 1933.

Publications of the Association for Moral and Social Hygiene. London : *The Shield, passim*.

RANDALL, R. G., *The Individual Aspects of Prostitution*, London, 1929.

Report of the Royal Commission on Venereal Diseases, Stat. Off., 1917.

ROBINSON, W. J., *Prostitution, the Oldest Profession*, London, 1929.

ROBINSON, W. J., *Sexual Truths*, Hoboken, 1932.

ROGEAT, M., *Moeurs et Prostitution*, Paris, 1935.

SCHAUDINN, F., *cf.* Winter in *Zoolog. Anzeiger*, 1906, Vol. 30.

SEMASHKO, *Health Protection in the U.S.S.R.*, London, 1934.

SPILLMANN, LOUIS, *L'évolution de la lutte contre la syphilis*, Paris, 1933.

STOKES, J., *Modern Clinical Syphilidology*, Philadelphia, 1934.

STORER, V., *Gonococcal Infection*, London, 1934.

TREVETHIN, *Report*, Stat. Off., 1923.

VAILLANT-COUTURIER, "Au secours de la famille, Enquête," *Humanité*, 1935.

Venereal Diseases and their Prevention. For men only. National Society for the Prevention of Venereal Diseases, no date, London.

TABLE OF EVENTS

1886 Repeal of C.D. Acts.
1889 DUCREY isolates the bacillus of Chancroid.
1898 BORDET describes Serum Hæmolysis.
      JADASSOHN'S first Questionnaire in Switzerland.
1899 First Congress in London against White Slave Traffic.
1902 Official Conference in Paris against White Slave Traffic.
1903 BORDET and GENGOU observe Spirochæta pallida without
      recognizing it.
      First Police Welfare Worker (a Woman) appointed in
      Stuttgart.
      METCHNIKOFF produces Syphilis in Anthropoid Apes.
1904 Thirteen States sign Convention in Paris.
1905 SCHAUDINN and HOFFMANN detect Spirochæta pallida.
1906 WASSERMANN'S Reaction Treatment.
1909 NEISSER'S Theory of the Phases of Syphilis.
1910 EHRLICH and HATA invent Salvarsan.
      New Convention on White Slave Traffic.
1914 Foundation of National Council for Combating Venereal
      Diseases (later known as British Social Hygiene
      Council).
1917 Venereal Diseases Act in England. First public Consulta-
      tion Centre for Venereal Patients opened at Lübeck in
      Germany, under Insurance Office.
1918 Foundation of Central Soviet for the Suppression of
      Prostitution as part of Commissariat of Health in
      Moscow.
      Lex veneris in Sweden.
1919 Medical Conference at Cannes. Foundation of League of
      Red Cross Societies to combat Venereal Diseases in
      collaboration with League of Nations.
      Foundation of Society for Prevention of Venereal Diseases
      in London.
1920 PINARD and HOCH discover Spirochætes in Human Seminal
      Fluid.
1921 Lex veneris in Czechoslovakia.
1923 Foundation of the Union internationale contre le péril
      vénérien in Paris.
      First All Russian Congress against Venereal Diseases.
      TREVETHIN Report published in London.
1924 International Agreement in Brussels for the Treatment of
      Venereal Diseases in all Ports, signed by fifty-seven
      States.
1927 Lex veneris in Soviet Russia and in Germany.
      Report of the League of Nations' experts on Licensed
      Houses and Traffic in Women and Children.
1928 Foundation of the Japanese League against Licensed
      Prostitution.

1930 Congress of the Union internationale at Copenhagen.
      Standardized Instructions for Treatment.
1933 Congress of Union internationale in Cairo.
      Abolitionist Programme adopted.
1934 Assembly of League of Nations accepts Resolution against
      Traffic in Women and Children.

CHAPTER IV

THE EVOLUTION OF THE SEX CONSULTATION CENTRE

I

THE fight against Venereal Diseases was the main factor in breaking down the nineteenth-century taboo on the discussion of sexual subjects. The urgency of this fight, the social danger of widespread infection were such incontestable matters of fact that the carefully cultivated emotional resistances of centuries could not prevail against the examination, discussion and practical application of the knowledge already available.

But the community consists of individuals, and after the war of 1914–18 it had become evident that these individuals were in as much need of mental and physical therapy as the social organism of which they are, as it were, the component cells. This in spite of the many reservations and reluctances to deal openly with the subject.

Here too the first impetus came from medical quarters and as an application of medical hypothesis. Not the hypotheses of pathology, but of racial hygiene, inspired by the work of Mendel, Darwin and Francis Galton. In 1891 the German sociologist Schallmeyer recommended the use of Questionnaires on the biology of heredity. The apothecary Breitfeld first took public action on the lines of modern "marriage-consultants," in 1908. He addressed a Memorandum to the German Reichstag, demanding health certificates from all those about to marry before the ceremony took place. He was strongly supported by the German Monists' League (Monistenbund), an organization of rationalists with a definite and consistent type of ethical theory, founded by followers of Haeckel and dedicated to the spread of biological knowledge. Breitfeld's demand was repeated in 1910, but the Reichstag did not even discuss it. The editor of the *Deutsche Medizinische Wochenschrift* (a professional paper corresponding to the *Lancet*), Dr. J. Schwalbe, addressed the Reichstag independently in the same sense; and in 1911 the Monists' League founded the first Eugenic Marriage Advice Bureau in Dresden on its own responsibility. This courageous innovation had some years of active existence—quite enough to show the crucial point of Eugenic Consultation. For only two per cent. of those who sought the advice and help of the Bureau had not already formed some sort of sexual relationship, legal or illegal. Thus, in practice, advice as to the wisdom and desirability of active sexual experience was not required ; the clients of the Bureau had made their own decision in this momentous matter, and came for advice as to details and methods.

Thus the term "Eugenic Marriage Advice" seemed hardly accurate. It was already obvious that in order to meet the deep-seated and widespread need for knowledge, marriage had to be interpreted as sex in its most comprehensive sense. It became irrelevant to enquire whether the patients and their partners were legally married or not ; or indeed had any intention of appearing in Registry Office or Church. It was too early to state this in public, although the whole logical sequence of observation and theory had already been worked out, in Great Britain, by Godwin, Shelley, John Stuart Mill, Ruskin and Edward Carpenter. William Godwin had proclaimed that compulsory marriage was obsolete as early as 1795, and practised what he preached in his free union with Mary Wollstonecraft. By the time that Carpenter formulated the demands in *Love's Coming of Age*—including the personal and economic independence of women, instruction in the physical facts of birth and love, recognition of emotional comradeship between members of the same sex and repeal of the English Divorce Laws—he was simply drawing the logical conclusions from the criticisms—and to use a contemporary term "*debunking*"—which began in the Age of the French Encyclopædists and the Revolution.

2

The nineteenth-century bourgeoisie recognized two sexual institutions : marriage and prostitution. They also professed to believe that no sexual manifestations should occur outside marriage. And so even biologists of erudition and experience at first confined themselves to helping within the marriage tie. As knowledge grew, they began to take premarital and "illegal" relationships into account and to recognize the realities—as distinct from the polite fictions—of marriage itself.

The great sexologist Iwan Bloch has recorded the opinion of Hoffinger, an unbiassed observer, before the dawn of the twentieth century.

"Although he (Hoffinger) had conscientiously and zealously investigated the number and percentage of happy marriages, his researches were always to this extent in vain : that he was never able to treat happy marriages as anything but very rare exceptions from the general rule" (*Sexual Life of Our Times*, p. 247). Bloch himself made a special study of 100 marriages, which he summarized as follows :

Definitely unhappy . . . 48
Indifferent 36
Unquestionably happy . . 15
Conventionally Virtuous . . 1

Among those marriages in this series which appeared to Bloch to merit the title of " happy " there were three (3) between elderly persons, three more between persons of " phlegmatic constitution," and thirteen in which physical conjugal infidelity was habitual. Wilhelm Reich has made a special study of eighty-eight cases, and published a summary of the results early in 1936. Sixty-six out of the eighty-eight ($\frac{3}{4}$) were " failures, accompanied with sexual infidelity," in thirteen the partners were " resigned or ill," six though " apparently tranquil " were " very doubtful," and three were " satisfactory." That is to say, these three seemed satisfactory in 1926, ten years ago, when the obser-

vations leading to Reich's summary were first made. But
by 1929 one still survived. Of the two others, the first had
been terminated by a divorce, and the second was disrupted
following a course of psycho-analytic treatment (*cf. Sexualität im Kulturkampf*, p. 123). These results may be compared
to those in Soviet Russia,[1] where biological factors have
freer play than in the archaic juridical framework of the
West. Madame Vera Lebedieva, the principal of the famous
Moscow Institute for the Protection of Mother and Child,
had the available statistics of the duration of registered
relationships collected and collated with these results :

> 19 per cent. lasted up to one year.
> 37   ,,   ,,   from three to four years.
> 26   ,,   ,,   from four to nine years.
> 12   ,,   ,,   from ten to nineteen years.
> 6   ,,   ,,   longer than nineteen years.

This would suggest between four and five years as the
practical average duration of an inclination between average
man and woman. The Russian and Western statistics make
us understand why V. L. Calverton termed his challenging
book *The Bankruptcy of Marriage*—at least in so far as
marriage is the expression of the sexual impulse. Society
as constituted in America and Western and Central Europe
could not blink these facts, and there were vehement—in
fact desperate—efforts to salvage the bankrupt institution
in some distinguished quarters ; to recognize and to some
degree meet the demands of primitive urges and developed
individual tastes, while at the same time maintaining the
social and moral *cachet* of the legal marriage. The most
famous of these salvage specialists is Van de Velde, the
leading gynæcologist of the Netherlands, and his famous book
Die Vollkommene Ehe (*Ideal Marriage*) started (in 1926) a
shoal of imitations and adaptations. But there is a deep
difficulty and inconsistency here. There can be no doubt
of the benefits conferred on many people by Van de Velde's

---

[1] They may also be compared to the laments and " modern instances "
in the work of such experienced medical men as Van de Velde (a passionate
upholder of the institution of marriage), R. L. Dickinson, the leading
American gynæcologist, G. V. Hamilton and others.—Translator's Note.

dignified, detailed and explicit instructions in the actual technique of approach, of intercourse, of the post-coital "afterglow." But the need for such knowledge means that whatever the advantages of marriage as a social and economic partnership may be, it makes companionship and contact into a habit, if not an obligation, and this is the surest way to blunt and fritter and destroy any emotional interest between the partners and any physical attraction. The knowledge of specific technique and of the possible coital postures is not the main content of Dr. Van de Velde's book, the ancient Hindoos of thousands of years ago were well versed in this art of love, and Van de Velde needed merely to refer to the *Kamasutra* and clothe its message in dignified and appropriate modern medical garb. So far, so good. But the kindly *savant* then strives to prove that the erotic resurrection he recommends is not in any way hostile or subversive to the established social order of Western and Central Europe ; and even harmonizes in every detail (as well as in general principles) with the Moral Theology and Discipline of the Catholic Church ! Nevertheless, these concessions do not succeed in obtaining freedom of purchase by any member of the public for Van de Velde's book, even in Protestant Great Britain ! There are restrictions to doctors, lawyers, teachers, clergy and serious students of social and mental problems. Thus a valuable and helpful book is treated as a poison which may only be administered to sufferers from the marriage malady, on special prescription in the form of a drug ! The general public may not learn how to escape seriously morbid consequences by timely knowledge and practice of its contents.

Another eminent student of human nature, Judge Ben Lindsey of the Children's Court at Denver, Colorado, U.S.A., tried to cure the marriage crisis by legal rather than medical means. He was a thoughtful and astute Conservative, and he suggested a slight alteration of the Marriage Law. As many young people are not able to afford the expenses of a married establishment, he advocated the formal recognition of " companionate marriage," a perfectly legal but intentionally childless union which could be dissolved, if so desired, without grave and prolonged difficulties. The first pregnancy was to change " companionate " into conventional matrimony, with all its obligations and implications. An inadequate solution!

Lindsey lost his official position, but was re-elected to the Superior Court of Los Angeles by a record majority of 600,000. He continues in California the work for social reform begun in Colorado.

Indeed, in actual fact " marriage " here is irrelevant. For the scientist and the humanitarian what matters *is the sore need of help and advice in every type of individual sexual proclivity and experience*, and the development of new possibilities of help and advice independent of legal and ecclesiastical quibbles. These were the considerations which led to the establishment of the first centre for Information and Advice on Sex, at the Berlin Institute for Sexual Science in 1919. The centre was free to all persons who believed themselves in need of its services.

3

It is significant that this centre sprang into life almost immediately after the war of 1914–18; for those years of agony and effort in all the countries involved had completely shown up the futility and failure of the hitherto accepted standards of the nineteenth century. In the course of the war millions of married couples hitherto entirely or mainly monogamous in their sexual habits had been separated for years, and had learnt the relativity of moral codes. At the same time all grades and classes of male citizens had been thoroughly instructed in the use of those appliances which are not only prophylactics against venereal diseases, but also against child-bearing; and concurrently female citizens had become conscious of their value to the State as substitutes and co-operators in " war work." Thus the moment was fully favourable for so radical an innovation as a Sex Advice Centre; the " hush-hush! ", the sexual silence-taboo, had been broken during the war in the campaign against venereal disease [1] and could not be re-imposed.

We were flooded with applications and enquiries, and for the first time were able to obtain some statistical evidence of the results of crass ignorance and dogmatic superstition in this field of human nature and needs. As a sort of introduction to individual consultations, Hirschfeld arranged a weekly " Evening for Questions " in the Ernest Haeckel Hall of the Institute ; this was open to all who cared to attend for several years, and personal privacy was guaranteed by the written question which was answered with equal care and thought ; and so deep a confidence, interest and obligation was established between questioners and instructors that anxieties and embarrassments were overcome and the shyest seekers for help came for subsequent individual consultations and (if necessary) treatments as well.

The Institute was a private venture, but in 1922 the Social Services of the Municipality of Vienna founded the first public and official Centre for Sexual Advice in that city, under the supervision of the gynæcologist, Dr. Karl Kautsky, son and namesake of the well-known Social Democrat and political writer. In 1924 the city of Berlin followed Vienna's example. But as soon as the Sex Advice Centre became part of the administrative machinery of town or state, the institution of marriage and the hereditary and biological aspect of the subject were stressed, rather than the individual right to know and the psychological and definitely sexual significance of knowledge. One of the Berlin newspapers of that time had an extremely apt cartoon ; a woman flanked by a child on either side, and wheeling a perambulator with a bouncing baby ; a man follows this little flock and a friendly neighbour advances to meet and greet them : " Hullo, where are you off to ? " The eldest child replies : " We're going to the Marriage Advice Centre, Mummy wants to know if she can marry Daddy ! "

The practical results of this conventionalizing of the official Centres were soon manifest. The biologically realistic and effective Centres, where instruction was given

[1] *Vide* the previous chapter.

without restrictions or discriminations to married and
unmarried persons equally, and contraceptives were recommended and supplied, were much more popular and successful than those which were only available for legally married
couples or at most for "those engaged to be married."
(Incidentally, the same strangely illogical restriction still
stultifies the admirable work of the British and American
Birth Control Clinics.) The right of all adults to birth control
information and appliances is a keypoint in any sociological
system based on the facts of human minds and bodies ;
but of course this basic axiom of sexual biology is sharply
opposed to the moral assumptions of our present social
order, and we need seek no further for the "reasons why"
the overwhelming majority of pioneer workers for sexual
enlightenment find no favour in official quarters. Nor is
it surprising that the year 1926 saw an official attempt to
limit the activities of the Official Centres still further.
The Catholic Hirtsiefer was then Minister of Public Welfare
for Prussia ; he was sincere in his faith and suffered grave
mal-treatment at the hands of National Socialists in a
Concentration camp in the Hitler era. His decree for
" The Promotion of Marriage Advice and Consultation "
(given in full in I.M.I. 535 (file No.), *Public Welfare*, 1926,
p. 299) limits the subject strictly " To the medical examination and testing of those intending to marry, in order to
ascertain their hygienic fitness for marriage." He continues
as follows :

" In the course of debates in the Landesgesundheitsrat
(Health Council) it was established that the Centres already
at work in some districts were mainly devoted to giving
advice to married couples and other persons as to how to
limit their families and how to employ contraceptives.
This kind of advice, as was made clear in the Landesgesundheitsrat, must be considered most undesirable and thoroughly
contrary to the real purpose of the Centres themselves."

In 1927 the Chief Medical Councillor of the city of Berlin,
von Drigalski, founded an " Association of Public Marriage
Advice Centres " on the lines laid down by Hirtsiefer. It
was and is a sterile hybrid, but genuine Sex Advice Centres

developed in every direction and found their best support in the laymen's and laywomen's Leagues for Sexual Hygiene and Birth Control.

4

These leagues were working-class organizations whose members were mainly either active Socialists or in sympathy with Socialist ideals. They interlocked with the " Workers-Samaritan Union," a Mutual Benefit Society which had always specialized in Health questions. The Leagues included thousands of intelligent and public-spirited working men and women in close contact with nurses, doctors and lawyers who sympathized with their aspirations, and supplied enlightenment and individual advice on these intimate subjects to the membership. The Leagues were mighty organs of propaganda in all German-speaking territories, not only in Germany itself, but in Austria, Switzerland and the German districts of Czechoslovakia as well. They had their own press ; in Germany alone—exclusive of Austria, Switzerland and Czechoslovakia—there were several monthly papers : *Love and Life* with a circulation of 60,000 copies, *The Call* with 30,000 and *Sexual Hygiene* with 21,000. In Austria there was an active and beneficent " Bund für Geburtenregelung " (" League for Birth Control ") founded by Johann Ferch, in collaboration with the German organizations. It did much good work until the clerical Dictatorship was re-established in Austria. At the moment when Hitler's henchmen were smashing the German Leagues, a League for Sexual Instruction came into being in Sweden (*Riksförbund for sexuell upplysning*), led by the indefatigable Elise Ottesen-Jensen. In Copenhagen the movement was led by Dr. J. H. Leunbach, one of the Presidents of the (now defunct) W.L.S.R. In Norway, Dr. Evang founded and edited a special periodical, and some single issues of this *Tidskrift for seksuell upplysning* attained a circulation of 30,000 copies in a country of less than 3,000,000 inhabitants !

Every organization, periodical and individual lecturer in this movement had absorbed the spirit of Hirschfeld's

" Question evenings," and was contributing towards a public policy of information and constructive statesmanship, based on the anonymous enquiries with which we were deluged. The same subjects appear in the forefront of interest, with amazing insistence, the same difficulties and perplexities, whether in North Germany or South, or in Hungary, Palestine, Belgium or Scandinavia ; my personal experience as public lecturer and private consultant, in many countries of various ethnic and social characteristics, merely confirms that of legal and medical co-workers throughout the world.

What are these main foci of mental curiosity and emotional stress ?

Whenever a new centre was opened there was a rush of patients who begged for the performance of abortions. Their entreaties could only be fulfilled in a small minority of cases, as the legislation of most European States is still on a mediæval level in this urgent matter. We were, however, able to convert most of our applicants to an ardent belief in the advantages of birth control by contraception ; and this subject " played lead " in those Question evenings which were attended by a majority of mature adults. But when young people formed a strong percentage of the audience, most of their enquiries showed unmistakable pre-occupation with " solitary habits," " self-relief " or " Onanism." And why were about 50 per cent. of these questions on Onanism addressed to us ? Simply because solitary methods of relief were chosen instead of more normal relations, out of fear of undesired offspring ! Ignorance of birth control is the great practical hindrance to normal sexual life for young persons who yet are sexually fully apt, biologically and emotionally.

Contraception on the one hand, self-relief on the other, have between them a whole cycle of clinical manifestations ; problems of male potency, of feminine insensibility or inadequate gratification, neuroses of all kinds, and theoretical controversies, philosophical rather than medical in their inception. These include the precise amount and methods of sexual instruction to children or young persons in their teens; they include such matters as Divorce, Marriage Laws, the Status of Illegitimacy, Sexual Deviations or Abnormalities. And then there is the special significance and fascination of the new experiments, economic and ethical, in Soviet Russia.

The modern consultant specialist in sexual matters must have mastered the wide field of relevant knowledge, from the medical, the psychological and—last not least—the sociological aspects. For inexperienced and uninstructed men and women forming the majority of the people have already been thwarted and perturbed and bewildered by the sex-phobia inherent in their traditional education and the influence of religion. Thus confidence is doubly difficult to win and keep. Only those doctors can succeed permanently in this office who themselves are in constant contact with the lives of the workers, and do not limit their efforts to so-called " better class patients " or to the mere routine of writing out prescriptions.

We learnt, in the course of several years' practice, that the interactions between social conditions and the intimate biology and, even more so, psychology of sex had hardly been recognized in professional tradition and literature. In 1927 I published the first systematic attempt in popular form at a Sociology of Sex, *Sex and Love in their Biological and Social Aspects.* It was based on the material collected at our Berlin Centre, under the auspices of the Institute for Sexual Science. Those to whom it was addressed welcomed the book with enthusiasm. Academic circles were very cool—with a few distinguished exceptions : the official view was " that book is not really science, but political propaganda." And that view demands an answer and an exposure.

According to the standards in question, anyone who limits their authorship to uncritical accounts of That Which Is, who gives the anatomy and physiology of reproduction, as it were *in vacuo* with no reference to social or economic contexts, is *ipso facto* " scientific " in approach. But he who depicts the relativity and interactions of social institutions and the manifestations of sex, and criticizes such existent institutions and customs from the point of view of the injury and degradation they inflict on the sexual emotions of humanity, is guilty of " political agitation." No Conservative in these matters can be guilty of political agitation, for he simply accepts the present state of things. But " political agitation " is a useful stone to throw at those who desire better things ; the name sounds menacing and dangerous to many worthy citizens. And the traditionalist is every bit as " political " as the reformer or revolutionary. The contrast between their views is the contrast between the stiff gloom of traditional theology and the clear light and fresh air of modern scientific hygiene. But, of course, no human parallel is ever wholly exact : there are mediæval minds in the ranks of the political left and personalities of high sexual and psychological evolution in the Conservative camp, as all experienced " agitators " will admit.

5

We may regard two of the main problems of the modern consultant in this field as practically solved—or at least, as solved in as much as we know that in practice they need present no insuperable obstacles. We know that sexual congress and reproduction are separable ; and we know that abortions performed by skilled professional workers in hospitals need hardly mean any risk for the woman concerned, while, on the other hand, abortions performed in uncleanly and unsuitable surroundings and by unskilled persons are highly dangerous and often fatal. We know also that these dangerous illegal operations cannot be stopped by legal penalties, however indiscriminate and atrocious, but only by adequate protection and care for expectant and nursing mothers and young children. It cost much effort and many precious years for us to reach this certainty, and the intrinsic importance of both birth control and abortion justifies their special treatment in separate chapters of this book. The more complex psychological problems revealed and treated in our work are still themes of fervent and incessant controversy.

The development of consultative and clinical work at the Centres soon showed a most regrettable lack in our equipment. Budding medical practitioners left their Universities without the least knowledge of the psychology of sex. This was the case in all countries round about 1920. And even our acquaintance with the physiology of sex was quite inadequate, outside the special departments of obstetrics and venereal diseases. For in the consulting rooms of the Centres there was revealed to us an amount of sheer inadequacy and grave dislocation of the bodily mechanism of sex in both men and women, for which no text-books had prepared us, and at which no lecturer had hinted. The function of orgasm, instead of being a universal joy and benefit, was shown to be an exceptional privilege. How should we deal with these difficulties ? We had to use our own discretion, apart from certain recourse to authorities on Urology.

Our women patients were often insoluble psychological puzzles. I remember well a lady of most fashionable and fastidious appearance who called one afternoon for a consultation. She stated that she had been married for some years, but had never experienced sexual satisfaction, " in spite of two pregnancies." She was entirely convinced that her " nervous state " was due to this lack, and wanted to know what I advised. I pointed out the unsatisfactory nature of " marriage consultation with 50 per cent. absent " and suggested that I should see her husband as well. She flatly declined : " That's out of the question, no one could mention ' that sort of thing ' to my husband." I enquired why not ? " Well, he lives in a provincial town—150,000 inhabitants—I grant you, but you know, Doctor, what provincials are like." " What is your husband's office or profession ? " " He's in charge of the Municipal Hospital for Women " ! ! I was speechless. But after consideration one had to admit that this Professor of Gynæcology was just a child of the Age, and of the Science of his Age, and therefore a victim of consecrated and systematized sex suppression and sex-phobia.

So we were led to investigate the individual difficulties and differences in attaining sexual gratification. The problem seemed relatively simple as regards men. The actual process of tumescence and detumescence, of accumulated stimuli and relief, seemed to follow the same lines in all our cases, although there were appreciable differences in individual intensity and rapidity of reflex action, and many individual disturbances of potency. In the course of the last decade and a half it has sometimes seemed that disturbances and defects of male potency are on the increase; and especially that premature climax or *ejaculatio præcox* is more frequent than formerly; and this has been attributed to the nervous irritability and unbalance of modern urban populations. I am inclined to believe that these pessimistic conclusions are based on an oversight. The former taboo on sexual discussions, even between doctors and patients, is disappearing, and many men now confide their difficulties and seek relief; whereas even a generation ago they would have concealed their sexual inadequacy as carefully as a secret crime, or put on the mask of sexual swagger and boasting, or simply accepted their fate as part of Life's Great Fiasco, without complaint or revolt.

Moreover we have now some detailed and precise knowledge of the actual nervous and glandular mechanism of masculine sexuality; and we are able to attack defective potency both by psycho-therapeutic and endocrine treatments. The results in both respects justify the following conclusions:

The specific genital potency of men is the combined result of accumulated stimulation and resistance. Disturbances of potency are disturbances of tension or resistance. Impotence resulting from defective erection is usually an endocrine inadequacy, due to the lack of stimulating endocrine secretions. Disturbed or defective potency due to increased resistance is generally psychological in origin. Shapiro analysed this group into the following psychological and mental categories (*Mediz. Klinik*, 1927, No. 31): dread of infection; inhibitions due to traditional religion, to ethical standards or to æsthetic considerations; doubt of being able to perform the act itself; dread of social consequences or of results of former masturbatory or auto-erotic habits. All these elements of fear and frustration exist, and by no means only among psychotic or neurotic individuals.

The various specific causes of defective erectile capacity may include the following factors, all of which must be taken into consideration and tested in each case :

" 1. An'injury to the gonad itself : this may be
" (a) mechanical, through external wounds or shocks ;
" (b) chemical, through such substances as alcohol, morphia, cocaine and nicotine ; or
" (c) bacterial.

" The injury to the gonad may be congenital ; such as anorchism or abnormally small organs, *i.e.*, eunuchoidism or infantilism or hermaphroditic anomalies.

" 2. Functional disturbances of other glands than the gonads ; such endocrine glands as interact with the gonads and may effect gonadic efficiency. These glands include the Thyroid, Hypophysis, Adrenals, Thymus and Pancreas.

" 3. Ionic disturbances in the tissues, even if the glandular function remains intact.

" 4. Disturbances of the vegetative nervous system operating the exchanges between gonad and specific organ ; and

" 5. Special peculiarities of individual psychology " (Shapiro).

The obvious methods of cure would appear to be increase of tension in cases of local disturbance, decrease of inhibition in cases of psychological and mental dislocation. But in practice there are so many complexities and varieties of impotence, that these elementary prescriptions are not feasible. There are always some psychological elements at work in such cases. Thus, every first occasion of erectile failure leads to sensations of disappointment and apprehension which are the bases of further fears and doubts ; and conversely primary erectile failures may be due to hitherto unknown constitutional peculiarities and deep-seated organic infantilism of the essential structures.

These complexities led us to have recourse to combined methods of treatment. Shapiro constructed two pharmaceutical preparations for the treatment of male impotence : Testifortan in 1926, Præjaculin in 1930. We were able to

analyse and distinguish the following diverse causes of
ejaculatio præcox :

The first cause is exhaustion and nervous irritability,
together, often, with deficient erectile capacity. These cases
are sexually hypotonic. The other and opposite cause is
excessive excitement frequently associated with facile and
rapid erection, and these cases are sexually hypertonic.
Hypotonic cases react successfully to the administration of
tonics and testicular preparations. Hypertonic cases are
unduly stimulated and aggravated by tonics, but improve
under the administration of sedatives, which calm and soothe.
In such cases præjaculin has proved its value, especially
when there is concurrent psychological treatment and
improvement of the external conditions in which the individual has to live. For we must not forget that this environmental treatment is relatively more important for patients
seeking help for sexual troubles than for those in any
and every other branch of medicine.

6

What of impaired or disturbed or absent sexual sensation
in women ?

In the course of consultations one is struck by the vagueness and ambiguity of the information given by all but a
very small minority of women patients : the Professor's
wife mentioned above was clarity itself in comparison !
Even in cases of women who are known to have had a
considerable amount of experience in these matters it is very
difficult to obtain precise or definite indications. " I don't
know." " How can I describe it ? " " It differs from time
to time." Can one imagine such answers on that topic
from a man ? Moreover, there is a further obstacle here,
both to expression and to comprehension ; for the terminology
for sexual manifestations has been built up on masculine
experience and by men. Thus, to refer to a " sexually
satisfied " woman was held to imply a woman in a state of
mind and body identical with that of the man after a successful and delectable coitus. It was assumed and without fur-

ther enquiry that such a state must or should ensue in women, and it was " expected."

Now sexual satisfaction in the male is the actual orgasm, the emotional accompaniment of the physical ejaculation or emission. What of the orgasm in women ?

In 1926 Bela Totis addressed the Psychological Society of Budapest and pointed out that orgasm is by no means the necessary sequence of libido, nor satisfaction of desire. Desire is certainly present in healthy women as an urge towards sexual union, and regular sexual activity has been long known to promote not only general health in women, but also their specific functions. Leunbach has made valuable investigations in this respect during the years between 1931 and 1934. He found that the frequent more or less pronounced menstrual irregularities and *malaise* to which many women are subject nearly always disappeared when these women were able to engage in regular sexual activity. But the distressing symptoms often reappear and promptly if the women are obliged to break off their sexual relationships or to cohabit infrequently and irregularly.

The " Moral " attitude of the Victorian era was accompanied by a strong economic and social pressure on women to conform to the belief that their specific desire was far less than men's. And there are echoes of this doctrine in many quarters still, notably even in such otherwise relevant and realistic works as the *Evolution of Sex* by the Spanish savant G. Marañón, who is of opinion that : " The feminine libido possesses as its characteristic precisely its rudimentary condition. This entitles us to suggest that in a certain sense the libido, as a differentiated energy, is a force of virile significance. We may say as much as regards the orgasm " (*Evolution of Sex*, English Translation, 1932, p. 72, Spanish original, 1930). So far as libido or specific desire in women is concerned, this statement is not merely questionable, it is inaccurate, and founded not on biological facts, but on social tradition. But there is some substance in the same writer's differentiation between orgasmic processes in men and women respectively, so far as can be observed or have been put on record.

He says : " It is unquestionable that the orgasm is totally different in the case of the woman and the case of the man ; so much so that in my opinion these differences may be assigned to the category of a sexual characteristic, not only by reason of their general physiological and biological importance. The sexual orgasm in the man is always a matter of a prompt act and a rapid sensation " (*l.c.*, p. 74). But the " feminine orgasm " is described as " very slow in general, in the first sexual relation." The extreme vagueness of this description corresponds to various statements made by patients in consultation and by other women who volunteer information on this difficult point. We may approach the question deductively and ask indeed whether we are entitled to expect an orgasm in woman ?

It has been proved, and repeatedly, that impregnation may take place without orgasm and without conscious participation on the woman's part as under the influence of drugs, drink or anæsthetics. Thus reproduction is not dependent on female orgasm ; as apart from consent to copulate. In the man, on the other hand, insemination implies ejaculation, and ejaculation requires the nervous climax of orgasm. Cases of masculine desire without the capacity to perform ejaculation or experience orgasm are pathological. The American sexologist Thorek recorded one of these cases in 1924. A negro patient had contracted parotitis, which led to toxic degeneration of the spermato-genic tubules and proliferation of the interstitial tissue of the organ.

In 1926 the first volume of Van de Velde's Marriage trilogy was published on the Continent, and it was believed and taught in our Consultation Centres that, as he said, a normal and healthy coitus means simultaneous orgasm, or, at least, orgasm in very rapid succession. The Dutch expert impresses on us that husbands should know that " every considerable erotic stimulation of their wives that does not terminate in orgasm, on the woman's part, represents an injury, and repeated injuries of this kind lead to permanent —or very obstinate—damage to both body and soul " (*Ideal Marriage*, p. 190 and *passim*). It is, however, probable that most women who seek medical advice for " lack of satisfaction in coitus " or " absence of orgasm " do not do so of their own accord, but are sent or brought by husbands who have taken Van de Velde's message to heart. We may approach this riddle either by way of biology and anatomy or of psychology and sociological history. Dr. E. R. Elkan has investigated from the zoological and comparative structural side. He consulted zoologists and observed many species of animal. He concluded that although there had never been any doubt or dispute as to the existence of orgasm even among the lower species of the animal world, it had not been observed even among the females of the higher anthropoids. But there were significant exceptions.

Among fish the females of the species *Selachiæ* have a definite orgasmic process. After amatory play and caresses between the partners, both extrude their gametes into the water ; thus fertilization does not take place within the female body, as among mammals, but as the male and female elements are deposited in rapid succession and closely in space, even the flow of the water does not prevent their merging.

In certain aquatic birds, *e.g.*, among swans, there seems to be a female climax of sensation, *i.e.*, an orgasm. At a certain stage in their coupling these habitually silent creatures utter a peculiar cry. This only occurs on other occasions when they are intensely excited.

In both species, fish and birds, there are no specialized genital fixation organs. Psychosensory reflexes seem to operate here and produce certain definite phenomena. Elkan could find no trace of " satisfaction " in the human and specific sense in any female of other species, whether during or after coitus (Elkan, 1933, p. 36).

There is, however, great individual diversity here among women. Certainly some women experience an intense climax of sensation in sexual relations, and many have a conscious yearning for this experience. The *Kamasutra* of ancient Hindustan contains this passage : " Here are the words of Auddalaki : The woman's condition is not as the

man's : she does not have the same delight as the man has
in the outpouring of the seed, for she has no seed. . . .
She has a special pleasure of her own, accompanied by the
joy of pride in herself. And she is aware of this pleasure.
This special pleasure of the woman arises in the beginning
and continues in uninterrupted sequence . . . but the
man's pleasure goes together with the out-pouring of the
seed.

" Now in the union of love, the man satisfies and feeds the
woman's longing and that we call ecstasy if it goes with
awareness of herself. The feeling of pleasure arising from
fulfilled longing, together with awareness of herself . . . is
called ecstasy or rapture among women." Elkan's comment
is " if we substitute the word ' orgasm ' for ' ecstasy ' this
would mean that in human beings the feminine orgasm is
interwoven with consciousness—with awareness. This
knowledge, gathered across millennia, in my opinion offers
us the clue to the mystery " (*l.c.*, p. 43). Again he says :
" Whenever the expression of sexual love coincides with a
high degree of personality or individuation in women, there
is the strong urge on her part to experience the equivalent
of the male climax of sensation " (*l.c.*, p. 49).

According to this view the orgasmic spasm in women
would be an occasional phenomenon, and moreover extremely
elusive and easily repressed or diverted : whereas in men
this experience is definitely cerebro-spinal as well as local,
and follows a fixed pattern of abrupt culmination and
subsidence. If this view is accepted we must conclude that
women are capable of orgasm, but only under certain
special circumstances. Further, it would imply that women
who do not feel definite orgasms are not necessarily incapable of any degree of sexual gratification, and still less
inherently " morbid " or " defective " in any way.

But this whole theory is most vigorously assailed from the
psycho-analytic standpoint ; and incapacity for orgasm or
absence of orgasm, whether total or partial, absolute or
conditional, and in man or woman, is interpreted as a
neurotic symptom, and indeed the major neurotic symptom.
This means that orgasmic absence or impairment would

require treatment *per se*, apart from any other circumstance, and was, in fact, the very crux and centre of all consultations and remedial treatments for these ills. Nor can we deny that the ethical patterns on which characters are formed in a social order with traditions of fear of sex and disgust for sex must lead as a rule to deviations and disturbances which can only be estimated in individual cases. If we grant these premises, we must also believe firmly that so long as present social and economic conditions prevail, it is useless and indeed derisory to attempt to give sexual advice and help without thorough psycho-therapy. There was no exaggeration in the comments of Dr. Doris M. Odlum, in the August issue of *Marriage Hygiene* for 1935 :

" To many women coitus even in marriage subconsciously represents an attack on their chastity, and in so far as it is associated with any feeling of satisfaction a deep guilt sense is aroused which frequently overshadows the pleasure and may lead to complete inhibition, to a neurosis or even to a psychosis."

According to this interpretation, the special prohibitions and traditions of the patriarchate form the soil in which impotence and insensibility, fear and shame, flourish like flowerless weeds. On these premises, the most recent investigations have been founded, as well as the special attention devoted to individual coital experience in sexual consultations. The results are of the most intimate and profound significance, although we have not yet, by any means, sighted our final goal.

7

The most recent investigations into the nature of the orgasm are based on experiences recorded in psycho-analytic circles in Vienna, from 1923 to 1927 inclusive. We may regard Wilhelm Reich's book *Die Funktion des Orgasmus* (1927) as a preliminary summary of efforts to understand and " place " this human problem from the psycho-analytic point of view. Official psycho-analysis took no notice of the endeavour to include the clinical aspects and interactions of the human orgasm in the general scope of neurology, apart from a few allusions in Fenichel's *Spezieller Neurosenlehre* which appeared in 1932.

But this discouragement did not check the flood of evidence which poured into the consultations of the "Socialist Society for Sexual Advice and Investigation" founded by Reich in Vienna (1929–30) and conducted under his supervision. The clue here appeared to be the connection between orgasm and anxiety in all its phases on the one hand, and between orgasm and the vegetative nervous system on the other hand. The greater the concentration of specific excitement in the genital apparatus, and the more complete the ebb and subsidence of this excitement throughout the vegetative nervous system, the more ideally perfect and satisfactory is the orgasm. The term "orgasmic potency" or "orgastic potency" was applied to "the capacity for excluding all inhibitions to a release of tension equivalent to the previous summation, and for registering this experience fully in the consciousness (*i.e.*, cortically)" (Reich, *Zeitschrift für politische Psychologie*, 1934, p. 31).

This advance in knowledge has been due to the efforts of psycho-analysis, and analytical changes of opinion have had considerable influence on sexual consultation centres ; the chief shifting of therapeutic attention being towards the structure of the respective neuroses. Sigmund Freud started his investigations into the realm of neurology from the "symptoms" ; but in the course of his researches the "neurotic character"—a definite biopsychic unity—took more and more the leading *rôle*. This tendency corresponded to the fruitful and illuminating change of trend in the whole realm of medicine, inaugurated by Friedrich Kraus's *Klinische Syzygiologie* in 1926. Individual personalities became once more the main objects of diagnosis and therapy alike, and were recognized as unities in their manifestations and reactions. Thus the disturbances brought to light in sexual consultations were viewed as integral features of special types of personality. If disturbances of the function culminating in orgasm, and the precise degree and duration of such disturbances were the measures of the intolerable conditions which drove people to seek advice in sexual consultation, then it followed that every special disturbance had to be regarded and treated as symptomatic for the whole personality of each individual, and that such treatment might imply solution by means of " Character Analysis."

Kraus's investigations have made it possible for us to state that living substances are mainly colloidal structures, and that the vital process may be defined as an independent current of certain fluids throughout the vegetative system.

Moreover, psychological currents and physical fluidic trends are in the closest interaction and obviously functionally identical. It appears that we may regard sexuality on the one hand and dread on the other as the two opposite primordial functions of living things ; and this theory throws quite fresh light on the well-known ambivalence of sexual manifestations, to which folklore and anthropology bear such striking testimony. Reich summarizes this hypothesis as follows : " The tension is felt centrally, in a state of dread or fear, manifesting for instance in disturbed heart action, but peripherally when the sexual urge is stirred (e.g., erection). In a state of fear, the bodily fluids, blood and lymph, ebb away from the surface, towards the interior of the organism. Sexual excitement has the exactly opposite effect ; the peripheral tissues become turgescent, the blood vessels of skin and mucous membrane are congested, the salivary glands and gonads secrete " (Vegetative Urform des Libido-Angst Gegensatzes, p. 207, 1934).

The research undertaken by Walter and Kate Misch (1932) has taught us that fear can be relieved by means of intramuscular injections of 0·1 acetylcholin ; and, contrariwise, that the prevention of sexual activity leads to dread and fear. These antitheses in the functions of that neuro-vegetative economy, the human body, may be systematized, on the basis of Kraus's discovery of the virtual identity and ambivalence of neural action, toxic action and electrolytic action in the hydration and dehydration of living tissue :

Vegetative Group (alternate increase and equivalence)	General Effect	Central-peripheral
I. Sympatheticus .	Lowering of Surface Tension	Systole Vaso-constrictor.
Calcium (Group)	Expulsion of Fluids (hydrophobia).	Cardiac Muscle active.
Adrenalin .	Striped Muscles slacken.	Intestines constricted.
Cholesterin .	Decrease of Electrical Sensibility.	
OH-Ions . .	Increase of Oxygen Intake. Increase of Blood Pressure.	
II. Vagus . .	Heightening of Surface Tension.	Diastole.
Potassium (Group)	Reception of Fluids . .	Dilator.
Cholin . .	Muscles tense and contracted	Cardiac Muscle relaxed.
Lecithin . .	Increase of Electrical Sensibility.	Intestines active.
H-Ions . .	Decrease of Oxygen Intake. Decrease of Blood Pressure.	

(See Reich, *l.c.*, p. 222.)

The first category may conveniently be described as the "Anxiety Group," the second as the "Libido Group." The facts already recognizable here are as follows:

1. There is a contrariety and alternate action of the potassium and calcium groups, vagus and sympatheticus; this implies expansion and contraction.

2. There is a polarity between centre and periphery as regards stimulation: Libido and Dread.

3. There is functional identity of the action of sympatheticus and vagus respectively with their distinctive chemical substances.

4. The nervous action of the specific organs depends on the functional unity and harmony of the organism as a whole.

And the functions of the whole organism must be conceived as founded on the polarity and interaction of two forces; the organism is a dynamic unity, and its mechanism is revealed to us by chemical processes; that is, by a dialectical evolution, the alternate action of the vaso-sympathetic system. It is not only an analogy based on external likeness if we use the terms current in modern sociology through "Characteranalysis" and coined by Karl Marx in his *Contribution to the Critique of Political Economy* in 1859.

According to Marx, dialectics is "the science of the general laws of motion, both of the external world and of human thinking." As we contemplate the working of these laws of motion we are able to perceive the occasional "transformation of quantity into quality" as Marx predicted. Moreover, we can also trace both chemically and psychologically the alternation of sexual tension and dread and sometimes the sudden metamorphosis of one fundamental motive into another. It is probable that the stimulus begins at the cœliac ganglion and the particular path then taken determines its manifestation, whether as desire or dread.

Thus we see that if human character is built up on a foundation of concepts and habits that set up a barrier against pleasurable and tonic experience, the emotional and especially the sexual life of the individual in question must be profoundly dislocated and thwarted. The general purpose of neuropathology is the study of the development of psychological structures and of the barriers against their external manifestation. The knowledge acquired by the study of neuroses can and should be used in the prophylaxis of neuroses. And sexual science gains an enormously significant key position thereby : for the regulation or the restoration of wholesome normal orgastic potency or capacity becomes the main focus of sexual consultation and advice, and indicates the sociological conditions which are veritable forcing houses for neuroses and neurasthenia, or conversely those favouring human happiness, health and achievement. Symptoms throw light on causes.

A comparison from another science may be relevant. When examining the ethnographical treasures in our Museums, one is often unable to repress a sense of aimlessness ; one asks " surely these are just curiosities—æsthetically often quite remarkable, but what is the meaning behind this selection of specimens ? " Museums receive and house the finest examples of ethnographical material. But if we ask the collectors what their prize specimens mean ; if we assume that the collector knows the train of social conditions and circumstances which would explain the purpose of individual objects—we are only too often, and severely, disappointed. Sociological anthropology is in its infancy ; the pathfinders for future discoveries have been Frazer and Malinowski, but we are still far from having reached the stage of anthropology which not only enumerates symptoms but traces causes.

Sexual science has also been mainly descriptive until the present time. The only possible illumination that might lead to knowledge of the origins of various types of sexual disturbance and deviation came from analytic psychology. In other words, sexual science until now has been more or less a phenomenology ; a record and investigation of the phenotypes of so-called " normality " and the aberrations therefrom. *We are at the parting of the ways towards a genetic science of sex.* The main corner stones of this structure will be Freud's material (including that collected by his disciples) ; Stekel's material collected and sifted for his series " Disorders of the Instincts and the Emotions " ; and the results of the latest investigations into the orgasmic process.

It is possible that the discovery of the precise mechanisms and origins of the aberrations and deviations of erotic emotion will provide a definite answer to the puzzling question as to the respective *rôles* of organic constitution and environmental pressure in sexual pathology. But we already know, without any doubt, that any helpful or intellectually honest advice in this field must take into account not only psychology and biology, but sociology as well.

To quote W. Reich : " As a medical man, one's duty is to consider the patient's health ; that includes the state of his or her emotional and instinctive life, but not his or her ' morality.' And let us suppose that we find an absolute opposition between these instinctive desires and needs, and the moral code of our present social order. It would be 'unanalytic' if we dismissed the patient's needs and desires as 'infantilisms' and manifestations of the 'pleasure-principle' and fell back on exhortations to 'resignation' and invocations to 'adjustment to reality' before having investigated the situation and decided for ourselves whether the clamant desires were really infantile regressions and the demands of external reality were really acceptable and compatible with human health. Thus we have no right to turn away from a woman who follows her own individual impulses by having sexual intercourse with many men, with the portentous judgment 'an infantile case'! Such a woman does not fit easily or happily into the framework of bourgeois society ; that is what ails her " (Reich, *l.c.*, 1936, p. 124).

8

The social order of to-day, which has not yet accepted women's equal humanity, in either theory or practice, is responsible for many consulting room dramas and difficulties. Some of these dramas have a streak of comedy, not to say farce. For example : a lady entered a certain consulting room, evidently in a state of severe depression and distress. She stated that she had been married for several years, but had no children and no prospect of any, although parenthood was the keenest wish of her husband and herself. " Oh, doctor, what can be the reason ? What is wrong with me ? "

The doctor replied that there were many possible causes. Had her husband been professionally examined ?

" My husband ? But what do you mean ? I don't understand. My husband wants your opinion of my case ! "

This woman had never imagined the possibility that a woman's failure to conceive the child she desired might possibly be due to some condition affecting the prospective father ! For thousands of years fertility has been the wife's " duty " ; women have accepted this obligation so whole-heartedly that they have no perception of the inequality of status and treatment of which such one-sided and un-scientific procedure is a symptom, in spite of all the democratic catchwords and trimmings of to-day.

The Sex Consultation Centre at Dresden collected very exact details on marital sterility under the direction of Professor Fetscher. These data contradicted the accepted view that the " barren woman " was necessarily in some way defective or at fault. Two-thirds of the childless marriages recorded at the Centre were childless because of azöospermia in the husbands (Notes, 1926–33).

It is much easier to detect the presence or absence of functional sperm cells in any man, by the use of the microscope, than it is to ascertain which—of all the many possible causes—is accountable for feminine sterility. Therefore it should be part of the regular procedure of all sex consultation, in cases of undesired sterility, to make first and foremost a thorough investigation of the spermatogenetic conditions of the male partner.

The fact that sperms are fully motile, *i.e.*, capable of the characteristic rapid movement of these cells, does not necessarily mean that they are capable of fertilizing the ovum. In 1931 G. I. Moench made detailed investigations, proving frequent structural and chemical anomalies in spermatozoa. But assuming that their functional capacity is perfect, pregnancy may be achieved, as a rule, by certain actions and positions, *e.g.*, the woman should remain recumbent some time after the act of intercourse, while if necessary a pad of cotton wool or lint should be inserted into the vagina ; and copulation should be timed to take place in the middle of the menstrual cycle.

What of artificial fertilization or artificial insemination ? This is as yet comparatively infrequent, for psychological reasons. It generally implies the use of seminal fluid provided by a third person, and this involves elaborate precautions and keeping all apparatus used to contain or inject the fluid at a special warm yet even temperature, as was explained by Stabel at the Congresses at Copenhagen and Vienna.[1]

A problem of far greater actual human appeal is that of

---

[1] *Re Artificial Insemination.* The possibilities of this technique are discussed in the *Eugenics Review* in an article by Brewer, '*Eutelegenesis*'' (January, 1936), and in H. J. Muller's eugenic philosophy based on Marxism, *Out of the Night* (Vanguard Press, New York). *Cf.* also Professor Julian Huxley, *Eugenics Review*, April, 1936, pp. 29 and 30.—Translator's Note.

sterilization; since the war of 1914–18 sterilization has been increasingly discussed and recommended in eugenic circles. The first specific law on the subject was passed in 1907, in the state of Indiana (U.S.A.), but promptly quashed, as "unconstitutional." However, the pioneering example of Indiana was followed (in 1909) by California. Under the Californian law, from its enactment till 1933, there have been 8,504 surgical sterilizations; the largest number of instances in any individual state. The other states supplying appreciable material for the investigation of the effects of sterilization are Kansas, Michigan, Oregon, Minnesota and Virginia; the number of cases in all, including the Californian, is 16,066. There have also been laws permitting sterilization in Alberta (1928) and British Columbia (1933), and some quite recent material from Europe. But we shall not go into details here, as all relevant facts are given in the Report of the Departmental Committee on Sterilization of December, 1933. (London, 1934, H.M. Stationery Office, Cmd. 4485.) This report gives so admirable and compact a summary of the problem that we cannot do better than refer to it.

9

The eugenic use of sterilization consists in the check on dysgenic, defective, diseased or dangerous heredity by possible future generations; such "minus-variants" or "sub-normals" would probably be unable to support themselves and might come into conflict with the law. They would thus be a partial or total burden on the community—in any case an undesirable circumstance.

At once we meet the moral and juridical objection that a compulsory surgical operation for the purpose of abolishing reproductive capacity is in contradiction to the bodily safety and integrity guaranteed to the citizens of civilized communities, e.g., it is directly opposed to the Offences against the Person Act of 1861 or to the Children and Young Persons Act of 1933, in Great Britain, and to Paragraph 224 of the German Penal Code, which has, however, been superseded or supplemented by the Hitlerist Law of 1933.

The juridical difficulty does not only apply to compulsory

sterilization. Even voluntary requests for the operation contravene conventional laws and customs, in so far as they are not specially provided for by " measures of exception." And such " measures of exception " can only be based on overwhelming scientific evidence, if they claim any scientific or biological sanctions. In comparing results from different countries we are at once confronted with the disadvantage " from the use of a vaguely descriptive terminology." This disadvantage " is increased by the fact that equally vague terms with a slightly different content are used in other countries. The term " oligophrenia " in use on the Continent is wider than the English term " mental defect " and includes cases which in England would be classed as " retarded " or " dull " (Report, p. 8). But it is possible to " strike an average " in estimating these differences of terminology. And on investigation we realize that our knowledge of inherited defect up to the present has been, and still is, extremely fragmentary and uncertain ; for " familial concentration alone should not be regarded as adequate proof that mental disease or defect have been transmitted by inheritance " (l.c., p. 11). Indeed—and this is a most significant admission—" It may be possible that in the light of future knowledge prevention will in some cases be effected by a modification of the environment " (l.c.). In these sober and exact statements we find the intellectual and civic responsibility of the best British tradition ; a favourable contrast to the levity with which German medicine has yielded to the commands and demands of Nazi sterilization mania.

These demands have been incorporated in the law for the prevention of hereditary disease in posterity, enacted on 14th July, 1933, and operative as from 1st January, 1934. This is the most drastic law as yet enacted on the subject. Persons will be considered as transmissibly diseased within the meaning of this act if they suffer from any one of the following :

1. Innate mental deficiency.
2. Schizophrenia.
3. Manic-depressive insanity.

4. Hereditary epilepsy.
5. Hereditary (Huntington's) chorea.
6. Hereditary blindness.
7. Hereditary deafness.
8. Severe hereditary physical abnormality.

Persons suffering from severe alcoholism may also be sterilized. The request for such procedure may be made by the patient or by his legal representative, or by a public body. Every lower court in Germany has an auxiliary court for the prevention of hereditary disease, which deals with such cases. It is interesting to note that this measure provides for the appointment of a special tribunal, consisting of a legal president and two medical members, one of whom is to be "specially competent in cases of hereditary diseases." The medical members of the court—this is without precedent in other sterilization laws—are not mere assessors, and as the decision is given by a majority vote, the doctors can outvote their legal colleague if they are in agreement. There is the Right of Appeal to a Higher Court, and the operation must be performed in a special hospital. The methods used are vasectomy in the case of males and salpingectomy in the case of females. Vasectomy consists in the division and ligature of the vas or duct, by which the spermatic fluid is conveyed from the testis. Salpingectomy consists in the removal of the whole or a part of the Fallopian tubes or oviducts which convey the ova from the ovaries to the uterus. In one European country, Denmark, the sterilization law allows castration, removal of the reproductive glands. But this law (enacted on 1st June, 1929) applies to "Persons whose abnormally developed sexual powers and tendencies predispose them to commit crimes and who become a danger to themselves and the general public" (Section 1). Therefore the Danish law is not primarily eugenic. Since 1935 Hitlerist Germany has special enactments, decreeing *castration* as the penalty for male homosexuality and exhibitionism.

Section XII of the German Law contains the crux of this social policy, in the following terms: "If the Court has finally decided on sterilization, it shall be carried out even against the will of the person to be sterilized, provided that the application did not originate with him alone. The medical official must request the police authorities to take the necessary measures. If other methods prove of no avail, the application of force is permissible." Both in English-speaking countries and in Scandinavia there have been severe and justified criticisms of this measure whose foundation is an ethnical and racial dogmatism expressed in Hitler's book *My Struggle*. According to this dogma, intricate problems of race and inheritance are not problems, but simple exercises in black and white ; Aryans and non-Aryans, Nordics and the rest. Under the law of 1st January, 1934, people are sterilized right and left, voluntarily and compulsorily, without any reliable records of these extremely significant operations. It would seem that both the individuals sterilized and the officials who sterilize them have an interest in concealing facts from public cognizance. There is a small but impressive omission in the 1936 edition of the great German Dictionary *Brockhaus*, Vol. 21. The word " sterilisierung " does not appear !

The objective and moderate pronouncements of the British " Brock Report " prove the complexity of human inheritance and social environment and the need for far more detachment and reserve than contemporary Germany has given to this matter. Thus the Report states that " The supposed abnormal fertility of defectives is in our view largely mythical " (*l.c.*, p. 18). Moreover, " the mortality rate among defectives and the offspring of defective stocks is abnormally high " : 22·5 per cent.—between one-quarter and one-fifth—of their children die ! " This high rate is doubtless due in some measure to the poor environment in which many defectives live and to their inability to take proper care of their children " (*l.c.*, p. 16). But there is undoubtedly a correlation between mental defect and inherent poor physique. What a warning against rash judgments and drastic mutilations is conveyed by the wise recognition that " The distinction between mental defect and retardation cannot always be made until the later years of adolescence." Note further that : " first children are more frequently subnormal than are later children in the same families " (p. 16). The exact mechanism of transmission is still largely unknown : " Heredity plays a large part in the causation of mental disorders, though except in the case of Huntington's chorea and myoclonus epilepsy, which are both rare types, there is no conclusive evidence that the transmission follows Mendelian ratios " (*l.c.*, p. 27). Voluntary sterilization may be eugenically defended and advocated in our present stage of genetic knowledge. Unfavourable results have not been noticed either in the United States of America or in the Swiss Cantons, which permit sterilization by request in certain more or less restricted conditions.

Thus the British Brock Report affirms that " We know that mentally defective and mentally disordered parents are, as a class, unable to discharge their social and economic liabilities or create an environment favourable to the upbringing of children, and there is reason to believe that sterilization would in some cases be welcomed by the patients themselves. This knowledge is in our view sufficient, and more than sufficient, to justify allowing and even encouraging mentally defective and mentally disordered patients to adopt the only certain method of preventing procreation. In this view, as in all our recommendations, we are unanimous, and we record it with a full sense of our responsibility." And again : " The case for legalizing sterilization rests upon the broad principle that no person, unless conscience bids, ought to be forced to choose between the alternative of complete abstinence from sexual activity or of risking bringing into the world children whose disabilities will make them a burden to themselves and society. If this principle is sound, to limit legislation to a particular class is neither logical nor equitable. We feel strongly that to impose any such arbitrary limitation will go far to defeat the object of the measure we advocate. Any measure which limits sterilization to mental cases will carry with it a stigma, much as certification does now " (pp. 39–40).

The decisive factor here is subjective and psychological ; the conclusions reached by the British experts are equally far removed from the mystical dogmatism of Catholic custom and from the militarist dogmatism of Nazi Germany. The sterilization mania—for it is nothing less—in the latter country is founded on what are assumed to be " objective " and scientific facts, and aims at the preservation of " racial integrity and purity of blood." Let us cite only one example, among many, of this " objective " attitude as it works out in actual fact. *Die Neue Weltbühne*, Prague, April 30th, 1936, has the following news item : " In Sommerau, near Reichenau in Saxony, a workman lost his left foot in a severe accident in the course of his employment. On leaving the hospital, the relevant office at Bautzen informed him that *he must be sterilized*, as his limited earning capacity made it impossible for him to support a family. The operation was performed forcibly, and the workman hanged himself three days afterwards." Professor Gauss, in Wuerzburg, believes that the average mortality amongst all women who are subjected to sterilization is about 5 per cent. About 28,000 women were certified for sterilization in 1934, so that, according to Professor Gauss' reckoning, about 1,400 died of the effects (*cf. Münchn. Med. Wschr.*, 1935, No. 3, and " Race Preservation in Germany," *Manch. Guard. Weekly*, June 5th, 1936).

It is justifiable and appropriate to include sterilization in our chapter on the Sex Education and Consultation Centre because the consultant is frequently asked how far sterilization is advisable as a method of " Birth Control " quite apart from eugenic considerations.

We may recall the famous case of Professor Schmerz of Graz, who performed 300 vasectomies on working-class patients, before the inauguration of Clericalist dictatorship in Austria, and was almost worshipped by his patients as a leader and friend. There is no record of psychological disturbances or disabilities following the vasectomies in Graz, or in any other state with humane and rational laws in this respect. Of course, Schmerz was brought into court for inflicting grievous bodily injury, for in a Catholic State no circumstances are held in public to justify sterilization even under the best medical auspices ! In 1931 Schmerz was imprisoned. In July, 1933, the second " Sterilization case " was heard at Graz, and twenty-one doctors were acquitted. But after the establishment of the present Clericalist *régime* in Austria the public prosecutor demanded that the case be reheard. As a result, on May 7th, 1934, the doctors in question and their literary protagonist and defender, Peter Ramus, received heavy sentences. Our readers will hardly suppose or impute any sympathy with Catholic dogma in the author of this summary ; but—quite independently of Canon Law and Papal encyclicals—I should only recommend sterilization in cases which showed both eugenic and social indications. In all other circumstances, contraceptive instruction carefully and individually adapted is to be recommended, although there are contraceptive limitations and problems which we shall proceed to consider. Before dealing with these, however, there are a few general results worthy of mention, arising from the work of Consultation Centres up to the present day.

10

Sex Education and Consultation Centres on the lines indicated in this book have been at work in Germany, Austria, Scandinavia and Switzerland. In Western Europe this particular sexological philanthropy and service has not been developed on any large scale [1] although individual medical practitioners do give enlightenment privately. In the English-speaking countries and in Holland, social service in sexual matters is limited to the organization of Birth Control facilities—apart from the legal and psychological pioneering to which we have already referred.

The latest political developments in Germany have crushed the work of scientific sex education and advice for working people ; although it appears that the " Union for Proletarian Sexual Reform and Maternity Protection " is still in being— our authority for this statement is a document issued by the Gestapo on the 3rd December, 1935. The Union was

---

[1] Although a beginning has been made at the Sex Education Centre founded in 1929 by Mrs. Janet Chance at the Century Theatre, Notting Hill, London, W., and at the quite recent Sex Education Centre under the direction of Dr. Edward Griffith, of Lindum House, Aldershot.—Translator's Note.

the most consistent and radical of all the non-medical associations for sexual reform in Germany and was able to make propaganda for contraceptives, even after the Nazi coup, as the Gestapo document complained. " Members of Marxist Leagues for sexual purposes and associations of that description are to be kept under observation and current reports are to be kept up to date." It may be supposed that the Proletarian Union has managed to survive under conditions of extreme danger and difficulty. In the Scandinavian states the work begun in Germany is being legally and publicly continued, with the advantage of the lessons gathered from previous experience. As this work may be undertaken on a large scale in English-speaking countrieṣ, it may be of some use to summarize the lessons of experience.

Whether the Consultations are arranged by private individuals or organizations, it is necessary that there should be at least two rooms in the available premises. One of these is the waiting room, the other for purposes of consultation. There is also an irreducible minimum of personnel : a medical practitioner and a social worker, whether colleague or secretary, to receive and register callers. Those in charge of each Centre should take trouble to rouse the interest and secure the co-operation of social workers, lawyers and economists, in order that possible enquiries from the patients may be answered by qualified experts who have their welfare at heart. For this work has ramifications throughout our financial and social fabric to-day : in the course of a consultation on possible pregnancy, whether desired or the reverse ; or on some defect of genital potency—with which the medical practitioner is quite competent to deal, the patient may point out that conditions of employment or marriage make it impossible to take the most direct way to recovery, and thus it becomes necessary to seek expert information there as well. In general, however, we must admit that the initiator of the work of a Sex Education Centre needs a knowledge of facts and a range of human sympathy far beyond what convention regards as the sphere of orthodox medicine.

It is, of course, possible to diagnose, advise and treat the same individual case on different premises ; but this is not altogether desirable if it can be avoided, although there are no substantial objections when medical practitioner, social worker and legal expert are in harmony. But it is a main requisite, both in principle and in practice, that there shall be prompt and competent " follow-up " procedure, when patients neglect to attend regularly for treatment, to their own detriment. This can be provided when the Sex Advice Centre works in conjunction with a Welfare Department of some philanthropic or provident institution, and thus has a right to the use of the funds of such an institution as well as access to its files.

There are immense practical advantages in such interaction of social service. But—no rose without some thorn !—Local, Municipal and Provident or Insurance Services are *ipso facto* part of the present social order, and dependent on public opinion for their life-blood. But the Consultant who is a genuine expert in sexual matters is forced to give expression to facts and rights which traditional moral codes either ignore or oppose. The greater the official influence and equipment behind a Consultation Centre, the stronger the tendency to give precedence to " morality " over sexual facts. There was a striking example of this inherent incompatibility in the recent history of the German and Austrian religious Associations, Catholic and Protestant, for purposes of education and social service. Their first attitude towards demands for sexual enlightenment was the most naïve and negative imaginable : how could they tolerate such abominations in a Christian Land ! But a large percentage of the working and middle classes expressed their approval of the innovation and attended the Centres. So the counterstroke followed : rival Centres were founded, under the direction of clerics or Committees chosen by Churchwomen. By 1933 the Roman Catholics had no less than fifty " Marriage Advice Centres " in Germany alone ; but these Marriage Advice Centres, like their Lutheran and Evangelical analogues, did not give any medical, physiological or psychological advice or instruction to those seeking their aid.

They confined themselves to the exhortations, the menaces and the platitudes of tradition.

The struggles to impart any adequate information or help in small towns and villages were memorable, and full of pitfalls. It may be taken as axiomatic that, in the present climate of public knowledge and honesty in these matters, the foundation of Sex Advice Centres in towns of less than 15,000 inhabitants is " Love's Labour Lost ! " Times and places of consultations would soon be public property in these small towns and every woman—if not every prospective patient—would fear to visit or even enquire after the sinister locality ! For if she had been observed in or near those premises at such and such an hour, all her neighbours and " friends " would soon be apprised of the fact, and why should she have been there if not on some business connected with—*horribile dictu*—Sex ? Sophisticated persons, with the immunities and opportunities that wealth and leisure and culture give, may smile at such preposterous paltriness. Granted : it is preposterous and paltry ; but it is a tragic and frequent psychological situation. In small towns and villages, sexual enlightenment and help can only be imparted in the discreet and private talks with individual medical and legal experts, within their usual office hours. For then, " professional secrecy," which convention accepts, offers protection against gossip and the malice of small minds.

At one time there was in my possession a dossier containing the addresses of all progressive and humanitarian medical practitioners, midwives, lawyers and social workers in all German or German-speaking regions. This information was of value to many suffering men and women, especially outside the larger towns and in Catholic districts. Fortunately I was able to destroy these lists before the burning Reichstag Buildings gave the signal for the terror still enthroned in Central Europe ! The police officials who broke into my house with a posse of twenty stalwarts, on the night of February 28th, 1933, had hoped to find enough incriminating material to " collar " thousands of progressive workers. They found—only myself : and that was far from pleasant ! But at least the quiet work of the experts in country places was not handed over to destruction. The workers remained unnamed, and their work in many cases may still continue in the shelter of anonymity.

BIBLIOGRAPHY

CALVERTON, V. D., SCHMALHAUSEN, S. D., *Sex in Civilisation*, London, 1929.

COSTLER, HAIRE, WILLY, *An Encyclopædia of Sexual Knowledge*, London, 1934.

DICKINSON, R. L., *Human Sex Anatomy*, New York, 1933.

ELKAN, R. E., " Über die Orgasmus-Unfähigkeit der Frau," *Arch. f. Frauenkunde*, Leipzig, 1933, Vol. XIX. English edition in the Press.

EVANG, K., *Tidsskrift for seksuell oplysning*, 1932–34, Oslo.

GODWIN, W., *An Enquiry concerning Political Justice*, 1793.

GRIFFITH, E. F., *Modern Marriage*, London, 1935.

GUETT, A., " Bevölkerungspolitik als Aufgabe des Staates," *Kongr. f. Bevölk. Politik*, Berlin, August, 1935.

HODANN, M., *Sexualelend und Sexualberatung, Patientenbriefe*, Berlin, 1928.

HODANN, M., *Amour et Sexualité*, Paris, 1933.

HODANN, M., *Geschlecht und Liebe*, Zürich, 1935.

KOPP, M. E., " Development of Marriage Consultative Centres as a New Field of Social Medicine," *Amer. Journ. Obst. Gyn.*, St. Louis, 1933, XXVI.

KRAUS, F., *Klinische Syzygiologie*, Leipzig, 1926.

LEHFELD, H., " Laienorganisation für Geburtenregelung," *Arch. Bev. Pol. Sexualethik and Famil. Kunde*, Berlin, 1931.

LEUNBACH, J. H., *Kvinder i nöd, breve til en læge*, Copenhagen, 1932.

LEUNBACH, J. H., *Könslivet og sundheden*, Copenhagen, 1935.

LINDSEY-EVANS, *The Revolt of Modern Youth*, London.

MARAÑÓN, G., *Evolution of Sex*, London, 1932.

MISCH, W. and K., " Die vegetative Genese der neurotischen Angst," *Nervenarzt*, 1932, No. 8.

MOENCH, C. L., " Studien zur Fertilität," *Zeitsch. f. Geburtshilfe and Gyn.*, Vol. 99, Stuttgart, 1931, Supplement.

NEISSER-SCHROETER, *Enquête über die Ehe- und Sexualberatungsstellen in Deutschland*, Berlin, 1928.

ODLUM, D. M., " Some Psychological Factors in Marriage," *Marr. Hygiene*, II, I, Bombay, 1935.

REICH, W., *Zeitsch. f. polit. Psychologie und Sexualökonomie*, Copenhagen, 1934 and 1935.

REICH, W., *Psychischer Kontakt und vegetative Strömung*, Copenhagen, 1935.

REICH, W., *Sexualität im Kulturkampf*, Copenhagen, 1936.
RUSSELL, B., *Marriage and Morals*, London, 1930.
SHAPIRO, B., " Neuere Gesichtspunkte zum Problem der Impotenz," *Med. Klinik*, 1927–31.
SHAPIRO, B., " Die Einteilung der Ejaculatio præcox," *Mediz. Welt.*, 1931, No. 38.
SCHEUMANN, F. K., *Eheberatung als Aufgabe der Kommunen*, Leipzig, 1932.
STONE, A. and H., *A Marriage Manual*, London, 1936.
STOPES, M., *Married Love*, London, 1918.
THOREK, *The Human Testis and its Diseases*, New York, 1924.
TOTIS, BÉLA, *Psychoanalyse und Gynäkologie*, Budapest, 1926.
VAN DE VELDE, *Ideal Marriage*, London, 1929.

TABLE OF EVENTS

1891 SCHALLMEYER recommends " Questionnaires on Biological Heredity."
1907 First Sterilization Law in the U.S.A.
1908 BREITFELD recommends pre-marital Certificates of Health.
1911 Eugenic Marriage Advice Centre opened in Dresden.
1919 First Sex Consultation Centre at the Institute for Sexual Science in Berlin.
1922 First public Sex Consultation Centre in Vienna.
1923 and years immediately following. Foundation of the lay Associations for Sexual Reform and Birth Control throughout Central Europe.
1926 VAN DE VELDE's *Vollkomene Ehe*. Simultaneous discussion in U.S.A. centring round B. Lindsey's *Companionate Marriage*.
      The Minister HIRTSIEFER tries to restrict Consultation Centres to Eugenics alone.
      SHAPIRO's chemical preparation " Testifortan."
1927 First attempt at a Sexual Sociology: HODANN's *Geschlecht und Liebe* (*Sex and Love*).
      First attempt at a Clinical Theory of the Orgasm : REICH's *Funktion des Orgasmus*.
1928 Sexual Consultations introduced into Scandinavian Countries following the W.L.S.R. Congress in Copenhagen.
1929 Three hundred workmen Sterilized by SCHMERZ, of Graz, as a method of Birth Control.
      Socialist Society for Sexual Consultation and Investigation founded in Vienna.
      Danish Castration Law for Criminals.
1931 MOENCH's monograph on Spermatozoa.   Professor SCHMERZ imprisoned.

1932 EVANG founds *Tidskrift for Sexuell upplysning* (*Periodical for Sexual Enlightenment*) in Oslo, with simultaneous editions in Stockholm and Copenhagen.
ELKAN'S paper before the Berlin Society for Sexual Research on the Orgasm in Woman.

1933 German Law of Compulsory Sterilization.
Riksförbund for seksuell upplysning (Swedish Sex Education Society founded under the direction of ELISE OTTESEN JENSEN).

1934 British Report on Sterilization (BROCK Report).

1935 REICH'S address on " Psychic Contact and Vegetative Current " at the Psycho-analytic Congress in Lucerne.

1936 British Labour Women's Conference demands Sterilization Law on lines of Brock Report.

CHAPTER V

THE HISTORY OF BIRTH CONTROL

I

BIRTH Control is a contribution of the English-speaking world to human knowledge and liberation. The term itself sprung from the active brain of Margaret Sanger, the courageous and far-sighted champion of the reform of current statutes in the U.S.A. In 1914 she coined this phrase, and since then " B.C. " has grown to imply a medical and social programme of world-wide scope.

And yet, strange to say, the *History of Medicine in the U.S.A.* which appeared in 1931, from the pen of Francis R. Packard, does not contain the words " Birth Control " on any of its 1266 pages ; nor in the index of medical terms ! Such is the remote sublimity of the professional mind, when confronted with a subject which has stirred the daily press throughout the U.S.A. and beyond the American frontiers from London to Tokyo. For Margaret Sanger is not a doctor of medicine, she is " only a nurse."

Yet American medicine has not always been so far from reality, before Margaret Sanger's work began Moses Harmann, a pioneer of social reform, championed the right of women to knowledge in his brave paper *Lucifer*. In 1906, when he was seventy-five years of age, he was condemned to break stones in Leavenworth Prison ! Then came Dr. William Robinson, who addressed his arguments mainly to doctors and " intellectuals " ; and in 1912 Dr. Abraham Jacobi roused a " sensation " throughout the States by dealing with contraception in his presidential address to the American Medical Association.

In her book *My Fight for Birth Control*, Margaret Sanger has depicted the growth of her personality and her life work. Years ago, as a nurse in the squalid tenements of New York's

East Side, she had the devastating and determining experience which we shall quote, for it is a profoundly typical human and medical experience, and not confined to the slums of any great city or of any powerful state :

" Mrs. Sack was only twenty-eight years old ; her husband an unskilled worker, thirty-two. Three children, aged five, three and one, were none too strong nor sturdy, and it took all the earnings of the father and the ingenuity of the mother to keep them clean, provide then with air and proper food, and give them a chance into decent manhood and womanhood.

" Both parents were devoted to these children and to each other. The woman had become pregnant and had taken various drugs and purgatives as advised by her neighbours. Then in desperation she had used some instrument lent to her by a friend. She was found prostrate on the floor amidst the crying children when her husband returned from work. Neighbours advised against the ambulance, and a friendly doctor was called. The husband would not hear of her going to a hospital and as a little money had been saved in the bank a nurse was called and the battle for that precious life began.

" It was in the middle of July. The three-room apartment was turned into a hospital for the dying patient. Never had I worked so fast, never so concentratedly as I did to keep alive that little mother. Neighbour women came and went during the day doing the odds and ends necessary for our comfort. The children were sent to friends and relatives and the doctor and I settled ourselves to outdo the force and power of an outraged nature.

" Never have I known such conditions could exist. July's sultry days and nights were melted into a torpid inferno. Day after day, night after night, I slept only in brief snatches, ever too anxious about the condition of that feeble heart bravely carrying on, to stay long from the bedside of the patient. With but one toilet for the building and that on the floor below, everything had to be carried down for disposal, while ice, food and other necessities had to be carried three flights up. It was one of these old airshaft buildings of which there were several thousands then standing in New York City.

" At the end of two weeks recovery was in sight, and at the end of three weeks I was preparing to leave the fragile patient to take up the ordinary duties of her life, including those of wifehood and motherhood. Everyone was congratulating her on her recovery. All the kindness of sympathetic and understanding neighbours poured in upon her in the shape of convalescent dishes, soups, custards and drinks. Still she appeared to be despondent and worried. She seemed to sit apart in her thought as if she had no part in these congratulatory messages and endearing welcomes. I thought at first that she still retained some of her unconscious memories and dwelt upon them in her silences.

" But as the hour for my departure came nearer, her anxiety increased, and finally, with trembling voice, she said : ' Another baby will finish me, I suppose.'

" ' It's too early to talk about that,' I said, and resolved that I would turn the question over to the doctor for his advice. When he came, I said : ' Mrs. Sacks is worried about having another baby.'

" ' She well might be,' replied the doctor, and then he stood before her and said : ' Any more such capers, young woman, and there will be no need to call me.'

" ' Yes, yes—I know, Doctor,' said the patient with trembling voice, ' but,' and she hesitated as if it took all of her courage to say it, ' what can I do to prevent getting that way again ? '

" ' Oh, ho ! ' laughed the doctor good-naturedly, ' you want your cake while you eat it too, do you ? Well, it can't be done.' Then, familiarly slapping her on the back and picking up his hat and bag to depart, he said : ' I'll tell you the only sure thing to do. Tell Jake to sleep on the roof ! '

" With those words he closed the door and went down the stairs, leaving us both petrified and stunned.

" Tears sprang to my eyes, and a lump came in my throat as I looked at that face before me. It was stamped with sheer horror. I thought for a moment she might have gone insane, but she conquered her feelings, whatever they may have

been, and turning to me in desperation said : ' He can't
understand, can he ?—he's a man after all—but you do,
don't you ? You're a woman and you'll tell me the secret
and I'll never tell it to a soul.'

" She clasped her hands as if in prayer, she leaned over
and looked straight into my eyes and beseechingly implored
me to tell something—something I really did not know.
It was like being in a rack and tortured for a crime one had
not committed. To plead guilty would stop the agony,
otherwise the rack kept turning.

" I had to turn away from that imploring face. I could not
answer her then. I quieted her as best I could. She saw that
I was moved by the tears in my eyes. I promised that I
would come back in a few days and tell her what she wanted
to know. The few simple means of limiting the family like
coitus interruptus or the condom were laughed at by the
neighbouring women when told these were the means used
by men in the well-to-do families. That was not believed,
and I knew such an answer would be swept aside as useless
were I to tell her this at such a time.

" A little later when she slept I left the house, and made up
my mind that I'd keep away from those cases in the future.
I felt helpless to do anything at all. I seemed chained hand
and foot and longed for an earthquake or a volcano to shake
the world out of its lethargy into facing these monstrous
atrocities.

" The intelligent reasoning of the young mother—how to
prevent getting that way again—how sensible, how just
she had been—yes, I promised myself I'd go back and have
a long talk with her and tell her more, and perhaps she
would not laugh but would believe that those methods
were all that were really known. But time flew past, and
weeks rolled into months. . . . I was about to retire one
night three months later when the telephone rang and an
agitated man's voice begged me to come at once to help
his wife, who was sick again. It was the husband of Mrs.
Sack, and I intuitively knew before I left the telephone that
it was almost useless to go.

" I dreaded to face that woman. I was tempted to send

someone else in my place. I longed for an accident on the subway, or on the street—anything to prevent my going into that home. But on I went just the same. I arrived a few minutes after the doctor, the same one who had given her such noble advice. The woman was dying. She was unconscious. She died within ten minutes after my arrival. It was the same result, the same story told a thousand times before—death from abortion. She had become pregnant, had used drugs, had then consulted a five-dollar professional abortionist, and death followed. The gentle woman, the devoted mother, the loving wife, had passed on, leaving behind her a frantic husband, helpless in his loneliness, bewildered in his helplessness as he paced up and down the room, hands clenching his head, moaning ' My God ! My God ! My God ! '

" The revolution came—but not as it has been pictured nor as history relates that revolutions have come. It came in my own life. It began in my very being as I walked home that night after I had closed the eyes and covered with a sheet the body of that little helpless mother whose life had been sacrificed to ignorance " (Sanger, *l.c.*, pp. 52 *ff*).

2

And Margaret Sanger's fight against ignorance began ; with enquiries from her—as a professional nurse—to the doctors in their professional capacity : what ought she to tell the women to do in such cases ? And the doctors did not know ! or they gave replies of the same description as the memorable practitioner who handed over Mrs. Sack to a death of torture. In France, Margaret Sanger had learnt the use of the " Wife's Pessary " invented by the great German healer and helper of women, Mensinga. She had formed friendship with the " génération consciente " group— Giroud, the Humberts, Nelly Roussel, Manuel Devaldès— for the anti-Birth Control Laws in France were only enacted in 1920. (The pessary, which had been invented in 1883, was introduced to the British public in 1887 by H. A. Allbutt, M.D., who was struck off the register by the General Medical Council in consequence !) At the beginning of 1914, on her first return to New York, Mrs. Sanger published a paper for proletarian wives and mothers: the *Woman Rebel*. At once there poured into her letter box a growing flood of correspondence; of women's agonies and appeals. And among them one fine day, an official communication with the stamp of the New York Post Office: "Dear Madam, You are hereby notified that the Solicitor of the Post Office Department has decided that the *Woman Rebel* for March, 1914, is unmailable under Section 489, Postal Laws and Regulations, (signed) E. M. Morgan, Postmaster."

The incriminating article dealt with the "Prevention of Conception," and was impounded under the Laws of 1873, known as the Comstock Laws, in memory of their instigator, the (as yet!) uncanonized Patron Saint of all the moral fanatics and sex-phobiacs from the Atlantic to the Pacific. In the disordered morbidities of Comstock's mind all mention of Sex was perilous to the sacred social order; and he became typical of the particular negative mental aberration from which he suffered. Bernard Shaw used the term "Comstockery" in 1905, and henceforward this word means any extremity of arrogant and perverted pseudo-Puritan hypocrisy. Even in the nineteenth century Comstock had been immortalized in caricature, but the letter and spirit of the law remained to stultify and destroy. Essays on the "prevention of conception" have been condemned and confiscated in the Land of Liberty long after 1914! For example, in January, 1935, 150 copies of a scientific monthly magazine, of most serious and responsible tone and with American and other contributors of the highest eminence—*Marriage Hygiene*—were despatched from Bombay, where it is published, to New York, for the purpose of distribution to editors of professional papers in the U.S.A. They never reached their destination. The American Customs held them up "under Section 305 of the Tariff Act of 1930, which prohibits the importation of obscene literature."

In September, 1914, Margaret Sanger was for the first time brought into court, on the charge of Birth Control propaganda. The case was postponed and the sentence quashed in 1916, as it was proved "that Mrs. Sanger was not a disorderly person." But there were endless legal complications. In 1914 Mrs. Sanger wrote a brief pamphlet, in clear and homely language for working women, entitled " Family Limitation." The vicissitudes of this pamphlet recall the most difficult propaganda efforts of revolutionaries in Tzarist Russia. " I took the manuscript to a printer well known for his liberal tendencies and courage. He read the contents page by page, turned deadly pale, and said : ' That can never be printed, Margaret. It's a Sing-Sing job.' I looked him straight in the eye and said : ' Well, what about it ? ' That question doubled him up. He stuttered something about having a family, and I replied that I had one too. Finally, after being goaded into shame and fury, he said that he did not believe in the damn thing and would not print it for a thousand dollars. I visited at least twenty printers within the next two weeks. No one would touch the job. I had to win the sympathy of some individual who would do the initial work, and trust the goods to do the rest. I am not at liberty to tell who did the work. The man is now a prominent leader in politics in another country. He did the linotype work after hours when his shop was supposed to be closed so that there would be no workers about to see him and his risky job. After that, there was still the question of printing, binding, and storing, all of which was accomplished by individuals of five nationalities over a period of three months, despite the careful watching of Uncle Sam " (Sanger, *l.c.*, p. 84).[1]

In 1915 (during Margaret's European tour to raise sympathy and funds), William Sanger, her husband, was entrapped into giving a copy of this pamphlet to a police spy ; he was arrested, put on trial and condemned to a month in prison. In November, 1915, the National Birth Control League of America was founded, next year the sentence pronounced in 1914 was annulled, but Margaret Sanger's propaganda had redoubled in the interval. On October 16th, 1916, she opened the first Birth Control Clinic in the U.S.A.,

---

[1] Many copies were posted from Great Britain, from addresses all over the country, by Margaret Sanger's sympathizers and supporters.— Translator's Note.

collaborating in its management with Fania Mindell, an interpreter, and her own sister, Mrs. Ethel Byrne. A female police spy visited the Clinic, received help as a patient and led the police to the premises. All three women were arrested, and the same fate befell Kitty Marion (who had already proved her courage in the British Suffrage movement) and who was seized by the indefatigable New York police as she distributed handbills on Birth Control. Ethel Byrne started a hunger-strike in prison, was forcibly fed after 103 hours, but held out for eleven days ; then she collapsed, and was released, almost at death's door. The Clinic was closed. The criticisms of the New York *Globe* after the annulled sentence of 1914 had been proved substantially correct :

" The quashing of the indictment settles nothing. The right of American citizens to discuss sociological questions according to their convictions is just where it was before—subject to the mutton-headed restrictions of some post office clerk and the complaisant persecution of a federal district attorney." In 1917 Margaret Sanger was imprisoned for a month for opening and running the Clinic. But in 1918 the New York State Court of Appeal made the majestic decision that medical men and women might lawfully give information to the laity about the prevention of conception : " for the protecting of health and the prevention of disease."

3

The New York Birth Control Clinic had been founded following on suggestions and support from England and Holland, where Margaret Sanger met distinguished and decisive adherents. Among them we may mention Havelock Ellis, Edward Carpenter, H. G. Wells, Professor Gilbert Murray and the Drysdale family, the standard bearers of the Neo-Malthusian philosophy, which is still the theoretical and intellectual background of British Birth Control. The Neo-Malthusian movement began with a sensational law suit, under remarkable circumstances, which are curiously parallel to those of the Sanger case in some respects and are among the crucial events of the nineteenth century.

In 1867 the Freethought Press issued a new edition of
the pamphlet *Fruits of Philosophy*, originally written by the
American Dr. Knowlton of Boston, Massachusetts, as early
as 1833. It contained directions as to how to apply such
knowledge of contraception as was then available. A Bristol
bookseller had inserted illustrations which were regarded
as transgressing decency, the book was confiscated, and both
publisher and retailer indicted. The social reformers and
indefatigable Rationalist agitators Charles Bradlaugh and
Annie Besant undertook a public protest against the attack
on freedom of discussion of population problems. They
reprinted the pamphlet afresh and informed the police that
they proposed to sell it to the public at a certain date and
place. The authorities acted promptly and thus great
publicity was secured for the legal proceedings which ensued.
On July 26th, 1927, the fiftieth anniversary of this memorable
trial was celebrated by a meeting, a Commemorative dinner
and significant speeches. The guest of the evening, *par
excellence*, was the octogenarian Annie Besant, who stated
the motives which had inspired Bradlaugh and herself, in
these terms : " We did not like the book, to speak quite
frankly. We did not say so then, but I say it now. It
was a very poor little book on the whole . . . but it
represented a great principle, the right to discuss the population question in order to do away with the poverty of the
people."
    The attitude taken by the Solicitor-General in 1877 is
unfortunately less obsolete to-day than we might wish.
Before stigmatizing Knowlton's pamphlet as " a dirty,
filthy book " he gave proof of his typically Victorian prejudices in words which remain psychological documents.
" I will point out one of the passages which, I think, evidently
not only shows the object of the writer but illustrates the
mischief and evil that the work is liable to produce. It is
really extremely painful to me (hesitating), very painful, to
have to read this. At page thirty-eight you will find . . .
(here the S.-G. read to the end of the chapter). Gentlemen, I
have read the whole of that, and I assure you that it has
been with extreme pain that I have found myself compelled

to read it." Incredible ? !—but "*plus ça change plus c'est
la même chose.*" On October 16th of the year 1935
proceedings were taken at the Westminster Police Court
against Mr. Edward Charles on account of his book *The
Sexual Impulse.* The magistrate, referring to three verses,
two of which were quotations from Aldous Huxley's
Brave New World, demanded to know whether one of the
expert witnesses, Janet Chance, the writer and director of
the first British Sex Education Centre, " considered them
fit and decent for people of the working class to read ? "
Mrs. Chance replied unhesitatingly " Yes." The magistrate
rejoined : " Then I will read them." (After a pause)
" No, I won't read them, I don't think they are fit to be
read " (*Evening Standard,* October 16th, 1935). Is there
not a remarkable similarity here, across the gulf of six
decades of " progress ? "

The particular aspect of the Bradlaugh-Besant agitation
which roused the representatives of " Law and Order "
to action, was, to quote the Solicitor-General, " that the
object of the whole book, the scope of this book, is to permit
people, independent from marriage, to gratify their passions,
independently from the checks which nature and Providence
have interposed." " It is a fact, universally admitted, that
unmarried females do not enjoy so much good health and
attain to so great an age as the married. What is the
inference from that ? Here are the means by which the
unmarried female may gratify her passions " (The Queen
versus Bradlaugh, p. 21). On October 1st, 1935, in the
course of the Charles trial, the magistrate asked the well-
known and eloquent woman preacher and Doctor of Divinity
Maude Royden : " In the case of unmarried people, don't
you think it is suggestive ? " Yes—fifty-eight years do not
mean much, in historical perspectives ! The inherent
fixations of an unbiological sexual system are stronger than
any of the pleas for social justice and convenience, so
incomparably voiced by Bradlaugh in the speech for his
own defence :

" It is said that this pamphlet tries to defend immorality.
You must contradict every page of it, ignore every word in

it, to warrant this assumption. You may say it is very unfair, for example, that the agricultural labourer should have children to burden the poor-rate. But put yourself in the position of the agricultural labourers. They have not the training and education that you have, and sometimes mere sexual gratification is the only pleasure of their lives. They cannot read Virgil ; they cannot read Dante. They cannot listen to Beethoven ; they cannot listen to Handel. . . . They have not time occasionally to run across the Alps. They have no opportunity of finding recreation in the Pyrenees. They cannot yacht in the North Sea. They cannot fish for salmon at New Brunswick or St. Johns. They are limited to their narrow parish bound, and their bound is only the work, the home, the beerhouse, the poor house, and the grave. We want to make them more comfortable and you tell us we are immoral. We want to prevent them bringing into the world little children to suck death, instead of life, at the breasts of their mother ; and you tell us we are immoral. I should not say that, perhaps, for you, gentlemen, may judge things differently from myself; but I know the poor. I belong to them, I was born amongst them . . . I plead here simply for the class to which I belong, and for the right to tell them what may redeem their poverty and alleviate their misery " (Queen v. Bradlaugh, p. 213).

Surely there has seldom been any nobler or wiser statement of the case for population control and social reform conjoined. Bradlaugh used, as Knowlton did, the theoretical basis of Malthus' famous argument which appeared first of all in 1798 and then more explicitly in his *Essay on the Principle of Population* in 1803. Malthus wrote : " The cause to which I allude is the constant tendency in all animated life to increase beyond the nourishment prepared for it." In this circumstance, Malthus beheld the main force " which has hitherto impeded the progress of mankind towards happiness " and also the point of departure for investigation " to examine the probability of the total or partial removal of these causes in future." Malthus was a clergyman of the Established Church of England, and consistently advocated late marriage and "moral restraint" till such marriage became economically safe. The more realistic Neo-Malthusians advocate Birth Control by means of contraception, as was definitely stated in their first anonymous pamphlet, the so-called "Diabolical Handbill," first circulated in Manchester in 1822. Its authorship is ascribed to Francis Place. In 1830 Robert Dale Owen presented the case for contraception in New York, in his work on *Moral Physiology*. He was the American Minister to France, and in 1831 the French birth-rate began to drop. In 1833 Knowlton's little manual appeared, and its re-issue in the latter half of the last century led to the legal and moral *cause célèbre* of 1877.

The most eloquent scientific advocate of this new tendency and new technique was Dr. George Drysdale. In 1854 he wrote and published his *Elements of Social Science*, the first complete presentation of contraception from the economic, philosophic and medical standpoints. Naturally and justly he became President of the newly formed Malthusian League, which began its active and honourable career on July 26th, 1877. Annie Besant was its first secretary. In the year of the great trial, 185,000 copies of Knowlton's pamphlet were sold, and 175,000 of Annie Besant's new manual, *The Law of Population*. At the Jubilee Anniversary Dinner in 1927, H. G. Wells made this estimate of the achievements of the Neo-Malthusian pioneers : " The trial marks an epoch in the history of mankind. For the first time we see human beings lay courageous hands upon their biological destiny. It is exactly fifty years ago that our League was founded and it inaugurated the greatest revolution in the whole history of human life, because for the first time we have the prospect of species escaping from the pressure of population, that is to say, from the grip of the struggle for existence that has hitherto controlled the whole biological process since it began."

Charles Darwin and Herbert Spencer greeted the new doctrines, though with some reserve. Neo-Malthusianism had started on the path to victory.

4

In 1881 the Nieuw Malthusiaansche Bund was founded in Holland. Although it had thirty-five " passive members " —or one might almost say " sleeping partners "—among the medical profession, only two, Dr. De Rooy and the first woman doctor of the Netherlands, Dr. Aletta Jacobs, ventured to advocate their aims and views in public. In 1882 Aletta Jacobs captured Trade Union help and started weekly consultations for working-class wives and mothers ; and as soon as Mensinga's pessary was patented and accessible, she gave contraceptive instruction as well as other much needed information on human health. In 1890 the League became responsible for the premises necessary for the increased attendance and thus the first Birth Control Clinic in the world began its beneficent work.

In spite of clerical opposition, the League received royal sanction in 1895, and in 1900 Dr. T. Rutgers became its Director in Chief. He founded the Birth Control Clinic at Rotterdam and in 1901 began to give theoretical and practical instruction to " competent assistants," often quite poor working women, daughters of the people, well acquainted with the realities of the workers' lives, who proceeded to give help on these lines in the provinces. This whole system anticipated the laymen's associations for sexual reform which appeared in Germany twenty years later. Unfortunately, however, as in so many enterprises of the Left, there was a " split." Some of the workers in the Dutch League disapproved of any recourse to lay help and Dr. Jacobs was among these. Simultaneously there was an intensification of Catholic propaganda ; the lay assistants were constantly represented as baby-farmers and quack abortionists. In 1904 the first clericalist Ministry of the Kingdom of the Netherlands attempted to penalize the League's work ; they failed then, but succeeded seven years later, following a large majority of Catholics in both Parliament and Administration. In 1911 Article 451 of the Penal Code was altered, and all practical propaganda for contraception was threatened with two months in prison and at least 100 gulden in fines. Since 1918 clericalist elements have been an integral part of Dutch Governments and their attacks have grown fiercer. The royal sanction was withdrawn in 1925, meetings were forbidden, Halls of Assembly refused, etc.

In 1924 Dr. Rutgers died, and in 1928 Dr. Premsela took over the helm. Under his vigorous direction, and in spite of cold-shouldering and petty persecution, the Aletta Jacobs Huis was opened in 1931. This institution provides Amsterdam with a Birth Control Clinic and a Sex Consultation Centre, fully equipped on Central European lines. In spite of the hostile propaganda of the Catholic " League of Large Families," individual Catholic women began to attend the Sex Consultation Centre in steadily growing numbers. Their enquiries are mainly focused on Birth Control; contraceptive technique forms the theme of six consultations out of every eight, according to Van Emde-Boas.

5

The father of French Neo-Malthusianism was Paul Robin, who lived from 1837 to 1912. He was a most forceful personality with an incessantly active, independent mind; he was a Darwinian, but at one time a Positivist ; an adherent of the First Socialist International, and in his educational profession constantly at loggerheads with his chiefs. He left his native land for London as a refugee after a political trial in 1872 ; in England he read Darwin's *Origin of Species* and Malthus' *Essay on Population*, and sought to win adherents for Neo-Malthusianism among the Marxian Socialists and Bakuninian Anarchists who were his fellow-exiles. He was offered and accepted the post of Professor of Mathematics at University College, and from that vantage point he addressed a Memorandum to the Socialist Congress in Marseilles in 1879, on behalf of the Malthusian League. " If we refuse to admit the necessity of restricting population, we are, in advance, sterilizing all reform and every revolution." Ferdinand Buisson invited him to return to France, where he became Director in charge of the Orphanage of Cempuies. There he became the pioneer of another crucial reform, co-education. In 1896 he founded the " *Ligue de la régénération humaine,"* and his Birth Control pamphlets and leaflets attained a circulation of 100,000 copies. In 1897 the Freethinkers' Conference refused to pass his Birth Control resolution, and in the following year he lost his post on account of his irreligious views. He went to New Zealand, but even in the antipodes he yearned for the fray against what he termed *" la prêtaille, la jugeaille et la soldatesque "*—in other words, the priestly, judicial and military castes. In 1899 France received him once more and in 1900 he succeeded in organizing the first International Neo-Malthusian Congress. This was held in Paris, and Dr. Charles Drysdale, brother of George Drysdale, was in the chair. His collaboration with G. Hardy (Giroud), Eugène Humbert and Dr. Klotz Forest so stimulated the movement in France that the re-populationists became alarmed and active " big-family " propaganda began. The Malthusian organization became divided and in 1908 Neo-Malthusian pamphlets were included in a new definition of obscene literature. The newspapers rejoiced and the professional moralists were delighted with their success in having an apostle convicted of pornography. Robin sustained a painful accident which destroyed his left eye. On August 31st, 1912, he committed suicide, though life lingered in his iron frame till the following day.

The war of 1914–18 was a forcing house for Nationalism in France as elsewhere. On July 31st, 1920, the Bill drafted by the Senator Lamarzelle and the Député M. Ignace became the Law of France. The country had lost heavily in man power during the war, and for the last ten years has been forced to import foreign labour, principally Italian and Polish. By the law of 1920, any act or attempted act which might in any way facilitate the reduction of the birth-rate if committed for the purpose of such reduction, was made illegal and punishable by one to six months' imprisonment and a fine of not less than 100 and not more than 5,000 francs.

Such Societies as *l'Alliance Nationale pour l'Accroissement de la Population française* and *le Conseil Supérieur de la Natalité* endeavour to counteract the trend towards limitation by means of agitation for further penalties as well as money prizes and concessions for large families. Their efforts are not successful, for coitus interruptus cannot be extirpated and " French letters " are obtainable by Frenchmen for prophylaxis against venereal diseases. The only effect of these restrictions is therefore to cast obstacles in the way of progressive and preventive medical technique. And there is already an audible opposition with both medical and political support. In 1931 *l'Association d'études sexologiques* was founded, under the chairmanship of Dr. Toulouse ; in February, 1933, the Deputy M. Quenin put forward a bill in the Chamber, which would have amended Article 3 in the Law of 1920, and legalized written or spoken propaganda for contraception once more. The Draft in question is No. 1384, and was presented at the Second Session of the 9th of February, 1933. In November of the same year, there was issued the first number of a quarterly periodical *Le Problème Sexuel*, the organ of modernist French opinion on sex questions. The Editress is Mme. B. Albrecht. Finally there has been a detailed and comprehensive draft for possible legislation " for the socially organized protection of Mothers and Children," dealing at length with contraceptive theory, which is at present the basis for discussion in France. This is the so-called " Lex Clamamus " (Parliamentary Document No. 1705, March 31st, 1933, Second Session).

6

Early in its career of active propaganda the British Malthusian League formed groups of adherents outside English-speaking countries. These groups were mainly medical, there were members in Amsterdam, Athens, Madrid, Naples, Paris, St. Petersburg, New York, and in various Indian cities, such as Shibtola and Pudukota. At the Congress organized by Robin and Drysdale in 1900, the League was formally internationalized. Between 1900 and 1913 offshoots sprung up in Bohemia, Spain, Belgium, Cuba, Switzerland, Portugal, Hungary, Sweden and Italy. Their Fourth International Congress was held in Dresden, in association with the Medical and Hygienic Exposition of 1911, and addressed a resolution to the Governments of the world, setting forth the aims of Neo-Malthusianism and the interaction between poverty, unemployment and over-population, on the lines traced in the *Principles of Population*. A more helpful and realistic result of the Congress was the issue of a pamphlet of practical advice on contraception by the Italian *savant*, Professor Luigi Berta, of Turin University. This pamphlet was prosecuted by the League of Public Morality, but the case ended in a victory for Berta and Birth Control ; the best brains of an Italy that still believed in liberty and justice aided his defence, and the next Conference was booked for Turin—when the war came down on Europe. In 1925 Mussolini expressly repudiated B. C. and later a law was passed against it. Following this law, married couples visiting Italy on their honeymoon, or at other times, have the curious experience of a search through their luggage by Italian customs officials for preventive appliances or preparations, which are confiscated if found.

Meanwhile, the British Malthusians had become aware of the " differential birth rate." The well-to-do limited their families, but the poorer and more ignorant sections of the wage-earners had less access than any other circles to this knowledge. So in 1913 Open Air Meetings, in Southwark, were held by the Drysdales and their co-workers, and nearly 12,000 copies of a " practical tract " were distributed. But Birth Control remained essentially " a middle-class demand " ; even in the arresting and appalling pages of *Maternity*, published in 1916 by the Women's Co-operative Guild, there is practically no mention of Birth Control as a solution, although the book shows the actual experience of women in working-class districts.

The war was a turning point. In 1918 the well-known authority on palæo-botany, Marie Stopes, D.Sc., published her book *Married Love*. Of this, Havelock Ellis remarked that it " seems to represent the most notable advance made during recent years in the knowledge of women's psycho-physiological life." It was promptly debarred from cir-culation in America as " an obscene book ! " but throughout

Britain and the English-speaking Dominions its success and influence have been enormous. " In emphasizing the value of a harmonious sex life to married couples, the right of women to happy motherhood, and the right of children to be wanted and loved, Dr. Stopes gave a new aspect to the B. C. movement which proved more popular than the exposition of the doctrines of Malthus " (How Martyn, 1930, p. 14).

In March, 1921, the first British Birth Control Clinic was founded by Marie Stopes, in London, and in May of the same year she held a propaganda meeting in support of Movement and Clinic which was an outstanding success for " Constructive Birth Control." A few months later the Malthusian League established a Centre at Walworth in South London. This centre became the focus of an international organization and under the indefatigable and devoted efforts of Mrs. Evelyn Graham Murray and Mrs. Evelyn Fuller it not only helped thousands, but became the parent of all the Clinics and Centres of the Society for the Provision of Birth Control Clinics (1923).

British Protestant opinion accepted Birth Control in the main as a " fit subject for discussion " after Lord Dawson of Penn, the King's Physician, delivered a speech to the Church Congress at Birmingham on " Sexual Relationships." This distinguished leader of medicine in Great Britain attacked the priestly doctrine "that marriage was instituted to prevent sin " and " that sexual intercourse should rightly take place only for the purpose of procreation." He did not hesitate to say " They ask for bread, you give them a stone."

In 1923 and 1924 there were two significant cases in London courts. One was a libel suit, brought by Marie Stopes against the Catholic medical man, Dr. Halliday Sutherland, for stating in a book that methods advised in the Clinic she had founded and conducted were "dangerous and harmful." The suit aroused tremendous interest and gave Dr. Stopes the opportunity of stating her case and of bringing to public attention both sides of this burning question. In March, 1923, the jury's verdict awarded one hundred pounds to Dr. Stopes, but the House of Lords reversed the decision on December 21st. The other trial was the prosecution of Guy and Rose Aldred for publishing Margaret Sanger's pamphlet *Family Limitation*, " the same work which was simultaneously being distributed by the Government of Yucatan, in the Republic of Mexico, to couples about to marry " (Sanger, *l.c.*, p. 262).

In 1920 Margaret Sanger had reopened her New York Clinic, and at the same time an independent organization, the Voluntary Parenthood League, with Mrs. Mary Ware Dennett as its Secretary, was formed in order to repeal the Federal laws against Birth Control in the U.S.A. Next year saw the inception of the American Birth Control League, which held its first Conference in New York in November of its first year. There was a public meeting at the Town Hall, which was interrupted by the police, following the interference of the Roman Catholic Archbishop. The Hall was cleared and Mrs. Sanger again arrested. In her own words : " At the thought of this official impertinence, this bullying, this arrogant dictatorship, this insolence of a Roman Catholic Archbishop, my resistance, my resolution became set " (*l.c.*, p. 206). Persecution seemed to keep pace with organization and propaganda. In 1923 the Birth Control Research Committee was founded, and in 1926 this was enlarged to form the Clinical Bureau, with Dr. Hannah Stone as chief officer. In March and April, 1929, the Clinic gave instructions and appliances to a supposed patient, Mrs. Sullivan ; she proved to be an *agent provocatrice* of the New York police, who were then under the most reactionary Catholic dictatorship. On April 15th the police again invaded the premises consecrated to the help of poor women, and arrested Dr. Stone, Dr. Pissoort and three nurses, behaving with unparalleled insolence and aggressiveness. On the 19th came the preliminary proceedings and the court was cleared. " A day after Mrs. Sullivan's (the *agent provocatrice*) demotion, the first public expression of approval of the raid was made, obscurely, to be sure, but enlighteningly. The Rev. Francis X. Talbot, S.J., said at a communion breakfast of the Holy Name Society in Jersey City that the raid had been justified. He condemned Mayor Walker for allowing the demotion of Mrs. Sullivan, and explained that the Roman Catholics had been very busy at the task of ' keeping God in the country ' " (Sanger, *l.c.*, p. 305). " Incidentally, it is worth noting in passing that several women patients whose cards were thus purloined have come to us pleading that we shall not use their names publicly as patients of the Clinical Research Bureau. Upon being questioned, they confessed that they had received mysterious and anonymous telephone calls telling them that if they continued to go to the Clinic their cases would be exposed in the newspapers. They happened to be Roman Catholic mothers, whose case-cards were taken and never returned " (Sanger, *l.c.*, p. 301).

In Great Britain, too, " the only serious opposition to Birth Control comes from the Roman Catholic clergy, who not content with preaching to their own people that any form of Birth Control other than abstention in marriage from sexual intercourse is immoral, refuse to allow others liberty of conscience " (How Martyn, 1930, p. 29). In considering the vigour and persistence of this Catholic opposition we must understand the ideology or the philosophical and theological premises on which it is based.

7

The great Bossuet wrote in his Méaux Catechism—for the use of children at their first Communion, that is, not later than twelve years of age—as follows :

" Tell me the evil we must shun in the use of the married state ? "

" It is the unjust refusal of conjugal duty. It is the use of marriage for the gratification of sensuality. It is to avoid having children, which is an odious crime."

On the other hand, we have a pronouncement by the Bishop of Beauvais, some centuries nearer our own day, to the effect that " God does not insist that married couples should crowd their homes with children." And it is significant that the Church of Rome has never forbidden the marriage of women who are sterile either by inherent constitution or subsequent operation or disease (*Canon* 1068, *Jus Canonici*).

There is a contradiction in logic here. But since the days of Augustine of Hippo and Thomas Aquinas, Rome has based her doctrines on a moral myth. Thus we read in the Encyclical *Casti Connubii* the pronouncement regarding Christian Marriage issued by Pope Pius XI on December 31st, 1930 : " Any use whatsoever of matrimony exercised in such a way that the act is deliberately frustrated in its natural power to generate life is an offence against the law of God and of nature, and those who indulge in such are branded with the guilt of a grave sin " (p. 27). For parenthood alone is assumed to justify the performance of the sexual act, just as was assumed in the Biblical passages, Gen. i. 27–28, ii. 22–23 ; Matt. xix. 3 *et seq.* ; Eph. v. 23 *et. seq.*, and the Twenty-fourth Session of the Council of Trent. So we have the following : " For in matrimony as well as in the use of the matrimonial rights there are also secondary ends, such as mutual aid, the cultivating of mutual love, and the concupiscence which husband and wife are not forbidden to consider so long as they are subordinated to the primary end and so long as the intrinsic nature of the act is preserved " (p. 28). All other exercises even in matrimony are denounced as " criminal abuse on the ground that they are weary of children and wish to gratify their desires without their consequent burden " (p. 25).

Here again, as in the days of Bruno and Galileo, the Vatican opposes science. The Epistle to the Ephesians is set up in opposition to what we already know of the significance and benefits of the profoundly complex mechanism of sexual satisfaction and the healing joy of the orgasm. Pius XI still maintains that sexuality is a bye-product of reproduction. But we have known for a long time that the converse is the case. We know that there is a primary instinct of conjugation but no instinct of reproduction, and therefore that " to gratify their desires " is a natural law of all vital and normal human beings. Nevertheless, in the face of biological achievements and social movements which can neither be ignored nor crushed, the Catholic church shows an amazing adaptability.   At the Catholic *Congrès de la Natalité* at Brussels, in 1933, an orthodox and permissible form of Birth Control was advocated, consisting of the observance of the so-called " safe period " in the woman's monthly cycle (*cf.* Chapter I, *supra*). Dr. P. Heymeyer, S.J., introduced what would appear to be a complete doctrinal anomaly, and was supported by his Colleague in Theology, Professor Duynstee, as follows : " The spouses perform the act in a natural manner and with no contradiction or incompatibility between the final consequences of nature and their individual method.   There is no destruction of life or of a natural sequence ordained by God—for there is no fertilization, and nature itself prevents it, for she denies impregnation to the women at such times."

So nature is for once " at fault " and not poor sinful humanity ! Q.E.D. Here we have the explanation of the totally uncritical acceptance and one may almost say " boosting " of Knaus's theory in Catholic circles, although in April, 1935, the Fascist-Clericalist Organ of the present *régime* in Vienna, the *Arbeiter-Woche*, had to find space to record many piteous complaints from unwillingly pregnant working-class women who had relied on " advice " given in the Confessional, which was usurping the office of Birth Control Clinic.   We also understand the arguments used by the Catholic clergy against any form of active and scientifically adequate Birth Control.   But there is no logical or tolerable defence of the venomous hostility displayed towards all Birth Control organization and propaganda among non-Catholics.

In a pamphlet against Birth Control published by the (Roman) Catholic Truth Society of London (56 thousandth impression, 1935, price 2*d.*) there is a reference to a certain " Note of Reservation," signed among others by the (Anglican) Canon Lyttelton, late Headmaster of Eton. " In addition to other evils . . . the most baneful will be the inevitable encouragement of immorality among unmarried people.   If contraceptives are in any circumstances permissible for normal married people. . . ." Then indeed it is not possible to prevent those outside that magic circle from " gratifying their passions " through the same instrumentality. Here—and not in any biological or æsthetic considerations—we have the core of the passionate opposition to B. C. which menaces and undermines the code of the Churches. But as that astute Conservative Lord Dawson of Penn warned the Church Congress at Birmingham : " The war has caused a hiatus and thought has broken with tradition. Thus, youth is no longer willing to accept forms and formulæ only on account of their age."

But what can sociological enlightenment avail against the Scholasticism of the Vatican ? Theology is a fantastic form of art—not an exact science !

8

Apart from Catholic hostility, Birth Control in Great Britain is not a matter of political alignment—still less a " party plank." No one class is predominantly for it, nor against it. There is an interesting contrast here with European experience, for the theory of Birth Control has had an earlier and warmer reception in Conservative circles than among other parties, although the Women's Co-operative Guild passed the following resolution as early as 1923 : " That this Congress urges upon the Ministry of Health and local authorities the advisability of information in regard to Birth Control being given at all maternity and child welfare centres in the country." A year after this, on May 9th, 1924, the Worker's Birth Control Group,[1] founded by Socialist supporters of feminism and Birth Control, organized a deputation to the Minister of Health in the first Labour Government—the Glasgow Catholic, John Wheatley—in order to demand prompt action on the same lines, but was refused. In February, 1926, a Private Member's (*i.e.*, non-Party) resolution was put forward in the House of Commons, by Mr. Ernest Thurtle, Labour M.P. for Shoreditch in the East

[1] This organization was very active in educative and propaganda work among Labour Women's Sections and at Labour Conferences from 1924 till 1930, when it was merged into the National B. C. Association. Among its leaders were Miss Dorothy Jewson, M.P. for Norwich, Bertrand and Dora Russell, Ernest and Dorothy Thurtle, Professor Harold and Frida Laski, H. N. Brailsford, H. G. Wells, A. F. Brockway, Hilda Browning, Stella Browne, and Maurice Newfield.—Translator's Note.

End of London, and son-in-law of George Lansbury. It was defeated by the following votes:

	Conservative	Labour	Liberal	Independent Prohibitionist
Against	113	43	10	1
For	53	26	3	

namely, by a majority of 85 (167 to 82), the majority of the House abstaining from voting. Of the four women M.P.'s, only Ellen Wilkinson went into the division lobby and in favour of the resolution. Most unfortunately Dorothy Jewson was absent from that Parliament.

The House of Lords, on the other hand, accepted a Motion by Lord Buckmaster on May 28th, 1926, by 57 votes to 44. The Motion was in these terms: " That H.M.'s Government be requested to withdraw all instructions given to, or conditions imposed on, welfare committees for the purpose of causing such committees to withhold from married women in their district information when sought by such women as to the best means of limiting their families."

The year 1927 is specially important, both in Great Britain and internationally. After fifty years of dignified and disinterested pioneering work, the Malthusian League was formally dissolved, and its task was carried on by other bodies in touch with contemporary needs. The B. C. International Information Centre was founded in London with Margaret Sanger as President and Edith How Martyn as Director, a position she held till 1935. At the same time Margaret Sanger expanded her field of action and summoned the first International World Population Conference at Geneva; Sir Bernard Mallet, the eminent British Civil Servant, took the Chair. But it was not all plain sailing; the Anglican and Protestant atmosphere of compromise and "tolerance" gave way to the excited protests of the Catholics, and Mallet was actually prevailed upon to remove all the names of participants, including Margaret Sanger's, from the pages of the official programme, as the proofs were being sent to the press! Why was this done? Was it through an antifeminist group? Or was it the influence of something

more pernicious, the order of some stage director behind the
scenes, who had given peremptory instructions to the actors ?
" Sir Bernard had pledged his word. to the representatives
of the Catholic countries, Italy, Belgium, Spain and Catholic
Germany, that B. C. contraception, and the conscious
control of population, would not even be mentioned. And
this in the free atmosphere of a scientific conference ! "
(Sanger, p. 285).

Mrs. Sanger was also the agent who brought Birth Control
into the Far East. In 1922 she accepted the invitation of a
group of progressive thinkers (the Kaizo) to visit Japan.
Her visa was refused, but she succeeded in landing on Japanese soil in circumstances of great dramatic and " publicity "
value, having won the support of Japanese politicians whom
she met on board ; and in 1929 the Health Department of
the City of Tokyo decided to set up Birth Control Clinics in
the municipal health advice stations. Interest spread to
China and India under the auspices of the intrepid Agnes
Smedley. In 1930 heads of Hospitals in Shanghai and
Peiping began to instruct their medical and nursing staffs in
contraception, and in the same year the first Government
Birth Control Clinic in the world was opened in the Indian
native state of Mysore. In November, 1933, there was a
Conference in the London School of Hygiene and Tropical
Medicine, organized by the B.C.I.I.C. on " B. C. in Asia."
It is a consistent and encouraging course of enlightenment,
of which a recent milestone is the publication of the quarterly
Marriage Hygiene, the most comprehensive scientific periodi-
cal on population and sex questions in the English language.
Marriage Hygiene first appeared in 1934, and is published in
Bombay, under the Editorship of Dr. Pillay.

A further decisive step in the course of 1927 has been the
centralization of contraceptive information and research
in the B. C. Investigation Committee, with Headquarters in
London. In 1931 the Investigation Committee was formally
associated with the National B. C. Association, founded
through the initiative of Mrs. Hubback under the Presidency
of Lord Horder and the Chairmanship of Lady Denman.
The Investigation Committee works independently, confining

itself to the technical and medical aspects of the subject. In 1928 and in 1929 and 1930 the Birth Control Information Committee (B.C.I.I.C.) and the Workers Birth Control Group began a vigorous electoral and parliamentary agitation in favour of B. C. at Welfare Centres, culminating in April, 1930, in a Conference attended by many representatives of organizations and Medical Officers from all over the country.[1] The Conference and the Departmental Report brought the Ministry of Health to terms. In July, 1930, was issued the Departmental Memorandum 153 giving sanction—under some vexatiously restrictive conditions, but everything must have a beginning !—that " the clinics will be available only for women who are in need of medical advice and treatment for gynæcological conditions, and that advice on contraceptive methods will be given only to married women who attend the clinics for such medical advice or treatment and in whose cases pregnancy would be detrimental to health." A few weeks later, on August 15th, 1930, the Lambeth Conference of Anglican Bishops, by a majority of 193 to 67, 41 abstaining, came to the following conclusion :

" Where there is clearly felt moral obligation to limit or avoid parenthood, the method must be decided on Christian principles. The primary and obvious method is complete abstinence from intercourse so far as may be necessary in a life of discipline and self-control. Nevertheless, in those cases where there is such a clearly felt moral obligation . . . and where there is morally sound reason for avoiding complete abstinence, the conference agrees that other methods may be used, provided this is done in the light of the same Christian principles."

On December 31st of the same year Pius XI issued his Encyclical on Christian Marriage (see *supra*). And the Irish Free State had already " grasped the nettle " by prohibiting any importation of B. C. literature or advertisements (!) in their Censorship Bill of 1928. In September, 1935,

[1] Shortly afterwards the Departmental Commission for the Investigation of the Causes of the Maternal Death-rate issued an alarming report, to the effect that 48 per cent. of such deaths were from preventable causes.—Translator's Note.

an account was rendered to the Celtic Congress at Cardiff of the fruits of this piety. The censorship of books and the regulation of dancing are the two outstanding efforts in this direction. The *Sunday Times* of September 15th, 1935, gives a significant account of the absurdities to which the policy of making people moral by act of Parliament will logically lead. " A certain dignitary decreed that, at dances, all cars should be parked under the supervision of an elderly person, presumably with the object that they should not be used to supplement the very inadequate sitting-out facilities that exist in most country halls." Mrs. Grundy and the Catholic hierarchy work in unison. But there is a most serious side to this preposterous paltriness : the pious Christian Celts, who have been the object of so much literary adulation, are " wedded to the soil " and could make excellent use of practical Birth Control to improve their economic status ! Official Irish statistics give £8 10 0 as the average *yearly* earnings of a boarded female worker, and £12 15 0 as the equivalent for a boarded male worker, and the board is sparse !

9

On January 15th, 1933, the Health Committee of the League of Nations gave official recognition to Birth Control —although here, too, the Delegate of the Irish Free State had entered a vigorous protest :

" Nevertheless it may become necessary to avoid pregnancy, in the interests of the mother's health ; and it is then preferable rather to prevent her from becoming pregnant than to interrupt a pregnancy which has already begun. It is not enough to tell a married woman suffering from tuberculosis, nephritis or cardiac disease that she must not have children ; it is indispensable that the necessary measures to prevent impregnation should be explained to the husband and wife by a medical practitioner."

This may seem the most obvious humanity and commonsense, in fact, almost a platitude, but it carries special weight, because it is backed by the prestige of the League of Nations and is an acknowledgement of the need for reliable and non-injurious methods. The results of contraceptive research have been recorded throughout the world in many different languages, in the pages of medical and biological periodicals and books, and this international diffusion makes it difficult to summarize and compare. But much progress has been made in collection and collation since the annual issue of the *Reports of the International Medical Group for the Investigation of Contraception* under the auspices of the B. C. Investigation Committee since 1928 (at 26 Eccleston Street, London, S.W.1). The Editor of these Reports, Dr. C. P. Blacker, the well-known Secretary of the Eugenics Society, writes in the fifth issue, 1934: " It is clearly futile in the present century to expect people drastically to alter their sexual habits and give up contraception as a result of propaganda to the effect that the practice is sinful; and practical steps to attain this end, such as the prohibition of the sale of contraceptives, would result, not in the suppression of B. C., but in the widespread substitution of harmful and unreliable methods such as coitus interruptus for better and safer methods " (p. 4).

Now how far are we practically justified in asking for " absolutely reliable methods ? " Dr. Hannah Stone, Directress of the New York Research Centre, has studied and dissected the results of an Enquête to American Hospitals dealing with about 150,000 patients (Report, 1934, p. 7). " From the statement of many of the medical men it would appear that the method : vaginal occlusive pessary with a jelly, was given to well over 90 per cent. of the patients." At our present stage of knowledge this combination of methods is the best, and in every individual case there must be examination and fitting in order to make sure whether the saucer-shaped diaphragm pessary on the *Mensinga* model or the cervical " cap " is the more suitable.

The commercialization of contraceptives is a serious problem in all those Capitalist communities which permit their sale and use; for there have been far too many instances of the enormous advertisement and profitable retailing of unsuitable and injurious preparations. The only state sensible enough to institute a Central Commission for the Study of Contraceptives is the Union of Socialist Soviet Republics. The Commission was formed in 1924, and nine years later was sub-divided into three sections, biological, clinical and statistical respectively. All available contraceptives are analysed and graded according to their efficacy and pleasantness and ease in use. Of late—since 1933— experiments have been made with biolactine, a preparation compounded by Dr. Dubintchnik, described in the B. C. I. Report of 1934 on p. 90. Biolactine is a lactic preparation and increases the acidity of the vaginal secretions.

J. R. Baker, C. I. B. Voge and other scientific investigators have made detailed studies of the chemical composition and physiological action of various preparations and pure substances, without demonstrating that any spermatoxin is at all applicable for clinical use. There have been cogent criticisms of the former favourite, quinine, by Robertson of Cambridge, 1925–28, and Dr. Cecile Booysen at the Doctor's Conference of the N.B.C.A. in London, December, 1935. As to the pessaries, the experience of Dr. Leunbach in his work at Copenhagen tends to prove that the sizes generally in use are too small for their purpose. The pessaries should be left in place for at least ten hours after coitus, but not continuously. The only intra-uterine or utero-vaginal method still considered worth discussion among responsible persons is the Gräfenberg ring, on which there are widely divergent opinions (cf. W.L.S.R. Congress Report, London, 1930, and B. C. Invest. Reports, 1930 and 1931, p. 62). Gräfenberg's tests were begun in 1919. He observed that appliances lying partly within the womb, and partly in the vaginal canal, involved risk of infection through the introduction of bacteria. He therefore introduced appliances wholly within the uterine cavity ; he first used silk, then silver rings bound with silk. Gräfenberg and Haire admit that the ring needs a high degree of gynæcological skill in order to be applied with safety, and is only possible in one-third of the patients needing contraception. Thus it must remain a minority method. Leunbach considers it unreliable.

All these individualized clinic methods are, as Dr. R. Latou Dickinson, the leading gynæcologist of the U.S.A., has declared, "approximately 95 per cent. effective, but so bothersome that fifty per cent. of those instructed return to simpler ways, even though these may embody a larger degree of risk " (Unmarried Adult, p. 191). So we must ask and ascertain the real value of contraception in the social order of to-day. There are several large treatises on reliability, but there is often a lack of distinction between " failures " and " unaccountable failures " (Investigation, 1931, p. 43). Comparative data show that even the double shield of the pessary plus chemical contraceptive gives an " accident " or " unaccountable failure " rate of 1⅗ per cent. (1·6) if the patients take the trouble to follow instructions correctly. For practical purposes this gives a very good " margin of safety." But psychological, emotional and mental factors are most important—and not easily calculable— here. In the words of Stix and Notestein, " contraceptives were less effective when used by Catholics than when used by people of other religious affiliations. For this group, contraception was most effective when used by Jewish couples " (1935).

The most comprehensive study of the methods of Birth Control in actual use is Raymond Pearl's, of 1932. His data included 13,008 cases, all American. The most recent analysis by Pearl deals with over 30,000 cases. His tables are models for all future statistical studies (Investigation, 1934, pp. 54–57). Dr. Blacker sums up Pearl's results as follows : " Both the white and negro groups in this sample favoured the douche over all other methods of contraception. This method would appear to be more used in America, as it undoubtedly is in France, than in England, where sheaths are the most favoured method, with coitus interruptus, or ' withdrawal,' second. The relative frequency of this douche technique is 37·1 for the white group and 55·4 for the negroes. . . . The sheath is employed by 29 per cent. of the total—more frequently, it will be observed, by white couples than by negroes." With-drawal was practised by only 17·4 per cent. " Thus the three most frequently used methods, those employed by 86·3 per cent. of the total, are the douche, the sheath and coitus interruptus. It is also worth noting that a technique involving the use of a pessary was employed by only 2·3 per cent. It would therefore appear that, among the present sample, relatively little influence is at present exerted by

COST OF CONTRACEPTION PER ANNUM :

Method	Price	Cost in shillings, occurring— times a week		
		1	2	3
Condom (A) . . .	6d. (a)	22/–	66/–	154/–
	3d. (b)	11/–	33/–	77/–
Dutch caps . . .	5/– (a)	10/–	10/–	10/–
Cervical . . .	(c)			
Suppositories (d) . .	2/– (a)	7/4	22/–	51/4
Ointments (e) . .	1/6 (a)	4/6	13/6	31/6
		21/10	45/6	92/10
Dutch (B) . . .	1/9 (b)	3/6	3/6	3/6
Cervix (C) . . .	(c)			
Suppositories (d) . .	1/– (d)	3/8	11/–	25/8
Ointment (e) (D) . .	1/– (c)	3/–	9/–	21/–
		10/2	23/6	50/2
Contraceptive Jelly .	8/6 (a), (f)[1]	31/–	92/–	217/–

[1] (a) Retail price.
(b) Clinic price.
(c) Recommended that two caps should be provided each six months.
(d) Twelve suppositories in each box.
(e) Fifteen applications in each tube, the ointment being smeared round the rim may readily deteriorate. In such circumstances it is recommended that a separate application of the ointment should be used in the dome of the cap so as to ensure the cervix being sealed. The cost would probably be the same.
(f) Single application tube.
(A) The condom if manufactured by a reliable process, really tested (regardless of the statements made), and dated, can give a percentage of success approaching 100.
(B) and (C) Caps when fitted by an experienced worker to appropriate cases, changed if any sign of perishing is found, and used with suitable chemical methods can be likewise exceedingly successful.
(D) Chemical methods : Theory and practice would indicate that single application methods of the jelly or foam jelly type alone are capable of almost universal application and a high degree of success. With others the chance of deterioration is higher and expectation of success less.
(E) Household methods : Tampons soaked in vinegar, dilute solutions of alum or lemon juice will at least lower the chance of pregnancy amongst those who financially or on account of isolation are incapable of employing one of the other methods. (Marriage Hygiene, 1/2, September, 1934.)

the B. C. clinics, which teach almost exclusively a pessary method" (*Investigation*, 1934, p. 59). That is also the case in England, as is shown by the comparative number of necessitous women and the attendance at the Clinics (N.B.C.A. Report, April, 1936). This *psycho-sociological aspect of Birth Control has not hitherto received the attention it deserves, and still less study has as yet been given to that profound and intricate domain of future research, the interactions between contraceptive technique and complete orgasmic potency.*

Voge has given a valuable illustrative example of the economic factors in contraception. In the table on p. 202 he estimates the year as comprising 308 days, making allowance for the menstrual periods. It thus contains forty-four weeks. Dickinson, Beam and Davis suggest that three times a week is the normal frequency of coitus.

10

The Seventh International B. C. Conference met in Zurich in September, 1930. The propaganda for B. C. on the Continent of Europe was closely allied and almost identified with the Left in politics, and had therefore become " Party politics " in strong contrast to the comparative detachment of the English-speaking world. Even in Scandinavian countries, where class conflicts had not approached anything like the vehemence of Central European conditions up to and until the World Crisis of 1929, the movement for Sexual Reform had always been linked with the political Left. Before the war of 1914–18 the Swedish economist, Professor Knut Wicksell, had tried to make Malthusian theories acceptable to a more or less Marxian working class. He coined the slogan " Two child system " or " Two child Family." In 1924 the first Birth Control Clinics were opened in all three Northern lands : in Oslo, by Dr. K. Anker Möller and her daughter, Dr. Tove Mohr ; in Copenhagen, by Thit Jensen; and in Stockholm, by Dr. Alice Nielsen. The further development of these Clinics combined B. C. with Sex Consultation and Advice, as described in our previous chapter. In Sweden the cause owes much to the efforts of Elise Ottesen Jensen, who was herself the seventeenth child of a Norwegian clergyman! She sought out the isolated cottages and hamlets in the forests of the Northernmost provinces, by motor-car in the summer, and on skis in the winter, in order to bring Birth Control and skilled medical advice on health in general to the peasant women. Her audiences number about 50,000 persons a year, and in addition to this rural spadework there is incessant activity at the polyclinic of Riksförbund for seksuell uplysning in Stockholm.

In 1928 the wave of public discussion and of public search for truth and help reached Spain.

In German-speaking countries the honour of the initiative in systematic propaganda belongs to the Zurich medical man, Dr. Fritz Brupbacher. He began to preach against excessive child-bearing in 1901, and was promptly " boycotted " by the Zurich Midwives. In 1903 he gave a lecture on family limitation. A man among the audience had brought his two children, aged respectively three and five years, and Brupbacher showed a pessary and explained its use. He was put in the dock by the public Prosecutor, on the charge of " public indecency and obscene acts before children." But the peasants who were summoned to condemn him acquitted him. His pamphlet *Kindersegen* (*The Blessing of Children*) reached half a million copies in circulation.

In Germany itself B. C. was always an integral part of systematic Sex Advice. The " *Bund für Mutterschutz* " or " League for the Protection of Mothers " founded in pre-war years by Dr. Helene Stoecker did specially valuable work here, in a logical and constructive spirit.

In 1928 Agnes Smedley, then in collaboration with Margaret Sanger, came to Berlin; a medical Committee was formed with Drs. Ruben-Wolff, Hodann, Bendix and Schmincke as members, and in the same year the first medical course of lectures and discussions on contraception was organized by this Committee, with financial support from the American leader. This action aroused violent opposition in the medical press and in middle-class reactionary circles. At the Medical Conference of 1926 the subject of B. C. was taboo and the Prussian Medical Board Committee (" *Aerzte-kammer Ausschuss*") passed the following resolution on December 8th, 1928 : "Contraception as a professional practice is to be considered as undesirable, both from the point of view of professional etiquette and of the opinion of the Medical Board Committee."

As has been mentioned already, the enlightened members of the medical faculty in Central Europe were closely associated with the Labour movement. It became imperative to clarify the theoretical basis of their championship of Birth Control. Marx had argued that the claim of the orthodox Malthusians, that social misery and poverty are mainly due to uncontrolled reproduction of the less fortunate classes, was merely a self-justification of the bourgeoisie and an attempt to push their own responsibilities on to the shoulders of a " Natural Law," for the misery and poverty of the poor is due to the economics of bourgeois capitalism, and the monopolies of land tenure and industrial production, whereby workers and employees can be exploited, to the profit of those in possession of the means of subsistence. If the misery that ensues is really the result of inexorable " Natural Law, " the bourgeois conscience may return to rest.

But this misery, this lack of food, of clothing, of housing, are not the fruits of any Law of Nature. *Modern methods of production and transport have so enormously multiplied the supply of foodstuffs as well as of other substances—and could further so increase this supply, under a system run not for Profit but for Service—that no hunger or deprivation of necessities need exist to thwart and stunt humanity.*

Modern mass production is not operated for the advantage of the human masses, but for the possessing and privileged classes. And therefore hunger and " mal-nutrition " and starved existence are not due to the numbers of those who suffer them. *The key to insufficiency is not Reproduction but Distribution.* The cure for insufficiency is not a biological problem, but one of politics and economics.

This was the view stated in pre-war Germany in the passionate debates " For and against the Birth Strike."

In *Pravda* (then the Organ of Russian revolutionary exiles) 29/16, June, 1913, Lenin wrote against the Sociology of Neo-Malthusianism and called it " a tendency made for the lower-middle class couple in isolation and egotism." But the greatest statesman of our age added " obviously, this does not hinder us from demanding a drastic change of the laws which prosecute abortion and the propaganda of practical contraception. These laws are mere hypocrisy of the ruling classes. They do not cure the ills of Capitalism, they only make these ills more disabling and more painful to the exploited masses. The liberty of Contraceptive propaganda and the protection of the elementary democratic rights of male and female citizens have nothing in common with Neo-Malthusianism as a social theory."

On the basis of human happiness, health and dignity, an understanding between Marxists and Malthusians was possible. Marxists were members of the Committee of German Centre for Work on Birth Control formed in 1931, on the lines of the London organizations. In 1932 an Information Bureau for Birth Control was instituted by members of the Left Wing in politics, and this Bureau worked in collaboration with the Centre founded under Mrs. Sanger's auspices. For although Socialist Medicine in Central Europe had no hesitation in rejecting the Malthusian doctrine as a general explanation of poverty and hunger, they fully admitted that *in the family and for the individual, as apart from the community*, numbers may be a decisive factor. The more mouths, the less bread, for within the family there already exists a form of Communal Distribution. Thus within each separate family conditions may be considerably improved by limitation of offspring.

Then came the Nazi *coup* of 1933, and the Nazi Medical Association directed their first blow against B. C. All sex Advice Centres were closed. All medical policy was under the spell of writers who preached : " German Race Improvement," " Uplift," " Race Hygiene." For women there was to be subjection and the compulsion to fertility : " The use of contraceptives means a violation of nature, a degradation of womanhood, motherhood and love " declared the official party paper for women, on May 5th, 1933. Theoretically Nazism stands against contraception because " the method is uncontrolled, it is against nature, as it strikes at procreation in general and not at disease in particular ; the population of a nation which exercises B. C. will at a date in the future be so reduced that a premium will be placed upon the weak, and contraception takes place under the whim of the individual. The individual thinks first of his own benefit rather than the benefit of the nation." National-socialism stands for sterilization because " the method is controlled " (cf. Chapter IV) " it is supervized by medical experts, and it strikes at hereditary and incurable diseases " (cf. Hitler, *My Struggle*, p. 144).

The Führer has formulated his programme in regard to sex and humanity in this one sentence quoted by the *Morning Post* of October 5th, 1935 : " The Education of Women has but one purpose : to make the mother of to-morrow "—the mother of fodder for guns and gas. Fascism is as opposed as Catholicism to Birth Control. The seriousness with which the German " League of Large Families " takes its work can scarcely be understood outside of the Third Reich to-day. But its seriousness to the rest of Europe should not be underestimated. We must never forget the bitter comment wrung by experience from Margaret Sanger : " It was flattering to know that enlightened public opinion was with us. But such opinion, based on tolerance, is seldom militant. It does not fight. While the other type, the ignorant, the prejudiced, the intolerant, is always pugnacious, egotistic, self-assertive. Therefore it seems to be all-conquering in this poor democracy of ours " (*Fight for Birth Control*, p. 329).

The American B. C. League is now under the leadership of Dr. Eric Matsner. It has tended towards reform of procedure, rather than radical change, ever since the decision of 1918, which permitted medical practitioners to practise and recommend contraception. A more militant body was founded in 1929 ; this was the National Committee on Federal Leglislation for Birth Control, on whose behalf Mrs. Sanger spoke before a Congressional Committee in

1931. The efforts and negotiations in this campaign go on incessantly, and are sharply opposed by the Catholics, who lamented in February, 1935, that the Bill then before the Senate (No. 4582) "will open the floodgates to all kinds of pornographic and obscene literature" (National Catholic Welfare Conference, in New York). Solicitor Charles A. Crowley, at the request of the Postmaster General (in Roosevelt's administration) Farley, demanded in a confidential letter to the Post Office Committee of the House of Representatives, that proceedings in cases of "unmailable" publications, which would include B. C., should in future not be confined to the sender or the place of despatch. For such matter was usually posted from large towns, where detection was difficult : "It should be possible to bring criminal action in the jurisdiction where the matter is delivered for that is where the real harm is done," writes Crowley. He knows well that in the Monkeyvilles and Main streets there is no public opinion to hold reactionary lawyers in check. This is the position in America to-day ; but we Europeans are concentrating attention and effort on the second great problem of population policy and sexual conduct ; namely, on abortion.

BIBLIOGRAPHY

ALLBUTT, H. A., *The Wife's Handbook*, London, 1887.
BAKER, J. R., "The Spermicidal Powers of Chemical Contraceptives," *Journal of Hygiene*, 31, 1931 ; 32, 1932 ; 34, 1935.
BENDIX, *Geburtenregelung*, Berlin, 1929. (A medical symposium and discussion on practical Birth Control.)
Birth Control. Pamphlet of Catholic Truth Society, London.
Birth Control and Public Health. Ten Years' Report of the S.P.B.C.C., London, 1933.
BELLAMY, H., "D'un Neomalthusianisme catholique et orthodoxe," article in *Le Problème Sexuel*, No. 5, Paris, 1935.
BRUPBACHER, F., *Sechzig Jahre Ketzer*, Zürich, 1935.
CHANCE, JANET, *The Cost of English Morals*, London, 1931.
CHARLES, ENID, *The Practice of Birth Control*, London, 1932.
COOPER, J. F., *The Technique of Contraception*, New York, 1929.
COX, GLADYS, *Clinical Contraception*, London, 1933.

DAWSON OF PENN, *Love-Marriage-Birth Control*, pamphlet, London, 1922.
DICKINSON, R. L., and BEAM, L., *A Thousand Marriages*, National Committee on Maternal Health, New York, 1931.
DICKINSON, R. L., and BRYANT, L. S., *Control of Conception*, Baltimore, 1931.
DRYSDALE, C. V., *The Malthusian Doctrine*, London, 1918.
DRYSDALE, G., *The Elements of Social Science*, London, 1854.
ELKAN-HODANN-GAMPE, *Schwangerschaftsverhütung*, Nürnberg, 1932.
VAN EMDE-BOAS, *Le B.C. en Hollande*—edt. in LUMIÈRE, Bruxelles, December, 1935.
FIELDING, M., *Parenthood : Design or Accident ?* London, 1927.
FIELDING, M., *Birth Control in Asia*, Report, London, 1932.
FIELDING, M., *Practical Advice on Birth Control* (India), B.C.I.C.
FLOREY, H., and CARLETON, H. M., " Birth Control Studies," *Journal of Obstetrics and Gynæcology*, 38, 1931.
GRIFFITH, E. F., *Modern Marriage and Birth Control*, London, 1934.
HARDY, G., " Paul Robin, a French Champion of Birth Control," *Critic and Guide*, October, 1925.
HART, H., and STONE, H., *Maternal Health and Contraception*, Newark, N.Y., 1933.
HOW MARTYN, E., *The Birth Control Movement in England*, London, 1930.
HOW MARTYN, E., " Contribution à l'Histoire de B.C.," *Problème Sexuel*, November, 1933, February, 1934.
International Group for the Investigation of Contraception, Reports since 1928, N.B.C.A., London.
KNOWLTON, CH., *Fruits of Philosophy*, Boston, 1833.
MALLESON, J., *The Principles of Contraception*, London, 1935.
MALTHUS, *Essay on the Principle of Population*, 2nd ed., 1803.
The Malthusian Handbook, London, 1911.
" Medical Problems of Contraception," *Brit. Med. Journ.*, July 15th, 1933.
MONTREVIL-STRAUS, " Le Birth Control," *Bull. Ass. franc. d. femmes-médecins*, Paris, No. 12, 1933.
MYRDAL, G. and A., *Kris i befolkningsfråagan*, Stockholm, 1934.
OWEN, R. D., *Moral Physiology*, 1830.
PEARL, R., *Human Biology*, Baltimore, 1932.
" Proposed Fed. Legislation for Birth Control," *Congressional Digest*, Washington, April, 1931.
SANGER, M., *My Fight for Birth Control*, New York, 1931, London, 1932.
SANGER, M., and STONE, H., *The Practice of Contraception*, Baltimore, 1931.

SELNITZKY and GUBAREFF, *Protiwasatotschnüye ssredstwa w ssowremennom nautschnom osswyeschtschenii*, Moskwa, 1927.

STIX, R. K., and NOTESTEIN, F. W., " Effectiveness of Birth Control," *Milbank Mem. Fund Quarterly*, January, 1934, to April 7th, 1935.

STOPES, M. C., *Married Love*, London, 1918.

STOPES, M. C., *Queen's Hall Meeting on Constructive Birth Control*, London, 1921.

STOPES, M. C., *Contraception, its History, Theory and Practice*, London, 1931.

STOPES, M. C., *Ten Thousand Cases*, London, 1933.

SWING, R. G., " Birth Control and Obscenity," *Nation*, New York, No. 3647, 1935.

VOGE, C. I. B., *The Chemistry and Physics of Contraceptives*, London, 1933.

VOGE, C. I. B., " The Applicability of Contraceptive Methods," *Marr. Hyg.*, 1/2, Bombay, 1934.

WILE, I., a.o., *The Sex Life of the Unmarried Adult*, London, 1935.

World Population Conference, Geneva, August 29th to September 3rd, Ed. 1927.

TABLE OF EVENTS

1798   MALTHUS' *Essay on the Principle of Population.*

1821   JAMES MILL states in the *Encyclopædia Britannica*, " The grand practical problem is to find the means of limiting the number of births."

1833   KNOWLTON'S *Fruits of Philosophy.*

1854   G. DRYSDALE'S *Elements of Social Science.*

1873   COMSTOCK Law in United States of America.

1877   BRADLAUGH-BESANT trial in London.
       Foundation of the Malthusian League.

1879   First number of *The Malthusian* published in London.

1881   Dutch Malthusian League founded.

1883   DR. MENSINGA constructs the Pessary known by his name.

1890   DR. ALETTA JACOBS founds the first Birth Control Centre in Amsterdam.

1896   Ligue pour la Régénération humaine founded in Paris.

1900   First Malthusian Congress meets in Paris.   International Malthusian League founded.

1901   BRUPBACHER initiates mass meetings on Birth Control in Zürich.

1905   Second International Congress at Liége.

1910   Third International Congress at The Hague.

1911   Fourth International Congress at Dresden.

1914 MARGARET SANGER invents the slogan "Birth Control."
1916 First American Clinic in New York.
1917 *Birth Control Review* begins publication in New York.
     MARGARET SANGER imprisoned.
1918 DR. MARIE STOPES' *Married Love* published.
     Court of Appeal in New York sanctions Birth Control
     Information from Doctors for medical purposes.
1920 Anti-Birth Control Law in France (July 31st, 1920).
1921 First British Birth Control Clinic founded in March by
     MARIE STOPES.
     Walworth Centre founded in November.
     First American Birth Control Conference in New York.
     Town Hall Meeting Trial.
1922 MARGARET SANGER visits Japan.
     Fifth International Congress in London.
     LORD DAWSON OF PENN advocates Birth Control at
     Church Congress at Birmingham.
1923 Foundation of Society for the Provision of Birth Control
     Clinics in London ; of Research Committee in New York.
     Marriage Law in Yucatan, and official distribution of
     Sanger pamphlet *Family Limitation* to newly married
     couples.
     The same pamphlet prosecuted in London.
1924 Deputation to WHEATLEY, British Labour Minister of
     Health.
     Workers' Birth Control Group founded.
     Birth Control Clinics founded in Scandinavia.
     Central Committee for the Study of Contraception in
     Soviet Russia (Moscow).
1925. MUSSOLINI penalizes Contraception in Italy.
     Birth Control Clinics in Japan and Mexico.
     Sixth International Congress in New York.
1926 LORD BUCKMASTER'S Motion accepted by the British
     House of Lords.
     Birth Control Clinic founded in Leningrad.
1927 Birth Control Information Centre founded in London.
     Birth Control Investigation Committee founded in London.
     World Population Conference in Geneva.
1928 Irish Censorship Bill.
     Berlin Birth Control Committee founded.
     Contraceptive Course for Medical Practitioners in Berlin.
1929 Workers at the New York Research Centre arrested.
     MARGARET SANGER founds Federal Legislative Committee.
1930 Government of Mysore founds a Birth Control Clinic.
     Lambeth Conference accepts Birth Control. Memorandum
     153 of the British Ministry of Health.
     Seventh International Congress in Zurich.

National Birth Control Association founded in London.
Papal Encyclical on Christian Marriage (*Casti Connubii*).

1931 ALETTA JACOBS Huis founded in Amsterdam.

1933 HITLER *régime* suppresses Birth Control in Germany.
Catholic Congrès de Natalité meets in Brussels.
League of Nations Health Committee accepts Birth Control.
Conference in London on " Birth Control in Asia."
Lex Clamamus submitted to French Chamber of Deputies.

CHAPTER VI

THE FIGHT FOR LEGALIZED ABORTION

I

In 1924 Dorothy Jewson, then Labour M.P. for Norwich, drew attention at question time to the connection between lack of Birth Control facilities and reliable information on the one hand, and the prevalence of illegal and septic abortion as one of the results. In April, 1936, Sir Arnold Wilson, K.C.B., an independent Conservative, of a type which seems almost peculiar to the British Isles, being strongly traditional in politics and economics, but bold and enlightened on certain aspects of individual liberty and happiness, pointed out the *rôle* of illegal and septic abortion in the increase of maternal mortality of recent years. He truly observed that " It is a matter of which it is exceedingly difficult for any member of Parliament to speak, because it arouses the greatest prejudice in the minds of those who have not given it the fullest consideration." He quoted from the Nation's Annual Public Health Report by Sir George Newman, that in the " view of an increasing number of experts and social workers " the " termination of cases of pregnancy under twelve weeks' duration, under surgical conditions in recognized hospitals, represents an advance in maternal care. The mortality under these conditions is reported as notably low." And, he added, " however little we may like to do so, it is time that we recognized and took stock of that fact."

In the course of this debate on the Health Estimates, there were thirteen speeches subsequent to Sir Arnold Wilson's. Only one of the thirteen speakers plucked up courage to follow Sir Arnold's lead ; this was Captain G. S. Elliston, who asked " whether the matter had been pursued further." The Minister ignored the subject in his reply.

On June 17th Maternal Mortality was again discussed, and Mrs. H. B. Tate, M.P. for Frome, in Somerset, pointed out that " one of the causes of the ill-health of mothers in the urban and industrial areas is the tremendous amount of abortion." She was followed by Lady Astor, who stressed the fact that one-sixth of maternal deaths were officially admitted to be due to abortion. Unfortunately, when attacked by Irish Catholic M.P.'s, Lady Astor took refuge in the Conventionality of Contraception, instead of vindicating women's right to really free motherhood. Lieutenant-Colonel Moore praised her " courage and openness of mind," but in spite of this tribute he " felt too embarrassed to follow in a discussion on matters which have either been reserved for the bed-chamber or the after-dinner port."

The press reporting of both these debates was significant. On the first occasion only the *Daily Telegraph* and *Manchester Guardian* gave brief but not unfair résumés of both speeches. On the second occasion most papers summarized ; but on both occasions *The Times* carefully omitted all reference to " this painful subject."

This attitude has been far too prevalent, even amongst active workers for contraceptive Birth Control. Thus, in 1929 Marie Stopes stated that she had received 20,000 requests for " criminal abortion " in three months ; and that in a given number of days one of her travelling clinics had " only thirteen applications for scientific instruction in the control of contraception, but eighty demands for criminal abortion ! " Strangely enough she actually thought fit in a letter to the *Freethinker* of November 30th, 1930, to refer to the demand for legalized abortion as " a fancied grievance " ; a really memorable psychological curiosity !

The British Law on abortion is laid down in Sections 58 and 59 of the offences against the Person Act of 1861. Agitation against it had already begun in 1915, when Stella Browne pleaded in the *Malthusian* of March 15th for women's right to freedom of choice in a matter concerning them so closely. In Germany, Austria and Scandinavia the demand had been vocal since 1909, and passionately expressed by Helene Stoecker, Oda Olberg, Marie Stritt, Camilla

Jellinek, Katti Anker Möller and other feminists of the Left. At the International Neo-Malthusian and Birth Control Conference in London (1922) Stella Browne argued for the Legalization of Abortion at the Woman's request, and referred to the pioneering practical example of Soviet Russia. The result was a horrified "hush-hush" and much wrath from the assembled Neo-Malthusian Orthodox. At the annual meeting of the Maternal Mortality Conference in 1929 Stella Browne returned to the charge. The only woman in an assembly of over a thousand who ventured to second her demand was the educational expert, Dora Russell. But the taboo of silence had been broken, and abortion became not only a most important reality in womens' individual lives, but a theme of public discussion, an "issue of public policy."

On June 7th, 1934, the Women's Co-operative Guild demanded legalization of abortion by an overwhelming majority.

On October 15th, 1935, the National Council of Women at Leicester accepted a resolution urging Government enquiry into the whole subject of legislation as well as administration. In the same month of October, 1935, there was published a Symposium of varying views, which roused considerable attention and discussion. In this book, entitled *Abortion*, Stella Browne demanded legalization of abortion, Captain Anthony M. Ludovici, the literary and artistic connoisseur, opposed it, and Dr. Harry Roberts drew conclusions midway between these extremes:

"I am not in favour of the complete legalization of abortion, though I sympathize with individual women whose pregnancy, if continued, will involve them in social or economic difficulties greater than society has any right to impose on them. So long as our conventions and our economic system remain what they are, I would reduce the legal penalties to a level more nearly in accord with contemporary opinion as to the sinfulness of abortion" (p. 142).

2

Dr. Harry Roberts is a fine humanitarian worker, but his

statement of opinion quoted above is so vague that exact legal minds must inevitably ask where the " penalties " are to begin ? And if lawyers are to have a voice in the matter we must recognize that the penalization of abortion is a part of the Canon Law and an obeisance to the Vatican by such States as preserve it in the twentieth century. The claim that abortion is in itself a " crime " is simply dogmatic theology. It has nothing to do with biological or psychological or economic factors, although these are often invoked —or invented !—in its support. The Papal Encyclical of December 31st, 1930, frequently mentioned in our preceding chapter, rejects abortion *in toto*, even when urgent " medical indications " exist. Its conclusions are based on decisions of the Congregation of the Holy Office on May 23rd, 1884, and August 14th, 1887, and these in turn are founded on the doctrine of Animation (*cf.* Article 2350 of the Canon Law), which forbade abortion under penalty of excommunication. This doctrine is that the immortal soul is attached to the fœtus from its earliest stages, *i.e.*, from the moment the ovum is fertilized. Thus a microscopic speck of protoplasm becomes a living human being and the immortal soul unfortunately implies the taint of original sin. Therefore the embryo must on no account be deprived of the possibility of baptism and a share in the Bliss of Heaven.

And as the expert in moral theology, Dr. Capellmann, has laid down in his *magnum opus* on *Pastoral Medicine*, all possible complications in the course of gestation are " due to maternal " and not to " fœtal conditions." It follows from these premises, that there can be no moral justification for destroying the fœtus in order to save the mother from death or invalidism. This is a regression even from the standpoint of Aristotle, who taught that the embryo only became animated after the lapse of a certain number of days after conception : he thought the exact date varied with the sex of the embryo. The soul entered the male fœtus at forty days, but the female at eighty ! The Christian Churches have certainly done their best to perpetuate and stereotype the subjection of women in practice, but so far as the animation of the fertilized ovule is concerned they admitted no loophole of escape, even on the basis of innate female inferiority ! The ovule had the right to salvation through Baptism at all costs.

The details of moral theology are sometimes strikingly suggestive of exhibitionistic and even scatological perversion. Rocaglia, a leading authority in the first field, expressed himself thus on the urgent need for certainty that an ovule has been expelled in cases of spontaneous miscarriage : "Owing to the ignorance of the obstetricians, the mothers themselves or those in attendance on them, embryos extruded in miscarriages are thrown down drains ; their souls, had they not been deprived of Baptism, would behold the Glory of the Lord in Eternity ; and their bodies, although not recognizable as human forms, at least deserve a more decent sepulchre " (Bellamy, *l.c.*).

3

Our readers may well ask " what have these ridiculous and revolting intricacies of Church dogma to do with modern knowledge of sex and modern ethics ? " Unfortunately they have great *indirect* power, for the mere fact that abortion is or can be treated as a juridical matter is the result of " moral theology " as interpreted by the modern bourgeoisie.

Let us turn from laws to the facts of women's lives. What *rôle* does abortion take, as regards both numerical quantity, quality and results ?

First of all—what is the proportion of Abortions to Conceptions and to full-term deliveries ?

In the proceedings of the Medico-Legal Society of London, in 1926, Dr. F. J. McCann said that " The amount of abortion is difficult to estimate. It is stated that about every fifth or sixth pregnancy ends in spontaneous abortion " (Slot, p. 37). This estimate is almost certainly an understatement. In 1930 the minimum estimate of persons in touch with Central European conditions was one abortion to every full-time birth. Of course, this was after the world economic crisis. Well let us take some available data before 1929, from the first precise and definite material on this subject, collected by Dr. H. Hecht of Prague. Dr. Hecht gave

lectures on venereal prophylaxis and general sexual hygiene, and distributed questionnaires among the women attending his lectures—with full respect for their confidential and anonymous treatment. He asked :
1. How old are you ?
2. How many children have you brought into the world ?
3. How often have you procured miscarriage ?
4. How many of your children are alive at present ?
5. What is your profession or trade, or your husband's ?
6. How many rooms has your dwelling ?

The first 500 women who replied were inhabitants of the industrial suburbs of Prague and of four Czechoslovakian provincial towns. These 500 women had given birth to 1,261 children and admitted 1,157 abortions. The 1,157 abortions were admitted by 305 out of the 500 women. One woman had had twenty, and three had had twenty-two each. Some in their thirties had procured miscarriages ten or eleven times. This questionnaire was issued and answered in 1928. In the same year the official statistics for Czechoslovakia recorded 344,441 births. Let us do a little arithmetic :

$$\frac{344,441}{x} = \frac{1,261}{1,157} = 321,955.$$

being the probable number of abortions in one year for Czechoslovakia. Hecht worked out further estimates on the basis of this questionnaire, and the official statistics of births from 1921 to 1927. He came to the staggering conclusion that the women in the Czechoslovak republic who were over fifteen years of age had committed over 10,000,000 " criminal abortions " in those seven years ! Thus his results implied that for every birth there was just under one abortion. This confirmed the estimated German averages, and the conclusions reached in France by Balthazard, Lacassagne and Doléris, as stated in the Draft Bill of the Deputé M. Clamamus.

In Newark, U.S.A., Drs. Hannah Stone and Henrietta Hart collected data from 2,000 patients attending the local Maternal Health Centre in 1933 :

Abortion induced by	Protestants		Jews		Catholics		Total	
	No.	Per cent.	No.	Per cent.	No.	Per cent.	No.	Per cent.
Physician .	214	40·4	170	61·0	72	31·2	469[1]	44·5
Midwife .	73	13·8	16	5·7	32	13·8	121	11·5
Self . .	243	45·8	93	33·3	127	55·0	463	44·0
	530	100·0	229	100·0	231	100·0	1,053[1]	100·0

[1] Including 13 cases among women without any religious affiliations (Investigation, V, 1934, p. 29).

These results are like those on contraception from similar American sources quoted in our preceding chapter. The Jewish mothers had the highest percentage of professional, *i.e.*, skilled attention in this respect and the Catholics were at the foot of the hygienic ladder *with* 11½ (11·5) *per cent. over the mean average of self-inflicted abortions.* Catholic education and environment are no more efficacious in preventing this " crime " than all the thunders of the secular law-makers. Careful sifting of available material throughout the world leads to the following conclusions : the four corner stones of practical reform :

1. Penalization does not prevent the wholesale procuring. of abortions.

2. Penalization does hinder the clinical control of abortions.

3. Penalization invites " criminal " abortion.

4. Penalization therefore is extremely dangerous to women's health.

4

The medical champions of the existing laws against abortion in the majority of States to-day constantly refer to the dangers of the artificial abortions *per se* to life and health. Let us admit that such dangers exist and are not negligible : nevertheless, they are as nothing in comparison with the perils of unskilled, septic, quack abortions. And there are only two remedial possibilities : (1) Unavoidable operations for the termination of pregnancy must be performed by skilled and competent practitioners with all modern resources ; and (2) There must be a great extension of reliable contraceptive knowledge and appliances.

These are the conclusions of human mercy and human reason, untainted by theology.

There is only one state which has acted consistently with human sympathy and modern science up to the present time as regards abortion, and that is the Union of Socialist Soviet Republics. On November 18th, 1920, the Commissars for Public Health and Justice respectively, Semashko and Kursky, signed a decree legalizing terminations of pregnancy up to three months if performed by qualified practitioners in specially designated Hospitals.[1] This drastic reform was continued and incorporated in the first Codification of the Soviet Penal Law in 1922 (Section 146). It was further laid down that only such abortions as were performed by unqualified persons and in unsuitable conditions were to be punished. The consent of the woman herself was to be necessary in any case. Only a year's imprisonment was to be the penalty for operations by unqualified persons, but in cases of death to the woman the operator might have up to five years' imprisonment. Women procuring abortions on themselves were not to be punished in any case, but looked after and taught contraception. The additions to the Penal Code in 1926 repeated these enactments.

Thus there has been only one country in which it has been possible to study the results of clinical abortion on an adequate number of cases. For in states under capitalism and traditional penal codes only " medical cases " are officially admitted to have been operated on and these " medical cases " are presumably women in less than normal average health. In the sixteen years of legal and scientific termination of pregnancy in the Soviet Union two problems have claimed especial attention. The interruptions of first pregnancies have occasioned grave doubt, and there has

[1] This positive measure followed the rescinding of the former Tzarist laws penalizing abortion immediately after the Bolshevik revolution of October-November, 1917, at the demand of the Russian women. The Women's and Children's Department of the Commissariat for Public Health was at that time administered by Alexandra Kollontay.—Translator's Note.

been much conflict of opinion as to " hormonic trauma,"
which may be set up by the termination of pregnancy in
certain individual cases (Kakushkin, 1934).
The leading theoretical exponent of the problems of
abortion in Soviet Russia is Dr. A. Genss, who attended the
W.L.S.R. Conference in 1929 at the Wigmore Hall and
stressed the fact that " from the medical standpoint, the
interruption of the first pregnancy is the most harmful of
all " (*Report*, p. 148). This statement has led to premature
announcements of the penalization of such interruptions;
even Karlin (1930) and Rongy (1933) made this assertion, but
it is misleading. In 1929 16·6 (16⅗) per cent. of these operations in the U.S.S.R. were performed on women who had
not previously borne children. Custom, as apart from actual
law, certainly favours all possible dissuasion from " first-
pregnancy abortions." The strong feeling among women on
this matter is confirmed by Lewis Fischer, who writes as
follows from Moscow to the *New Statesman and Nation* of
February 22nd, 1936 : " Yet when the party and the government initiated an intense campaign last year (1935) against
the innumerable abortions . . . there was such a wave of
resentment that the campaign ceased and the contemplated
legislation denying abortions to childless women is still in
abeyance. Even this mild form of puritanism provoked
widespread opposition." [1]

5

The second objection has been thus formulated by Kakushkin in 1934. He refers to sterility and reduction of sexual
desire : " It is probable that in these cases, more than in
other post-abortive disturbances, a hormone trauma is at
the root of the trouble ; but we should also reckon with the
possible effect of anatomical injuries connected with the
abrasion of the gravid uterus. The violent drawing down of
the uterus, the forcible dilatation of the cervical canal, and

[1] In June, 1936, the Soviet Union re-enacted serious penalties on
abortion except for medical indications alone. This regrettable and
retrograde step has been undertaken with a view to attaining a population
of 300,000,000 by 1971, and in reply to the menace of Germany and Japan.
Cf. Chapter IX, § 1.—Translator's Note.

the traumatic curettage of the wall of the uterus may possibly injure the nervous mechanism on which sexual sensations depend, which lies in the region of the ligamenta sacro-uterina " (Ludovici, *l.c.*).

This extreme pessimism is in accord with various criticisms heard at the Pan-Ukrainian Gynæcological Congress at Kieff in 1927. Dr. Genss declares the impression these views convey to be misleading, and founded on incomplete and partial material (*cf. Betänkande*, 1935, p. 69, and the reports sent to the Norwegian Government : *Innstillingen*, p. 40). The death-rates after abortion show a striking decline. In ten years 266,000 clinical abortions were performed in Moscow. Their average death-rate was 1 in 17,000 or 0·06 per thousand. In Leningrad we have interesting half-yearly data : for 1933, from January to June, 0·06 per 1,000, from July to December, o. The number of cases was 47,000. There are still some illegal abortions, and the women who venture on these are more and more seeking hospital help after the first interference. The mortality here is 6 per 1,000. In Sweden it is 7½.

There are, of course, in some cases complications and accidents immediately due to the operation. In 300,000 cases the percentage of perforated uteri was from 0·04 to 0·08. In 192,000 cases there were 0·03 per cent. of sepsis ; inflammatory symptoms in the uterus and ovaries 0·47 per cent. ; and uterine sub-involution 1·4 per cent. There were feverish symptoms (rise of temperature to over 100° F) in 2·03 per cent. out of 288,000 Moscow cases ; and in sixteen Leningrad clinics these symptoms affected from 1·3 to 3·3 per cent.

But late sequelæ are obviously very slight. Levit stated that frequent curettages on the same woman often caused sterility. But in 1935 the Swedish Legation in Moscow, investigating the subject at the request of the Swedish Government, could find no confirmation of these statements. And they reported that " it is not known that psychic injuries followed " (*Betänkande*, p. 70). I may add that my own experience and observation of several hundred cases in which my German colleagues had disregarded a merciless law, tend to the same conclusion : " psychic injuries " of a permanent kind are extremely rare, and practically only occur after first pregnancy abortions. It is true that Arnold Zweig has immortalized a case of frustrated mother-love in his gripping story *Young Woman of* 1914 ; but I repeat, this is exceptional, and not usual.

The comparatively safe and satisfactory results of the Russian clinical abortions are due to the encouragement of skilled professional work by the Soviet Law. The method in use is curettage, and this procedure in the Abortaria takes only a few minutes in the vast majority of cases. Curettage has been found superior to the injections so widely attempted and recommended throughout Central Europe since 1924. These injections are associated with the name of Heiser, a Berlin pharmacist who was the defendant in a tremendous *cause célèbre* in 1924. He had performed illegal operations on over 3,000 women, without any fatal accidents ; the method used by Heiser was the introduction of a paste into the gravid uterus, by means of a piston-like instrument. The paste was compounded on a recipe of his own, and induced powerful contractions and then expulsions of the product of conception. The large number of " criminals " involved, and the public sympathy for Heiser, led the authorities to drop the case. At the time I made experiments on animals with the paste, and there was no septic effect. The paste was bacteriologically harmless, but there were severe post-operative hæmorrhages in 10 per cent. of the cases, which made it necessary to supplement the paste with curettages.

The exact ingredients of the paste were kept a secret by its inventor. But many imitations were put on the market by other individuals. On October 25th, 1932, the Prussian Ministry of Health made it illegal to supply Heiser's paste, Antigravid, Interruptin, Antiathon and Provocol, except to a doctor's order. The last word has not yet been said on this method. With all its defects there is little risk of embolism.

One of the arguments brought forward by Ludovici against the legalization of abortion is the continuance of illegal, *i.e.*, non-clinical, quack abortions in Soviet territory even under the wide and humane provisions of the law of 1920. He is right in maintaining that quack abortions and self-abortions still went on, but what of the special conditions prevalent in Soviet Russia, and different to those obtaining in " Western Christendom " ? The territories of the Soviet Union are one-sixth of the total land surface of our planet, but the transport facilities are still very inadequate and there is a dearth of sufficient trained medical practitioners relative to the population to be attended and the standard set in public health work. And in spite of enlightened laws and fear of punishment for recourse to quacks, many Russian peasant women have more faith in the " wise woman " of their locality than in strange doctors, in white coats, with glittering instruments. After all, Soviet Russia is not the only country in which tradition is stronger than reason in many individual minds ! It is a question of time : medicine must have time to vanquish the fears and rituals of primitive magic.

6

No, with all his eloquence and versatile ingenuity, Ludovici has missed, or avoided, the real core of the opposition to free and safe termination of pregnancy. Dr. Vollmann, the spokesman of this opposition within the medical faculty of Germany, even before Hitler's advent, made no bones about physical risks or clinical considerations. He spoke out, and as follows : " The harm done to morality and to our whole social fabric would be far worse ! The fear of pregnancy is a barrier against temptation and sensual impulse ; it is the only barrier between thousands of girls and ' free love ' ; the promiscuous indulgence in sexual relationships. If these girls can feel sure of being able to get rid of the possible results of such indulgence with impunity, the last defence against sexual licence would go down. Then there could be no more holding them back and the demoralization which would ensue must inevitably infect the whole moral sphere and drag down our people's

souls and bodies " (1925, p. 59). Not gynæcology, but the morality of the past and of fear ! And Dr. Genss hit the nail on the head in his " Open Letter " in reply :
" Now we have the real objection ! . . . When the conflict of classes becomes embittered and conscious, marriage ties and religious scruples prove so rotten that they vanish at the breath of any strong human need. If we permit abortion, we ' desecrate ' bourgeois morality and virtue, and bring ' materialist considerations ' into the ' sacred ' sphere of marriage. We cause ' confusion,' for does not marriage lose all its ' sacred ' aura as soon as a skilled surgeon is summoned to regulate offspring, instead of leaving the matter in God's hands ? No ; tradition on the one hand and definite financial interest on the other are the main motives of those doctors who oppose the legalization of abortion, and who in doing so become the servants of that bourgeoisie which still rules us."

Ludovici has made a final objection on very fundamental lines. He maintains that to leave abortion to the free choice of the individual woman is to act on a mistaken and " monomorphic view of sex." He claims that for woman sexual fulfilment demands childbirth, and not only coitus, as is the case with man.

Let us grant that a woman who has never borne nor reared a child is unlikely to experience the full emotional possibilities of her nature, though there are not one but many types of temperament among women. Nevertheless, we must beware of confusing the sexual needs of women with their reproductive power. If a woman deeply desires a child, the social order should make it easy for her to fulfil her longing. Until now, no state in actual recorded history has made such definite arrangements on those lines as Soviet Russia. Pregnant women must not be put to heavy manual labour in the U.S.S.R. They have two months' holiday before their confinements and the same period of holiday afterwards, with full pay for all four months ; they may not be dismissed from their work during this time, and for a further seven months they have the right to have two half hours off work, with no reduction of pay, for the purpose of nursing their baby ; they have also other privileges of various kinds.

How different from the actual conditions in most other communities, as distinct from their official phrases. Economic help here is worth thousands of lyrical phrases about maternity as a social service.[1] And this callous neglect bears its consequences ; consequences recorded in the plaintive laments of officials and ministers of Church and State, in their denunciations of those responsible for the falling birth-rates, for the risks to national prestige, and the unbalance in the age composition of modern populations. But the exhortations to be fruitful and multiply, however urgent and incessant, fall on deaf ears.[2] Population experts of the eminence of Burgdoerffer in Germany, Carr Saunders in Great Britain and the Myrdals in Sweden concur in pointing out the deceptive nature of the present slight excess of births over deaths in Northern and Western Europe. For their annual population increase is not now enough to keep their numbers constant. In 1935 R. Kuczynski contributed a most valuable essay to *Economica* in which he dealt fully with the declining actual fertility of Atlantic peoples and introduced the concept of the " gross reproduction rate " :

" If we assume again that fecundity would be realized to the full if every female from seventeen to forty-six years had a child every eighteen months, the total number of children born to a woman passing through child-bearing age would be twenty, and the gross reproduction rate (which comprises girls only) would be 9·8 " (p. 131). " Wherever the gross reproduction rate is constantly below one, the population must die out even if every newly born girl reaches the age of fifty. Wherever the gross reproduction rate is constantly above one, the population will reproduce itself if a sufficient number of newly born girls passes through child-

[1] The late Winifred Holtby has an excellent summary of the relevant facts, at least as concerns Great Britain, in her manual on *Women in the XXth Century* (1934).—Translator's Note.

[2] " Many among the more imaginative and sensitive types are restricting their families sometimes to zero, because they feel that they cannot bear to bring children into a world exposed to such a risk of war and chaos " (Professor Julian Huxley, Galton Lecture for 1936).

bearing age. The best method of ascertaining the net reproduction consists in multiplying the specific fertility rates (ratio of female births to female population) of the individual years of age by the numbers of females living at those ages according to the life table. The sum of these products is the net reproduction rate. It shows (on the basis of present fertility and mortality) the average number of girls born to a newly born girl, or, what amounts to the same, the average number of future mothers born to a mother of to-day. The net reproduction rate, of course, must always be smaller than the gross reproduction rate. . . . The highest rate which I have found for any large country was for the Ukraine in 1896–97. It amounted to 1·96, which means almost a doubling within a generation. In Western and Northern Europe it was 1·3 fifty years ago. In 1933 it was 0·76 . . ." (p. 134).

The logical conclusions from these facts and mathematical calculations are startling :

" No conceivable decrease of mortality or increase of nuptiality can thus prevent the dying out of the population of Western and Northern Europe. The only factor which may prevent it is an increase of matrimonial fertility. . . . A great and permanent rise of fertility can be obtained only through a restriction of birth control. . . . But it should be realized that with a net reproduction rate of 0·76, fertility would have to increase by over 30 per cent. in order to insure the maintenance of the population. . . . We thus have to choose only between two policies : either make the raising of children more attractive, or adapt our economic and social structure to the needs of a decreasing population. Each of these policies involves a gigantic task which certainly will not become easier by delay " (pp. 140–141).

Yes, it is easy to perceive why the Nationalists under every flag in Europe are doing their utmost to discourage Birth Control and outlaw abortion, in the hope to raise fresh squadrons of battle fodder and machine minders. The Draconian laws of Nazis in Germany and Fascists in Italy are examples of futile ferocity. The Italian birth-rate has fallen steadily since 1925, and in spite of a rise in the German birth-rate in late 1933 and 1934, it is now evident that economic stress and psychological disillusionment have had their effect in the Third Reich as well. Burgdoerffer himself was at pains to point out that the sudden spurt of marriage and breeding could not be maintained, having regard to the age composition of the German population in 1935.

Thus the recent reaction in population policy has not had the desired results.

In 1919 the peoples of Europe saw more clearly ; they had passed through four years of agony, and they were not inclined to listen to further invitations to mutual slaughter. And there were widespread efforts towards abortion law reform ; stimulated by the interest of the sexual states-manship in the Russian People's Republic, and by the improvement in women's status in many countries after the war. In the Swiss Canton of Bâle, the General Assembly accepted a draft Bill which rescinded the penalties on abor-tion on the occasion of its first reading. But at the second reading it was rejected, mainly owing to the passionate opposition of Professor Labhardt, the Chief Gynæcologist of the local Hospital for Women. It is significant that one of the main " arguments " in the press was the assertion that Bâle would be invaded and " swamped out " by women from all countries of Europe if the Bill went through ; and these wicked women would ruin the reputation of that godly city for all time. This is almost on a level with the epoch-making remark of Professor Sellheim, of Leipzig, some years later, when the agitation was rousing intense public interest throughout Germany. Professor Sellheim declared that if abortion were legalized, there would be an immediate " siege of our hospitals " by hordes of frantic women. Q.E.D.

In 1920 and 1921 the Left Wing Socialists of Germany brought the demand for the legalization of abortion (whether absolute or partial) into the Reichstag debates. In 1926 a few concessions were made in the extremely severe law surviving from the Imperial Code. The punishment of imprisonment with hard labour was changed to simple detention. But the agitation for adequate reforms was only whetted to greater activity. A projected revision of the Penal

Code (1927–30) suggested further alleviations. In France, Victor Márguéritte wrote his remarkable and courageous problem novel *Ton Corps est à Toi;* it was translated into most European languages and widely discussed (1927). In Germany two medical men with a grasp of social and psychological facts, Friedrich Wolff (in *Cyankali*) and Credé-Hoerder (in *Paragraph* 218), put the case for reform on to the stage. Those of us who took part in the movement for Sexual Education and Reform throughout Central Europe, in that decade of hope and effort, all spoke to the audiences who crowded the theatres where *Cyankali* and 218 were performed, and urged them to demand better laws and better conditions for mothers and children. We also organized and addressed mass meetings on the subject in the popular campaign which reached a climax between 1930 and 1932. Friedrich Wolff was prosecuted under the law, and while all Germany rang with the protests of his friends, the National Socialists were capturing the political key-positions and preparing for the *coup* of March, 1933. Many factors combined to bring about this reactionary revolution ; first of all we must admit that the world slump of 1929 had hit all Liberals and Socialists doubly hard. Of course, these Draconic laws failed to stop all illegal abortions in Germany. Even in 1934 many women travelled from Denmark to Berlin in order to have the benefit of a wider choice of doctors and facilities than Copenhagen could offer. And the Scandinavian Exchange was more persuasive than all the moral fervour of the Berlin Medical Council. Laws against abortion may be never so severe, but the facts of human nature and economic circumstance persist, and the countries in which this " crime " is most stringently penalized—at the present time Germany, Italy and France—are simply examples of the truth in the statements of the famous Norwegian medical official Heitmann, which Schlyter, the Swedish Minister of Justice, made the text for his address at the Oslo Juridical Conference of all Scandinavian countries in 1934 :

" The chief argument for this necessary reform is the absolutely intolerable nature of present conditions under the penalization of abortion. Both doctors and other persons qualified to form an opinion in our country are entirely unanimous about this, so I will hold myself excused from detailed discussion."

7

The point of view enunciated by the great Swedish jurist has become increasingly vocal throughout Europe of recent years. As a rule, projects of reform have been limited to admitting medical grounds. But eugenic, social and humanitarian " indications " have sometimes been advocated or even accepted. An example of the " humanitarian indication " would be the termination of pregnancy due to rape, criminal assault or incest, or occurring in a girl of fourteen or under that age.

The crucial point is "social justification." In 1926 a revision of the Czechoslovakian law in this respect was discussed, and the Minister of Justice, Meissner, proposed a redraft of paragraph 286 in these terms, thus definitely accepting social indications :

" The expulsion of the embryo is not punishable if it is performed with the consent of the pregnant woman by a physician authorized to public practice in a public hospital, if

" . . . 4. It be undoubtedly established that the pregnant woman would not carry the child till birth, or would not be able to fulfil her duty to maintain (economically) the child without menace to her own livelihood or the existence of another person, whom she has to maintain and who is as near to her as the child whose birth she is expecting, would be.

" . . . If the abortion cannot be performed in a hospital, the consent of another physician is necessary."

The reform has not yet been incorporated in the Czechoslovak code, but has stimulated discussion both in that country and throughout Europe, in a most useful manner.

In 1932 the Swiss Canton de Vaud accepted eugenic indications : " Article 130 : Abortion is not punishable when it is practised on a person suffering from mental illness or mental infirmity and whose offspring will in all likelihood be tainted, but the operation can be performed only with the authority of the Health Council."

In the Polish Republic brave work has been done by Dr. Żeleński, who wrote fine propaganda essays and novels under the pseudonym " Boy." His tragic story *Piekło kobiet* (*The Women's Hell*) depicts the suffering inflicted by the complacent ignorance of those who do not suffer. In 1933 Poland accepted both medical and humanitarian reasons for permitting abortions, in paragraph 233 of the Penal Code. By a wise interpretation of " humanitarianism," pregnancies caused through seduction or compulsion on the part of men in a position of authority, are treated as in this category.

Latvia accepted medical indications and to some extent social grounds also in 1933, in paragraph 440. Unfortunately the latter concession was withdrawn again in March, 1935.

Outside Europe a remarkable advance is to be recorded, to the credit of the Argentine Republic, which accepted medical indications, including insanity and pregnancy due to rape, in 1921. The centre of the movement for reform to-day is in the Scandinavian lands, where it is one of the most frequent themes of public discussion, in speech and print. Already some actual alleviations have been made. Thus in 1930 Denmark permitted " remission of punishment in extenuating circumstances " (paragraph 242).

On November 7th, 1932, a Committee of investigation was appointed in Copenhagen. At the same moment the Danes learnt that " a great court case on abortion " was imminent ! The defendant was Dr. J. H. Leunbach, the Co-President of the W.L.S.R. An extraordinary game of " hide and seek " took place. The august Committee repeatedly postponed its Sessions, as its members wanted a " lead " from the verdict on Leunbach ; while the representatives of the Law refused to call the case, until they knew what the Special Committee thought ! Finally the case was heard in 1935, after three years' delay, to the accompaniment of the most virulent onslaught against the defendant in the Conservative press of the whole country. For Leunbach had been very frank about the motives behind the opposition. As long before as

1929 he had said in the course of a public lecture that "many medical men refused poverty as an indication for abortion, but readily accepted wealth."

The occasion for the prosecution were three fatalities among the poor working women who flocked to the doctor for advice and help. But in the course of the defence it was proved that this percentage of deaths among his patients was actually less than that in the Danish National Hospital (Rikshospitalet). Three out of 320 in Leunbach's list, and two out of 200 for the Hospital ! The result was an acquittal and a tremendous popular ovation. Leunbach was nominated as a candidate for the National Assembly in the autumn elections and fought on a detailed sex reform and Left Wing political platform. He was defeated, but he had achieved immense things for the cause of freedom. In both Norway and Sweden special Committees of medical, legal and sociological experts are working out detailed suggestions for reform. Unfortunately Sweden suffers at the moment from a population mania, which is largely due to the influence of the Myrdals, but the theses published by the Ministries of Justice in both countries in 1935 contain material of great value and are among the best contributions to the study of abortion. Far out in the storms of the North Atlantic, Iceland has almost escaped European public attention, but on December 10th, 1934, the Alting accepted a Draft Bill entitled " The Instruction of Women in Contraception and Abortion." This measure not only permitted but enjoined hygienic instruction in Birth Control methods, and laid down rules for termination of pregnancies on medical grounds. Then, in paragraph 9, it proceeded as follows : " . . . In estimating the amount of risk to life or health in full-term deliveries, in each case of pregnancy, it should also be taken into consideration whether the woman has had a large family at short intervals, or suffered greatly in her last confinement or lives under very poor financial circumstances, owing to large families, unemployment or illness among members of her family."

This law, which is in actual operation, since 1935, was

drafted by Vilmundur Jónsson, the Chief Medical Officer of Iceland, and is the widest measure of reform as yet achieved in any non-Socialist community.

In Great Britain the Medical Association has set up a special Committee to consider reform of the existing law, in so far as it affects therapeutic and eugenic abortion. This Committee has reported and its recommendations were considered by the Assembly of the B.M.A. at Oxford in July of the current year. The recommendations of the special Committee were significant in tone, though their scope was necessarily limited by their terms of reference. They recommended extended and precise medical indications, and also the following eugenic indications : (1) Both parents certified mental defectives. (2) Father and one child certified mental defectives. (3) Father psychopathic, and one child a certified mental defective ; and (4) Two children certified as mentally defective, even if neither parent is apparently defective nor psychopathic.

The report also indicates that in the opinion of the Committee, " the legalization of abortion for social and economic reasons would go far to solve the problem of the secret operation." They point out, however, that it is for the community to discuss and demand this reform. At the beginning of the year 1936 an Abortion Law Reform Association was founded in Great Britain. Its first Conference was held in May, and its Report has just been issued. The personnel of this Association is a guarantee that economic and psychological factors will be given as much weight as technically medical considerations in its policy and propaganda.[1] For we must never forget that the psychic state during pregnancy is hyper-sensitive and swayed by profound and obscure tides of emotion ; and that the whole case for this reform is not so much gynæcological as economic and psychological.

Dr. Beckwith-Whitehouse was quite right when he emphasized the uselessness of talking man-made law and

---

[1] The Hon. Secretary is Mrs. Alice Jenkins, 17 Mount Carmel Chambers, Kensington, London, W.8. The Chairman of the Executive Committee, Mrs. Janet Chance, the social reformer and writer.—Translator's Note.

traditional reason to any pregnant woman who insists on demanding release :

" What always amazes me is the extraordinary moral mentality of a woman, married or single, who sets her mind upon the termination of a pregnancy. It almost seems to become an obsession at the time, and no argument or threat will turn her from her path. It is not the slightest use pointing out the criminal nature of the action inasmuch as the patient's mental outlook so frequently appears to be obscured. Neither is it of any avail to dwell upon the immediate physical risks involved as a woman always seems to think that the dangers of terminating a pregnancy are magnified and out of proportion to the advantage which she will gain."

These comments were made in the course of an address to the Medico-Legal Society of London, and show acute insight into the psychology of pregnancy : but surely there is a certain spiritual arrogance in the term " extraordinary moral mentality." Any one in touch with reality and aware of the social and economic background of all sex problems to-day needs no further assurance that abortion cannot be settled on medical grounds alone or by medical practitioners alone.[1] In the words of a veteran of French medicine, Professor Couvelaire, formerly in charge of the famous Hôpital Baudelocque :

" Premature terminations of pregnancy are most frequently due to the over-strain and exhaustion of mothers who have been compelled to hard work without any alleviation during their gravid state and in conditions to which no breeder of live-stock would subject the animals under his care ! "

BIBLIOGRAPHY

ANDERSEN, K., *Abortus provokatus med henblikk paa dens mulige indikasjoner*, Oslo, 1930.
ARNORSSON, E., *Nordisk Tidskrift f. Strafferett*, Copenhagen, January, 1936.

[1] At the end of July, 1936, the B.M.A., in its Annual Assembly, accepted the report of the Special Committee on Abortion after a long and vehement debate.—Translator's Note.

BATKIS, G. W., *Sexualrevolution in Russland*, Berlin, 1925.
BELLAMY, H., " L'ovule fécondé dans la théologie catholique,"
 Prob. sex., November, 1934.
BROWNE, LUDOVICI, ROBERTS, *Abortion*, London, 1935.
BURGDOERFFER, F., *Volk ohne Jugend*, Berlin, 1934.
BURGDOERFFER, F., " Zur Kritik der neuesten deutschen Be-
 völkerungsentwicklung," *Deut. Allg. Zeitg.*, March 3rd,
 1935.
CAPELLMANN, C., *Medicina pastoralis*, 4 Ed., Aix, 1879.
CAPELLMANN, C., and BERGMANN, W., *Medicina pastoralis*, 19 Ed.,
 Paderborn, 1923.
CHANCE, JANET, *The Cost of English Morals*, London, 1931.
CRAIG, ALEC, *Sex and Revolution*, London, 1934.
CREDÉ-HOERDER, *Paragraph 218*, Dresden, 1929.
EDIN, K. A., *Undersökning av abortförkomsten i Sverige*, Stock-
 holm, 1934.
ELLIS, H., *Studies in the Psychology of Sex, V.: The Psychic
 State in Pregnancy*, Philadelphia, 1906.
*Erfahrungen mit der Freigabe der Schwangerschafts-Unterbrechung
 in der Sovietrepublik (deutscher Bericht über Kiew-Kongress
 1927)*, Stuttgart, 1933.
FISCHER, L., " A Reply to Joad," *New Statesman*, February 22nd,
 1936.
HARMSEN, H., *Bevölkerungsprobleme Frankreichs*, Berlin, 1927.
HECHT, H., " Schwangerschaftsunterbrechung der Proletarierin,"
 Soz. Arzt, 1932.
HOELLEIN, E., *Gebärzwang und kein Ende*, Berlin, 1930.
GENSS, A., " Der künstliche Abortus," *Arch. soz. Hyg.*, 1928,
 554 *ff.*
GENSS, A., W.L.S.R. Congress, *Report*, London, 1930, and *passim*.
GOLDBERG, E., " Die psychischen Wirkungen des künstlichen
 Aborts," *Aerztl. Vereinsbl. f. Deutschl.*, December, 1929.
GROTJAHN, A., *Hygiene der menschlichen Fortpflanzung*, Berlin,
 1926.
GROTJAHN, A., *Eine Kartothek zu Paragraph 218*, Berlin, 1932.
GROTJAHN-GROSS, E., " Die italienische Gesetzgebung zur
 Bekämpfung des Geburtenrückganges," *Arch. soz. Hyg.*,
 1930.
Innstilling No. 1 angaaende forandring i straffeloven, paragraph
 245, Justisdepartementet, Oslo, 1935.
KAKUSHKIN, N., " Funktionelle Störungen d. weibl. Geschlechts-
 organe nach Künstl. Abort.," *Zentr. Bl. Gyn.*, November,
 1934.
KUCZYNSKI, R. R., *The Balance of Birth and Death*, II,
 Washington, 1931.
KUCZYNSKI, R. R., " The Decrease of Fertility," *Economica*,
 1935.

KUCZYNSKI, R. R., *The Measurement of Population Growth*, London, 1935.

LABOUR PARTY, Report on Maternal Mortality, National Conference of Labour Women, Sheffield, 1935 ; London, 1935.

LEWINSOHN, R., " Die Stellung der Sozialdemokratie zur Bevölkerungspolitik," *Schmoll. Jahrb.*, 46, 1922.

MARGUÉRITTE, V., *Ton corps est à toi*, Paris, 1927.

" Medical Aspects of Abortion," *Brit. Med. Journ.*, II, 1932, 968 *f.*

MYRDAL, PROFESSOR and A., *Kris i befolkningsfraagan*, Stockholm, 1934.

" Nationalsozialistisches Strafrecht," *Denkschrift d. preuss. Just. Min.*, Berlin, 1933, 65–66.

NEMILOV, A., *The Biological Tragedy of Woman*, London, 1932.

PARRY, A., *Criminal Abortion*, London, 1932.

PELLER, S., *Fehlgeburt und Bevölkerungsfrage*, Stuttgart, 1930.

Plan, organ of F.P.S.I., London, 1934–36, *passim.*

Report of Fifth International Neo-Malthusian and Birth Control Conference, London, 1922 (Heinemann).

Report of A.L.R.A. Conference, London, 1936.

RONGY, A. J., *Abortion, Legal or Illegal ?* New York, 1933.

SCHARFFENBERG, J., " Befolkningsspörsmaalet fra socialistisk synspunkt," *Arb. blad.*, Oslo, October 21st, 23rd, 25th, 1935.

SCHLYTER, K., *I foster fördrivningsfraagan*, Oslo-Stockholm, 1934.

SLOT, G., and DICKSON, E., *Transact. of the Medico-Legal Soc.*, XXIII, Cambridge, 1930.

Statens offentliga Utredningar, 1935, 15, " Betänkande med förslag till lagstiftning om avbrytande av havandeskap," Stockholm, 1935.

Statens öffentliga Utredningar, 1934, 50, " Utredning ang. Revision av 13 paragraf, Strafflagen," Stockholm, 1934.

STOPES, M. C., *Mother England*, London, 1929.

Veröffentlichungen d. Preuss. Medizin. Verwaltg, XXIII, Berlin, 1926, " Ueber die Zunahme der Fruchtabtreibungen."

VOLLMANN, *Fruchtabtreibung als Volkskrankheit*, Leipzig, 1925.

WINTER, " Der künstliche Abort im neuen Strafrecht," *Reichsgesundheitsblatt*, Berlin, 1926.

WOLFF, F., *Cyankali*, Stuttgart, 1929.

ZWEIG, A., *Young Woman of 1914*, Translated, London, 1934.

TABLE OF EVENTS

1913 KATTI ANKER MÖLLER demands legalization of Abortion for Norway.

1915 STELLA BROWNE advocates legalization of Abortion for Great Britain in the *Malthusian*.

1919 First Reading of Legalization Bill passes the Council of the city of Bâle. Professor LABHARDT succeeds in preventing acceptance at Second Reading.

1920 Soviet Russia legalizes Abortion performed by Medical Practitioners.

Independent Social Democrats and Communists start agitation in Germany against Paragraph 218.

French Law of July 31st increases penalties for Abortion.

1921 Argentine Republic permits Abortion for Medical Reasons, and in cases of Insanity and Rape.

1922 New Abortion Law codified in Soviet Russia.

1924 DAME JANET CAMPBELL'S Report on Maternal Mortality in Britain.

HEISER trial in Germany.

1926 New and revised Soviet Penal Code. Abortion still legal (paragraph 140).

German Law slightly alleviated.

Agitation in Czechoslovakia.

1927 Ukrainian Gynæcological Congress. Discussion on Abortion.

New Draft Bill submitted to German Reichstag.

1929 Legalization of Clinical Abortion up to three months proposed in Esthonia, but not finally passed.

1930 Danish Paragraph 242 rescinds penalties in " milder cases."

1931 JANET CHANCE'S book *Cost of English Morals*.

MR. JUSTICE McCARDIE denounces the British Abortion Law on many occasions.

1932 Poland accepts Medical and Humanitarian grounds for Abortion.

The Swiss Canton de Vaud accepts Eugenic grounds.

MEISSNER reform drafted in Czechoslovakia.

1933 Latvia legalizes Abortion on Medical, Social and Eugenic grounds.

Nazi Government in Germany proceeds rigorously against Abortion.

1934 Scandinavian Juridical Congress in Oslo. Abortion discussed.

LEUNBACH trial in Denmark.

Iceland legalizes Medical and Social grounds.

Women's Co-operative Guild Congress in Great Britain demands drastic reform.

1935 Latvia rescinds Social indications.

1936 Abortion Law Reform Association formed in London.

Soviet Union rescinds social indications.

CHAPTER VII

SEX EDUCATION

I

THE Czech educational magazine *Mládá kultura* (*The Culture of Youth*) in the third number of its Second Volume published this piece of news from a secondary school :

"*Lesson on Philosophy:* 'Then your books have a chapter about the most splendid thing on earth, about—about—Love. There are different kinds : Mother love, love between friends, and finally—eh—er—um—well, the love of husband and wife.' Red as a turkey-cock in the face, our teacher turns rapidly to the subject matter of the following chapter.

"Then in the lesson about the Human body. The textbook contains a chapter entitled ' The Organs of Sex.' The teacher sends the girl pupils out of the room ; then he reads through the whole chapter very quickly, in order to comply with the educational regulations. One of us laughs aloud. His name is entered in the punishment book, and then the embarrassed and disconcerted girls are summoned to rejoin us, and the pedagogue begins an explanation of the nervous system, stuttering and stammering as he does so ! Incidentally that sort of thing is about all that young people are taught about sex in the secondary schools of to-day, excepting, of course, the threats that are heard when some love secrets become public property or when some sixth form stripling is discovered on the premises of a disorderly house, and reported to the Board and threatened with dismissal. And so, for these young people, Sex is something unclean, mysterious and forbidden."

In estimating the purport of this, we must bear in mind that the school in question is far from " backward " in comparison with most other schools ; on the contrary.

There is a certain amount of co-education ; and the textbook in use actually admits the fact that human beings have genital organs. Whereas most of the anatomical diagrams and illustrations in use throughout the schools of Christendom reveal the bones, veins, nerves and intestines unsparingly, but boggle and come to a full stop before the sexual apparatus. So that secondary school at Liberec-Reichenberg in Czechoslovakia was quite progressive and advanced, as schools go to-day. But the teacher in charge was visibly embarrassed ; one of the boys laughed out of nervous excitement and self-consciousness. The girls were sent out of the room, and " the rest is silence " and the repression of sexual knowledge and interest, out of open discussion into secret talk and secret action.

And that is really as far as we have got to-day.

For we cannot expect that a social order which is on principle hostile to sex or ashamed about it should suddenly become affirmative, in the one domain of the instruction of young people, and teach accurately, proudly and gladly. Any reference to this matter in state schools under official auspices is characterized by

1. A strict limitation to the reproductive and parental aspects of sex, and emphasis on plant life and animals,[1] without drawing comparisons with our own species, and with the most careful omission of the possibility of preventing reproduction.

2. Systematic terrorization about venereal diseases in particular and the " dangers " of sex in general ; and reprobation of auto-erotism or masturbation in children.

3. And as a result of these two tendencies, ignorance and intimidation, the formation of habits of embarrassment and sense of guilt in the children, of distrust of the information sparsely doled out by grown-ups, who themselves wince and flush at the mention of sex ; and finally a double helplessness before the primitive urge of their own puberty.

" But," our readers may ask, " Is this not a purely

---

[1] Though, as will appear later on, the L.C.C. educational authorities were doubtful about mammals in this connection and thought them unsuitable for the class instruction in senior schools.—Translator's Note.

negative and pessimistic view of the serious efforts now so widely made at some sort of rational instruction ? " Well, let us examine available evidence.

2

In 1927 the syllabus for the Board's Final Examination of students in Training Colleges laid down that :

" Instruction in sex hygiene is left to the discretion of each individual college. The Board, however, suggest that it should be included, but the manner of dealing with it must depend on the qualifications of any lecturer available."

This is in the tradition of British individualism and elasticity of method, and in some respects preferable to the rigid systems and courses of continental countries. Nevertheless we cannot avoid suspecting that this indecision and flexibility are not wholly due to Liberalism in the teaching profession, there are other motives. Under the authorization of the education officer, the London County Council has issued Memoranda on Curriculum I., Science for Junior Schools. Under the date July, 1935, when London was administered by a Labour Party Majority, we find the following :

" . . . IV. Reproduction.

" The increase in size of living matter through division of cells and the cell as the unit of living structure are matters of interest and importance. Suitable objects for microscopic study in this connection are amœba, blood corpuscles, yeast, etc.

" Reproduction of flowering plants :

" (a) Study of pollen, i.e., male cells. Forms of pollen grains ; experiments on germination of pollen.

" (b) Pollination—self and cross.

" (c) Fertilization—growth of pollen tube.

" (d) Seeds and development of fruits.

" (e) Seed dispersal.

" The life histories of the frog and of birds have been suggested above as appropriate for study. The development of the frog from spawn and of the chick from the hen's egg may be taken up more fully as illustrations of animal reproduction.

" It will generally be agreed that class instruction in senior schools should not include mammals in this topic. The pupils will, however, be familiar with the notion that the other essential processes of life, breathing and feeding with their resultant growth and excretion, are common to almost all living things ; they will have been trained to think about such processes in a relatively impersonal way when the processes are considered in relation to human beings. Thus, the pursuance of the four topics suggested in this section will be some preparation for facing the problem of sex, and the knowledge gained should at least act as a steadying influence when such problems become insistent in the individual lives of young pupils."

So in the year 1935 the London child is officially referred to the generative history of the frog as an adequate key to " The Mysteries of Life." Ilya Metchnikoff made an observation in his *Études sur la Nature humaine*, thirty years ago, which biology has not yet had occasion to revise : " In the case of frogs, which have nothing better to do, coitus lasts for several weeks." The analogy is surely misleading ! But it is the direct result of the *Hadow-Report* (Section 52, p. 67) of 1926, which recommended " that instruction in elementary physiology and hygiene developing out of the lessons in elementary biology should be given to all boys and girls in modern schools and senior classes." Quite so ; but need it be so " elementary " ?

The battle in Berlin for adequate instruction in these matters to school children, was long and hard. After ten years of effort on the part of social reformers and public health workers a " memorandum on Enlightenment for the Practical Instruction about Venereal Diseases " was issued by a Social Democratic Member of the Landtag, who was at the head of the special Bureau for the Inspection of Schools, under a Municipal Council which also rejoiced in a Social Democratic Majority. That was in 1931. The Memorandum begins with the following memorable words :

" A warning of boys and girls alike, against the dangers

of careless intercourse and of alcohol, is necessary. . . .
Attendance at these lectures is not obligatory for pupils ;
parents who do not wish their children to attend this course
should inform the School in writing, and should be given
timely notice of this provision. Medical men are to deliver
the lectures to boys' schools, medical women to girls'."

After some further rules of a cautionary and restrictive
kind, the document proceeds :

" The lectures should be confined within certain limits of
subject matter. Detailed mention is to be made of the
results of alcoholism, the existence of infection and the nature
and effects of the specific organisms in lues and gonorrhœa,
as well as of the sequelæ of venereal diseases. The prevention
of pregnancy must not be mentioned. We would specially
recommend that these matters should be treated with the
care due to their intrinsic nature and to the youth of the
audience."

This document was issued on December 14th, 1931. On
receiving a copy I sent the following enquiry by registered
letter post to the President of the Council on March 17th,
1932.

" I should be personally much obliged to you for information as to the need for including the sentence ' The
prevention of pregnancy must not be mentioned ' in the
Memorandum. I ask for this further explanation because
of objective facts. As you know, our modern methods of
instruction do not consist in delivering ' lectures ' but
in discussing the subjects treated with the children, thus
collaborating with their minds. My experience in such instruction is that it is quite impossible to avoid questions
from the children about the prevention of pregnancy.
Both in middle-class and in proletarian homes the subject
is so frequently discussed, that it would be merely a symptom
of mental dullness and deficiency for the children not to
ask questions. How is the person in charge of this instruction
to meet such questions, conformably to your Memorandum ?
It would be indefensible and a shirking of responsibility
to reply : ' That does not come within our subject, this is
not the place for talking about that.' The immediate and

well-merited result would be sly grins and titters, and the whole result of this innovation would be undermined and endangered."

The President and Chairman of the Educational Committee in the Prussian Parliament preferred not to answer this inconvenient enquiry. He took refuge in a silence unbroken to this day.

Norway offers a third instance of contemporary Sex Education and its practical hindrances. The Schools Committee of the Oslo Town Council had a Labour majority and in February, 1935, they formally resolved to give " instruction on reproduction." The Conservative paper *Aftenposten*, commented as follows on February 13th, 1935 : " Oh, well, we think that the Labour Party will not get much co-operation for this. The parties of the Right will not take the responsibility of demanding this instruction from the staff ; for the majority of teachers will certainly decline to impart information for which they consider themselves unqualified." Nevertheless, on May 8th, 1936, it was finally decided to include this subject as part of the obligatory curriculum for all seven grades. Teachers who preferred not to give the instruction were to have substitutes for those lessons. Seventy five pounds (1,500 kroner) were allocated for special instruction of the teachers themselves. The most forcible objection raised in the debate on this allocation by a Conservative lady was that " In this question, particularly, parents do not want to have their children told by any chance school-teacher." She opposed the resolution " because she did not want youth to be deprived of modesty, illusion or romance."

Let us ask the children's opinion on a matter which concerns them. There is a senior school in the London area in which British individual freedom has had a significant and progressive result. Miss Zoe Dawe has given the girls under her charge instruction on sex for some years. She has encouraged them in criticism and expression on these lessons, and in 1934 they wrote essays on " What I think about reproduction." Violet, fourteen years of age, wrote : " In my opinion I think we should have lessons on repro-

R 2

duction because no one would dream of telling us at home.
I think it is only right to learn of it at school, as we should
have to find it out for ourselves, and very likely would hear
a good deal wrong. All children know a certain amount
about it, so they might just as well know the rest. If you so
much as touch on reproduction in conversation, people
change the subject immediately and so we get the impression
that it is not nice to talk about and are just as much in the
dark as ever. If we did not have these lessons, when we went
out to work people would think us ignorant, as well as this,
if we were ill in any way we would feel uncomfortable, not
knowing how to put things."

Florence wrote with definite realism :

" There is a lot of mothers who do not like telling us these
things, but I think that is silly, because we have all got to
know about it when we get older."

And Marjorie wrote tersely :

" An ignorant child is a danger to the community."

So youth is already far clearer in the vision of what is
needed, and how it should be attained, than hesitant middle-
age. Even Herbert Spencer in the mid-nineteenth century
demanded " Education for Parenthood." The present
position in many households has been neatly summarized
by Mary Ware Dennett :

" The modern child who quizzed her mother as to her own
origin, and was given the traditional answer : God sent you—
' And how did you get here, mother, did God send you, too ? '
—' Yes, dear.'—' And grandma ? ' ' Yes, dear.'—' And
great-grandma ? '—' Yes, dear.'—' Do you mean to say,
mother, that there have been no sex relations in this family
for over two hundred years ? '—The story, as I have heard
it, never included what mother said after that. Possibly she
began to grow up herself " (*Sex Education of Children*,
1932, p. 99).

3

The recognition of the need for antivenereal instructions
and warnings to the senior classes of Schools had to be
tempered by psychological and pedagogic experience, for it

was soon observed that the lectures on " Enlightenment " and " Moral Hygiene " lost their objective value and weight because of their highly sensational subject matter. On the other hand, sexual knowledge built into the biological courses, and thus treated as an organic part of the science of Life, vivifies interest, and in Leicestershire educational circles Davidson formulated the definite rule that " There should be no isolation of the course in sex hygiene " (1930, p. 58).

Nevertheless and in spite of all practical and pedagogical advantages of frank and comprehensive treatment, it became obvious that the teaching profession in many different countries did not dare to run counter to the ideology of the social order which still survives. And this although the sexual standard of values has changed appreciably since the twentieth century began. Fiction and the stage prove this : " In the Edwardian period, the sexual life was presented in literature with a frankness, sincerity, and knowledge forbidden to the Victorian. . . . Promiscuity is coming to be an accepted convention in modern fiction as monogamy was in Victorian " writes the American historian of literature, Robert Morss Lovett in *The Sex Life of the Unmarried Adult* (1934, pp. 270–74). Alas, these changes have not penetrated into the sacred area of education. Wherever this immensely complex subject has been admitted to the curriculum of any State-supported or fashionable and long-established school, it has been after severe struggles and under protest from religious bodies ; and it must be treated " with due discretion and caution " and so far as possible confined to reproduction. Even the reproductive process should be taught so far as possible " along botanical lines " as Monsignore Miley urged in the *Scotsman* of February 23rd, 1932, when commenting on the discussions of the Scottish Primary and Secondary School Committee about " the matter of making provision for the teaching of biology." A similar pronouncement was made by the director of the Municipal Girls' High School in South German (and Catholic) Regensburg in 1925 : " A general incorporation of the study of Biology into our curriculum so that this

Science replaces humanistic and mathematical branches—
does not seem compatible with reverence for female modesty"
(Kammerer, 1926). In the school syllabus approved by the
British Social Hygiene Council we read of " The boys and
girls having separate lessons on this occasion only on human
reproduction and general sex hygiene." In " extension to
human beings " the subjects to be discussed are : " Organs
concerned in Reproduction and their Function. Menstruation. Secondary sex characters. Period of gestation.
Birth. Early life and parental care of the young." In the
film " Gift of Life," " Reel 4, on human reproduction is not
included here as it is only shown to young people at the
special request of those responsible for them."

Obviously the determining factor in the whole system is
the fear of saying too much. Otherwise how could an experienced medical woman and authority on the technique of
contraception, Dr. Gladys Cox, express herself as follows in
her manual for young people : *Youth, Sex and Life :* " The
precise details of the sex act in humans do not concern you
until you are about to be married, and for various reasons
it is wise to postpone seeking such detailed information until
that time arrives " (p. 160). No : all these limitations and
fumbling timidities do not arise from " various reasons "
but from one alone : they arise and exist because all those
persons who are sufficiently enlightened to see the need of
dealing with sexual matters, but, on the other hand, not
sufficiently emancipated to reject the present social order
and ethical code, are constantly in dread of undermining
order and morality if they " say too much." To say too
much in this connection means to speak not only of the
structures of sex but of its dynamic function ; of the impulse
of sex. This would mean, not only an outline of the mechanism of menstruation to girls in their early teens, it would
imply some reference to the psychological awakening, the
waves of emotional excitement and the ebb of depression
which are apt to coincide with the monthly cycle. Full and
helpful information would also mean that the formation of
ova and spermatozoa, gestation and birth were not treated
as more or less mechanical processes, but that mention was

made of sexual desire and pleasure, and the emotions which have so great a power over life, whether in their primary form or their irradiations and secondary manifestations. But such honesty would mean a definite choice between the negation of sex and its affirmation, between Pauline Theology and scientific humanism; and as the theories of scientific humanism have their equivalent tendencies in the political and economic world, the development of human personalities on their sexual side is thwarted, in order not to " bring politics into the schoolroom." But politics must affect the whole of life, and *vice versâ*.

To ignore the emotional side of sex in this formally sanctioned biological instruction is to return implicitly, if not frankly, to the theological point of view; to urge the presentation of these facts " on botanical lines " is to assume that " animal " sexuality is inextricably connected with " sin," and an irrelevant and evil factor in an otherwise morally perfect world. Here too there is a deep inconsistency, for the emotions of sex and their irradiations may be presented and appreciated *in the literature lessons*, as to wipe out erotics would be to wipe out the bulk of lyric poetry, at least in the Western world. A further accepted rule of conduct is that youth should refrain so long as possible from sexual activities. The idealistic formulation of this aim is Sir J. Arthur Thomson's " Ordinary people should be bigger than their endocrine glands." But in practice this amounts to a " Great Refusal," a neglect to face and estimate facts in the light of modern biology. As an example of this new light shed by science on many secret places, and much human suffering, we may take the more objective and optimistic attitude which is now possible towards juvenile and adolescent masturbation and auto-erotism in its wider sense. " Possible "—but not by any means frequent, even among doctors and teachers who are generally smitten with something like panic at any auto-erotic or (even more at any) hetero-erotic experience among those under their charge. Investigators who are not afraid of reality, nor blinded by the shadows of the past, come to conclusions which make the pusillanimities of the orthodox both pitiful and comic. Let us quote, for example, Dr. Havelock Ellis's summary of the conclusions reached by a famous American psychologist and social investigator, with which he entirely concurs :

" . . . That Dr. Katherine Davis did not find any markedly greater proportion of later happiness in girls who had not masturbated or had sexual play in childhood, as compared to those who had had such early sex experience. Dickinson and Pearson state that there is a real difference in the way of better health among those women who keep on with the habit of masturbation than with those who drop it after early life ; this might be considered due to greater health and vigour in those who continue the habit, and it is a common experience for women to find that improved health means increased or resumed auto-erotic activity "(*Psychology of Sex*, p. 134, 1934).

Or hear Professor J. Dueck in Robinson's series of essays, *Sexual Truths* (*cf.* Chapter III) on " Sexual Abstinence in Men and Women " :

" Continental students, even when they are well prepared, take their examinations with a good deal of fear and trepidation. Students who have normal sexual intercourse are in good condition and even the most stupid of them show in the course of the examinations an amazing degree of confidence. This type of man succeeds, the undersexed and those who indulge in self-abuse, fail. . . ." (p. 200).

These are realities. But what of the consequences of sex-phobia and theology even in the present century ? In a few decades historical criticism may be in a position to estimate their sorry price.

For instance, Professor Max Gruber, a light of academic Munich, has called sexual atrophy to aid the timidities and obsessions of " education " so called. He declares that the seminal fluid elaborated by the male glands is retained and " resorbed," if not " wasted " by emissions, whether by intention or accident. He admits that : " It might be thought that this resorbtion could only be beneficial in strict moderation and become harmful if carried any further. But we must remember that nature has provided against excessive accumulation, by means of the automatic emissions during sleep, known as ' nocturnal pollutions.' Moreover, the secretions of the testicles diminish when the organs are not used. The testicles are bodily organs and respond to use or inactivity as other organs do. If they are not in active use they receive a diminished blood supply, and if they have less blood supply their whole state of nutrition and vitality is lowered " (*Hygiene des Geschlechtslebens* (*Hygiene of Sex Life*), pp. 72–73).

Here we have the consistent result of the bourgeois trend of thought under the auspices of theology and applied to a wider field than the education of the young : Sexual atrophy as a Prescription and a Programme ! As Reich remarks (1936, p. 44) : " It is not to be wondered at, that nearly 90 per cent. of women and 60 per cent. of men are sexually debilitated, and that neuroses have become a symptom and a problem of the masses."

4

The treatment of auto-erotism—self-relief, self-excitement, auto-sexuality, solitary relief, onanism or ipsation—shows the ban on juvenile and puberal sex manifestations in the most acute form. The English healer or quack, Bekker, published a solemn warning which roused much interest in the eighteenth century, under the pompous title *Onania or the Heinous Sin of Self-Pollution, and all Frightful Consequences in both Sexes, considered with Spiritual and Physical Advices.* This work gave Professor Simon André Tissot, of Lausanne, the occasion to attempt the first discussion of " Onanism " which had any pretentions to scientific method. His *Traité de l'onanisme* appeared in 1764, in Lausanne, and he roundly put Bekker into his place with the comment : " The only tolerable portions of this book, for sensible readers, are its Notes " (p. 28). Nevertheless he too treated auto-erotism as a grave danger, and in spite of the commendable courage shown in a serious approach to this theme, Tissot's conclusions are quite untenable in the light of our present knowledge. But for a long time Tissot was an acknowledged authority, and his views were promulgated by Hufeland in his treatise on the prolongation of human life. Hufeland compared " victims " of this habit to " withered roses and walking corpses." He spoke of their " fear, remorse, shame and despair," and of the cause of the " self-loathing and weariness of life peculiar to our times "—" our times " were the years round about 1796, which cannot be described as lacking in action or excitement. (Quoted from *Makrobiotik*, vol. II, p. 16.)

There are echoes of this sort of thing even in the works of Krafft-Ebing and Moll. In the first edition of *Psychopathia sexualis*, Krafft-Ebing maintained that homosexuality might be the result of prolonged and habitual " self-abuse." He believed that " self-abuse " " produced neurasthenia and that psychological disorders, such as paranoia, and maniac depressive insanity (' Folie circulaire ') may develop on the basis of this neurasthenia " (*l.c.*, p. 70). Moll was of the same opinion, and stressed the extreme risk and harm of solitary indulgence to homosexuals (*Contr. Sex. Empfindung*, p. 221, 1891), for in his days it was still believed that deep-seated aberrations could be " cured " and brought to achieve " normal coitus." Even to-day the ghoulish prophecies of Tissot are spread among young and ignorant people, under religious auspices and with much talk of " self-pollution," " youthful lusts " and " youthful errors." Young persons who read and believe this rubbish and have no access to reliable sources of information become thoroughly terrified and obsessed with dread and guilt ; and of course the results of such prolonged depression and tension are often very serious. Grosser and Gurievitch have recently published a comprehensive and detailed study of *Sex in Contemporary Life*, based on Ukrainian material, and this contains many illuminating cases. A peasant, twenty-three years of age, stated : " Onanism has really had a bad effect on me. *Of course, I didn't notice it, at first, but only after friends and books had enlightened me* " (1928) ! And we must admit that the first impressive and effective protest against such lying intimidation, came from the Swedish writer August Strindberg and not from the medical profession. In his autobiography *A Servant's Son*, Strindberg vehemently protested against these methods, but the special object of his wrath, Bishop Kapff's *Warning by a friend of youth, against youth's worst enemy*, continued to appear, with its text unrevised and unaltered, since its first appearance in 1843, and had reached its twenty-second edition in 1911. In 1920 the Christian Moral White Cross League of Germany published 160,000 copies of a pamphlet by Dr. Seidel :

. . . " Thus silent sin slinks like a secret poison among the ranks of youth, stealing their strength and their life itself. No vice is so destructive to body and soul as self-abuse, *which by its very nature may be easily and incessantly practised.* . . . But the sad results are inevitable," etc. (pp. 20–25).

Even a trained medical authority like Dr. Vermeil wrote in *Der Ruf*, a Church periodical for young men, that those who thus indulged would become impotent and lose their memories. The sole remedy, he said, was " Christ Jesus, our Salvation."

In England we have Arthur Trewby's *Healthy Boyhood*, which appeared in 1909. It is used in 230 public and preparatory schools and in the Royal Navy. Here are three sample extracts :

" This vice enfeebles the intellectual powers, inducing lethargy and obtuseness, and incapacity for hard mental work. And last, and most of all, it is an immorality which stains the whole character and undermines it for life."

" The private parts of the body (!) are closely connected with the spine, and the spine is closely connected with the brain. It follows, therefore, that if you meddle improperly with these parts your brain will suffer, and you will be unable to concentrate."

" Should this be your case, if you have been already led astray, then kneel down at once as soon as you have read this, at the latest before you lie down tonight, and make a full and frank confession to God of what you have done."

The book received quite favourable reviews from a number of papers, including the *Lancet* and the *British Medical Journal*. Even to-day Max Huhner can bring himself to write as follows in *Marriage Hygiene* for November, 1934, basing his view on many bulky but unsound treatises :

" Onanism . . . is not a disease of imagination. It is a real disease. . . . When masturbation has been firmly established, you can no more talk your patient out of masturbating than you can talk a child suffering from scabies out of scratching. The latter is caused by an irritation in the skin, and the former by an irritation in the prostatic urethra."

The form of " education " based on these medical myths is characterized by the recommendation of T. Schilgen, S.J., in *Youthful Purity* (*Reinheit der Jugend*), p. 92 : " In all such temptations, the best course is to pray and then occupy oneself in some other way." Gutmann's *Science of Education* has received the Catholic Imprimatur, and 45,000 copies have been printed since the first edition in 1913. In the 1923 issue there appears this passage :

" In order to detect the sin, many educational authorities recommended that the blankets and sheets should be turned back about half an hour after the child goes to sleep. If the child's hands rest on the lower part of its body, there is cause for anxiety. If the night-clothes and bed linen show traces—the anxiety becomes certainty. The main method of cure is to work on the conscience of the child ; this will bring admission if one is able to win the child's confidence. Let the admission by the poor sinful little mortal be facilitated by treating the act as a misfortune rather than as an offence. . . . It is suggested that some such enquiries be made as follows : ' Have you touched yourself on those parts of the body which one always keeps covered ? ' ' Were you alone ? Was it only for a minute ? ' If such was the case, we are probably dealing only with thoughtlessness and self-will. ' Decent people don't do that, for God has forbidden it ; it mustn't happen to you again, or we shall have to punish you.' If the child admits more prolonged manipulations, it would be advisable to enquire whether much pleasure were felt. If this should unfortunately have been the case, the appropriate measures should be taken at once. Bodily chastisement is only suited to very young children, for they are not yet open to moral suasion, and chastisement is apt to discourage children at later stages of their growth. . . . The child should be admonished with the most sacred seriousness, to make an honest admission of sin in the Sacrament of Confession. . . . In very hardened cases the only safe means of rescue is the regular, frequent and reverent reception of the Blessed Sacrament " (pp. 334–5).

Such are the menaces which torment millions of mothers for their children's future, and turn the sap of youth to gall and tears. Medicine has no part in such superstition. The writers from whom I have quoted—and the quotations might have been multiplied indefinitely !—are incapable of any unbiassed judgment of sexual matters. They are inspired by sheer sex-phobia, hatred and terror of others' joy. There is only one tolerable and adequate criticism of these Obscure Men, and that was uttered by Havelock Ellis after a more than thirty years' war with these successors of the witch-burners and the Inquisition :

" The extravagant horror of ' perversity,' the mania for finding and dwelling on ' perversions ' in the young, is itself the most perverse of perversions." (*Psychology of Sex* 1931, p. 131).

5

" Only a handful of writers had been capable of looking at the matter calmly. By seeing it in perspective, coupled with other auto-erotic activities, Ellis helped to make a sane view possible." Thus writes Peterson in his biography of Ellis (p. 268). The first study of auto-erotism by the great sexologist was published in 1898 in the *Alienist and Neurologist* (XIX, 260–99). Since then the term " auto-erotism " has become part of the vocabulary of sex-psychology, and especially of psycho-analysis. Sigmund Freud gratefully accepted this new word and scientific concept in his *Three Contributions to Sexual Theory*, which appeared in 1905 (p. 43).

Ellis's view that auto-erotism was essentially a biological

process has been confirmed with every subsequent decade. Most of the present-day sexologists will agree with Norman Haire when he says : " The truth is that over 90 per cent. of people masturbate and that very few of them experience any lasting evil effect. When evil effects occur, they are due, in the vast majority of cases, to worry about masturbation, and not to masturbation itself " (*Encyclopædia of Sexual Knowledge*). Meirowski made the first systematic enquête on the subject among practising physicians and medical students. He received affirmative answers in 88 per cent. of his totals ! Julian Markuse's estimate is 93 per cent. without professional distinctions, Dueck's data even amount to 90·8 (90⅘) per cent. ! and this material suffices to prove that the habit is not in itself pathological. The only sex specialist of experience and repute who stands by the former view is Rohleder, of Leipzig, and his attitude has earned the nickname of " *Tissot Redivivus*." Finally the certainty of error reached the inmost circles of specialists. In 1923 Stekel published a Monograph on auto-erotism (onanism) based on psycho-analytic work. He sought for the key to the superstitious dread of " ill-effects." He wrote :

" It is high time that the widely promulgated myth of the noxiousness of onanism should be thoroughly exposed. The medical profession can hardly see clearly here, for they are both judges and accused : the haunting sense of guilt which has become attached to the habit of self-relief affects the doctors ; for doctors are human beings and like their patients they themselves have masturbated, more or less frequently. And therefore so much nonsense and so much hypocrisy is declaimed with the stentorian accent of vigorous conviction " (p. 103).

In 1929 I published a selection of letters from young people who were habitual masturbators or auto-erotists. Their contents confirmed the sequence of cause and effect traced by Grosser and Gurievitch at Kharkoff a year previously. Self-relief is in itself a physiological occurrence, *i.e.*, normal ; but the fear and shame inculcated on sexual matters at an early age can cause neurotic disturbances, general and functional, which are then laid at the door of

the habit itself. (*Cf. Onanism, neither a Vice nor a Disease.*[1])
Light reaches unexpected quarters, though slowly. By
1932 even the Christian Student Movement admitted that
" Popular fallacy is that masturbation in the early ages
has a tremendous ill-effect on the body and mind of the
boy " (girls might not exist, so far as this document is
concerned).[2] " The truth is that we have the highest
authority for saying that in the actual act of masturbation
during early ages the child does no physical or mental harm
to himself whatever " (Smith, 1932).

This sweet reasonableness is not only a little late in the
day, but also not wholly spontaneous. The wide commercial
circulation of preventives, in the U.S.A. especially, has
enabled many young people to form relations with members
of the opposite sex without spying or interference from
" grown-ups " in school, home or " business " ; and to
have some sort of " normal " experience at an age when
their parents were just emerging from the chrysalis ! There
is, however, we must note in passing, often considerable
confusion here in the minds of the vigilant censors of the
other generations. At puberty both boys and girls incline to
idealist sentiment and may often feel extreme attraction
towards persons of the opposite sex, without venturing on
any conscious declaration of their feelings, or any attempt
at physical approach. It is shallow psychology to assume that
in the " teens " the desire necessarily means the act !
Nevertheless, the sexual situation in post-war America
had reached a point which made the official representatives
of morality concede that auto-erotism was relatively harm-

[1] *Cf.* Dr. Robert Latou Dickinson, the leading gynæcologist of the
U.S.A., wrote in 1935 : " If then, as implied by several series of studies,
the frequency of auto-erotism among women is found to run from two-
thirds to four-fifths it would seem to be so general an experience as to
warrant calling it a natural phenomenon, possibly a provision of nature,
looking toward a response in later completed sex activity " (*Sex Life of the
Unmarried Adult*).—Translator's Note.

[2] For instances to the contrary, see Dickinson and Beam, Katharine
Bement Davis and Frances Strakosch, although the latter deals mainly
with psychopathic subjects.
In 1915 Stella Browne wrote : " A certain amount of self-excitement
and solitary enjoyment seems inevitable in any strongly developed sexual
life " (*Sexual Variety and Variability among Women*, B.S.S.P. pamphlet,
No. 3).—Translator's Note.

less—as well as so much " less wrong " than normal sex
relations !

Thus even the appearance of enlightenment in Smith's
pages is really a manifestation of sex-phobia ! Well, let us
admit that Smith has captured a modicum of reality, *for
auto-erotism is certainly preferable to compulsory abstinence !*

On March 22nd, 1926, the British Social Hygiene Council
issued a " Statement on Continence in Relation to Social
Hygiene " which was very much a work of supererogation
and misleading at that. The Council majestically put it on
record that :   " There is no evidence either from physiology
or from experience that for the unmarried sexual intercourse
is a necessity for the maintenance of physical and mental
health."

Every neurological specialist can easily prove the exact
contrary, and one is amazed that persons of distinction in
medicine and psychology could bring themselves to sign
the B.S.H.C.'s thesis ! For auto-erotism is certainly preferable to abstinence, but we must never forget that a prolonged
habit of self-relief " becomes unsatisfactory and causes
deep disturbances for the lack of an equally responding and
sharing partner is soon definitely felt. And if auto-erotism
ceases to satisfy, it provokes satiety, weariness and sense of
guilt, but is not discarded because of the urge of sex. The
result is a compulsive neurosis. There is a further disadvantage . . . when the relief is obtained mainly or partly
through mental imagery it tends to foster childish, pre-
genital attitudes towards sex, *i.e.*, it becomes a regression.
And the danger of full-blown neurosis grows with the length
of time during which self-relief is practised " (Reich, 1936,
p. 100).

Of course, there is a great difference between auto-erotism,
plus a certain conscious mental content, and the purely reflex
actions of very young children ! We refer in this chapter, as
in the appended table, to the former. The table was compiled
from Central European material by O. Schwarz, the well-
known Viennese psychologist, in 1935.

Masturbation begun or intensified during puberty is often
the result of homosexual practices between boys or girls

Age . .	under 10	10–11	12–13	14–15	16–17	18–19	over 19
Percentage of Cases .	4·3	5·1	22·5	42	16·7	7·2	2·2

in their teens, or of intense homo-erotic relationships. The first psychological analysis of this emotional factor in the German Youth Movement of pre-war days (the Wandervögel or " Birds of Passage ") was made by Hans Blueher in 1913. His acute and honest conclusions raised a storm of wrath ; they were described as a vile slander, smirching youthful purity. But there can be no doubt of the substance of Blueher's book to-day. " It remains true that a certain liability to more or less romantic homosexual affection is found among boys, while girls, much more frequently, cherish enthusiastic devotion for other girls somewhat older than themselves, and very often for their teachers. Even, however, when these emotions are reciprocated, and even when they lead to definite sexual manifestations and gratification, they must not too hastily be taken to indicate either a vice calling for severe punishment or a disease demanding treatment. In the great majority of these cases we are simply concerned with an inevitable youthful phase " (Ellis, 1934, p. 203).

Blueher's observations were collected in 1913, but in 1917 he made them the basis of a comprehensive theory of psychological and social evolution. His book *Rolle der Erotik in der männlichen Gesellschaft* (*Rôle of Erotic Emotion in Male Communities*) has much valuable and significant material, although his conclusions are in some respects biassed and extreme. He points out that romantic associations, military cliques and educational relationships between teacher and pupil of the same sex are seldom quite without homo-erotic elements however below the level of consciousness. The vehement asseverations of sexually repressed people against such conclusions, their outcry of " nonsense ! " and " vile aspersions ! " are ample confirmation of Blueher's hypothesis.

M.M. 8

There has been striking confirmation in recent history : for instance, the official " justification " of the Massacre of June, 1934, in Germany and the remarkable statement by Gorki, that to destroy the homosexuals was to destroy Fascism—a statement uttered in support of the renewed penalization of homosexuality in Soviet Russia in the same year. In Germany at the present day homosexual acts between male persons may be punished with penal servitude up to ten years ! (Law enacted June 28th, 1935, Article 6). Moreover, the amendment to the law for the Prevention of hereditarily Diseased Offspring (June 26th, 1935), § 14, makes castration the punishment for male homosexuality and exhibitionism in cases of possible progeny.

This type of mind enthroned in high places makes it impossible to give due weight to the psycho-sexual instability and plasticity of puberty. Every accurate and impartial statement of facts in this region, whether the facts be heterosexual, bisexual or homo-erotic, is deemed to corrupt the morals of the youth. Accusations are made that " young people are systematically tempted to homosexuality " and *every facility is provided for the political manipulation of sexual urges and sexual ignorance.* At present England can pursue an isolation policy which makes it difficult to realize the treatment of serious scientific and educational work on the Continent in post-war years. In 1932 Wilhelm Reich was threatened with murder unless he " made tracks for Russia " ; and after my study of the difficulties of young people in their teens (*Lad and Lass—Bub und Mädel*) a well-known military periodical made the amiable recommendation that I should be removed from my post " and sent to the North Pole " (April 16th, 1925. *Der alte Dessauer*).

These attacks on sexual science are only one wing of the battle ; imaginative literature and pictorial art, whether graphic or plastic, are subjected to an ignorant and prurient supervision, nosing busily for " Pornography." There have been many conspicuous cases. In the nineties of last century Henrik Ibsen and Gerhard Hauptmann were declared " obscene," and in 1934 and 1935 respectively Sweden and Norway permitted prosecutions of advanced thought and expression. The whole gamut of Obscenity Laws from Anthony Comstock to the attacks on Radclyffe Hall's *Well of Loneliness* and D. H. Lawrence's *Lady Chatterley's Lover* are manifestations of one constant tendency. The social background of these prosecutions shows only too clearly the wholly negative effect of such " sex-education," juvenile or adult, as present economic and ethical conditions provide.

6

" Popular education was introduced by Forster's act in England in 1870, despite the alarmed satirists who had pictured houses burning down while their cooks read hydrostatics in sixpenny tracts. The Civil War marked the same turning in America. It is more than an extraordinary coincidence that Lord Campbell's Act, the final establishment of obscene libel as a crime at Common Law, the Comstock Acts in America, and the publication of the *Origin of Species*, all occurred approximately in a decade. The cluster of the dates 1857, 1859, 1868, 1872 indicates that the late Puritanism which flowered in what we call mid-Victorianism was beginning to struggle with the Frankenstein Monster it had created " (Ernst-Seagle : *To the Pure*, p. 169).

Actions at law against " Obscenity " and " Pornography " are a direct result of the Democratization of " Culture." So long as a small inner circle of the governing class amused itself by spicing sex with literature, all was well. The Courts of princes and prelates up to the end of the eighteenth century were not sanctuaries of " Morality," but when the masses were able to read, and to choose their reading—danger threatened ! Books priced at round about two guineas are seldom attacked, but sixpenny pamphlets with equivalent material are obscene. The Purity Crusades of the various and numerous Societies for the Suppression of Vice are the negative instruments of our special phase of social development, and therefore dearer far to those in authority over us than the efforts of progressive societies.

This particular negative legislation has three main purposes. The first purpose is to restrict and if possible penalize the distribution of literature which deals with " sex " and therefore, according to a certain type of mind, with " dirt." The use of Post Office facilities is denied to the authors and vendors of such literature in the U.S.A. Secondly, to restrict the widespread advertisement of sexual commerce of all kinds ; and finally to provide an impenetrable zareba of pretences and penalties between young persons and this monstrous thing.

To Comstock anything remotely touching upon sex was obscene. " The English meaning of the word is, primarily, ' offensive to the senses, or to taste or refinement ; repulsive, filthy, foul, abominable, loathsome ' ; and secondly ' offensive to modesty or decency ; expressing or suggesting unchaste lustful ideas ; impure, indecent, lewd ' " (Obscene Publicat. Act, 1857, 20 and 21 Vict., c. 83). Note that the individual element of pleasurable experience in sex is threatened with dire penalties, whilst the social or reproductive factors are comparatively immune. Nevertheless, the Judicial Proceedings Act of 1926 (16 & 17 George V.) (to cite only one instance) in V, c. 61 (Regulation of Reports), forbids the mention in judicial proceedings of " any indecent matter or indecent medical, surgical or physiological details, calculated to injure public morals "—which is quite vague enough to justify the most preposterous circumlocutions. " Private parts of the body " instead of sexual organs or genital organs ; " a certain condition" instead of pregnancy are witnesses of our contemporary sex-phobia. Then there is the Post Office Act of 1908 (8 Ed. VII, C. 48., Section 63) which has a certain unconscious humour. Indecent or obscene prints, etc., are excluded from the Post, together with " live animals and anything of an explosive or inflammable nature," under penalty of £10 fine or twelve months in jail. And specially sensitive and vicariously moral persons have been known to class scientific work under this category !

The subject of sexual advertisements is a mine of curious information and also of the art of " getting away with it " in spite of the Draconic Law ! We will not further dwell on this, except to point out that by the Indecent Advertisement Act of 1899 (52–53 Vict., c. 18) " Any advertisement relating to any complaint or infirmity arising from, or relating to, sexual intercourse shall be deemed to be printed or written matter of an indecent nature, within the meaning of the above section." This simply means that the most discreet ingenuity is employed so that appearances be preserved, while, nevertheless, they that seek, shall find ! As indeed in all countries with similar laws.

In post-war Germany, after vehement Catholic propaganda, a law was passed for the protection of youth from " Dirt and Trash." The borderline here was even vaguer than in Britain and the " glorious uncertainty " of what exactly constituted crime even greater ! For, as Ernst and Seagle contend : " The available literature in support of censorship is based on philosophies of infant damnation and salvation by ignorance. . . . The stronger jurists flounder in a morass of illusory tests, while the weaker indulge in purely subjective interpretations " (*l.c.*, p. 291).

I am of the opinion, after fairly careful study and some experience in human nature, in various countries of the Old World, that the results of Moral Censorship in the last half century exactly correspond with the fruits of the " Regulation " of Prostitution. The defects of both systems far outweigh their advantages. *And in any case, the futile and clumsy negative and repressive treatment of sexual manifestations and available knowledge, so far, does not deserve to be called Enlightenment or Education.* So far, there is only a form of *Education against Sex*, plus inadequate information on the Mechanism of Reproduction and menacing warnings against " illicit intercourse." To create and direct a positive Sex Education is a task for the Mental Hygiene of the future. So long as established European hypocrisy confiscates photographs of the Venus of Milo from shop windows in Budapest, and makes no protest when Victor Margueritte is deprived of his Légion d'Honneur because of his " Garçonne " ; so long as we treat Desire as something Sub-human, and Affection as something Anæmic—for so long we shall have to wait before we are able to achieve wholesome knowledge and dignified acquiescence towards Sex.

BIBLIOGRAPHY

ALMKVIST, J., *Sexuell Kultur*, Stockholm, 1933
ARKIN, E. A., *Doschkol'nij wosrastj*, II, Moskwa, 1929.
ARMITAGE, G., *Banned in England*, London, 1932.
ARTZYBASHEFF, *SANINE*, London.
BLUEHER, H., *Der Wandervogel als erotisches Phänomen*, Berlin, 1913.
BLUEHER, H., *Die Rolle der Erotik in der männlichen Gesellschaft*, Jena, 1917.
BOURBON, *De l'influence du coit et de l'onanism sur la production des paralyses*, Paris, 1857.
BROUN, H., and LEECH, M., *Anthony Comstock*, London, 1928.
BUEHLER, CH., *Das Seelenleben der Jugendlichen*, Jena, 1923.
CHANCE, J., *Experiments in Sex Education*, London, 1935.
CHANCE, J., *Cost of English Morals*, London, 1931.
COX, G., *Youth, Sex, and Life*, London, 1935.
CRAIG, ALEC, *Sex and Revolution*, London, 1934.
DAVIDSON, J. F., "Discussion of the Teaching of Sex Hygiene in Elementary Schools," *Ann. Rep. Sc. Med. Off.*, Leicestershire, 1930.
DENNETT, M. W., *The Sex Side of Life*, New York, 1928.
DENNETT, M. W., *The Sex Education of Children*, London, 1932.
Education of the Adolescent (Hadow Report), Stationery Office, London, 1926.
ERNST, M., "Changing Laws and Changing Attitudes," in *Sex Life of the Unmarried Adult*, Edited by I. WILE, London, 1935.
ERNST and SEAGLE, *To the Pure*, London, 1929.
GAUFEYNON, *La masturbation*, Paris, 1925.
GROSSER and GURIEVITCH, *Geschlechtsleben der Gegenwart* (Ukraine), Kharkoff, 1928.
GRUBER, MAX V., *Hygiene des Geschlechtslebens*, Leipzig, 1907.
Handlingarna i maalet, Stockholm, 1934 (Process against Sex Educational Review).
HODANN, M., *Onanie weder Laster noch Krankheit*, Berlin, 1929.
HODANN, M., *Bringt uns wirklich der Klapperstorch?* Berlin, 1932.
HODANN, M., *Bub und Mädel*, Berlin, 1932.
HODANN, M., "De l'onanisme des enfants en bas âge," *Probl. sex.*, Paris, 1934.
HUHNER, M., "Disorders of the Sexual Function," *Marr. Hyg.*, November, 1934.
HUXLEY, J., *Biology and Society*, London, 1928.

KAMMERER, P., "Die unsittliche Biologie," *Neue Generation,* Berlin, 1926.

LANVAL, M., *L'éducation sexuelle et les parents catholiques,* Bruxelles, 1934.

LOWETT, R. M., *The Sex Life of the Unmarried Adult in English Literature.* Cf. WILE, *Sex Life of the Unmarried Adult,* London, 1935.

"Masturbation," *Out of Bounds,* I, June, 1935.

MOHR, O. L., *Forplantningslære som fag i vaare skoler,* Oslo, 1935.

OGNIEFF, N., *Diary of a Communist Schoolboy,* Translation, London, 1928.

REICH, W., *Der Sexuelle Kampf der Jugend,* Berlin, 1932.

REICH, W., *Die Sexualität im Kulturkampf,* Copenhagen, 1936.

ROHLEDER, H., *Die Masturbation,* Berlin, 1921.

RUSSELL, DORA, *The Right to be Happy,* London, 1928.

SCHWARTZ, O., *Psychology of Sex and Sex Education,* London, 1935.

SELO, H., "Bibliographie traitant l'onanisme et education sexuelle et l'enfance," *Probl. sex.,* July, 1934, Paris.

SMITH, F. V., *The Sex Education of Boys,* London, 1932.

Social Hygiene and Biological Teaching, London, 1931.

SPRANGER, E., *Psychologie des Jugendalters,* Berlin, 1928.

Statement on Continence in Relation to Social Hygiene, London, 1926.

STEKEL, W., *Onanie und Homosexualität,* Berlin, 1923.

STEKEL, W., *Briefe an eine Mutter,* Zürich, 1928.

STERN, W., *Psychologie der frühen Kindheit,* 5 Ed., Leipzig, 1928.

STOLPE, SV., "Den svenska striden om diktens frihet," *Samtiden,* Oslo, 1936.

TAMM, A., *Ett sexualproblem, onanifrågan i psyko-analytisk belysning,* Stockholm, 1930.

THOMSON, A., *Education and Social Hygiene,* London.

TISSOT, *Traité de l'onanisme,* Lausanne, 1764.

TUCKER, T. F., and POUT, M., *Sex Education in Schools,* London, 1933.

WALKER, K., *Preparation for Marriage,* London, 1935.

WEBB, B., *The Teaching of Children as to the Reproduction of Life,* London, 1932.

WEDEKIND, F., *Frühlingserwachen,* Berlin, 1909.

WIKANDER-BRUNANDER, S., *Handledning för undervisningen i sexualkundskap,* Stockholm, 1935.

Zeitschrift für psycho-analytische Paedagogik, Sonderheft " Onanie," Vienna, 1928.

TABLE OF EVENTS

1764 TISSOT's book on Masturbation.
1857 Obscene Publication Act in Britain.

1873 COMSTOCK Laws in U.S.A.

1886 STRINDBERG criticizes the Scaremongers.

1898 HAVELOCK ELLIS volume on Auto-erotism (published in U.S.A.).

1903 Third International Public Health Congress in Paris. LANNOY's address on " L'Education Sexuelle."

1907 Congress of the German Society against Venereal Diseases at Mannheim. Sexual Instruction in Schools discussed. After the suppressed Russian Revolution of 1905 erotic groups and clubs formed in Russian schools and universities under the influence of ARTZYBASHEFF'S SANINE.

1909 British Medical Press praises TREWBY'S *Healthy Boyhood* in spite of misleading information on Auto-erotism. FRANK WEDEKIND'S *Frühlingserwachen (Spring's Awakening)* gives the signal for the widest discussion on Sex Enlightenment in Continental Europe.

1913 BLÜHER analyzes Erotic components in German Youth Movement.

1918 Intensified Anti-venereal Propaganda as a result of the War. More energetic demands for Instruction in Schools.

1923 STEKEL'S Monograph.

1925 Discussion in the Berlin Town Council on Sex Enlightenment. HODANN forbidden to mention Contraception to his pupils.

1926 HADOW Report in Britain. Statement of the British Social Hygiene Council on Continence. German Law for the Protection of Youth against Dirt and Trash.

1927 Board of Education recommends Sex Instruction.

1930 W. REICH'S *Geschlechtsreife, Enthaltsamkeit, Ehemoral,* the first affirmative analysis of the problems of Sex Education.

1932 Christian Student Movement concludes that " Masturbation does no physical or mental harm."

1933 Conference on Sex Education in London (Report by JANET CHANCE).

1934 Law suit against Sex Education Press in Sweden. Acquittal on charge of Pornography.

1936 Oslo Education Council decides on obligatory instruction in knowledge of Reproduction.

CHAPTER VIII

THE ANALYSIS OF THE SEX TABOO

I

WHY is there such discrepancy between biological knowledge and social resistance? For it is mere verbiage to reply that the community is by its very nature hostile to the sexual impulse of its individual members. No: the answer is more complicated. After the evolutionary trend of research since the epoch-making work of Darwin, Haeckel and Hertwig, we must delve into human motives and find the particular vested interests which are incompatible with the rational application of our knowledge of sexual functions and emotions.

For no artificial and wholly external system of rules could be imposed on humanity if there were no emotional acceptance of such a system. Sex-phobia is very deep seated, it is cultivated by education and sanctified by religion in most of our contemporaries, and we must know the irrational and subconscious mechanism of sex-phobia before we can judge how best to apply conscious enlightenment to the community for a better and happier to-morrow.

And this means that we must outline the theory which furnishes the most forcible and intellectually distinguished suggestions concerning the irrational and instinctive elements in the human psyche. We must take counsel with psychoanalysis; for—as has been pointed out in the Preface—Sigmund Freud is as fruitful an explorer as Copernicus and Darwin. The intellectual world and the press have apparently recognized Freud's eminence and services at last; for they gave him an ovation on his eightieth birthday (May 6th, 1936). But what of the long years of injustice, misrepresentation and abuse through which Freud's psychological genius and purpose fought their way? And the motive of all the mud throwing and distortion is not in doubt ; it was an example of sex-phobia, for Freud had hardly formulated the main outlines of his theory in the earliest years of our century when " the storm broke loose, especially in Germany ; and those who attacked psycho-analysis were far from scrupulous in their methods or their arguments . . . of course it is in the very nature of psycho-analysis to provoke the most acute resentment and hostility. Psycho-analysis infringes the prejudices of civilized humanity at a particularly sore point ; the very theory of psycho-analysis became personal at once, by exposing to the light of day that which all were agreed should be concealed in the subconscious mind ; and thus all our contemporaries became ' cases,' displaying their deep resistance before the psycho-analytic probe " (Freud, *Collected Works*, XI, p. 192).

Malinowski has referred to " the consideration of the unofficial and unacknowledged sides of human life " ; and this was undoubtedly the chief stone of stumbling in the new science, as Freud realized would be the case in the light of a remark by Charcot, under whom he had worked for years in the treatment of hysteria. This remark was not made in the course of a clinic, but at a social gathering. Charcot said suddenly and with great vivacity, " *Mais, dans ces cas pareils, c'est toujours la chose génitale, toujours, toujours, toujours !* "

Freud's comment was, " I know that for a moment I was almost paralyzed with astonishment, and I said to myself : Yes, but if he knows this, why does he never say so ? " (*History of Psycho-analytic Movement*, p. 7). Well, Freud did say so ; and the mere fact that he revealed and insisted on the immense *rôle* of sexuality in the unconscious mind of man, a *rôle* that is so great just because of the repressions exercised by the consciousness, and that he fought this truth into the fullest general recognition, in the teeth of the academic word—this perception and this persistence are among the intellectual treasures of our time.

One must keep a sense of proportion here, and I feel bound to quote a passage from Freud's letter to me, dated October 9th, 1935 : " I beg of you not to use the term

Sexual psychology for Psycho-analysis; Sexual psychology was the phrase coined for it by a hostile Berlin man of letters, and it was meant to imply contempt and depreciation." No one could suppose that the author of these pages would use the term " sexual " with any shadow of reprobation ; but let us admit and state explicitly that psychoanalysis is much more comprehensive than any exclusively sexual psychology could be. But it is a historical foundation for any dynamic concepts or treatments of the sexual impulse, and for the scientific disregard of the traditional taboo. And in the present chapter we shall deal with this particular facet of psycho-analysis, alone.

2

It is known that psycho-analysis grew out of therapeutic medicine, from the attempts to find a cure for symptomatic neuroses, hysterias and phobias, disorders which had hitherto proved refractory to all treatments. The research into their origins revealed a mass of curious evidence, which appeared with significant regularity, and indicated that sexual sensations and activities began " almost simultaneously with extra-uterine existence " (Freud, in an article on " Psycho-analysis " in 1923). This meant the extension of the concept of sexuality, in order to include its juvenile and infantile manifestations. It became evident that the pleasurable acts performed by young children with their own bodies followed a definite sequence of phases or stages in the formation of sexual personality ; and that these phases might be distinguished as oral, anal, and genital, and in that order of appearance. Thus, infantile or juvenile manifestations form a primitive pattern which is considered " perverted " or " arrested development " if it survives into adult life. The " polymorphous " and, as it were, nebulous sexuality of the child becomes normally focussed in the genital organs when the child grows into maturity.

Freud's initial name for these emotions and actions typical of infancy was " polymorphous-perverse " ; a term which has since been superseded by " phase of auto-

erotism," and more recently by Ellis, who finds " the pre-
genital phase " more appropriate (*cf. Psychology of Sex*,
p. 131).

The most significant aspect of the new concept of sexuality
is not only its extension in time, but its psychological
ramifications. According to Freud, " Sexuality is delivered
from an exclusive association with the genital organs, and
revealed as a comprehensive function, an urge towards joy,
which is only secondarily and incidentally ancillary to
reproduction. And, further, the sexual emotion is understood to comprise all those tender, benevolent and sympathetic sentiments which are included in that protean word
' Love ' " (*Collected Works*, XI, p. 149).

Psycho-analysis has been labelled " Pansexualism." The
reply is not difficult, when once the peculiar mental reactions
of established orthodoxy are given due weight ! The
medical faculty throughout Germany was incensed at
Freud's exposure of traditional morality, and when the war
of 1914–18 began to bring in its harvest of mental ruin and
derangement they were triumphant at being able to retort
that here was good, clean, honest insanity, with no taint of
Sex ! These worthy medicals ignored the factor of Narcissism
and the Narcissistic neurosis, although psycho-analysts had
put this particular deviation on record in 1914. Nearly all
the cases of war-neuroses—or " shell-shock " as it is more
colloquially termed—were more or less Narcissistic in origin,
and resulted from an emotional trend turned inward
towards the Ego itself, however subconsciously. In the
words of Freud : " That is to say, psycho-analysis was
blamed as a rule for undue and unjustifiable extension of
the concept of sexuality ; but when it happened to be
convenient on any particular occasion, this ' extension '
was forgotten and psycho-analysis was reproached for
taking the narrowest possible view of the sexual sphere "
(*Collected Works*, XI, p. 167).

These controversial methods are cheap and easy enough
so long as the theory of libido has not been worked out in
relation to a general concept of instinct and emotion, as
Freud admitted in 1925. Libido is here defined as " The

quantitatively variable and measurable force of the sexual
urge, directed towards its object, in the extended sense
revealed by Analytic theory " (*Collected Works*, XI, p. 195).
These extensions and definitions are not only valid for the
" mind diseased " and the paralyzed will. They are the
bridge that leads from *descriptive* to *dynamic* psychology ;
and the corner stones of the bridge were Freud's investigations into the nature of dreams, for in dreams the unconscious of sane, satisfied, and normal persons, reveals
itself (1900). Freud brought modern methods into the
study of dreams, and he wrote : " The dream is built up
in the same manner as a neurotic symptom. It is a compromise between the demands of a repressed instinctive
urge, and the resistances of a power that exercises censorship
within the Ego. As a result of this origin, the dream is as
unintelligible as the neurotic symptom, and in equal need
of interpretation " (*l.c.*, XI, 157).

After dreams the " common light of day." The *Psychopathology of Everyday Life* was published in 1904. In this
study Freud pointed out that the trivial failures to keep
promises or lapses of memory with which our everyday life
is strewn, even though we may not be consciously aware of
them, are generally manifestations of unknown or unacknowledged emotional complexes.

In 1906 Bleuler and Jung, the Zürich savants, began to
take an interest in their Viennese colleague's results.
Bleuler persuaded Dr. Eitingon to visit Freud and study
analytic methods on the spot, and as a result the first
psycho-analytic clinic in Berlin was founded in 1920 and
conducted until the Nazi counter-revolution drove Eitingon
from Germany ; he continued his work in Palestine. It is
an interesting commentary on Nazi mentality that those
German analysts who have accepted the Hitler *régime*
emphasize their patriotism by removing the portrait of
Freud from the clinic in which they practise. For Freud—
horrible to relate—was a Jew.

Bleuler's approval broke the ban of isolation and misrepresentation. In 1908 the first International Psycho-
analytic Congress was held at Salzburg. In the same year

Freud made the first attempt at a systematic study of character formation on his special lines, in his work on *Character and Anal Erotism*. In 1909 Freud and Jung were invited to the United States by the Rector of Clark College, Worcester, Massachusetts, and so Freud was first privileged to speak publicly on psycho-analysis at an American University (*cf. American Journal of Psychology*, 1910).

In the same year the second International Congress was held at Nürnberg, and the " International Psycho-analytic Association " was founded, with Jung as its President.

In 1911 a great co-worker and pioneer in knowledge and liberation, Havelock Ellis, recorded that " Freud's psycho-analysis is now championed and carried out, not only in Austria and Switzerland, but in the United States, England, in India, in Canada, and I doubt not in Australasia."

3

The process of subdivision and varying opinion was soon to begin within the school founded by Freud. Between 1910 and 1911 the leader of the Viennese research group, Alfred Adler, left the group, and developed a theory emphasizing the non-sexual elements in human psychology. There seems to have been a certain " inferiority complex " behind Adler's apostasy (*History of P.A. Movement*, p. 42).

" Adler's theory emphasizes . . . that all libidinous feeling contains an admixture of egotism. This would have been a palpable gain if Adler had not made use of this assertion to deny, every time, the libidinous feelings in favour of the impelling ego-components (*l.c.*, p. 44). The picture which one derives from Adler's system is founded entirely upon the impulses of aggression. It has no place at all for love. One might wonder that such a cheerless aspect of life should have received any notice whatever; but we must not forget that humanity oppressed by its sexual needs is prepared to accept anything, if only the ' overcoming of sexuality ' is held out as bait " (*eodem*).

As early as 1912 Jung had proclaimed to Freud in a letter from the U.S.A., " that his modifications of psycho-analysis had overcome the resistances to it in many persons who hitherto wanted to know nothing about it." Freud was sceptical from the first. "The modification was nothing more or less than the theoretical suppression of the sexual factor " (l.c., p. 49). "The sexual libido was replaced by an abstract idea, of which it may be said that it remained equally mysterious and incomprehensible, alike to fools and wise " (l.c., p. 54).

To-day, twenty years after the modifications by Jung and Adler, it is evident that Freud put his finger on their essential defect. We need not here discuss their reasons or their arguments, but it is indisputable that both ignored the clear and explicit positive attitude towards sexuality, which psycho-analysis never hesitated to proclaim. Neither the individual psychology of Adler, nor Jung's doctrine of psychological types were thus able to furnish fresh material and results in the sphere of sex.

The fact of infantile sexuality was the first new discovery of psycho-analytic method. Here the most important element, in both theory and practice, was the exact amount of localized, i.e., genital sensation and action, even in the " pregenital " phase of development. The study of infantile sexuality had at first to be by way of adult " regressions," but since 1909 analytic technique has been used on children, with certain adaptations (Three Contributions to Sexual Theory, p. 68). Great opposition was provoked by Freud's statement that :

" At any rate, at the height of the development of childhood sexuality, the functioning of the genitals, and the interest in them reaches predominant significance, which comes little short of that reached in maturity " (Collected Works, V, p. 233, English in I.J. of P.A., 1924, p. 125).

This view of early genital activity is the logical deduction from the theory which is the Alpha and Omega of psychoanalysis ; the theory of the " Œdipus Complex," which assumes that intense emotional experiences in early childhood form the basis of the adult personality : the particular individual sexual capacities, tastes and trends being determined by the extent to which the Œdipus Complex has been overcome and absorbed into the growing character, or survives in the form of neuroses.

4

Orthodox psycho-analysis insists on the universality and intensity of this emotional situation : it is regarded as the " keypoint of all future developments " (*Collected Works*, XI, p. 168). Freud was even more explicit in his essay on " Resistances to Psycho-analysis " (published in *Imago* for 1925 and in *Collected Works*, XI, p. 233). He claimed that it needed " a great effort not to perceive anything so obvious, as the culmination of early infantile sexual emotion in a fixation on the parent of opposite sex, combined with a sense of rivalry towards the parent of the same sex. And that this rivalry and emotion become direct desire of a sexual kind before the age of five years."

Here criticism is justified—but not criticism founded on prejudice against sex. Rather is our objection here founded on realistic observation ; it is empirical but sound. Freud is far too sweeping in his generalization.

He puts on record his view that " with boys the desire to beget a child from their mother is never absent, with girls the desire to have a child by their father is equally constant, and this in spite of their being completely incapable of forming any clear idea of the means for fulfilling this desire " (*Collected Works*, V, p. 354. *Int. Journal of P.A.*, 1920, p. 384). Stekel, who has left the orthodox Freudian fold, but continues to develop his own analytic investigations and treatments, states that " boys never wish to be fathers " (1921, p. 48). We may cite one further example of the extreme and absolute insistence on the Œdipus complex in the publications of Freudian experts : the specialist from whom we quote is the child-psychologist Melanie Klein. She analyzed a girl child of two years old, and " discovered " that this infant " already wished to rob her mother, who was pregnant, of her children, to kill her and to take her place in coitus with the father " (*Int. Journal of P.A.*, VIII (1927), pp. 26–29, after Westermarck).

The analysis of children's minds hitherto made was based

mainly on dreams. But we cannot obtain or reasonably expect coherent, *i.e.*, " freely associated," accounts of either dreams or waking experiences from children under five years of age ! Now every experienced student of the psychology of testimony knows the incalculable amount of suggestion which may be brought to bear on witnesses whose evidence is not completely spontaneous and " first-hand." And we must recognize the difficulty of preventing the " projection " of genital concepts from the adult mind of the analyst into the pre-genital phase of the analysed " patient."

Moreover there is a further factor, thus described by the well-known analyst, J. C. Flügel :

" Now the parents in virtue of their developed heterosexual inclinations tend very frequently to feel most attracted to those of their children who are of the opposite sex to their own and thus (consciously or unconsciously) to indulge in greater manifestations of affection towards such children ; this unequal distribution of affection being in turn perceived and reciprocated by the children themselves " (1929, p. 15).

Indeed we are here on very uncertain ground, in spite of the supreme self-confidence of many practising psychoanalysts. But just because we must make serious reservations and criticisms of these more detailed developments in Freud's work, it is due to truth and loyalty to acknowledge most fully his achievement and our debt. The Œdipus complex is a stupendous intellectual construction with most significant implications for early historical achievements in social organization, religion and art ; it is as inspiring a creation as the great Drama of Sophocles, from which Freud took its name.

Freud has said that " the oracle and the doom of Œdipus are alike materializations of inward necessity " (*Collected Works*, XI, p. 175). For every young child has the first experience of sexual desire in the endogamous (or to use the term invented by adult ethics, incestuous) wish for union with that parent whose sex is complementary ; and the fulfilment of this desire is aimed at, through the removal of the other parent, whose sex is the same as the child's.

Thus endogamy or "incest" lies at the very core of the psychology of sex.

And indeed there have hardly been any civilizations without some form of "Table of forbidden degrees of kindred and affinity." But these degrees vary considerably. The widest taboo was that which ruled the exogamous clans of primitive man. Robertson Smith, of Cambridge, made investigations into the records of animal sacrifice among the Semites, and Freud was led to trace the development from the Incest Taboo of primitive exogamy to the rituals of totemism. He concluded that the Totem animal symbolized the father; it is sacred, "taboo," it may not be destroyed. But on specially solemn occasions it is slain and devoured by the tribe in a communal ceremony. What is the origin of this rite? Freud maintains that it symbolizes the murder of the Old Man of the primeval horde by the younger men, his sons, who were jealous of his possession of the horde's women and girls. But when they had slain their begetter and tyrant—remorse and fear returned, and the parricides renounced their desires in so far as women of their own horde were concerned. Exogamy was born, and with it the Totem Taboo; religion and civilization were launched on the seas of time.

5

There is grandeur in the unity of this theory, and numerous illustrative examples may be found in Myth and Legend and Custom, for the conflict between father and son appears to be the universal human drama—quite apart from individual analyses—in the history of human evolution.

But where are adequate and definite proofs, in sufficient quantity? For as Malinowski has perceived: "The answer to evolutionary and historical questions must always be given in the form of a functional explanation and not in that of an empty evolutionary scheme or historical hypothesis" (Ingese Congress Proceedings, I, 1926).

Malinowski is Professor of Anthropology at the London School of Economics. He was the first investigator to furnish detailed studies of a matriarchal community, based not on deduction, but on first-hand field-work. His name is forever associated with the people of the Trobriand Islands, the Melanesians through whom he has taught valuable lessons to the White West. Malinowski shows that in this Melanesian matrilineal world the affectional and emotional ties between parents and children take their own distinctive forms and that : " The social arrangements of the Trobriand matriliny are in almost complete harmony with the biological course of development, while the institution of father-right found in our society crosses and represses a number of natural impulses and inclinations " (*Sex and Repression*, p. 76). And this implies that " we might say that in the Œdipus complex there is the repressed desire to kill the father and marry the mother, while in the matrilineal society of the Trobriands the wish is to marry the sister and to kill the maternal uncle " (*l.c.*, p. 81).

Thus we find that Freud's great construction is not absolutely but relatively valid. This relativity has been somewhat aggressively proclaimed by S. D. Schmalhausen : " When psycho-analysis speaks of instincts, it really means social habits, economic compulsions, historical determinants. When psycho-analysis speaks of man, it means, though it knows it not, man's class struggles, institutional coercions, capitalistic ways of life. The psycho-analysts think they are talking subtle psychology, when what they are really discussing is crude sociology " (1935, p. 210).

The belief of some psycho-analysts in the primary nature and absolute supremacy of the Œdipus complex goes so far that Ernest Jones, the leading psycho-analytic practitioner in London to-day, has claimed that " the matrilineal system with its avunculate complex arose . . . as a mode of defence against the primordial Œdipus tendencies " (1925, p. 128). This view would describe matriarchy as " a decomposition of the primal father into a kind and lenient actual father on the one hand and a stern and moral uncle on the other " (*l.c.*, p. 125).

Here, " as in most psycho-analytic interpretations of folk-lore, custom and institutions, the universal occurrence of the Œdipus complex is being assumed, as if it existed

т 2

independently of the type of culture, of the social organization and of the concomitant ideas. Wherever we find in
folk-lore hatred between two males, one of them is interpreted
as symbolizing the father, the other the son, irrespective of
whether in that society there are any opportunities for a
father and son to conflict. Again, all repressed or illicit
passion which we find so often in mythological tragedies
is due to the incestuous love between mother and son, even
though such temptations could be shown to have been
eliminated by the type of organization prevalent in that
society " (Malinowski, *Sex and Repression*, p. 140).

6

Such distorted interpretations cannot be accepted by
serious students ; for, however intellectually tempting by
their symmetry and completeness, such hypotheses are contradicted by obvious facts and masses of first-hand material
evidence. They move in a vicious circle. Freud's totem
theory bases the origin of culture on psychological sentiments which are themselves the fruit of centuries—if not
millennia—of cultural concepts and controls. Malinowski
has developed this objection in detail, in Part III of his
Sex and Repression in Savage Society. He declares that
remorse is foreign to very archaic emotional life. And when
Freud contends that " without the assumption of a mass
psyche, or a continuity in the emotional life of mankind
which permits us to disregard the interruptions of psychic
acts through the transgression of individuals, social psychology could not exist at all," this theory makes the assumption
of " the methodical figment of a collective soul. As a point
of fact no competent anthropologist now makes any such
assumption of ' mass psyche.' . . . Frazer above all rules
this conception consciously and methodically out of his
work " (Malinowski, *Sex and Repression*, p. 157).

The quotation from Frazer's *magnum opus* has special
force, because Freud has called Frazer as a witness in favour
of his incest theory, at least to a certain degree. The
assumption that a super entity or " mass-psyche " has actual
existence is only a step on the road to the totalitarian State.

The "mass-psyche" was the theoretical basis for the doctrines of anti-Liberal and anti-democratic political philosophers of all shades of Conservatism from Menenius Agrippa to Friedrich Stahl and Jellinek. The "mass-psyche" has nothing to do with the facts revealed by anthropological and social research and experience.

The problem of exogamy is by no means *chose jugée*. The Cambridge scientist, Sir James G. Frazer, has the following comment at the end of his fourth volume on *Totemism and Exogamy* :

"Men eat and drink and keep their hands out of the fire instinctively for fear of natural not legal penalties, which would be entailed by violence done to these instincts. The law only forbids men to do what their instincts incline them to do ; what nature itself prohibits and punishes it would be superfluous for the law to prohibit and punish. . . . Instead of assuming, therefore, from the legal prohibition of incest that there is a natural aversion to incest, we ought rather to assume that there is a natural instinct in favour of it, and that if the law represses it, as it represses other natural instincts, it does so because civilized men have come to the conclusion that the satisfaction of these natural instincts is detrimental to the general interests of society " (Vol. IV, p. 97).

The other great historian of human ritual and conceptual evolution, Edward Westermarck, questions the existence of incestuous inclination as a rule of human emotion ; that is, he doubts the primary doctrine of Freud. Westermarck writes " there is a remarkable lack of inclination for sexual intercourse between persons who have been living closely together from the childhood of one or both of them. This has been recognized by various writers as a psychological fact proved by common experience and is attested by statements from different parts of the world " (*Three Essays*, p. 72. *Hist. of Hum. Marr.*, II, 193 *sqq.*, 1921 Ed.).

Havelock Ellis is of the same opinion, as mentioned in Volume IV of his great *Studies*, p. 205, and in the more recent *Views and Reviews* (1932), p. 168. Thus authorities in very diverse fields have found their observations concur, and it is no valid reply to simply throw doubt on the reliability of expert witnesses, after the unfortunate manner of E. Jones. Westermarck comments as follows on Jones' method of defence :

" I have sometimes wondered that psycho-analysts who claim such intimate acquaintance with the unconscious part of the mind, display so little knowledge of the conscious part of it " (*Three Essays*, p. 74).

There are psychological complications here, and the infant and the adult are not identical in their reactions. Anthropology and folk-lore seem on Frazer's side, and Malinowski makes the following distinctions :

" In the first place, under the mechanisms which constitute the human family serious temptations to incest arise. In the second place, side by side with the sex temptations, specific perils come into being for the human family, due to the existence of the incestuous tendencies. On the first point, therefore, we have to agree with Freud and disagree with the well-known theory of Westermarck, who assumes innate disinclination to mate between members of the same household. In assuming, however, a temptation to incest under culture, we do not follow the psycho-analytic theory which regards the infantile attachment to the mother as essentially sexual " (*Sex and Repression*, pp. 244 *ff.*).

He continues : " . . . Freud . . . tries to prove that the relations between a small child and its mother, above all, in the act of suckling, are essentially sexual. . . . This theory it is impossible to adopt. . . . Instincts must be defined not simply by introspective methods, not merely by analysis of the feeling-tones such as pain and pleasure, but above all by their function (p. 245). . . . The pleasure index cannot serve to differentiate instincts, since it is a general character of them all (p. 246). . . ."

According to Malinowski the exact function of the taboo on incest depends on the attitude of children towards their mother, attitudes based on social motives. " In any type of civilization in which custom, morals and law would allow incest, the family could not continue to exist " (p. 251). As we have already indicated, the majority of orthodox analysts take refuge in psychology without any social context, psychology, so to speak, *in vacuo*, and refuse to consider the economic bases of the sexual customs and institutions in successive grades of evolution. But anthropology and sociology cannot tolerate this vacuum, and fill it with significant discoveries. The great social anthropologist Malinowski thus defines his divergence from the Freudian view, which " consists in the fact that Freud assumes a continuous persistence from infancy, of the same attitude towards the mother. In our argument, we try to show that there is only a partial identity between the early and the later drives, that this identity is due essentially to the mechanism of sentiment formation ; that this explains the non-existence of temptations among animals ; and that the retrospective power of new sentiments in man is the cause of incestuous temptations " (*l.c.*, p. 249).

We have said enough to indicate the contradictory present stage of the controversy among experts on the incest taboo, from the functional and social aspects. But if we consider the more individual and imponderable " feeling-tones " here, folk-lore can throw unexpected light. Thus the vernacular slang of every Slavonic people has among its most offensive expressions the command to have sexual congress with the mother. Malinowski tells us that in the matriarchal communities he has investigated, the insulting curse includes the sister as well. Now this primitive and vehement explosion of obscure emotions seems to be independent of social institutions, and we can hardly avoid the guess that they include some ambivalent wish fantasies. Malinowski tells us that there is a *gradation* of heinousness in these curses :

" The invitation to maternal incest is but a mild term used in chaff or as a joke . . . the mention of sister incest in abuse is a most serious offence . . . but the worst insult . . . is the imperative to have connection with the wife. This expression is so bad that . . . no native would pronounce it but in whispers, or consent to make any jokes about that incongruous mode of abuse " (*Sex and Repression*, p. 106). " The real cause is the plausibility and the reality of the act, and the feeling of shame, anger, and social degradation at the barriers of etiquette being pulled down and the naked reality brought to light. For the sexual intimacy between husband and wife is marked by a most rigid etiquette " (*l.c.*, p. 107).

What is the kernel of this manifestation ? Is it indeed the same shame and dread of sex as Europe knows so well, in the incongruous setting of a community in which sexual repression in practice seems non-existent ? Or are these " curses " the first beginnings of patriarchal " morals " in a matrilineal community ? We have no answer as yet. But according to Malinowski *the Trobriand community is free from neuroses, because there is no sexual repression.* And this is the most impressive body of evidence yet offered for the view that neuroses are simply " sequelæ of thwarted sex life " (Reich, *Einbruch der Sexual Moral*, p. 19).

These ritual or vernacular " curses " are a key to a wide and obscure field of primitive psychology. In the most recent decade investigations have been made hand in hand with psychiatric research, and the results may foreshadow the answer to our question : From whence has humanity learnt to dread sex and be ashamed of it ?

7

What is the specific response of the archaic and primitive to sex ? What indeed is the special definition of the archaic personality ? Not any deficiency in craftsmanship or technique in any field, but the attitude taken as a rule towards the world (the not-self) and the Ego.

Goetz has given the following summary of the essential difference between " primitive " and " civilized " :

" As soon as human beings have explicitly sensed their separateness from the world around them, and have learnt to distinguish rapidly and surely between animate and inanimate objects in that world, and to control and deal with these objects by means of rationally conceived actions, they are no longer to be termed primitive. Human beings are no longer primitive if they perceive their own individuality and construct their own individual universe of

conditions, tendencies, emotions, and associations. A main
characteristic of archaic or primitive minds is the belief in
Magic. It is archaic to attribute to thoughts, words and
gestures the power to deal at a distance or create or change
objects afar off. . . . But every evolutionary psychologist
knows that the most mature and highly evolved minds have
their archaic streaks, just as the most primitive human
beings exercise reason and induction in many aspects of
their lives. And ' we moderns ' have our magic of religion,
orthodox or outlawed ; just as primitives eat and drink and
hunt, with careful vigilance and purpose, although they call
magic to aid them " (Goetz, 1933, p. 2).

Thus there are strata in all of us that recall the remote
past, and their exact power over us depends on our degree
of individuation. This is a factor of extreme significance.
Individuation is the opposite pole to the primitive merging
into the group, the race and the community, the gang, the
party, the species. And we know beyond any doubt that
erotic emotion reduces the individuation of the most
clearly defined personality and obliterates the sharp barrier
between self and not-self. The whole world quivers and
glows or threatens in accord with the fortunes of the lover ;
there is sometimes an indescribable exaltation, well-being
and benevolence towards all created things. The barriers
of time and space waver, there are hallucinations and vivid
telepathic experiences. Much of the. emotion of those in
love has a dream-like quality, something of divine madness.
Reason and self-preservation flicker and vanish.

> " I ask not, I care not
> If guilt's in thy heart ;
> I know that I love thee,
> Whatever thou art."

Whatever the *rôle* of neurons and hormones in creating
this mental state, its subjective force is one of the primary
human experiences. The world of erotic magic is typical
of puberty, and the " exaltations, agonies " of first love, with
the illusions and despairs of youth, that are so close to the
pit of madness and the convulsive ecstasy of the primitive
ritual dances.

The most difficult problem for primitive minds is Death.
The work of the psychiatrist, B. Goetz, has elucidated the
interrelationships of dread of death and sexual emotion ;
his work is as comprehensive as that of Freud, constructed
on material which includes the psychic symptoms of
contemporaries as well as of the child and the primitive
" savage "; myths, folk-lore, symbolism and the evolution
of decoration in dress, and buildings, weapons and utensils.
Slowly he was able to trace an evolutionary process which
enabled him to see how human beings had come to terms
with sex under this or that social system, and also why
they had chosen just those methods of restraint or release.
The *Sexual History of Humanity* (*Sexualgeschichte der
Menschheit*) was first planned in 1929, and the work of
Mannhardt, Graebner, P. M. Schmidt, Frazer, Freud,
Preuss, Anckermann, Andree and other experts was used in
the material, sifted and discussed.

We may form certain main conclusions, based on folk-lore
and ethnography. Apparently the male human being has
always been more inclined to ask " Why ? " and follow
trends of reasoning (however strangely) than his mate.
And for so far back in history and prehistory as we can
glimpse or guess, woman and child have been objects of
dread, of uneasy curiosity and in some manifestations, of
repugnance, alternating with violent attraction. Women
and children were alike—yet in some respects so different.
Menstrual phenomena were the cause of extreme perturba-
tion and a whole system of " sympathetic " exorcisms. The
emergence of the child from its mother's body, the smallness
and strange appearance of the new-born baby and its
misshapen " twin," the placenta, were also profoundly
mysterious and menacing. And by a strange " identification " the child becomes one with the ancestral dead, the
womb with the grave. Frazer has collected much evidence
in *The Fear of the Dead* (I, pp. 20, 24, 26). Not only such
primitive cultures as remain open to observation, furnish
such evidence, but the world of folk-lore and underground
belief and custom, overlaid by the churches, in Europe.
What of the " Little People," the Dwarfs and Gnomes,

small as little children in stature, but potent for good or ill, in energy and wisdom ? These Gnomes are blends of babe and ancient, and in them are concentrated the forces of birth and death ; while the adult man, at the summit of life, fears them, for they are his past and future in one. A further identification is that of the ancestor or forefather with Death itself. Europe has the skeleton in Holbein's pictures and Goethe's *Totentanz*, while Africa and the Islands of the South Seas have the " spirits of the dead " of which Frazer observes that they influence " the general attitude of primitive man . . . by fear rather than by affection " (Frazer, *l.c.*, I, p. 10). Thus even the new-born babe becomes " Death " ; the son who strives for life and survival thrusts his begetter into the Land of Shades. And this is the kernel of the eternal strife between father and son, between the individual and the community, between the desire of immortality and the dread of death. Thus in Greek myth Kronos tries to evade the doom pronounced by the oracle—death at the hands of his children—by devouring each new-born babe. Gea, Mother-Earth, the woman side of the Universe, saves her babies by deceiving him, and gives him a stone to swallow instead of Zeus. And the oracle is fulfilled.

Turn to the Semites. Abram is commanded to sacrifice his son to Yahveh. But a way of escape is opened to him ; he becomes the father of a great people, Aw Raw Haam. The individual may die, the race remains. He destroys his ancestral totem-idols, and in symbol or sympathetic magic this implies that his father is also destroyed. And the Hebrew ritual knows of no " other side " ; it is concentrated on this world.

Christianity turns away, to the Beyond. The " Father " sends his " Son " to die on the Cross that the people be " saved." From what ? From the " World " and the " Flesh." And the Cross is a form of the ancient fire symbol, the Swastika.

" And actually represents the Father himself, the eternal begetter kindling the spark of life, *i.e.*, the son. And if the symbol of life becomes a death token, it means nothing

more or less than the death of the son at the Father's hand ;
his sacrifice. Humanity—or the Congregation of the Faithful
—yearns for the goal attained by this sacrifice ; the Kingdom
of Heaven, likeness to God, eternity, life eternal ; and
thence, the sacrifice of the Son of Man is consummated
forever anew " (Goetz, *l.c.*, p. 137) in the Communion of the
Christian Churches.

The range of possible primitive symbolism is not wide,
and the symbols used are found in many distant cults and
climates. Fire is a typical symbol of virility, and is
associated with the worship of male gods. In India one of
the names for the male principle is Prhamanta, the firestick,
which is driven into the soft wood to enkindle it, as the
male organ penetrates the body of the woman. In old
Teutonic and Scandinavian bridal rites a hammer, the
symbol of Thor, was laid in the lap of the seated bride ; and
Thor was the Storm God, the Lord of Lightning and Flame.
There are other cases, known to us all, though unexpected
perhaps. A great star of fire led three Wise Men from the
East to the cradle where the Son of God was lain in the
straw. Straw catches alight and the great flame spreads
throughout the world. But the Child in the cradle is the
seed of the firestick, *i.e.*, of the awl ; for His Father is the
Carpenter.

Ever again the sex of mankind or the fruit of sex is at
enmity with the spirit, *i.e.*, the individual. And so we have
" the belief that sex is what has made Man, creator of the
world, subject to mortality" (Goetz, *l.c.*, p. 167). But sex
cannot be extirpated, so it is depreciated, vilified, denied.
It is labelled " Sin." And the sacrifice of the Son is the
ransom for sin.

The mythical way to salvation and eternal life is the
destruction of sex in beings who are sexual and of different
sexes. Again and again we find this doctrine and its legends
from the Adam and Eve of Genesis to the Purusha myths
of India and Plato's Symposium. Thus there develops an
attitude towards life, founded on sheer wish-fantasy, and
persisting in spite of all that Darwin and Freud have
taught us. The late Jacob Wassermann, psychological

novelist and imaginative writer, has expressed this attitude
in the words of the fifteen-year-old Jewish lad, Michael
Hoffmann, who puts the conflicts and terrors of his teens
before Christian Wahnschaffe:
" The Soul is Pure, the body is unclean ; a Sister—she is
something holy, a Sanctuary. But to look at, she is a
Woman ; and one broods over it night and day. A Woman—
and Woman's name is fear. She is the Body, and the Body
is a living dread. Were one once free from the Body—one
could understand the whole world ; but for Woman one
could know God. And so long as we know not God—we are
tormented and in dread " (*Wahnschaffe*, II, p. 341, 1919).

8

". . . and there be eunuchs which have made themselves
eunuchs, for the kingdom of Heaven's sake. He that is
able to receive it, let him receive it " (Matt. xix. 12).
  In Tzarist Russia, and in that eighteenth century which
brought the Encyclopédistes and the French Revolution,
Selivanoff founded the sect of Skoptzy, who still survive.
They preach and practise two forms of castration as tokens
of salvation and mortification of the flesh : the " Lesser
Seal " implies removal of the testicles ; the " Greater Seal "
amputates the penis as well. But the majority of the
human race have preferred to " renounce the flesh " by
symbol, or in the extremely attenuated form of circumcision,
which is practised widely and with great variations of
method throughout the world. And the peoples who
circumcise their children or young adults have forgotten the
original motives for this rite, and invented endless good
reasons for the practice—æsthetic reasons, as when the
negroes questioned by Bryk replied proudly that " it was
fine, like that " ; theological reasons, such as those advanced
by Hebrew Orthodoxy ; whilst Western civilization now
elects to praise the " admirable hygienic wisdom " of
Moses ! But " hygienic wisdom " has unfortunately never
sufficed to keep ritual customs alive through thousands of
years. The son of Islam declares that " the Prophet has
commanded us." But let us for a moment consider the

form of circumcision best known in Europe : the Hebrew
rite. The prepuce is caught up in a vessel full of sand, *i.e.*,
it is " buried." It symbolizes a body that is consigned to the
desert. Bryk reports that among many negro tribes the
prepuce is eaten by the child's mother, again a symbolic
interment ; and the Hova of Madagascar give the severed
portion to the father to eat ; this symbolizes a cremation.
For the archaic analogies are definite and almost universal :

Man .	. Woman.
Father .	. Mother.
Fire. .	. Cave.
Cross .	. Rhombus or Lozenge.
Serpent .	. Tree.
Sky .	. Earth.
Kronos .	. Gea.

The psycho-analytic interpretation of circumcision is a
mitigated form of castration, inflicted by the father in order
to prevent the son's approach to the mother, who is still
desired. Goetz comments with a bitterness easy to understand that " many people, of course, find it easier to
imagine a jealous male parent than to put themselves in
the place of a devout believer in religion " (*l.c.*, p. 232).
Then he reminds us that primitives have a very rudimentary
sense of time, and that the primitive male parent would
scarcely muster enough forethought to castrate his little
son, because the son might be a danger to his own mother
in twelve or fifteen years' time ! Should such be the case,
the father would by that time have consoled himself with
younger and more attractive partners. The whole interpretation is a misreading of facts, for sexual emotion in children
is different from sexual emotion in adults. Havelock Ellis
pointed this out as long ago as 1911 in a paper on *Psycho-
analysis in Relation to Sex* read before the Medical Congress
at Sydney, Australia :

" Freud himself has encouraged this error, and exposed
his position to quite unnecessary attacks by speaking of
childish sexual psychology in terms of adult physical facts.
This is notably the case as regards Freud's introduction

of the term 'incest-complex,' and by his acceptance as typical in this respect of the altogether adult story of Œdipus and Jocasta. . . . True, the 'incest-complex' is a terminological absurdity, since the sexual theories of childhood are absolutely unlike those of the adult, and the adult's attitude has no more meaning for the child than, it would usually seem, the child's attitude has for the adult" (*Philosophy of Conflict*, 1919, pp. 214 and 219).

Goetz has suggested a *modus vivendi*, but I fear that the orthodox psycho-analysts will reject it :

" If Freud would declare that his doctrine is meant symbolically we could then work as one ; and he is the greatest master of symbolism in all recorded history, as we acknowledge without doubt or hesitation. For our dispute with Freud will be at an end if he means by the functional word ' Mother '—Woman herself ; and if he means the ' World ' when he speaks of Woman herself, the most desirable treasure in the whole world ! For—father and son fight each other with the world as prize ; the son, the rising generation, drives his begetter out of life, into death. . . . The son strives to overthrow his father and reign in his stead. . . . Freud's theory becomes intolerable if reduced to the merest material literal formula. But in its sublimated aspect it would be the greatest imaginable intellectual construction " (*l.c.*, p. 229).

Critical psycho-analysts, who give due weight to social and economic factors, agree that the Œdipus complex is potent in and for the patriarchal stages of human history. And these phases are of special interest to us ; we live in one of them. And the history of its life and institutions may throw light on the question we have to answer : How does the sex taboo survive in twentieth-century civilization ?

The Œdipus complex is not essential to the answer ; the evolutionary psychology of religious belief will suffice, together with the analysis of the sense of shame. Goetz has shown that shame is *not solely refusal of what is not desired ;* and in this he is more adequate than Havelock Ellis in a passage quoted in the work referred to (*l.c.*, p. 193). *A sense of shame implies some awareness of self.* And there is a difference between anatomical shame—*i.e.*, shame of the naked body—and physiological or functional shame. Functional modesty is the significant emotion, psychologically. It is correlated with individuation ; it diminishes almost to vanishing point as the threshold of consciousness blurs and merges into the group ; *e.g.*, in the Saturnalia of Old Rome, where there were neither masters nor slaves and time stood still.[1] In some European countries the Saturnalian ghosts still walk through carnival nights. But as soon as the accentuated individual difference brings the consciousness of conflict between ego and " species," mankind " knows its own nakedness," and confesses " That he is no more than the beasts that perish ; a confession totally opposed to the lofty station that his own pride has always claimed. Now the most vividly concrete manifestation of mankind's earthliness is sex in its primary functions and impulses. It becomes gentler, more dignified, more ' human ' when it seeks communion of sentiment and feeling as well as of bodies, when it becomes sublimated and transmuted into love. But then—there is no occasion for shame. Only crude sex is set against a background of storm and shame ; and it is nevertheless humanity's very root in the earth, in the flesh, in this mortal life " (Goetz, *l.c.*, p. 198).

On this profound emotional basis the traditional sex taboos of patriarchal societies in our Western world have grown and flourished. They have cloven love in twain, calling one side " Heavenly," the other " Earthly." What are the psychological and economic forces tending to perpetuate this cleavage ? Who are the obscure men, the sons of darkness, who seek to cultivate and exploit the primitive elements in contemporary minds ? Our search for these motives and protagonists will lead out of the relatively quiet domain of folk-lore and ethnography into the strong currents and undercurrents of to-day's battle of interests and ideas.

---

[1] A vivid and well-documented picture of this primitive ritual group merging is given in the anthropological novel of Naomi Mitchison, *The Corn King and the Spring Queen.*—Translator's Note.

BIBLIOGRAPHY

BACHOFEN, J. J., *Das Mutterrecht. Eine Untersuchung über die Gynaikokratie der alten Welt nach ihrer religiösen und rechtlichen Natur*, Stuttgart, 1861.

BREND, W. A., *Sacrifice to Attis*, London, 1936.

BRIFFAULT, R., *The Mothers*, London, 1927.

BRUNNER, C., *Liebe, Ehe, Mann und Weib*, Potsdam, 1924.

BRYK, F., *Neger-Eros*, Berlin, 1923.

DURCKHEIM, E., *La prohibition de l'inceste et ses origines*, Paris, 1898 (L'Année Sociologique).

ELLIS, H., *The Philosophy of Conflict*, London, 1919.

FLÜGEL, J. C., *The Psycho-Analytic Study of the Family*, London, 1929.

FRAZER, J. G., *Totemism and Exogamy*, I–IV, London, 1910.

FRAZER, J. G., *The Dying God*, London, 1911.

FRAZER, J. G., *The Golden Bough, IX, The Scapegoat*, London, 1913.

FRAZER, J. G., *Folklore in the Old Testament*, London, 1919.

FRAZER, J. G., *The Fear of the Dead in Primitive Religion*, I–II, London, 1934.

FRAZER, J. G., *Creation and Evolution in Primitive Cosmogonies*, London, 1935.

FREUD, S., *Collected Works*, Vienna, I–XI.

FREUD, S., *History of the Psycho-Analytic Movement*, London, 1916.

GOETZ-HIRSCHFELD, *Das erotische Weltbild*, Dresden, 1929.

GOETZ-HIRSCHFELD, *Sexualgeschichte der Menschheit*, Berlin, 1929.

GOETZ, "Ein Schema präkategorialen Denkens," *Allg. Zt. Psychiat.*, 1932.

GOETZ, "Irrte hier die Entwicklungspsychologie?" *Fortschr. d. Med.*, 1933.

GOETZ, *Volkskunst und Volkskunde, Gestalt und Bedeutung*, Prague, 1934.

GOODLAND, R., *Bibliography of Sex Rites and Customs*, London, 1931.

HUGH-HELLMUTH, H., "Zur Technik der Kinderanalyse," *Int. Zt. Ps.-An.*, 1921.

JONES, E., "Mother Right and the Sexual Ignorance of Savages," *Int. Journ. Ps.-An.*, 1925.

KLEIN, M., "The Psychological Principles of Infant Analysis," *Int. Journ. Ps.-An.*, 1927.

KRISCHE, P., *Das Rätsel der Mutterrechts-Gesellschaft*, Munich, 1927.

LAWRENCE, D. H., *Psycho-analysis and the Unconscious*, London, 1923 and 1931.

Lévy Bruhl, *Les fonctions mentales dans les sociétés inférieures*, Paris, 1910.

Loewenthal, J., " Hakenkreuz und Raute," *Zt. Sexwiss*, 1928.

Malinowski, B., " Baloma ; the Spirits of the Dead in the Trobriand Islands," *Journ. R. Anth. Inst.*, London, 1916.

Malinowski, B., *The Argonauts of the Western Pacific*, London, 1922.

Malinowski, B., *The Anthropological Study of Sex*, Ingese Congress I, Berlin, 1927 (read 1926).

Malinowski, B., *The Sexual Life of Savages*, London, 1927.

Malinowski, B., *Sex and Repression in Savage Society*, London, 1927.

Malinowski, B., " Magic Science and Religion," in Needham, *Science, Religion and Reality*, London, 1926.

Malinowski, B., *The Father in Primitive Psychology*, London, 1927.

Mannhardt, W., *Korndämonen und Feldkulte*, Berlin, 1875 and 1904.

Moll, A., *Das Sexualleben des Kindes*, Berlin, 1908.

Money-Kyrle, R. E., *The Meaning of Sacrifice*, London, 1930.

Money-Kyrle, R. E., *Aspasia*, London, 1932.

Preuss, K. Th., Lévy Bruhl's " Seele des Primitiven," *Baessler Arch.*, 1931.

Rank, O., *Das Incestmotiv in Dichtung und Sage*, Leipzig, Vienna, 1926.

Reich, W., *Der Einbruch der Sexualmoral*, Copenhagen, 1935.

Reik, Th., *The Ritual*, London, 1931.

Reitzenstein, F. v., " Der Kausalzusammenhang zw. Geschlechtsverkehr u. Empfängnis in Glaube und Brauch der Natur-und Kulturvölker," *Zt. Ethn.*, Berlin, 1909.

Roheim, G., *Australian Totemism*, London, 1925.

Roheim, G., " Psycho-Analysis of Primitive Cultural Types," *Int. Journ. Ps.-An.*, 1932.

Schmalhausen, S., *The New Road to Progress*, London, 1935.

Seligman, C. G., " Anthropological Perspective and Psychological Theory," *Journ. R. Anthr. Inst.*, 1932.

Shand, A. F., *The Foundations of Character*, London, 1920.

Smith, Robertson W., *Lectures on the Religion of the Semites*, 1889. Third Edition by St. A. Cook, London, 1927.

Stekel, W., *The Depth of the Soul*, London, 1921.

Stekel, W., " Der Abbau des Incestkomplexes," *Fortsch. Sexwiss*, 1926.

Stern, Cl. and W., " Erinnerung und Aussage in der ersten Kindheit," *Beitr. z. Psych. d. Aussage*, Leipzig, 1905.

Storfer, A. J., " Zur Sonderstellung des Vatermords," *Schr. angewandte Seel-Kunde*, XII, Vienna, 1911.

Storfer, A. J., *Maria's jungfräuliche Mutterschaft*, Berlin, 1914.

THE ANALYSIS OF THE SEX TABOO 291

VOLOSHINOV, V. N., "Freudism, Krititscheskij otscherk," Moskva, 1927.
WESTERMARCK, E., The Origin and Development of Moral Ideas, London, 1917.
WESTERMARCK, E., Ritual and Belief in Morocco, London, 1926.
WESTERMARCK, E., Three Essays on Sex and Marriage, including "The Œdipus Complex," London, 1934.
ZUCKERMANN, S., The Social Life of Monkeys and Apes, London, 1932.

TABLE OF EVENTS

1914 FREUD'S Study of Narcissism (term coined by HAVELOCK
      ELLIS).
1920 Psycho-analytic Congress at the Hague and clinic founded
      in Berlin by EITINGON.
1925 KRISCHE collects the available material from Matrilineal
      Communities.
1927 MALINOWSKI'S *magnum opus* on the Trobrianders.
1929 GOETZ'S *Sexualgeschichte der Menschheit*, with historical
      interpretation of the conflict between father and son
      throughout human religions.
1931 W. REICH shows the material and economic bases of the
      exogamous clan in *Einbruch der Sexualmoral*.
1934 WESTERMARCK'S criticism of the Œdipus Complex.
1935 SCHMALHAUSEN'S criticism of FREUD from the Sociological
      Point of View.
1936 REICH'S *Sexualität im Kulturkampf*.

CHAPTER IX

THE PATRIARCHATE IN DISSOLUTION

I

ON the 28th of June, 1936, this passage appeared in *Pravda :* " In no country of the world has woman such complete equality and opportunity in all departments of life, whether political, social or domestic, as in the Union of Socialist Soviet Republics. In no country does she who is responsible as citizen and mother, for the bearing and rearing of citizens, enjoy such respect and support as in the U.S.S.R."

Proud words, and justified in their pride. But they were the preamble to the new " Law of Family Life," which made the interruption of pregnancy a penal offence once more ! For sixteen years the Soviet Union's initiative had given an example to the advocates of abortion throughout the world. But—what now ?

The Soviet Government's Draft Law of May 26th, 1936, was discussed for several weeks, with unparalleled fervour both of opposition and advocacy, in all the factories, collective farms, railway trains, club houses and last, not least, in all organs of the Press. All Soviet citizens have had an opportunity of participation in discussion and criticism of this new Family Law. Moreover, the law has been proclaimed as justified by and logically consistent with that great achievement of Russia's Soviet Revolution of October-November, 1917 : the full human and civic equality of the sexes.

The Soviet Statesmen are fully aware of the handle they have given to all the opponents of legalization beyond their frontiers, and indeed there has been a chorus of reactionary triumph and derision : " Even those Communists have thrown that over ! " *Pravda* scores a definite point, however, in its leading article of June 28th, 1936, by reminding these scoffers that " in countries under a bourgeois *régime* the penalization of abortion becomes an instrument of torture for women ; it is no measure of protection but of subjection and insolent scorn," and the paper proceeds to show the hypocrisy and economic exploitation to which this Draconian law gives full scope. *Pravda* remarks that talk of protection for women's health is, to say the least, inconsistent in communities which expose thousands of their mothers to unemployment and what is termed " malnutrition." In a word ; penalties on procuring abortion are one thing in the Soviet territories and something very different under Capitalism.

In examining *Pravda's* vehement and confident claims we must not forget that the new Law of June, 1936, is much more detailed, constructive and comprehensive than any anti-abortion law on the statute books of the West. The complete official title of the June Soviet Law runs as follows : " Law concerning the prohibition of abortions, the extension of material help at childbirth, the establishment of subsidies for large families, the increase of maternity homes, crèches and nursery schools, the more effective prosecution and penalties for the non-payment of affiliation dues, and certain changes in the divorce laws."

This is a gigantic programme. Certainly other countries have admitted the right of motherhood to help and support, in their social Insurance measures, and local grants in aid, but on a painfully inadequate scale. But Soviet Russian women have already very substantial privileges in maternity. Practically every one of them is engaged in some form of productive work, mental or material ; and these women have the right to fifty-six days before and fifty-six days after childbirth as a holiday from work, with full pay, as well as further humane and helpful concessions during the period of lactation. The plans for an enlarged maternity service include 11,000 maternity hospitals to be in operation by January 1st, 1939, and Midwives Central Stations are to be added up to 14,400. The crèches are to be enlarged so as to provide for 2,000,000 Soviet citizens ; 800 new milk stations are to be constructed ; there is to be nursery school provision for three times the present number of young children, *i.e.*, 2,100,000 instead of the present 700,000. A sum of between 692 and 693 millions of roubles has been allocated to this work.

The Soviet rulers point to the plans they have made, and the solid advantages they already offer, and declare that in future their women citizens should have no need to evade motherhood, but can undertake it gladly and safely. Another element was active in the evil conditions previous to the law of 1920, which has lost its sting : the preamble to the 1920 law argued that " The moral prejudices of the past and the economic difficulties of the present, have compelled many women to have recourse to these operations." But there are now no illegitimate children in Soviet Russia ; all children are wards of the State, none are hurt or handicapped because of actions by their parents before their conception ! And the increased and increasing material prosperity of the Soviet territories, both European and Asiatic, since the second Five-Year Plan, seems to exclude the fear of starvation which hung as a menace over the People's Republic for many years.

In the criticisms of the Government's draft which filled the press in May and June, it was repeatedly mentioned that there was no reference to contraceptive Birth Control. This objection was correct. But we must bear in mind that the former law (the positive, pro-abortion enactment of 1920) did not explicitly mention all the conditions and considerations relative to its main content.

There was another factor quite as important as the urgent economic considerations ; the feminist principle, which claims woman's right of self-determination, of disposal of her own body, and development of her own mind ; and the fundamental requisite to such mental and bodily freedom is the power to decide whether she will bear children, and if so when. The social and sexual programme of the Soviet Russian Revolution demanded the deliverance of women from those " four C's " of tradition : " Clothes, Church, Cookery, Children." But the years since the revolution of 1917 have been so full of storm and stress, of victory and achievement that the new law has lost sight of the need for women's freedom and individual rights in a flood of economic optimism, submerging even any reference to contraception ! And as Soviet Russia has no such restrictions and pro- hibitions of Birth Control as Italy and Germany and even still to some extent the United States of America, we may hope that future sexual statesmanship may be built up round Birth Control. The new law deals with the collective and communal aspects of sex. But communities are after all com- posed of individuals, and we may reasonably doubt whether individual needs and differences have been sufficiently met, and whether the renewed penalization of abortion must not inevitably lead to a sharp rise in the number of illegal operations, with their train of invalidism and death, in spite of all the constructive work for maternity now promised and planned. Only the future can tell.

Lewis Fischer has made extensive observations and enquiries in Moscow, and has come to this sceptical con- clusion (*Neues Tagebuch*, July 18th, 1936 ; *cf. Nation*, June 25th, 1936, New York) :

" How many human tragedies will follow the enactment of this law ! ' Black ' (*i.e.*, secret) lairs for abortions without safeguards, will kill or cripple the women who have recourse to them. The women who are forced to beg for this relief from door to door will become violently hysterical. Young people will suffer intolerably. Perhaps—who can tell ?— before many months have passed, the misery and agony inflicted will have become sufficiently vocal to compel the first Soviet Russian Parliament (whose inaugural session is fixed for 1937) to rescind this wholly unjustifiable measure, and thus erase a blot on the record of Soviet Democracy."

2

During the last century women have become increasingly individualized and differentiated in all the countries of Europe, since Caroline Norton wrote in 1838 " The natural position of women is inferiority to man." And the liberator of woman has been neither church nor chivalry, but the machine. For it soon became evident, even in the early stages of the Industrial Revolution, that in many cases machines could be tended and " fed " as well by women as by men ; and much more cheaply. This meant the absorption of many women into industry outside the four walls of their homes, and large-scale machine production took over many forms of necessary work formerly done by women at home. Gina Lombroso-Ferrero has even suggested that the Industrial Revolution was a usurpation by men of women's place and tasks. But whether we approve or regret it, this process has not yet culminated, it is still spreading ; thus soap and candles are manufactured wholesale in Europe, except perhaps in certain remote mountain recesses ; stockings are sometimes hand knitted, but even so they are bought in shops and more and more shops become items in " multiple stores." In Western and Central Europe the buying, cooking, serving and washing up of meals is part of the housewife's daily routine, below a certain level of income. But the Soviet State has been a pioneer here as well. Communal kitchens and dining halls are part of the Soviet Communist system, and the paper table napkins in these public dining halls are printed with such sententious mottos as " To eat in common is a way to the new life."

Comparisons between men and women in large-scale industry have demonstrated the greater average energy and activity of the former, but the longer life and perhaps greater power of endurance at a lower rate of pressure, at least under present conditions, characteristic of women. And during the appalling tensions of the war of 1914–18 women " did their bit " in professions and occupations hitherto reserved for men, in a very creditable and adequate manner.[1]

The psychological and economic regression known as Fascism in Europe to-day proclaims that " Woman's place is the home." But this is the logical—though desperate—attempt of a tottering oligarchy to retain their power over the mass of the people by the incendiarism of sex conflict as of conflict between nations.

[1] And in Soviet Russia to-day the shock troops of industry have many and indefatigable *udarnitzas* as well as *udarniks*.—Translator's Note.

The status of women is founded on the technique of productive industry on the one hand ; and on that of prevention of conception on the other. In many countries to-day public opinion holds that " adultery " is " worse " in the wife than in the husband, and many legal codes have crystallized this verdict, with more or less vindictiveness. But the " double standard ". is doomed, since women are now able to experience coitus without impregnation as an inevitable result, and more and more of them are becoming fully aware of this possibility. The commercial plasticity of rubber and the expansion of our biochemical knowledge have had a drastic influence on conduct, within a very few decades. In Western Europe and the U.S.A. there is a steady decline in the once supreme value attached to anatomical virginity ; and this decline continues, coinciding with shifting economic conditions, although various social classes, creeds, occupations and even regions of the same country show such differences in this respect. The process is not of uniform rate. But it is incontestable, whether by those who praise or deplore ; and it is the living proof that the objective, external and eternal " Moral Law " is in fact fluid and relative.

As sociologists and historians began to realize this relativity, they accentuated it by their criticisms and comparisons. In 1928 the well-known Italo-Swiss sociologist, Roberto Michels, made an attempt at " ethical statistics " ; and in doing so threw as much light on his own standard of values as on the shifting sands of popular custom and practice. For he dealt mainly with illegitimate births, especially pre-marital illegitimacy ; the marriage ceremony was thus the Magic Ring of his particular ethical theory. Well, let us take this inadequate and formal standard as our test of the survival of traditional morality. Both in Great Britain and in Germany there were extensive official enquiries into private lives, in connection with the allowances for the children of combatant soldiers during the world war of 1914–18. These investigations proved what a gulf existed *between the conventional assumptions and the actual facts of thousands of humble, laborious and respectable lives.*

Irene Clephane has admirably summarized these results in her study *Towards Sexual Freedom*. She reminds us that " the authorities found themselves compelled to give the same recognition in regard to allowances to the ' unmarried wives ' in these unions, and their children, as to legally married women " (*l.c.*, p. 216). It has been estimated by cautious and experienced sociologists and medical observers that considerably more than half the total amount of sexual activity in Western European and American communities, now takes place outside legal marriage. But, there is still tragic ignorance and tragic cowardice. To quote Clifford in *Lady Chatterley's Lover* (p. 215) : " People can be what they like and feel what they like and do what they like, strictly privately, so long as they keep the form of life intact, and the apparatus." And the ghosts of archaic fear, in the minds of modern people, are still powerful for evil ; working mental havoc and social misery and deceit.

3

Sexual science and especially neurology have revealed the psychological damage inflicted by this perpetual conflict between obsolete standards and actual emotions and conditions, in the majority of adults with healthy minds and bodies to-day. It is a conflict involving almost every trend and manifestation, auto-erotic, " normal," *i.e.*, hetero-sexual, or deviation. Any just and honest and humanly merciful standard is twisted and spoiled by the intrusion of conventional lies and tyrannies. And in sheer self-defence, to keep their livelihood, to avoid endless misunderstandings, to spare pain to those who care for them or depend on them— people bow the knee to Rimmon and do lip service. Com-promise is almost inevitable. A psychologist in Copenhagen, H. Gottschalk, has studied *Some Problems of Jealousy* (1928) and come to significant conclusions on the economic factor, in the usually unmistakably different reactions of husbands and wives. He made studies of actual concrete cases of jealousy, carefully documented and cross-questioned. It appeared that the traditional attitude, " the proper thing to do " in the circumstances, was very powerful in deter-

mining behaviour, even in enlightened men and women
who were intellectually critical of the conduct expected of a
" wronged " partner. There was also a difference typical
of the patriarchate, even in decline. The men were all
more or less jealous of their wives in a physical and specifically sexual way ; they were comparatively indifferent to
their wives' " friendships " with other men, if such friendships had no bodily expression. The women, on the other
hand, were inclined to condone or ignore sexual divagations,
but became seriously angry and distressed at relationships
involving the emotional tenderness, pre-occupations and
refinements which we designate under that elastic term
" love."

The subjects of Gottschalk's studies were middle-class
couples, by nationality either Danes or Germans.

Surely it is obvious that the different reactions of husbands
and wives respectively were still determined by the economics
of the patriarchate. The men were on guard lest children
begotten by another man should inherit the putative
father's " name " and " means "—even in cases where the
names were far from illustrious and the " means " a minus
quantity ! The women, dependent on their husbands for
livelihood and even pocket money, were ready to make
biological, and even psychological, concessions for their daily
bread.

But what a change is taking place, especially in large
towns and in every social stratum, since the invention and
circulation of even partially reliable preventives ! The
unmarried women—especially those employed as wage-
earners in industry or clerical work or in the professions—
are by no means willing to accept the restrictions which
could still be forced on them by relatives and employers a
generation ago. Pre-marital sexual experience—often as a
form of " trial marriage " with the future partner, but, of
course, not by any means always permanent even in
intention—is increasingly frequent among young women
in social circles which demanded virginity as a *sine qua non*
at the beginning of the twentieth century. And there is
more and more mutual tolerance within legal marriage,

although the education and evolution of a proprietary feeling developed throughout millennia, into reciprocal consideration and comradeship is, of course, a very slow, complex and piecemeal process.[1] The double standard is indissolubly connected with a property economy and inheritance through male descent. Originally based upon this system of property inheritance, father right and sharp economic inequalities, it has become a shield and weapon of defence to perpetuate patriarchal ideals. The interaction of family and property was traced by F. Engels in 1884, and his diagnosis has been proved correct by the events of the crowded years in which the patriarchate of Tzarist Russia was liquidated and transformed by the Soviet Revolution. When the private, *i.e.*, domestic production of the necessities of life (food, clothing, means of transport and shelter) was taken over by large-scale organizations or by the State itself, the economic basis for the bourgeois family, with its customs and codes, became a thing of the past. This meant the obliteration of the difference between sexual relationships sanctioned by Church and State and those which had not secured the protection of these magic formulæ or judicial concessions. And therefore no children could be handicapped and

---

[1] A very sound and subtle account of the present situation, especially in the U.S.A. under the pressure of the " economic blizzard " and the great slump of 1929 and after, is given by Lorine Pruette, Ph.D., in *The Sex Life of the Unmarried Adult* (London and New York, 1935). There are also most interesting case studies in the *magnum opus* of Dr. Katharine Bement Davis' *Factors in the Sex Life of 2,200 Women*, also dealing with American material, and mainly of the professional classes. There is plenty of ignorance, cowardice and prejudice amongst them, and some pitifully wasted lives. But there is also refreshing courage and intelligence, as, for example, in the woman who writes : " I ' thought through ' my experiences to a sane conclusion, but not all women can. . . . I succeeded in winning the game of sex after all. . . . I don't know that my life would be as full and rich or my marriage as happy as it is, had I never gone through and won out against these experiences." Recently there has been a development of the questionnaire method ; carefully compiled queries have been sent to educated persons, in both Europe and America, with strict precautions as to anonymity, by such authorities as Taylor, K. B. Davis, Peck and Wells, Achilles, G. V. Hamilton and Exner. Men and women alike testify that " sex has never been socially controlled ; it has merely been driven into underground channels, often more objectionable than prostitution " (*New Generation*, June, 1936, p. 64). *Cf.* also Dr. R. L. Dickinson.—Translator's Note.

humiliated by the stigma of illegitimacy ; all children became both " natural " and " lawful."

The history of economic change has, however, a perceptible " time-lag " on the cultural and psychological side. The traces of patriarchal thought and feeling are deep seated, even after the material basis of existence has been remodelled. A communal organization is not well adapted to a patriarchal moral code ; but this anachronism has not prevented the most extraordinary and incongruous " rationalizations." Thus the " aim and goal " of the Soviet anti-abortion law of June 28th has actually been proclaimed to be " The fight against levity and frivolity in family life and neglect of family obligations " (*Pravda*, June 28th, 1936). These phrases belong to the past. Indeed the social laboratory of Soviet Russian life from 1917–34 has provided remarkable evidence of the interdependence of bourgeois marriage and the repression of early sexual activity. The Russian social psychologist Barasch has (" Sex Life of the Workers of Moscow," *J. of Soc. Hyg.*, Vol. XII, No. 5, May, 1926) collected extensive statistical material on " the adaptability to monogamous behaviour " and the actual age at which sexual practices began, and has calculated that the earlier the efflorescence of sex, the less happy in and suitable for, monogamous ties in adult age. Here is the logical explanation of conventional indignation at the mere mention of juvenile sexuality, not to speak of its actual manifestations. And here is the theoretical chain, which makes the pillars of the Capitalist state like the pillars of the Christian churches, into exploiters of the shame and dread of sex ; a phobia which is perhaps not inherent in human nature, but must have developed in the earliest stages of the patriarchate (as has been suggested in our eighth chapter).

4

Historically and clinically psycho-analysis is of the first importance, but it has been interwoven with the traditional marriage taboo on sex. The leaders of accepted thought, and the doctors not less than any other bourgeois, were furious in their repugnance and resistance to Freud's revealing theories. But all except the most arrant Comstockites have become reconciled to "sublimation." For Freud has expressly repudiated any intention of letting loose "unbridled instincts." He keeps to his original view of the precise mechanism of emotion, but he advocates canalization and transmutation of primitive urges into safer and superior forms, that is, by sublimation, and analysis claims to reveal "repressed desires" in order that the patient may learn their control. Freud declares that "Civilization has been built up on the denial and control of instinctive urges, and every single individual should repeat the history of the ascent of the human species on his path through life with understanding and resignation. Psycho-analysis has shown that the instinctive urges which must go through the transmutation into civilization are mainly—though not solely—those of sex" (Freud, *Collected Works*, XI, p. 198. *Cf.* also "These Eventful Years," *Enc. Brit.*, published 1924).

Psycho-analysis has entered the pulpit and the drawing-room ; it has "lined up" on the bourgeois front. The early error of analyzing individuals *without reference to their social environment* has borne its fruit ; and proved inadequate and misleading. "Legitimate" and "illicit" sex manifestations have been re-labelled, in a new terminology, but on the traditional lines, thus throwing a vaguely "scientific" aura around such pronouncements as that the British Social Hygiene Council addresses to youth. In their *Sex in Life* manual for "Young Women" the B.S.H.C. write : "Believe me, it is worth while waiting until you are married to express the fullness of your love for each other" (p. 25). The manual intended for "Young Men" is much more definite in its language ! "Apart from this higher control, physical attraction alone leads to Lust. Lust degrades ; Love ennobles" (*Sex in Life : Young Men*, p. 25).

Here is simply the Catholic moral theology in the disguise of an active and eminent public health organization ; a doctrine and a vested interest essentially "at enmity with joy," and well equipped to suppress and twist unwelcome truth. Let us give only one recent instance of how this doctrine works. During 1935, a large printing agency in Hertfordshire received an order to adapt the case papers used by the Society for the Provision of Birth Control Clinics at the London headquarters, for distribution to their patients, for the use of a local clinic just established. The order was booked, and then came a letter from the proprietor of the printing press, dated December 12th, 1935 :

" . . . When we quoted you for this work we did not realize the intimate nature of it, and as we have a number of apprentices and juniors employed here (male and female), we do not feel that we should be doing the right thing in passing these jobs through the works. . . ." [1]

5

The propaganda of sex-phobia is part of a social doctrine and a social system. Anthropologists are aware of this, though they have not been explicit on the subject, restricting themselves to such brief allusions as Malinowski's to " specific perils " " for the human family " (*Sex and Repression*, p. 244, *cf.* Chapter VIII, *supra*), and Frazer's " satisfaction of these natural instincts is detrimental to the general interests of society " (*Exogamy*, IV, p. 97). These " specific perils " and " general interests " refer to the economic structure of the patriarchal family. According to the present conclusions of anthropology " the theories which maintain that marriage in its monogamous form has always existed are now generally accepted " (Malinowski, 1926,

---

[1] In the autumn of 1931 there was a controversy in the correspondence columns of the independent *Week-End Review* arising from a letter by Stella Browne pressing the need for abortion law reform. There were numerous and vehement letters both for and against, and both sides were given a " fair show " by the very able Editor, Mr. Gerald Barry. But the defenders of the *status quo* were not content to argue their case ; they wished to suppress all mention of the facts and considerations in favour of legalized abortion, and several threatened to withdraw their subscriptions if the correspondence were not closed. Gerald Barry at once refused all dictation, and in the issues of November 21st and 28th he gave an account of the pressure which had been put, and stated his belief that the case for legalization was sound. Fortunately the enlightened readers rallied round the paper, made up the subscriptions which had been cancelled by fresh ones, and showed that " it does not pay to be hectored." In the following month Mr. Justice McCardie made his famous comments from the Bench, on the need to reform the statute of 1861.—Translator's Note.

pp. 92 *ff.*). And, of course, individual sexual preference, individual love has always existed, but has had to beat its wings against social barriers ; it was first openly recognized *as valuable in itself* in the Romantic and Revolutionary movements of the eighteenth century, coincidently with the more definite differentiation and individual emancipation of European women. The gulf between love and livelihood, between the desires of individuals and the demands of the social order, has not yet been built over, in spite of the systematic efforts of the revolutionary phase in Soviet Russia (1918–34) to liberate Eros from the cash nexus.

Constantin Brunner, from whom I have already quoted, has remarked that : " Illegitimate children are often termed ' Love-children ' ; a proof that love is apart from and outside marriage." As this deep conflict was recognized by an increasing section of public opinion, sexual reform was born, in the effort to mitigate or conquer the evils of the Capitalist social order. The World League for Sexual Reform on a scientific basis (W.L.S.R.) was born in Copenhagen in 1928 (*cf.* Chapter II), and has undoubtedly done fine preliminary and organizing work. There was also the " Bund für Mutterschutz " (League for the Protection of Motherhood), founded by Helene Stoecker, Ph.D., one of the pioneers of German University Education for Women, and a social idealist of great courage and delicate insight (1905–33). On the eve of the war, the " British Society for the Study of Sex Psychology " was founded in London, with Edward Carpenter as President, and a small group of active and distinguished members, and carried on educative propaganda under difficult circumstances.

The World League (W.L.S.R.) was initiated by the pioneering efforts of Magnus Hirschfeld (1867–1935). He, Havelock Ellis and Auguste Forel were the appropriate and illustrious trio of Presidents from 1928 to 1931, when Forel died, and Havelock Ellis retired. The final trio were Hirschfeld, Norman Haire in London, and J. H. Leunbach in Copenhagen. The programme of the W.L.S.R. was comprehensive and within its wide limits consistent ; it included the complete equality of the sexes, the abolition of the handicaps on unmarried mothers and illegitimate children, the abolition of laws against Birth Control and abortion, positive and constructive sex education, and reform of the marriage and divorce laws. Valuable material was presented in the papers and discussions at its four congresses, in Copenhagen (1928), London (1929), Vienna (1930), and Brno (1932), but at the same time strong currents of divergent opinion became manifest in its membership. Moreover, the international political and financial situation grew rapidly worse immediately after 1928. There was an ameliorative influence on the legislation of Central Europe and Scandinavia. But in Great Britain the W.L.S.R. had far less result than might have been hoped. The electoral equality of women was granted in two instalments, in 1918 and 1928, before the W.L.S.R's. activities extended to this country, and their professional equality was accepted in theory, though often denied in practice. There remain the two main stumbling blocks ; the status of the illegitimate child and the English law of separation and divorce.

There have been ingenious attempts to defend the Bastardy Laws through a somewhat tardy process of " rationalization." The British Social Hygiene Council offers this humane explanation for inhumanity to woman : " Every child has the right to the love of two parents and to . . . a home where father and mother both take part in his upbringing. Therefore society frowns (!) on the unmarried mother, because among other reasons (!) the child under these circumstances has not its full chance of proper development " (*Sex in Life : Young Women*, p. 16). There is no trace of the recognition that the community should be responsible for the children it permits to be born.

The most flagrant examples, both of the tyranny of the past and of irrational and unsatisfactory compromise between past and present, in England to-day are the laws of separation and divorce (the Scottish law allows many more grounds for divorce and is more humane and reasonable in details of procedure).

The need for reform of the Divorce Law was proclaimed in

both the Majority and Minority Reports of the Government Commission which reported just after the war. There have been, since then, certain reforms in procedure which make it possible for persons of less than moderate means to obtain relief, if they are very persistent and know the ropes. Also by the Act of 1923 wives have the right to divorce their husbands for adultery, even for a single act uncomplicated by other offences. But what a fantastic mixture of absurdity and cruelty remains! A. P. Herbert's striking novel *Holy Deadlock*—obviously a study from life—has shown the law in operation, even in the case of educated persons of some means and with influential and competent advisers. Eminent legal opinion has spoken again and again of the urgent need for cleaning up the divorce laws. Thus Lord Hewart of Bury declared in the *Daily Telegraph* last year that " divorce law needs reform " and " should be in accordance with reason, fairness and good sense." Yet nothing thorough and adequate is done, though the Royal Commission was appointed a generation ago.[1]

The lamentable psychological effect of the present English divorce law is manifest in a morbid obsession with the " guilt " of extra-marital sexual relationships, as compared with conduct that may be far more destructive to health, happiness and human dignity. This curious pre-occupation has been recorded in memorable terms in that far from radical but intensely respectable paper the *Sunday Times* of September 29th, 1935, in commenting on the trial of Mrs. F. Rattenbury. " A British judge pointed out to the jury, for the first time from the Bench, that guilt of adultery is

---

[1] Many legal experts, writers and divines of the Established and Free Churches in England have denounced the present divorce law from different points of view. We may cite amongst others Lord Salvesen, the late Lords Gorell and Buckmaster, the late Mr. Justice McCardie, Mr. Claud Mullins, the magistrate, and the late Dr. Bernard Hollander, the neurologist. Mr. E. S. P. Haynes has kept the anomalies and cruelties of the law before the public with immense vigour and caustic humour, and there is a capital summary of the present position, particularly as it affects the poor, *i.e.*, the majority of our people, in Mr. Alec Craig's *Sex and Revolution*. There is this benefit, however, from the refusal of successive governments to alter the law. An increasing number of men and women are learning to despise and defy it ; and in some cases, at least, to build up their lives and achieve happiness on a basis of reality.— Translator's Note.

not necessarily presumptive guilt of murder. Hitherto, one would have gathered that, in the opinion of both juries and judges, it was! "

6

The years 1933–34 were as heavily disastrous for sexual reform as for many other international efforts towards peace and progress. The Fascist victories in Germany and Austria completely hamstrung the movements in those countries. The number of qualified experts with a turn for propaganda and leadership, as well as research, was and still is extremely small; they occupied a disproportionately important position, and if they were imprisoned or killed, their students and patients were doubly deprived. Thus the Spanish section of the W.L.S.R. ceased all its activities after the murder of Hildegart in 1933; and the death of Hirschfeld in exile in 1935 was the signal for a crucial stocktaking and discussion between the two surviving Presidents as to whether the organization should continue or close down; for the French section had virtually isolated itself and the Dutch had severed all connection with the parent body.

The co-Presidents, Dr. Leunbach and Dr. Haire, issued a joint declaration: " Among the members of various national sections, schisms have arisen as to how far the League should preserve its original non-political character. Some members believe that it is impossible to attain the aims of the W.L.S.R. without fighting at the same time for a social revolution. Dr. Haire insists that the programme of the League should be kept free from political activity. Dr. Leunbach is of opinion that the W.L.S.R. can attain nothing because it has not attached itself to the worker's revolutionary movement, and cannot attach itself to that movement."

Thus Haire advocated compromise as the way to effective results; and Leunbach advocated an open declaration of solidarity with the most radical sections of Europe's working class, with emphasis on the incompatibility of effective change and bourgeois economics or theological ethics. He demanded the reconstruction of the social order, so that health and happiness should be made possible for humanity.

This appreciation of the factors at work against sexual enlightenment led Leunbach to identify himself with the work of Wilhelm Reich. The Sex-Pol agitation (Sexual-policy) has been built up by Reich as a result of his experiences in the German worker's movement in the course of many strenuous years. Leunbach appeared as a candidate for the Danish Parliamentary Elections in 1935, on an independent Sex-Pol platform (cf. Chapter VI). The items in his programme were as follows :

1. A campaign for the possibility of happiness and harmony for all human beings, through a satisfactory sexual life.
Therefore : The abrogation of all laws limiting the freedom of normal and mutual sexual experience. Planning and public recognition of affirmative enlightenment.
2. Removal of all compulsion in marriage or divorce.
Therefore : Legislation enabling the community to take over the costs of rearing children, so that all who desire children can have them, without being socially and financially penalized for parenthood.
Complete abolition of the status of and stigma on "unmarried mothers" and "illegitimate children."
3. Education of children to be healthy, independent individuals capable of reproducing a healthy future generation.
Therefore : Expansion of child care, under direct public control. Abolition of the authoritarian principle in schools.
4. Support for young people in their struggle for independence and their social and sexual rights. Preparation of young manual workers and "intellectuals" for their historic task and destiny ; the Social Revolution.
Therefore : Fight against unemployment. Organization of young people for the discussion and solution of their special difficulties.
5. The housing problem to be adequately met. A room for each person, in which they are "at home."
Therefore : Increased provision of residences at public expense, so that even the unemployed may be decently and safely housed. Higher taxes on luxury dwellings should be one of the means of raising necessary funds.
6. Complete equality of men and women, economically, socially and sexually.
Therefore : Free, gratuitous and public access of all to sexual instruction, to contraceptive information and all the necessary appliances. Unrestricted right of women to the termination of pregnancy, by skilled and qualified practitioners. Leave from

work with full pay for women, for at least two months before and two months after every birth. Free medical attendance during pregnancy. Free hospital care and anæsthesia in childbirth. Provision for crêches and nursery schools, so that all mothers wishing to do so may leave their children in skilled care.

7. Expert therapeutic treatment for all sufferers from psychoses, neuroses, and erotic disturbances. Abolition of penalties for sexual abnormality as such.

Therefore : Instruction of physicians and pedagogues in sexual economy, provision of an adequate number of clinics and training centres.

8. Rational prophylaxis against venereal diseases.

Therefore : Public instruction in the most effective methods of prevention. Venereal clinics to be provided and to be accessible all night and in the morning.

9. The liquidation of prostitution.

Therefore : Abolition of unemployment and underpayment of women. Provision of special free prophylactoria.

10. The Campaign for a Socialist Community founded on the prosperity, health and personal happiness of all its members.

Therefore : A revolutionary attack on exploitation and oppression, in the name of freedom and Socialism.

7

The organization whose programme we have just outlined is at present the only international body of a scientific character aiming at a sexual renaissance. Its programme takes into consideration economic and administrative necessities as well as specifically sexual factors, and recognizes their interdependence. In Scandinavia there was animated public discussion following the Danish elections of 1935. In the course of this controversy, the upholders of the *status quo* constantly declared that the Sex-Pol programme, if realized, would lead to " Sexual Chaos."

In April, 1936, the Sex-Pol replied to this objection in the organ of Norwegian University students *Kamp og Kultur*. Their manifesto placed the old and the new codes in graphic juxtaposition.

Until now, Socialism has suffered shipwreck as a cultural movement, because it has shared the same fear as Conservatism and believed in the inherent opposition of Sex and Civilization. Socialism did not dare to probe into the exact nature of that bugbear, " Moral Chaos," with which we were menaced and reproached. But a Socialist civilization can never be hostile to Life itself ; but must advance and create in the service of life : Let us examine this concept more closely.

What is sexual chaos ?

In our opinion it means :

1. Insistence on " conjugal duties " and " rights " if the partner is unwilling.

2. Entrance on a lifelong sexual contract without previous experience of the partner's private tastes and qualities.

3. Liaisons with working-class girls because they are " good enough for that sort of thing " ; but rigid self-restraint towards a bourgeoise *fiancée* who is considered " far above all that."

4. To lay special stress on the " bridal night " as a central point of indecent fantasy, leading to total abstinence or crass brutality in practice.

5. To prize the " seduction " of " maidens " as the summit of male sexuality.

6. To practise self-excitement by means of pornographic pictures at fourteen years of age. But in later phases, as a full-grown Nazi or member of the Oxford group, to become fervent in praise of " Woman's Honour and Purity."

7. To punish children for auto-erotic acts, and persuade boys in their teens that seminal emissions cause " spinal atrophy."

8. To take part in the pornographic Press and picture trade.

9. To do profitable business out of films of a kind which stimulate young people unbearably, but at the same time to put obstacles in the way of their natural joys and loves, in the name of morality and civilization.

What is not sexual chaos ?

1. Bodily and mental conjunction and satisfaction between two people who love one another irrespective of present laws and customs.

2. The deliverance of children and young people from a sense of guilt, so that they may taste the experiences suitable to their stage of growth.

3. To avoid marriage or alliance with a partner until there is the knowledge of mutual harmony, bodily as well as otherwise.

4. Never to bring children into the world, unless they are loved and wanted, and can be properly cared for.

5. Never to demand love or bodily contact as a duty.

6. Never to seek the services of prostitutes, but to choose a partner on an equal footing.

7. Not to perform coitus under archways, in cellars or alleys, but in the privacy of a room of one's own.

8. Never to keep up the appearance of an unhappy marriage out of " moral considerations."

And so forth.

In actual practice, the attitudes described above as really
" chaotic " are those of custom and tradition and are
associated with support of things as they are. Here is an
example of " moral chaos " quoted from a British observer
very well informed of the realities of contemporary politics
and journalism :

> " The contrast in circulation between the surviving political
> papers and the new popular ones is strikingly illustrated by the
> fact that the *Manchester Guardian,* famous throughout the world
> for the quality and fearlessness of its news and comment, has less
> than 100,000 circulation, while of the *Daily Mail, Daily Express*
> and *Daily Herald* all aspire to a circulation of two million, and
> the *News of the World, which specializes in sex and crime* for
> Sunday reading, has a three million circulation. . . . The best
> every-day seller in England is sport, and side by side with it we
> must put crime and stories which excite sexual interest. *A sex*
> *crime is the sub-editor's happiest windfall.* Sex is found in England
> to be particularly for Sunday reading : the largest circulations
> belong to those Sunday papers which specialize in sex and crime
> stories " (*l.c.,* pp. 22 and 27).

The pamphlet by Kingsley Martin on *The Educational
Rôle of the Press,* from which we have quoted, was published
by the League of Nations in 1930. Or let us turn to two of
the most distinguished sociological students and experienced
practical politicians now alive, Beatrice and Sidney Webb,
who comment as follows in their encyclopædic work on
Soviet Communism : a New Civilization :

> " When in the Western countries we talk about a moral or an
> immoral man, still more about a moral or an immoral woman, it is
> understood to refer to their sexual relations rather than to any
> other form of morality or immorality. This concentration on
> sex is unknown in the U.S.S.R." (p. 1034).

We find, therefore, a consistent moral theory as well as a
consistent economic doctrine and practice in Sovietism on
the one hand, and the highly specialized industrial capitalism
developed in Great Britain together with political democracy
during the last 150 years, on the other. There are, of course,
minor anomalies, but the two general trends are distinct.
But the latest form of capitalism which has thrown aside
democracy in favour of frank terrorism shows certain

further anomalies and inconsistencies of a significant kind, especially in its German form ; for Italian Fascism confines itself rigidly to enforcing the moral dogmatism of the Roman Catholic Church in this sphere of conduct. Nazism, however, is suffering as a philosophy of life from the tactical dishonesty of its first propagandists. There can be no doubt of the inherent antagonism to sex among its leaders—the destruction of the Berlin Institute, that centre of light and help, was not only a very material barbarity but a symbolic gesture as well. For the leaders of Nazism, sexual science, like Marxian Socialism, was simply " a Jewish invention " and therefore to be insulted, hunted down and destroyed. And this hostility was really perfectly logical, for the Nazi branch of Fascism is the latest weapon of a class oligarchy against the growing activity and power of a new way of life.

But the support of the masses was only won for Nazism by delusive promises and phrases, economic and social, which could not have been materialized within the Capitalist framework, and which are now of course no longer heard.[1] The really revolutionary and constructive elements in National Socialism were doomed from the moment of the February coup in 1933, although the blow did not fall till June 30th, 1934, when Roehm was murdered. For it should not be forgotten that Roehm was at least an outspoken enemy of certain forms of hypocrisy. On November 26th, 1933, at the summit of his power, and on terms of close friendship with his " leader," he issued the following order to the troops under his command :

" The revolution was won not by the canting humbugs or moral cranks, but by revolutionary fighters, and I forbid all leaders and Storm Troopers to continue their activities as ' crank moral æsthetes.' "

Roehm fell, and the official leaders of Nazism carry on an exaggerated propaganda " on behalf of family life," lay stress on authority in home and school, and insist on the

[1] To take a striking example, outside the purview of this study : the promises to tackle the large landed estates, either by taxation or by subdivision. The Junkers, especially of Eastern Prussia, have had the casting vote in German politics since Bismarck's day, and they now share it with the armament kings of Essen and the Ruhr.—Translator's Note.

public and domestic subjection of women. Herewith one illustrative instance, which might be multiplied *ad nauseam*. Rosenberg, author of the *Myth of the Twentieth Century*, is the mouthpiece of the N.S.D.A.P. and one of its leading officials. In formulating the philosophy of Nazism, he declares the gravest sin of the feminists to be their demand for political and civic equality with man ; and as their second most serious offence—their fight against the " double moral standard " in the androcratic state of to-day (*l.c.*, pp. 494–502, German Edition). This insistence on the whited sepulchre of conformity has gone so far as to enact a law penalizing officials " taken in adultery " with dismissal from their jobs ! (1936).

But there is a flaw in this structure which has already become uncomfortably perceptible, although so far as possible denied. The totalitarian State has necessarily encouraged the regimentation and collective education and discipline of children and young people ; there are two nation-wide organizations for boys and girls respectively, the Hitlerjugend (Hitler Youth) and the Bund deutscher Mädel (League of German Girls). And these organizations are shot through and through with individual " indiscipline " and insubordination ; in sexual matters as well as otherwise, although without any basis of rational and humanitarian ethics, and in a " hole and corner " fashion which cannot lead to any very helpful results. The claims and aims of these two giant organizations are directly hostile to the claims of the family and undermine parental authority, at the very moment of its " reinstatement " from above.

There is a similar split between philosophy and practice in the treatment of illegitimacy. In September, 1934, the juridical section of the N.S.D.A.P. drafted an Amendment to the Law, suggesting that illegitimate children should " in every case bear the name of their father and share the rights of inheritance on an equality with those born in wedlock " (*Frankfurter Zeitung*, Nos. 506–7, 1934). And the joint responsibility of several possible fathers of the same woman's illegitimate child was advocated in these terms : " It has been objected that . . . such joint responsibility is practically the infliction of a heavy fine. Those who have had occasion to observe the licence and immorality which cause such joint responsibility, will consider a heavy fine quite appropriate." Thus we find on one hand the infringement of the marriage taboo in the recognition of illegitimate children's rights, and on the other hand, simultaneously, a lapse into the moral standards and phrases of tradition.

Which means that the most authoritative of terrorisms is no longer able to " iron out " the contradictions which arise whenever the patriarchate is enforced to-day ; whether in sexual matters or otherwise.

Nor is even Soviet Russia by any means free from psychological regressions and contradictions, owing to the survival of traditional standards. We have referred to examples at the beginning of this chapter and in Chapter II (*cf.* S. and B. Webb, *l.c.*, p. 1060).

For we have as yet no sound and detailed biological philosophy of civilization. Freud's theory of sublimation has simply superseded moral theology as a scientific " façade " for the social fabric of yesterday and to-day ; by the theory that all " higher values " are only achieved by the repression of instinct. The leader of reaction in Denmark, Professor E. Geismar, has put this clearly :

" Belief in the spirit was a firm basis for sublimation even after religion had lost some of its influence. But I fear that now, in spite of much talk of sublimation, there will in actual fact be less and less of it. And that must have sinister and disastrous consequences for our civilization " (*Dag. Nyheder*, October 21st, 1934).

Can scientific research provide a theoretical basis for deciding whether the demands of moral theology—as formulated by St. Paul and St. Augustine, St. Tertullian or even Freud—are indispensable for the material and social and psychological creation which is human culture ?

8

We have known for some time that the skin has electrical and motor functions, that its quality is that of a membrane. The actual potential of the skin cannot be normalized, but it certainly responds to affective stimuli by oscillations. We have already referred to the interaction of emotion and the vegetative system (Chapter IV, § 7).

The knowledge of this mechanism is due to the electro-physiological tests made by Wilhelm Reich, in collaboration with the Psychological Institute of the University of Oslo. He found that stimulation of the erogenous zones increased the potential of the skin, but that there was a definite "difference" between turgescence caused by mechanical means and the fluid current of sensation peculiar to voluptuous pleasure. The latter was the crucial factor. Reich was able to combine his electric apparatus with an Oscillograph, and to photograph the vegetative currents of pleasurable sensation in the form of oscillations in the electrical current of the surface of the erogenous membrane (Reich, 1936, p. 10). At the present stage in his investigations the following conclusions are justified :

"Sexual excitation is functionally identical with an electrical charge of the genital zones. Dread is accompanied by a decrease of this surface charge . . . 'libido' as a term for the sum of psychic energy is no longer a figure of speech ; it applies to electrical processes, and includes the manifestations of sex in the vast electric economy of the Universe.

"Epidermis and mucous membrane alike have a latent potential corresponding to a quiescent or negative condition. In each individual this potential varies, between certain limits. The vegetative centres, or sympathetic ganglia, are the mainsprings of this electrical mechanism in the surface of the organism, in association with the whole biological membranous and electrolytic system.

"The sexual zones are supplied with specially acute sensory capacity and electric potentiality. Moreover, their negative or latent potential is generally higher and their range of sensation greater. This entirely corresponds with the greater intensity of the psychic and cerebral emotions, accompanying their excitation and function.

"In test experiments dread and joy can be as sharply distinguished as in mental hospitals.

"Passive congestion by mechanical means does not raise the latent potential. The sensation of specific pleasure is an indispensable condition.

"Thus sexual friction is a form of biological activity, dependent on the alternations of charge and discharge. The discharge is felt as specific pleasure. The intensity of sensation depends on the degree of electrification of the superficies, and *vice versâ*. " The degree of potential in the superficies and the intensity of erogenous—*i.e.*, vegetative—sensation are functionally identical."

Thus it appears that erotic excitement is a form of organic production in itself. The formula " Tension, Congestion, Distension, Relaxation " would then be manifestly a biological summary of the vital process.

Side by side with electrical and biological tests, we must consider the analytic study of the formation of characters and habits. Is not the conclusion justified that protracted sublimation and sexual repression lead to a special frame of mind, wholly adapted to follow and maintain the " civilization " of tradition ? Sociology confirms this view. The average individual character in the present stage of evolution is liable to an immense variety and degree of neurotic fixations. In complete contrast is the freedom both from impotence and from "deviations", to which Malinowski testifies, among the matrilineal communities he has so carefully studied. For in those communities there is no sexual repression in childhood and puberty and comparatively few prohibitions for adults. May we not conclude that sexual repression forms the human material at the basis of the class State, and continues to provide the class State's surest guarantee of survival ? For sublimation in theory and practice acts as a permanent depressor of human energy and human capacity.

The capacity to fully experience the process of orgasm is the best measure of health and freedom from neuroses in individuals (*cf.* Chapter IV, § 7). But such vigour is notoriously rare in modern communities. Therefore the repression of traditional codes is unbiological, harmful to life and health, and not necessary to intellectual or material achievement. Individuals who have retained their genital capacity unimpaired are as a rule correspondingly " potent " and able in other directions, more active, more creative, more aware of themselves and the world—and certainly less adapted to the colourless and subordinate lives of the exploited. These are the facts which give such impetus to the Sex-Pol move-

ment and its message to the social and political confusion
of to-day. The campaign against the Things That Are has
hitherto been fought mainly on the economic front. The
present social order has defended itself by means of Church
and School as effectively as by its armies and police forces,
in fact the services of priests and school teachers have generally made recourse to " direct action " superfluous.

After the Boer War the serenity of the Victorian era was
shaken, and since the world war of 1914-18 certainties have
given way to questions and doubts, and search for a doctrine
in which mankind can believe and for a rule of life which it
can follow with hope and pride. Of course, no student of
human nature would attribute the world unrest of to-day
to the increase of rational and conscious processes, *per se*,
but it is doubtless partly due to the undermining of accepted
codes and expectations. Reason has gained relatively, both
individually and collectively. Modern machine production
is complicated and exacting in its demands, and necessitates
a higher degree and a wider diffusion of exact knowledge ;
and those *who know a lot need to believe less !* People begin
to criticize and make demands. This is the dialectical process of the age in which we live. It is a process so vast in
scope and significance that no branch of science can honestly
or safely ignore it ; and sexual science least of all !

One illustrative example among thousands may throw a
light on the changes now taking place throughout human
habits and therefore throughout the human environment.
In 1933 the public health expert Professor Schioetz published
a study of pediatrics in collaboration with Borgny Seland,
based on Norwegian data. It was entitled *The Birth Month
as a Factor in the Child's Future*, and was illustrated by
detailed graphs, showing how rapidly the traditional Yule-
tide Weddings of the North are being abandoned in favour
of unions consummated in the summer, and how the distribution of conceptions has shifted in consequence. For
from the year 1906 to 1910 the majority of births took place
in September, when mothers and babies had to face the long
northern winters after their mutual ordeal of birth. But
from 1926-30 the month with the highest number of births

was April, which meant much more favourable conditions for the young lives in the ascending rhythm of the annual cycle. Thus our atavistic survivals wane before the process of social evolution, and individuals gain in health and happiness.

For primitive man the whole of life, food, as well as mating and birth, was and is saturated with taboos and ringed with fears.

In Malinowski's phrase : " Eating is for primitive men, an act surrounded by etiquette, special prescriptions and prohibitions, and a general emotional tension to a degree unknown to us " (*Magic and Religion*, 1926, p. 42). We have passed out of this phase, but sex is still in the realm of taboo ; shrouded in ignorance and fear for the majority. The decline of the patriarchate is the signal for the breaking of these bonds, although as Havelock Ellis has reminded us in his profound essay *The Function of Taboos*—no community will ever be able to dispense with some restrictions on conduct. And everyone of us to-day is responsible for the development of the taboos of the future, for the standards of rational humanity as distinct from the Shamanism of the past and the exploitation of human hates and fears. But speculations in ignorance and savagery are only profitable so long as the leaders of scientific thought are content to isolate themselves in their laboratories and lecture halls, under the discreditable excuse that " science has nothing to do with politics." The lamentable result has been that " politics " have had nothing to do with scientific fact or the scientific spirit.

A further factor here is the increasing individuation in both sexes. Until the eighteenth century the majority of human beings appear to have lived almost on the vegetative level ; their consciousness would seem to have been both more limited and more collectively diffused than that of even the majority to-day. But the technique of machine production in the Atlantic civilizations of the last 150 years has given the signal for intense and deep-seated changes, which have by no means reached their climax. The pace of change has quickened in an astounding manner. The democratic Liberalism of the nineteenth century is seriously rivalled by the Concepts and Plans of Collectivism whose first experimental pattern is found in the civilization of Soviet Communism. The combined though contrasting forces of wider and more intricate yet closer Collectivism, and more acute individual differentiation and consciousness have furnished the material for the sexual science of the future.

The keynote is the separation of sex from reproduction. The aim of sex is the release of tensions in the individual. Tensions arise biologically in the functions of the endocrine glands and the sympathetic nervous system. This release of tension needs no justification or excuse or certification, either by the magic of the altar or the " price " of parenthood, as concerns the individuals. But when once new lives begin, sexual activity becomes social and communal in its responsibilities. And so we have the human conflict which no programme of reform or reconstruction has so far solved : the conflict between individual sexual demands and the interests of the child.

Hitherto, communities have considered the social aspects of this matter, almost to the exclusion of the individual, in their laws and institutions. The longing for personal happiness has been sacrificed to the rearing of children in the framework of the family and the interest of the ruling classes in the supply of gun-fodder, of the " Unemployment Reserve " in industry or of serf labour on large feudal estates. While amongst those born to ownership of property and exercise of power, there were available alleviations ; by persuasion or purchase or sheer compulsion they could gratify their desires without danger to the " social fabric."

Now, the conflict between the reproduction of the species and the fulfilment of individual needs has become clamant. In every capitalist community of America and Europe the rearing of children has become a burden of which the burden-bearers are entirely aware. The Soviet Union now believes it can make this burden tolerable by social services to the mothers (cf. § 1 in this chapter). It hopes by this means to balance the claims of the community and the individual.

Time alone will prove whether this hope is justified ; whether the provisions of the law of June 28th, 1936, win the justification of success or new conflicts arise and demand fresh re-adjustments. The dawn of Collectivism means the end of the patriarchate whose latest phase was the type of social conventions which we term Victorian. What is the new shore towards which we steer ? Not the matriarchate, but a new adjustment between the sexes and between the generations ; an equipoise which neither sacrifices the Many nor the One. To take part in this cosmic evolution is far from comfortable ; we are on the verge of change, perched on the perilous range between two watersheds. But it is an inspiration and a profound responsibility to strive with all our powers so that the results of science may be placed at the service of the new world, so that the Shamans of to-day may no longer be able to blind men's eyes, and lead their feet into the paths of Death and Pain.

BIBLIOGRAPHY

BODEN, REV. J. F. WORSLEY. *Mischiefs of the Marriage Law*, London, 1932.

BRITISH SOCIETY FOR THE STUDY OF SEX PSYCHOLOGY. *Policy and Principles*, London, 1914–29. *Sexual Variety and Variability in Women*, Pamphlet 3, London, 1916.

BRUPBACHER, F., " Die neue Abortgesetzgebung in der Soviet-Union," *Intern. ärztl. Bull*, Prague, Juni, 1936.

CONUS, E., *Mutter- und Kinderfürsorge in der Sovietunion*, Moscow, 1933. (Translated, London, S.C.R.).

CRAIG, ALEC, *Sex and Revolution*, London, 1934.

ELLIS, H., *The Philosophy of Conflict*, London, 1919.

ELLIS, H., *The Function of Taboos*. In " Everyman's Library," No. 930, London, 1936.

ENGELS, F., *Ursprung der Familie, des Privateigentums und des Staates*, Hotting, 1884.

EPSTEIN, J., "Das neue Homosexuellen Gesetz Soviet-Russlands," *Ztsch. f. pol. Psych.*, Copenhagen, 1935, II, 1.

FISCHER, L., " Erziehung zur Demokratie," *Neue Weltbühne*, Prague, June 18th, 1936. *Cf. Reynolds Weekly*, June 7th, 1936.

GEISMAR, E., *Selvtugt eller Utugt. Dag. Nyheder*, Copenhagen, October 21st, 1934.

GOTTSCHALK, H., *Skinsygens Problemer*, Copenhagen, 1936.
HAYNES, E. S. P., *Divorce as it Might Be*, Cambridge, 1915.
HERBERT, A. P., *Holy Deadlock*, London, 1934.
LORD HEWART OF BURY, "Divorce Law," *Daily Telegraph*, October 21st and 22nd, 1935.
HODANN, M., *De Strijd om de sexueele Moral*, Hilversum, 1934.
KAMINSKI, Vratch i abort., *Izvestiya*, October 18th, 1936.
LAWRENCE, *Lady Chatterley's Lover*, Paris, 1930.
LEUNBACH-HAIRE, "Von der bürgerlichen Sexualreform zur revolutionären Sexualökonomie," *Ztsch. f. pol. Psych.*, Copenhagen, II, 1–2, 1935.
MALINOWSKI,B.,*The Anthropological Study of Sex,*Ingesekongress, 1926, I, Berlin, 1927.
KINGSLEY MARTIN, *The educational Rôle of the Press*, Paris, 1930.
LORD MERRIVALE, *Marriage and Divorce*, London, 1936.
MICHELS, R., "Sittlichkeit in Ziffern?" *Kritik der Moralstatistik*, Munich-Leipzig, 1928.
MORGAN, L. H., *Systems of Consanguinity and Affinity of the Human Family*, Washington City, 1870.
MULLINS, CLAUD, *Marriage, Children and God*, London, 1933.
Pravda, June/July, 1935, and May 26th to June 28th, 1936. Leading article June 28th, 1936, *Stalinskaya sabota o materi i djetjach*.
REICH, W., *Dialektischer Materialismus und Psychoanalyse*, Copenhagen, 1934.
REICH, W., *Experimentelle Ergebnisse über die elektrische Funktion des Orgasmus*, Erste Mitteilung, 1936. Publication pending also in French.
ROSENBERG, A., *Der Mythos des 20, Jahrhunderts*, Munich.
SCHIOETZ, C., and SELAND, B., "Welche Bedeutung hat der Geburtsmonat für die Zukunft des Kindes?" *Ztsch. Kinderheilk*, Berlin, 1933.
STRACHEY, P., *Memorandum on the Position of English Women in Relation to that of English Men*, London, 1935.
WEBB, B. and S., *Soviet Communism: A New Civilization?* I, II, London, 1935.
WESTERMARCK, E., *The History of Human Marriage*, I–III, 5 Ed., London, 1921.
WOLFSON, B., *Sociologiya braki i ssemi*, Minsk, 1926.

TABLE OF EVENTS

1856   GUSTAVE FLAUBERT begins the publication of "Madame Bovary" in the *Revue de Paris*.
1857   FLAUBERT tried and acquitted.
1869   Agitation for Women's Suffrage begins in Great Britain and U.S.A.

1870 MORGAN'S *Systems of Consanguinity* published.
1879 BEBEL'S *Woman and Socialism* (*Die Frau und der Sozialismus*) (Translated into fourteen languages; published in fifty-one editions).
IBSEN'S *Nora* (*The Doll's House*).
1893 Women's Franchise in New Zealand.
1901 Women's Franchise in the Australian Commonwealth.
1904 FOREL'S *Question sexuel.*
1905 The Suffragettes under the leadership of EMMELINE and CHRISTABEL PANKHURST begin to use terrorist methods (till 1914).
1905 Bund für Mutterschutz in Germany advocates equal rights for Illegitimate Children.
1907 Limited Franchise for Women in Norway, the pioneer European state in this respect.
1913 Universal Franchise for Women in Norway.
1914 Foundation of the British Society for the Study of Sex Psychology.
1915 CASTBERG Law in Norway gives equal rights to Illegitimate Children.
1917 Beginning of the Sexual Revolution in Russia. ALEXANDRA KOLLONTAY Commissar for Maternity and Child Welfare. Social and Political Equality of Women.
1918 People's Act gives Vote to British Women over thirty years of age.
German Republic and Austria give Franchise to Women.
1923 New Divorce Law in England.
1926 Personal Property Act for Women in England.
1928 Universal Franchise for Women over twenty-one years of age in Great Britain.
1931 Legal Equality of Women in Spain.
1934 W.L.S.R. dissolved.
LEUNBACH stands as candidate for Danish Riksdag on a Sex-political platform.
1936 Adultery made a ground for dismissal of German officials.
DR. PILLAY founds the Society for the Study and Promotion of Family Hygiene, including Sex Hygiene in India.

EPILOGUE

THIS book is the first attempt at an historical synopsis of a new science, and the author is well aware that this first attempt must necessarily fail to present a complete picture of all the efforts and influences out of which modern sexology has emerged. Thus, it has not been possible to include details of the most recent and very valuable Russian and Spanish work, nor to follow events in the Far East. But even as it is, the book could not have been written without the active sympathy and support of the leading experts in many different countries, and I herewith thank these authorities for all their helpful information and suggestions.

First and foremost amongst them is the great master and pioneer, Dr. Havelock Ellis, then Professor Bronislav Malinowski, the British Social Hygiene Council, The Eugenics Society, the International Birth Control Information Centre, the Society for Providing Birth Control Clinics, the National Birth Control Association, Mrs. Janet Chance, Miss Irene Clephane, Miss Zoe Dawe, Miss Alison Neilans, Mr. R. Elkan and Mr. N. Haire, all of whom have forwarded my work in London. Important American material has been furnished, through Mrs. M. Sanger, by the Office of the National Committee on Federal Legislation for Birth Control in New York City and Washington ; Dr. Pillay, of Bombay, has given information about India. The latest developments in the U.S.S.R. have been described by Professor Bronner of the People's Commissariat for Health, in Moscow, by the Soviet Embassy in London, and the Soviet Minister in Oslo, Mr. Yakoubovitch. Other experts who have always been most ready with their help are Dr. Fritz and Dr. Paulette Brupbacher of Zurich, Dr. W. Reich, Dr. Evang and Dr. Nic. Hoel of Oslo, Fru Ottesen-Jensen of Stockholm, Dr. J. H. Leunbach of Copenhagen,

Professor S. Freud of Vienna, and Dr. Goetz of Tel-Aviv. I wish to express particular thanks to Miss Stella Browne of London, not only for the English translation of my work, but also for her many valuable annotations and information on the movement in Great Britain. Equally cordial thanks are due to Fröken Heddy Aubert of Oslo, for the zeal and disinterested efficiency with which she gave her secretarial services.

Misinterpretations or errors of fact, in the light of the extremely rapid pace of present developments—whether progressive or reactionary—can hardly be avoided. But the author will sincerely welcome any additions or corrections, which should be sent to him, c/o W. Heinemann (Medical Books) Ltd., 99 Great Russell Street, London, W.C.1. The task of recording and of realizing the Scientific System of Ethics must be a collective task. And it must be undertaken as expressed by Havelock Ellis in the preface to his great *Studies*, and as long ago as 1897, the year in which the modern Psychology of Sex was born :

" Sex lies at the root of life, and we can never learn to reverence life until we know how to understand sex."

POSTSCRIPT TO CHAPTER IX

In the autumn of 1936, a Marriage Reform Bill drafted by Mr. A. P. Herbert, M.P., and presented by Mr. G. de la Bere, M.P., was given a second reading in the House of Commons, and is now under consideration in Committee. This Bill implements the suggestions of the Majority Report a generation ago, but adds the regrettable stipulation that a marriage cannot be dissolved under five years.—*Translator's Note.*

INDEX

Abderhalden, 51, 52
Abolitionists, 95, 98, 100, 109
Abortion, 140, 142, 213, 304
 and maternal mortality and
  morbidity, 214
 attitude of Roman Catholic
  Church towards, 216
 British law on, 214
 British Medical Association Committee on, 233
 by curettage, 223
 complications and accidents of,
  221, 222
 in first pregnancy, 221, 223
 in Russia, 220, 223, 293
 injection methods, 223
 legalized, fight for, 213 ff., 230 ff.
 legislation against, 228, 229
 method used in Russia, 223
 mortality of, 222
 penal laws against re-enacted in
  Russia, 293
 prevalence of, 217 ff.
 reforms and concessions in various
  countries, 230 ff.
 sequelæ of, 221, 222
Abortion Law Reform Association,
 233
Abstinence, sexual, 248, 249, 256
Adler, and individual psychology,
 271
 leaves Freudian group, 270
Advertisements, sexual, 260, 261
Albrecht, Mme. B., 187
Aldred, Guy and Rose, 190
Algolagnia, 65, 66
Allbutt, Dr. H. A., 176
Allen, W. M., and discovery of the
 luteal hormone, 22
America, birth control in, 172, 178,
 190, 207, 208
American Birth Control League, 207
Andersen, Hans Christian, 40
Andrin, 51
Annual for Sexual Intergrades, 39
Anxiety, and libido, 153, 154
Apes, production of syphilis in, 84
Aschheim, 23
Asia, birth control in, 196

Association d'études sexologiques,
 187
Astor, Lady, on abortion, 214
Augusta Victoria, Empress, 81
Auto-erotism, Havelock Ellis on,
 253
 (*See also* Masturbation.)

Baer, Karl Ernst von, discovers
 human ovule, 7
Baker, J. R., 200
Bâle, proposed Bill to legalize
 abortion in, 228
Bang, Hermann, 40
Barker, "Colonel," case of, 48
Bayliss, and discovery of secretin,
 17
Bayly, H. Wansey, 88
Bechterev, V. M., 18
Beckwith-Whitehouse, on abortion,
 233, 234
Bedborough case, 74
Behne, on spermatozoa, 25
Bekker's *Onania*, 249
Belgium, decline of syphilis in, 116
Beneden, Eduard van, on the
 gametes, 7, 8
Benjamin, Harry, on hormone
  treatment of homosexuality,
  56
 on hormone treatment of im-
  potence, 29
Benkert, first uses term "Homo-
  sexual," 40
Bernard, Claude, and internal secre-
  tion, 16
Berta, Professor Luigi, pamphlet on
 contraception by, 188
Berthold's experiments on gonadic
 transplantation, 15
Besant, Annie, and birth control,
 180
 Secretary of the Malthusian
  League, 183
 The Law of Population, 183
Bestiality, 64
Binet, coins term "Erotic
 fetishism," 63

327

Related Titles by James DeMeo
from Natural Energy Works
http://www.naturalenergyworks.net
Also available from your favorite on-line or main street bookstore

James DeMeo: *In Defense of Wilhelm Reich: Opposing the 80-Years' War of Mainstream Defamatory Slander Against One of the 20th Century's Most Brilliant Physicians and Natural Scientists*, 2013.

James DeMeo: *The Orgone Accumulator Handbook: Wilhelm Reich's Life-Energy Discoveries and Healing Tools for the 21st Century, With Construction Plans*, 3rd Revised Edition, 2010.

James DeMeo: *Saharasia: The 4000 BCE Origins of Child Abuse, Sex-Repression, Warfare and Social Violence, In the Deserts of the Old World*, 2nd Revised Edition, 2006.

James DeMeo (Editor): *Heretic's Notebook: Emotions, Protocells, Ether-Drift and Cosmic Life Energy, With New Research Supporting Wilhelm Reich*, 2002.

James DeMeo (Editor): *On Wilhelm Reich and Orgonomy*, 1993.

www.ingramcontent.com/pod-product-compliance
Lightning Source LLC
Chambersburg PA
CBHW071622270326
41928CB00010B/1745